A VOLUME IN THE NIU SERIES IN

Slavic, East European, and Eurasian Studies
Edited by Christine D. Worobec

For a list of books in the series, visit our website at cornellpress.cornell.edu.

RECOLLECTIONS

IVAN BUNIN

Translated and edited by Thomas Gaiton Marullo

NORTHERN ILLINOIS UNIVERSITY PRESS
AN IMPRINT OF CORNELL UNIVERSITY PRESS
Ithaca and London

First published 2024 by Cornell University Press

Library of Congress Cataloging-in-Publication Data

Names: Bunin, Ivan Alekseevich, 1870–1953, author. | Marullo, Thomas Gaiton, translator, editor.
Title: Recollections / Ivan Bunin, translated and edited by Thomas Gaiton Marullo.
Other titles: Vospominanii͡a. English
Description: Ithaca [New York] : Cornell University Press, 2024. | Series: NIU series in Slavic, East European, and Eurasian studies | Includes bibliographical references and index.
Identifiers: LCCN 2023046158 (print) | LCCN 2023046159 (ebook) | ISBN 9781501776137 (hardcover) | ISBN 9781501776144 (paperback) | ISBN 9781501776151 (epub) | ISBN 9781501776168 (pdf)
Subjects: LCSH: Bunin, Ivan Alekseevich, 1870-1953. | Bunin, Ivan Alekseevich, 1870-1953—Friends and associates. | Authors, Russian—20th century. | Soviet Union—History—Revolution, 1917–1921—Personal narratives.
Classification: LCC PG3453.B9 V6713 2024 (print) | LCC PG3453.B9 (ebook) | DDC 891.78/309—dc23/eng/20231127
LC record available at https://lccn.loc.gov/2023046158
LC ebook record available at https://lccn.loc.gov/2023046159

Contents

RECOLLECTIONS

Introduction

Thomas Gaiton Marullo

The Salle Gaveau stands only steps away from Avenue Champs-Élysées, Place de la Concorde, and the Arc de Triomphe in Paris. Built by the architect Jacques Hermant in 1906–1907, the Salle Gaveau was designed primarily as a concert hall, replete with great organs, grand pianos, special acoustics, and seating for a thousand spectators. The Salle Gaveau was a center for the intellectual and cultural life of the French capital, including an afternoon lecture on April 13, 1930, by the famed Russian writer Ivan Bunin in a rare public appearance since his arrival in Paris from Russia a decade earlier.

As noted by the critic Vladimir Talin, the place was filled to overflowing with the "flower of the Parisian literary and political emigration . . . the pillars of the émigré elite."[1] There was Pavel Milyukov. There was Pyotr Struve. There was Vasily Maklakov. There was Metropolitan Yevlogy (sitting in the first row). The excitement was palpable but bittersweet. Spectators had come to hear an avowal of old-world law order and art by an individual whom they saw as the foremost representative of prerevolutionary Russian literature, culture, and civilization.

They had every reason for such a view. The sixty-year-old Bunin, like everyone else in the group, had lived to tell his story of struggle and survival in repeated revolution and war.[2]

Speaker and spectators shared an even more poignant fate. For more than a decade, they—and the more than two million Russians like them—had sat on their suitcases, waiting for the moment when the Soviet state collapsed and they could return home. By 1930, though, such hopes were dimming. With each passing day, Bunin and the Russians in the Salle Gaveau and elsewhere were acknowledging the unthinkable: permanent exile abroad. Indeed, it was the cruelest blow in their shattered lives that they, not the Bolsheviks, were being swept into the dustbin of history. In anger and grief, Bunin and company had cursed Alexander Kerensky and others for losing Russia. In shock and awe, they had watched at how first Vladimir Lenin and now Joseph Stalin were transforming their ancient (if chronically backward) homeland into a brave new world. Only two years earlier, in 1928, Stalin had initiated the first of his five-year plans to industrialize Russia. Equally stunning and disturbing, he was laying the foundation for a new proletarian culture, for socialist realism, which, with its demands for "idea," "party," and "nationality," threatened a radical break with Russian culture, in particular its most treasured feature, the national literary tradition.

The Russians who had come to hear Bunin knew that although they were losing the battle with the Bolsheviks politically—France had recognized the Soviet Union in 1924—they were far from finished aesthetically. They and their fellow expatriates lived by a unifying and comforting truth: it was they, not their Soviet counterparts, who lay claim to classical Russian literature, to the legacy that had begun with Alexander Pushkin, reached an apex with Leo Tolstoy, and lived on in the man about to appear before them. That is why they had come—as Talin wrote, to hear the famous Russian writer Bunin read from his personal recollections of Russian writers, living and dead. This meeting between Bunin and his fellow émigrés had a historical, if biblical, cast. The encounter was not unlike the *zemskie sobory*, or "assemblies of the land" in Russia of the sixteenth and seventeenth centuries, to which the tsar or patriarch summoned nobles, priests, bureaucrats, merchants, and townspeople to discuss problems, to pass laws, and, in 1613, to choose Mikhail Romanov as Russia's new ruler, thereby ending the Time of Troubles, a fifteen-year dynastic crisis that, not unlike the events of 1917, threatened to dismember the nation.

In the meeting between Bunin and his expatriate colleagues, there were also echoes of the book of Exodus, as forlorn exiles from the Russian Eden looked to Bunin as Moses carrying aloft the sacred tables of Russian literature and also as a Chrysostom—in Russian, *Zlatoust* or "golden-mouthed"—from "whose lips," Talin noted, "they could feel the [national] creative literary pulse and breathe its literary atmosphere."[3]

Bunin, his émigré listeners agreed, was an exemplary writer not only of Russia's past but also of its present and future. The solemn event, Talin continued, featured the "spokesman of that time-honored Russian literature that has died out almost completely in Russia . . . [an individual] who had gathered a large crowd . . . to resurrect the incarnate image of the remarkable past . . . of Russian culture, and to bring it to a younger generation who has forgotten or does not know such a thing."[4]

Hopes for Bunin were indeed high: what else could one expect, Talin asked, from a great Russian artist who had lived in "that epoch of Russian literature before it was severed into two parts . . . 'Soviet,' buckled by the yoke of party dictatorship . . . and 'émigré,' bent by a homeless, but free exile."[5]

Since his arrival in the West, Bunin had not disappointed as a writer. He had published a steady stream of poetry and prose, including two novels, *Mitya's Love* in 1925 and the first three parts of *The Life of Arseniev* between 1927 and 1929. He was not only preserving the literary heritage of Pushkin and Tolstoy but also scaling new heights in artistry and expertise. As did Moses and Chrysostom, he was keeping the faith—politically, socially, and aesthetically. Émigré critics were enthusiastic, if relieved. "Bunin continues the classical tradition in Russian literature," Mikhail Tseitlin wrote apropos of Bunin's collection of stories titled *The Rose of Jericho* in January 1924. "But it is only now that we are beginning to notice how precise his texture is, how profound his worldview. . . . Bunin is alien . . . to the influences of Dostoevsky and symbolism . . . to all that is unclean, confused, and halfhearted, to all lies and compromise . . . and to everything that is now hailed as a cultural achievement, a norm." In that same year, Zinaida Gippius continued: "Ivan Bunin is, without a doubt, first among contemporary artist-writers. . . . Writing about days gone by, he re-creates the past as something that is alive, now, and almost charmingly deceptive; he turns back time. Contemporary literature in Europe has retained its Russian prime minister. . . . Bunin is Russian in bone, flesh, and blood; he is truly a writer of the *Russian* land."[6]

Bunin enjoyed boundless popularity with readers, every new piece hailed as cause for celebration and hope. "We are already accustomed to the fact that we await every new story of Bunin's with impatience and that we almost always greet it with enthusiasm," Nikolai Kulman wrote in a review in mid-December 1925. "That is why it is both natural and understandable that one . . . hears from readers with every new work: 'Truly, this is the best thing that Bunin has ever written.'" A month later, Fyodor Stepun polished Bunin's halo further by noting that his "prose is like Sacred Scripture itself." Others, including Dmitri Svyatopolk-Mirsky, saw Bunin as the way, the truth, and the light. "People talk about Bunin's holiness," they said. "He is the 'pride and joy' of the Russian emigration, a pillar of Conservatism, a highly held banner that flies Great, Powerful, and Free . . . over the vileness of Soviet . . . and Futurist perversions."[7]

If Bunin's listeners in the Salle Gaveau in 1930 thought that he would meet their expectations, they were sadly mistaken. In fact, they were in for the shock of their lives. To their dismay, the object of their affection was neither as a Moses nor as a Chrysostom. Rather, as reported by Talin, Bunin was a "Mephistopheles . . . [who mocked] everything that was humane, profound, touching, and insightful"; a "talentless artist . . . [who painted] from a palette of tar and soot"; a frenzied gymnast who "performed caustic acrobatics on a trampoline"; a crazed warrior who shot "cannons and cries"; a raving lunatic who spewed forth "coarse spit and hate"; and an embittered patrician who took on all comers with "aristocratic rancor . . . and the mournful mastery of one who has had too much to drink."[8]

For two hours, Bunin, Talin wrote, read from a notebook "filled with malicious entries of malicious feelings and malicious thoughts."

"'Russian literature? What Russian literature?'" Talin mimicked Bunin's voice. "'Good God, pal, you have no idea, you cannot imagine what have I not seen . . . what I have not had my fill of seeing in my lifetime: poseurs, frauds, braggarts, liars, scandalmongers . . . shameless admen and self-promoters.'" The abuse was unending. Alexander Blok, Bunin dispatched into a "basket of laughable nonentities." Maxim Gorky, he indicted for writing "loathsome things" and for carrying the "false passport of a tramp."[9]

Even more outrageous, Talin fumed, was Bunin's claim that amid self-styled scoundrels and swindlers, he alone had been the man of the hour, the white knight who, singlehandedly, had slain dragon-hacks and phonies to save Russian literature from perdition. "How monstrous," Talin wrote, "to hear from Bunin ravings of narcissistic superiority and excellence . . . [rants that were] coarsely provincial, anti-artistic, and Mephistopheles-like." Could Russian literature before 1917, Talin asked in disbelief, have been only "malice, charade, caricature, gossip, and slander"? Could all of Bunin's literary encounters and acquaintances have been only with "poseurs, frauds, and fools"? What about the "most noble and exalted representatives of Russian literature"—Tolstoy and Anton Chekhov were significant examples—who had fallen Bunin's way? No, Talin continued, any "love and nobility" Bunin showed only for himself.[10]

Talin, though, did concede to Bunin this victory. The content of his remarks was grating, but the form of his comments was grand. Bunin had listeners in the palm of his hand. Like an orator, he read in a way that was "splendid, biting, and aristocratically caustic." Like a composer, he syncopated "pauses and stresses . . . [with] rests and rushes, surges and swells."[11]

Even more commendable was that Bunin, in his reading, assumed poses dear to the Russian heart. At times, Bunin was a "master of unrestrained exposé." At other times, he was a scientist who "devilishly insightful and piercing . . . used an x-ray machine to see . . . inside." Still at other times, he was an actor who "imitated the speeches and readings of his subjects." Indeed, so moved was Talin by Bunin's dramatic bent that awe trumped anger. "I must confess," he wrote, "that Bunin rendered [his subjects] . . . with such skillful mastery, in such a murderously brilliant way . . . that if I did not know that he was a great writer, I would have been convinced firmly that he was a great professional impersonator."[12]

If Talin was unsure whether to censure or sanction Bunin's antics, his colleagues in the audience were not. Stunned by Bunin's "collection of the villains of Russian literature," they laughed often, long, and hard at his imitations and portraits. "How could they not restrain themselves?" Talin was forced to admit. "Such was the great force of Bunin's talent."[13] Both Talin and company had to acknowledge an unpleasant truth: Russian writers were not gods for admiration or worship, but mortals like themselves, with similar failings and flaws.

Talin, though, sought to rein in the fun. Russian literature was for him too sacred to be cut down by its last viable practitioner. He did what others did when they were confused or angered by Bunin. He sought to relegate the writer to the gossamer mists of a Russia gone by. If Bunin showed a "nihilistic stance" to colleague-writers, Talin opined, it was because of his "profoundly protective-conservative worldview." Notwithstanding the events of 1917, Russia remained for him a land of masters and men. Only recall, Talin countered, in *The Life of Arseniev*, how "lovingly and pathetically" Bunin had described a "richly tanned giant-hussar in a red dress uniform." With a chin that "jutted out slightly" and nostrils that were "thin and curved in an energetic and somewhat suspect way," such a figure "overwhelmed [all] with his superhuman height, his long thin legs, and the sharp-sightedness of his heavenly eyes!" Also recollect, Talin continued, how many years later, "at the grave of this representative of this irretrievable and condemned Russian past, young Arseniev fell on his knees, pursed his lips, and cried bitterly."[14]

Talin and his compatriots at the Salle Gaveau should not have been surprised by Bunin's truculence. In their exuberant mythmaking of the man, they had forgotten how Bunin rocked Russia with his 1909 *The Village* and his 1910 *Dry Valley*, his damning exposés of indigenous landowners and serfs. They had also let slip from memory his 1917 "Loopy Ears," in which Bunin parodied Fyodor Dostoevsky's 1865 *Crime and Punishment* with his hero Sokolovich, a modern "extraordinary man" who does what Raskolnikov could not do: he murders a prostitute without remorse.

Talin and company were also ignorant or heedless of earlier *skandaly* by Bunin. At a gathering of writers in Moscow in early 1918, Bunin attacked both the February and October Revolutions and what he considered to be their literary apologia: Blok's recently completed "The Twelve." Even more eyebrow-raising were Bunin's lectures titled "The Great Narcosis," where, in Odessa on November 17 and 24, 1919, he stunned and shamed listeners with a diatribe against Russia and Russians.

Country and citizen, Bunin proclaimed, had done it again. They had entered into their latest cycle of "enormous and bloody carnival . . . [of] sedition, internecine strife, boiling-overs and absurdities." For the umpteenth time, they had succumbed to the national "proclivity . . . for savagery and tears"; strayed in their "boundless steppes, impenetrable forests . . . [and] endless backwaters"; laid bare their "immaturity before their neighbors"; and ceded to their "fatal peculiarity of always moving forward in circles."[15]

Even worse, Bunin continued, was the psycho-spiritual treachery. Russia and Russians, he thundered, had "sold their souls to the devil." They had been seduced by "that new and vulgarly absurd word 'bolshevism.'" They had become "narcotized" by Soviet drug-dreams, by the "hundred-fold absurdity . . . of worker-peasant power." They were a "deeply emotional people" who had ceded to "starry-eyed idealism and faintheartedness . . . [and to] an "estrangement from genuine life, an ignorance of existence, even an *unwillingness* to understand reality."[16]

Bunin's reading at the Salle Gaveau was not his last word on Russia and Russian literature. On October 23, 1948, at another public lecture in Paris, he repeated the charges that he had made against his literary confreres eighteen years previously. This time, though, two things were different. First, although Bunin remained among émigrés as the Moses and the Chrysostom of the diaspora, he was now seventy-eight years old, in his twenty-eighth year of exile, and past his prime, physically and aesthetically. In fact, he was seriously ill. Even more distressing, perhaps, Bunin was facing a different audience. With the exception of Maklakov, the star-studded cast that had attended Bunin's 1930 reading was gone: Milyukov had died in 1943, Struve in 1944, and Yevlogy in 1946. Talin was also gone. Writers who followed Bunin abroad after the revolution and who remained in the West also had passed away: Dmitri Merezhkovsky in 1941, his wife, Gippius, in 1945, and Konstantin Balmont in 1942.

Further, with the victory of the Soviets in World War II, Bunin was facing a change of heart by Russian exiles toward their confreres in the East. Émigrés, outraged over the devastation of ancestral nests, had cheered their compatriots in the triumph over fascism. Not unexpectedly, if naively, they also had hoped that Stalin would move from dictatorship and terror to democracy and peace. After almost thirty years of rancor and animosity, expatriates sought to accept Soviet reality and to extend the olive branch to Russians on the other side of the border. Even more revealing, perhaps, émigré critics and reviewers moved to reevaluate, even praise writers who had supported the revolution and the new Soviet state. Velimir Khlebnikov, Sergei Esenin, and Vladimir Mayakovsky now entered the Russian literary pantheon.

With such reconciliation and renewal, Bunin disagreed violently. Willingly, he became the thorn in the rose that Russian exiles offered to Soviet prodigals. He was deemed by many émigrés as a relic and an obstacle, even an embarrassment for the hoped-for reunion of Russians on both sides of the border. Fading into the sunset, he was seen as a false prophet who, frothing at the mouth, vaunted a Russia of memories and dreams, with no one to blame but himself for his misery. Even his status as a Nobel laureate—in 1933, Bunin was the first Russian and the first writer in exile to win the coveted award—held sway no longer.

To be sure, Bunin had cheered Russians in the worldwide struggle. Even before the outbreak of the war, he told his fellow exile Vasily Sukhomlin on April 6, 1941: "If Russia would declare war on Hitler, I would walk to Moscow on my knees to thank Soviet power." Even as Russians were being trounced by Germans, Bunin's faith in his homeland remained absolute. "First one place falls, then another," he noted in his diary on September 19, 1941. "But will Russia be defeated? I find that difficult to imagine." As Alexander Liberman wrote to Alexander Baboreko about Bunin in mid-August 1942: "Ivan Alexeevich was a hundred percent Russian patriot. He thought only about saving Russia from the barbarians."[17]

Still, after geopolitical hostilities ceased, aesthetic ones continued. During the lecture in Paris in 1948, his final appearance in public, Bunin again took on pre- and postrevolutionary writers for what he saw as the harm they had caused Russian literature. As recalled by Tatyana Loginova-Muravyova, Bunin was sickly and drawn. Suffering from emphysema, he coughed, wheezed, and gasped for breath. With an ingratiating smile and a carafe of cognac before him, Bunin fulminated against such self-styled "cretins" as Fyodor Sologub, Valery Bryusov, Balmont, Esenin, Mayakovsky, and Blok.[18]

The matter did not end there. When Mark Veinbaum, editor of *New Russian Word*, the major postwar newspaper of the diaspora, published Bunin's remarks on December 27 and 29, 1948, ripples became tsunamis. Bunin was bloody, but unbowed, writing to Andrei Sedykh on January 20, 1949: "I kiss you for defending me against those individuals who swear at me for my 'Autobiographical Notes,' and for the fact that on their account, I did not burst out into tears for what I said about Blok and Esenin (about whom I did not hear a peep [from the audience] when I read my 'Notes' in public and when I insisted that *in no way were they the history of Russian literature*). [I kiss you also] that old man

Bunin allowed himself to have a personal opinion about the poetic talent of Mayakovsky, who, for all his servile lack of talent, is one of the greatest lackeys of Russia poetry."[19]

The shots that Bunin fired in 1930 and 1948 at pre- and postrevolutionary Russian writers for their failings, particularly for what he saw as their betrayal of indigenous culture and civilization, did little to stem his anger. Rather, they were the opening salvos for what would be his final work, *Recollections*, published in Russian by Vozrozhdenie (Renaissance) Press in Paris in 1950.[20]

On first glance, in *Recollections* Bunin seemed intent on continuing literary vendettas: the final spasms of a vitriolic, demented, and bitter old man losing his grip on literature and life. He trounced not only the subjects of his public readings—Blok, Esenin, Balmont, Bryusov, Sologub, and Gorky—but also such individuals as Maximilian Voloshin and Alexei Tolstoy. Having gifted Zinaida Shakhovskaya with a copy of *Recollections* on October 27, 1950, Bunin felt compelled to write: "When your Highness writes her memoirs, do not abuse [others] as I abuse [people] here."[21]

Reviewers responded in kind. "I have read your article [on Alexei Tolstoy]," Mark Aldanov wrote to Bunin on January 15, 1950. "I think that it will create an impression . . . of an exploding bomb." Nine months later, he continued: "[*Recollections*] has affected me greatly. It is a book that is intrepid, terrible . . . [and] written with great force. Those people who abuse it would do better if they could find untruths in it. I can only ask you this question: Was it necessary to tell the entire truth?" Everyone in *Recollections* was a cretin, Praskovya Stepanova noted succinctly, with Mayakovsky—"the cretin of cretins"—leading the pack. Speaking about *Recollections* in general, Georgy Adamovich repeated not only Talin's censure of Bunin's remarks but also his grudging sanction to the writer's truth. "One cannot but think long and hard about [*Recollections*]," Adamovich wrote. "If there was a decline [in Russian literature], from where and when did it occur? Did it ever happen at all? Could it really be the case that in the course of a quarter century, Russian literature was in the power of shameless chatterboxes, poseurs, cheats, frauds . . . [and] naive, trusting simpletons? Could it only have been decline and collective deception and clamor—in many cases beyond question and judged correctly by Bunin? . . . But recalling his past repugnance and repulsion, Bunin has triumphed. He has proven himself to be the victor."[22]

In contrast to his 1930 and 1948 lectures, though, Bunin filled *Recollections* with new images and ideas. Mindful that his life was drawing to a close—half of *Recollections* was written in bed—and anxious to leave this world with more than curses and condemnations, Bunin countered memories of villainous foes with flashbacks of heroic friends: individuals who, though wise in the ways of the world, sought to make it a better place. Beyond Gorky, Alexei Tolstoy, and the avant-gardists, the cast of characters in Bunin's recollections included writers Leo Tolstoy, Chekhov, Alexander Kuprin, and Alexander Ertel. Stories of the singer Fyodor Chaliapin, the musician Sergei Rachmaninov, and the artist Ilya Repin mingled with accounts of the geographer Pyotr Semyonov-Tyan-Shansky, Prince Pyotr Alexandrovich of Oldenburg, and the English writer Jerome Jerome. There were even nods to family members: the poet Anna Bunina; brothers, Yuly and Yevgeny Bunin; and a nephew, Nikolai Pusheshnikov.

As was the case with much of Bunin's memory-driven fiction—his 1900 "Antonov Apples" and *Dry Valley* were pertinent examples—the people breathing new life in *Recollections* were seen by Bunin as painfully human. Some were seriously flawed; others, less (and more tolerantly) so. Indeed, the ways that the figures in Bunin's final work confronted their faults and failings were a key theme of the work. Like Uncle Pyotr in *Dry Valley*, the failed master of the Khrushchev household, villains in *Recollections* dissembled in mask and masquerade. Like Natalya, the faithful servant of the work, heroes in *Recollections* assumed a more prosaic, if credible, cast. They accepted who they were. They took their lumps and bumps in stride. They lived sadder, but wiser, lives, knowing that what had not killed them made them stronger. Like Natalya, they were the ones with stories to tell.

An equally seminal feature in *Recollections* is that, in his final work, Bunin showed himself in a way that he had not done previously. Whereas in his fiction, Bunin hid behind his characters, he now stepped forth boldly with his views on literature and life. Nothing was left to the imagination. What Bunin loved, he really loved; what Bunin hated, he really hated. If others styled him as a Moses and a Chrysostom, he saw himself as a Luther, with "here I stand" theses on issues and ideas that were near and dear to his heart.

Like Vladimir Nabokov, Bunin commanded that memory speak, but even more than his archrival, he scoured the past to inform the present. Via psycho-spiritual sojourns to the past, Bunin resurrected and refashioned Russian literature, culture, and civilization in his own image and likeness. Often, he had the facts straight. Equally often, he colored them with his own spin on people, places, and events. When Bunin reflected on life in *Recollections*, he told it as he thought it was or as he wanted it to be.

As with his readings in 1930 and 1948, Bunin knew that with his final work, he was confronting readers and reviewers with images, ideas, and ideals that they had forgotten, that they had rejected, or, worse, that they did not know or wish to know. Biography and history became *pouchenie* (exhortation), on one hand, and *apologia pro vita sua* and last will and testament, on the other. The pose

Bunin struck in *Recollections* was not unlike the portraits of deathbed stances of his famous nineteenth-century predecessors—Vissarion Belinsky and Nikolai Nekrasov come to mind—in that he, too, reiterated values and virtues even as, metaphorically, he lay propped up on a couch and stared icily, with a pointed hand, into a distance that transcended self and, by extension, time and space itself. Given everything that had happened to Bunin and his homeland, the stakes for personal and cultural redemption had never been higher.

In 1950, Bunin was eighty years old. Unlike the proverbial cat, he had lived more than nine lives. He had endured the decline of imperial, patriarchal Russia; the revolution of 1905; the First World War; the February and October Revolutions of 1917; and the first years of the Russian Civil War. Exile to France in 1920 brought little peace. Economic depression, together with sociopolitical struggles between rightists and leftists, struck Bunin as déjà vu. Even more traumatic were the conflagration of World War II and the onset of the Cold War, where, it seemed, Stalin could realize Adolf Hitler's dreams for world conquest and domination.

Still another sign of the apocalypse for Bunin was that Russian literature was declining rapidly on both sides of the border. Looking east, he lamented how its foremost representatives were dead or hounded by socialist watchdogs. Looking west, Bunin mourned how equally famed practitioners of Russian poetry and prose had died, with no one to take their place. Nabokov was alive, but his 1936 *The Gift* was his last Russian novel.

If the wolves were howling outside the door, they were also growling from within. Bunin was falling victim to the three things he dreaded most: old age, sickness, and death.

Given the way Bunin thought he and life were going, he feared not only for the loss of Russian literature but also for the memory of national writing. Although Bunin published sketches and articles on Russian writers and artists in émigré journals and newspapers almost from the beginning of his time abroad, it was only in 1950, with death seemingly imminent, that he felt compelled to pen *Recollections*. His goal was literally a matter of life and death. That is, by leaving for posterity a summa of his thoughts and impressions on people, places, and events, and on the issues, images, and ideas in indigenous art, Bunin sought to fashion a canon of Russian culture and civilization—a Moses-like set of tablets, so to speak—for wandering Russians to carry with them until they returned to Russia.

Recollections leaves four immediate impressions. The first is vastness: Bunin spanned Russian culture and civilization from the eighteenth century to his present day. The second is urgency: he preserved Russian literature and art from the ravages of politics, time, and space. The third is salvation: he identified for Russians saints to revere and sinners to censure. The fourth is authenticity: he sought credibility for his likes and dislikes via a plethora of facts and figures.

The last impression is the most striking. Bunin was not a modernist, but he was certainly modern. As he had done throughout his writing, particularly in his pre-1917 novels and stories, Bunin rooted *Recollections* in a freewheeling collage of dialogue, polyphony, and a "literature of fact" of fictional and extrafictional sources. Citations from Russian poetry and prose appeared among excerpts from critical articles and reviews. Selections from letters and diaries moved in sync with snippets from books and encyclopedias, notepads and albums, newspapers and journals, telegrams and letters. Appeals to anecdotes and tall tales merged with summons for gossip and hearsay.

Like any avant-garde writer, Bunin also had *Recollections* embrace diverse kinds of performance. If Bunin was not singing songs, declaiming verse, and mimicking colleagues, others were. Tableaux-montages struck diverse tones and moods. Carnival reigned supreme. At times, *Recollections* sounded a decadent strain as Bunin and company ate, drank, and made merry, for tomorrow they died. At other times, *Recollections* resembled a three-ring circus, in which, metaphorically, writers and artists swallowed swords, swung from trapezes, and flew from cannons. Still, at other times, *Recollections* moved to vaudeville, burlesque, and shtick as literati and others seemed willing to do anything for a laugh. Finally, *Recollections* often assumed a somber cast as writers and others underwent deathbed conversions before God and humankind. Like his two lectures in Paris, Bunin's *Recollections* played to a diverse crowd with no holds barred. In true modern fashion, he broke the fourth wall in intimate tête-à-têtes with readers. They were for him participants in proceedings, the sole objects of his attention.

Bunin moved *Recollections* to a second dynamic. The world, he divided into good guys and bad guys, with the latter claiming his energy and attention.

The bad guys were, of course, the Russian avant-gardists, the root of all evil in Bunin's world. Bunin objected to the group for several reasons. Most obviously, he was jealous of the attention and acclaim that individuals such as Andrei Bely and Blok had garnered from readers.[23] Even more shallow, perhaps, Bunin's vaunted, if at times shrill, stance as an aristocrat cast him as a patrician amid proletarians, the hoi polloi, especially those of the Russian literary world, inviting derision and disdain.

Close inspection of Bunin's dislike of the modernists reveals more understandable, if viable, grounds for his enmity. Chief among them was his understanding of Russian writers in society. Bunin held fast to the time-honored national view that practitioners of prose and poetry were more than scribblers and scribes of the trials and travails of heroes and heroines. Rather, they were priests and prophets who sought to answer, with a nod to Winston Churchill, the riddles, enigmas, and mysteries of Russian—and human souls. If, in the public's and Bunin's imagination, Russian-born writers understood life, it was because they had loved and lived it to the fullest. Not unlike the hussar in Bunin's *Arseniev*, they were hale and hearty individuals, without pretense and pose. What readers saw was what they got. The national consensus was also that indigenous literati did not fear life but engaged it head-on. They overcame obstacles and challenges; they defeated injustices and vicissitudes; they relished frays and fights. Even with metaphorical guns to their heads, they were the conscience of the nation and the world.

Further, if Russian writers lamented sickness, old age, and death, it was because they wished to live forever. They did not sweat the small stuff; rather, they relished it as the building blocks of a meaningful existence. For Bunin and Russian readers, national literary masters looked on creation and, like God, saw that it was good. Classicists in mind, body, and soul, they saw the world as bright, rational, and ordered: heaven on earth. Having gifted readers with new senses to see, smell, hear, and touch, they returned them to Genesis and paradise.

Against such standards, Bunin believed that the avant-gardists failed at every turn. If their predecessors upheld Eden, these individuals championed the fall and deserved the exodus—spiritual and social, political and aesthetic—in which they found themselves.

For Bunin, the avant-gardists were cretins and cavemen, Mongols and Huns who scourged literature and life with insanity, sickness, and death. The regression, he opined, was physical and moral. Physically, the avant-gardists were wasted and wan. Bodies were stunted, heads were huge, skulls were bare. The avant-gardists were for Bunin also grotesquely androgynous. Priapic midsections attended womanly breasts, feminine faces, and ringlet curls. Drunkards, miscreants, and pedophiles marched in step with sodomites, addicts. and devil worshippers.[24]

In the regressive allure, Bunin also saw the avant-gardists as stuck in childhood, adolescence, and youth. In their self-inscribed worlds, life was all about them. Often, the fun and games were physical. Sex, drugs, and alcohol fueled hijinks and hooliganism, scandals and scenes. The avant-gardists, Bunin continued, were hotheads and brats who engaged the world with sneers, leers, and fisticuffs. Small wonder, he mused, that life treated them so harshly. Justly did they deserve their lumps, bumps, and black eyes.

In the physical and metaphysical posturing, the avant-gardists were for Bunin everything and nothing. At a moment's notice, they posed as patriots and monarchists, masters and men, Westerners and Slavophiles. Without warning, they were snobs and snivelers, Zeuses and zanies, Greeks and geeks. At the drop of a hat, they were devils and demons, angels of vengeance and chairmen of terrestrial globes. Many were the hats that they wore.

Whatever the pretense or pose, Bunin continued, the avant-gardists displaced imagination with image, substance with style, heart with head, reality with reality show. In fact, it amazed Bunin that the avant-gardists wrote at all. They could not sit still, externally and internally. If Bunin traveled the world as a seeker and a pilgrim, they joyrode through creation, galloped into philosophies and beliefs, and bolted over paradoxes and problems. Mornings, they cried "Eureka!" Evenings they were baffled and perplexed. As Bunin saw it, the modernists moved from producers staging sacrilegious plays to doomsdayers auguring the end of the world, to politicians promising quick fixes in new worlds, to dictators threatening violence on crowds, to rakes and roués burning candles at both ends. Ultimately, and unsurprisingly, they died in sanatoriums, hospitals, and asylums or with ropes around their necks or pistols to their heads.

For Bunin, they were also opportunists and careerists. As much as the avant-gardists allegedly wanted to leave this world, they wanted very much to remain in it. Cold and cunning, craven and crass, and hell-bent on power, money, and fame, they did everything and anything to secure their place in life. They lied about their education, concealed their backgrounds, and fantasized adventures and exploits. They also could be seductive and charming; flattery got them everywhere. Onstage, the avant-gardists professed asceticism and simplicity. Offstage, avant-gardists lived the good life. Even as they condemned the bourgeois, they were exemplar arrivistes. They gadded about in silk underwear and ties, bowler hats, and patent leather shoes. They relished elegant prints, silk bedspreads, and dark tablecloths with vases of fruit. At the expense of others, they were the life of the parties, wining and dining at the best restaurants, taverns, and inns. With impunity, they sold themselves to the highest bidder, the Bolsheviks heading their list. Lenin, Stalin, and Felix Dzerzhinsky filled—and paid—their bills.

To Bunin's even greater annoyance, the avant-gardists were uproariously successful in their quest. Whereas the writer of *Recollections* climbed the ladder to success slowly and painfully—Bunin attracted widespread attention only with *The Village*, twenty years into his literary career—the avant-gardists were overnight sensations and for a straightforward reason. Patrons and lovers, fans and groupies did the work for them. They proclaimed the avant-gardists geniuses and "God's people"; they provided shelter and funds; they opened doors to circles and salons. Dostoevsky-like, they loved when their hands were bitten by those they had fed.

Bunin had even greater difficulties with their poetry and prose. Content and form provoked his fury. The avant-gardists, Bunin asserted, were clueless, without issues, images, or ideas. They copied European fiction and fashion. They catered to cart-horse poetics; to accordions and drums; to spit, snot, and vomit; and to the tastes, demands, and passions of the mob. It also irked Bunin that the avant-gardists wrote about people, places, and things about which they knew nothing. From their nests in Moscow and St. Petersburg, they waxed eloquently, if ludicrously, on provincial masters and men, on rural flora and fauna.

The avant-gardists, Bunin continued, also cared little for Russia or their own front door. They climbed mountains, sailed the seas, dwelled in deserts, and camped in caves. They circled the planets and shot to the stars. They ascended into heavens and descended into hells, mythic and real. Bunin was also annoyed when the avant-gardists blessed the future and spat on the past; when they mocked gentry classicism with worker art; and when they wrote what he saw as nonsense: flutes with backbones, clouds wearing pants. Bunin also cared little that the avant-gardists bypassed the prosaic of life for cosmic visions, thoughts, and emotions, a worldview that, in his view, exposed unease with existence, not insight into it.

Most damning for Bunin was the call of the avant-gardists for revolution, violence, and blood. Their support for the Bolsheviks, whether momentary or lifelong, was a sin he never forgave. It was incomprehensible and outrageous to the writer of *Recollections* that although the modernists had never known hunger or want, they screamed eye for eye, tooth for tooth. Nothing to them was sacred. Christ, they crucified anew; the Mother of God, they called a whore. Nicholas II was a pup, a geek, and a snob. Lenin was God; the rabble, apostles and disciples. The avant-gardists, Bunin continued, abhorred compromises and middle grounds. All who were not with them—politically, socially, and aesthetically—were against them. Enemies were to be whipped, slashed, stabbed, shot, hanged, and crucified. Friends had it worse. They were baptized with blood and confirmed with sweat and tears. They were dispatched to destroy the world, not save it.

Even more startling, perhaps, Bunin charged that the avant-gardists welcomed revolution and war, demagoguery and dictatorship as circus and carnival, pageant and parade. In the events of 1917, they claimed, squall and storm advanced to symphony and song, to sunrise and spring. With Lenin, Stalin, and others, paradises and edens merged with resurrections and second comings.

If Bunin saw the avant-gardists as villains, he deemed other Russian writers as heroes. His pantheon included such "classicists" as Ivan Turgenev, Yakov Polonsky, and Afanasy Fet. He also applauded writers with a more experimental, if modern, bent: Vladimir Korolenko, Nikolai Leskov, Vsevolod Garshin, and

Vladimir Solovyov. Even Dostoevsky, whom he once promised to remove from his pedestal, received, vis-à-vis *The Brothers Karamazov*, grudging respect.[25]

In *Recollections*, two writers claimed Bunin's special attention and love. The first was Leo Tolstoy. He was not the idol or god—"He, His Very Self"—who had seized Bunin's boyish imagination. Rather, Tolstoy was for him an unassuming mortal who lived in an unpretentious home with an unobtrusive wife amid unremarkable cares and concerns. To Bunin's surprise, Tolstoy did not strut boldly into encounters, breathing fire and brimstone and bearing the tablets of *War and Peace* and *Anna Karenina* in his hands. However contradictorily, he portrayed primitive strength in physical weakness. On one hand, the Tolstoy in Bunin's *Recollections* appeared as a diminished individual with hair that was gray and sparse, a beard that was uneven, and legs that were bowed. On the other hand, Tolstoy conveyed an aura of strength with hands that were huge, jaws that jutted out, and eyes that were penetrating and sharp.

Even more intriguing is that, with Bunin, Tolstoy was not only a perfect gentleman but also a surrogate father who, sadder but wiser, passed on prosaic admonitions and advice. The messages were quintessential Tolstoy: *War and Peace* and *Anna Karenina* in nutshells. With tender handshakes, the great writer bid Bunin to love and live with women only in marriage. With enchanting smiles, he added that life should be lived not for career, self, or the future or on one's sleeve. Rather, it should focus on a present that is simple, purposeful, good, and rich with glimpses into happiness.

The most poignant aspect of Bunin's memories of Tolstoy in *Recollections*, however, is when he presented the object of his filial affection as confronting the onset of sickness, old age, and death. As noted by Bunin, Tolstoy had already known mortality in the passing of his seven-year-old son, Vanya. Although never a believer in the conventional sense, Tolstoy was so stunned and saddened by his loss that he had no choice but to affirm eternal life. Bunin was quick to note, though, that what Tolstoy believed for Vanya, he could not do for himself. Bunin left his self-styled father as aged, cold, and bitterly unhappy, but he also made his point. Tolstoy was, after all, human and flawed. He was, after all, every man and woman.[26]

The other hero in Bunin's *Recollections* was Chekhov. If Tolstoy functioned as a surrogate father for Bunin, Chekhov was a stand-in brother. Only ten years younger than Chekhov and a frequent and welcome guest in his home, Bunin looked to the writer as a role model and mentor and as someone who had overcome obstacles of class, education, even genetics to claim a place in literature and life. Although Bunin clung desperately to his aristocratic roots—his noble heritage was often his only defense against the modern world—he did what so many of his group did with people outside their rank and station. He recognized individuals from other castes as intellectuals, artists, and equals who contributed greatly to the genius of the Russian soul.

If the modernists were for Bunin arrivistes, Chekhov was for him salt of the earth. Joyfully, he noted Chekhov's modesty, restraint, and happiness over talent, where and whenever it appeared. Bunin was also at one with Chekhov's likes and dislikes. He esteemed Chekhov's love of Tolstoy, that in the great writer's fiction the sun was the sun, nothing more. He affirmed Chekhov's dismissal of the avant-gardists as peasants, card sharps, and horse thieves and as scorpions, crocodiles, and snakes. He applauded Chekhov's objections to what he saw as the shish-kebab structure of Gorky's *Foma Gordeev* and the political shrillness of his "Song of the Stormy Petrel" and "Song of the Falcon."

More personally, perhaps, Bunin empathized with Chekhov's distress at readers who dismissed him as a lightweight and at critics who, as they had done to Bunin, typed him as cold, crystal, and pure, on one hand, and, on the other, as a moaner and groaner in valleys of tears. He also took to heart Chekhov's prosaic advice: to write daily, to be bold in prose, to avoid verbiage and pomposity, and to accept failures as steps in growth and resolve. For Chekhov, the sea was big, period; or, in a nod to Bunin, it smelled like watermelon.

Most important, and as he had done with Tolstoy, Bunin presented Chekhov also as dealing with the final things. Consumption had darkened Chekhov's face, thinned his body, and muffled his voice. It also had made him quiet, preoccupied, and reserved. At the same time, however, Bunin showed Chekhov not only as accepting his fate but also as determined to make the most of his remaining days. As with Bunin's memories of Tolstoy, the flashbacks of Chekhov are rich with everyday details. Along with fits of coughing and of handkerchiefs soaked with blood are portraits of Chekhov playing pranks, telling jokes, catching mice, and tending flowers and trees. Strolls on moonlit nights and anxieties over dress for visits to Tolstoy accompany wishes to be a pilgrim-monk and hours in silence, musing about the meaning of it all. Even more poignant are scenes of Chekhov, akin to Tolstoy, confronting his own end, but with this difference—dread of demise and confusion over immortality ceded to fear of aesthetic oblivion: readers would forget his works after his death.[27]

Bunin's pantheon in *Recollections* included other representatives of the folk, with even greater indulgences and allowances. Alexander Kuprin was for him a Mongol who terrorized publishers and editors. Unlike modernist-Asiatics, however, Kuprin was an Oriental whom he deemed worth his time and effort.[28] It was Bunin who had set Kuprin on the writing path. More than anyone else, perhaps, Bunin lamented the tragedy of Kuprin's life: his final days as an alcoholic and, worse, as a returnee to the Soviet state. Still, in *Recollections*, Bunin saw much to admire and applaud in Kuprin. Like Tolstoy and

Chekhov, Kuprin, too, was simple, quiet, and shy. He, too, cared little for money and fame. He also did his best when he wrote simply and honestly.

Another proletarian who captured Bunin's admiration in *Recollections* was Alexander Ertel. Ertel was for Bunin a model of Russian manhood. Polished and pragmatic, he pursued success straightforwardly, without the Hamlet-like hesitations that paralyzed other Russian writers. In Bunin's view, everything that Ertel thought, said, or did was sensible and sane. Coming from nowhere and nothing, without pretense or pose, Ertel moved at will between cattle dealer and lord. His life was rooted in Russian values and verities. The men in Ertel's family were self-made: stable and solid, human and humane. They were also self-schooled, particularly in history, politics, and literature. Such formation, they instilled in their offspring. Classics and farming were required courses of study. Ertel was also no stranger to life. Intimately, he knew peasants, merchants, innkeepers, even convicts. Unlike many Russian writers (Bunin included), he worked for a living, managing farms and estates. Indeed, Ertel understood the Russian soul and soil in a way that Leo Tolstoy and Bunin did not.

The energy and resilience Ertel knew in life he brought to literature. Unlike homegrown literati, Ertel eschewed theories and trends, fashions and fads. Rather, he vaunted common sense and pragmatism in art. As a writer, Ertel had the respect not only of Bunin but also of Tolstoy, owing to his knowledge of common people, particularly their language. Equally noteworthy, perhaps, Ertel's two feet on earth caused Bunin to champion him as a philosopher who, not unlike Platon Karataev in Tolstoy's *War and Peace*, knew life from bottom up.

Bunin's reflections on Ertel show that his subject, for all his rootedness in life, also steered clear of socio-politico-economic explanations of existence. Such stances, Ertel thought, were futile. They enervated bodies with ire; they confused souls with "-isms" that were part pathos, part nerves. Also akin to Karataev—and, for that matter, to Bunin, to other Russian "classical" writers, and even to Dostoevsky on a good day—Ertel discerned life principles that affirmed a logical and ordered world. First among them was surrender to an inscrutable God. A close second was fidelity to the teachings of Christ, and a third, balance and moderation in life. To Bunin's delight, Ertel held fast to two additional life rules. One was Karataev's idea of "healthy egoism" whereby individuals discover self and life when they do what needs to be done: when, for themselves and their families, they earn their daily bread—no more, no less—in a sincere and steady way. The other was the search for absolute truth in relative and conditional terms: the need for composure and compromise in the world.

Bunin's stock of saints was not without nepotism. With pride, he pointed to a distant relative, Anna Bunina, a poet of the late eighteenth and early nineteenth centuries. First and foremost, Bunina was for him a woman who, like himself, had triumphed over challenges and obstacles to win a coveted, if lone, place in literature and life. If Bunin was the last of male gentry writers, Bunina was the first of female ones. Bunin was not pro-woman. To his wife and others, he brought the passions and prejudices of the patriarchal male. Flashes of misogyny, as well as of racism and homophobia, pierce the narrative. Although Bunin revered such beloved Russian heroines as Tatyana Larina in Pushkin's *Eugene Onegin* and Natasha Rostova in Tolstoy's *War and Peace*, he avoided these types in his own writing. The heroines of his fiction oppressed or were oppressed; they destroyed or were destroyed. Katya, in *Mitya's Love*, drove the hero to suicide. Young One in *The Village* was raped and hanged naked before being married off to the cruel peasant Rodka. Even Natalya, the serf girl who served as the surrogate mother and memory keeper in *Dry Valley*, was first humiliated and sent into exile by the master Pyotr before she, too, was raped by the devil-incarnate Yushka.

All the more surprising, therefore, was Bunin's championing of Bunina. His story of the woman in *Recollections* has a modern ring. Bunina is presented by her admiring descendant as a being who was two hundred years before her time: From the beginning, she knew what she wanted in life and how to get it. Hands down, Bunina was the most fulfilled and successful individual in *Recollections*, dwarfing even Chekhov and Tolstoy. Her accomplishments were impressive. Rejecting life in the village, Bunina opted for existence alone in St. Petersburg. Self-educated in the classics, she enjoyed success as a poet, ties to the writers of the time, praise from readers and reviewers, pensions and gifts from the tsar and tsaritsa, and membership in the Russian Academy of Sciences. (Bunin himself was named an "academician" in 1909.) Like Tolstoy and Chekhov, Bunina also faced final things bravely. Even as everyone assisted her last days, she passed from this life as gracefully as she had lived it.

The admiration and affection that Bunin had for the heroes of *Recollections*, though, did not preclude objections to their ways and writing. They were, Bunin reaffirmed, human. Chekhov topped the list. The writer, he claimed, knew nothing about landowners, orchards, and estates. His plays were false, far-fetched, and inferior to his prose. He had not seen cherry orchards or even cherry trees. In the famed play itself, Ranevskaya was a ninny; Gaev, a fop; and Lopakhin, a loser. Trofimov was a Gorky look-alike. Firs had outlived his time and type. Kuprin was similarly flawed: guilty of tawdry realism, vulgar platitudes, cheap ideology, and pandering to the times.

In *Recollections*, Bunin also considered heroes in other arts. Once again, the focus was on the everyday, on patricians and plebians. With the former, Bunin recalled not stirring concerts by Rachmaninov, but an initial encounter on the Black Sea. With the latter, Bunin remembered not stunning paintings by Repin, but a visit to the artist's dacha in Finland. Similarly, Bunin recollected not operatic triumphs by Chaliapin, but impromptu recitals and wild rides in troikas with the singer, as well as one evening when Chaliapin carried a drunken Bunin five stories to his hotel room.

The most painful and poignant parts of Bunin's *Recollections*, however, were not the heroes or villains in his life, but those who fell in between. Gorky headed the list. Of all the characters in *Recollections*, it was Gorky who caused Bunin the most hurt and pain, and for a straightforward reason. Gorky was for Bunin the ultimate Judas, as unfaithful to himself as he was to others. With Gorky, Bunin came out swinging. Like Kuprin, Gorky was for him a Mongol but one who merited scorn, not praise. From behind shifty eyes, bushy eyebrows, flat nostrils, wide cheekbones, a wrinkled face, and huge folds of dark and dry skin, Gorky, Bunin charged, played life and people like harps. Exploiting his good fortune, Bunin continued (with envy and bitterness), Gorky seemed always to be the right person in the right place at the right time. It was not talent but political, social, and aesthetic change that had propelled Gorky to glory.

Gorky, Bunin added, was a master actor-chameleon. Depending on his mood, his audience, and how much he smoked and drank, Gorky could be sweet or sour, beatific or battered. On good days, he was a proletarian who boasted schools of hard knocks. On bad days, he was a politician who barked out slogans and maxims with broad strides, raised shoulders, and extended necks. Throughout, he summoned tears, turned pale, frowned fiercely, and spoke in a deep bass. Like a puppet, Gorky raised his eyebrows and the folds on his forehead. Like a *raisonneur*, he soliloquized in tones that were severe, didactic, and dry. Like a bourgeois (and the avant-gardists), he loved money and lavish lifestyles. Foppishly, he waved batons. Equally dandy-like, he sported silk shirts, wide capes, Caucasian belts, and broad-brimmed hats.

As a writer, Bunin charged, Gorky continued the charade. His autobiography reeked with lies. His fictional heroes bordered on self-parody: barefoot bums waxing eloquently on freedom, folk giants vaunting might and right, and freedom fighters tearing flaming hearts from their chests. With Gorky, Bunin went on to say, politics and rage overtook perspective and restraint. New York was for him not a bustling metropolis of skyscrapers and strivers; rather, it was a behemoth with jaws of black crooked teeth and stomachs of iron and stone.

For all the vituperation and anger, though, Bunin could not let Gorky go. Deep-seated affection, even love, rose to the fore. Periodically, Bunin forgave and forgot, confessing between himself and Gorky an intimacy and admiration that grew stronger with time. Despite the hagiography, personal and Soviet,

Gorky was for Bunin also prosaically human, especially when the two men were alone. When Gorky was not shouting from rooftops, he was soft-spoken. When he was not burly and brash, he was gentle and genteel, even clownish and comic. Uncomfortable with followers and crowds, Gorky sought out select friends. Hands, he clasped in a pleasant and priest-like way. Faces and lips, he kissed lovingly and longingly. Shyly, Gorky showed to Bunin pictures of his family, even material for a dress he had bought for his wife. For all the proletarian hype, Bunin also took care to note, Gorky devoured world literature and culture and wrote in a competent way. Indeed, the difference between Gorky's private and public selves was, in Bunin's view, so profound that, in exasperation, he felt compelled to ask: Will the real Gorky please stand up?

With Gorky in *Recollections*, though, Bunin claimed primacy in the relationship: it was Gorky who praised Bunin, not vice versa. More to the point, perhaps, it was also Gorky who proclaimed two things that Bunin, throughout *Recollections*, wanted himself and everyone else to hear. One looked back: Bunin was the last writer of the gentry, of the culture and civilization that had given to the world Pushkin, Turgenev, and Tolstoy. More importantly, perhaps, the other looked forward: Bunin was a teacher and a model for new writers and readers in Russia and beyond. True, Bunin accepted such encomiums as gift horses from Gorky's mouth, but the circumspection—and humility—were short-lived. Gorky could tell the truth, Bunin acknowledged, especially if it was about him.

Bunin was even more conflicted about Alexei Tolstoy. As he saw it, Tolstoy never had a bad day. He was perennially, if annoyingly, cheerful and upbeat. If the glass was empty, Tolstoy saw it as full or next to the tap. He was also ultimate Teflon. Nothing—images and ideas, people and politics—stuck to him. If others in *Recollections* landed on their head or other parts of their anatomy, Alexei Tolstoy always wound up on his feet, and for a straightforward reason. He triumphed in war or peace. Whatever united and divided people and nations, Tolstoy transcended with the greatest of ease. Simultaneously, with impunity, he was an aristocrat, a bourgeois, and a revolutionary: a comrade and count. In equal parts, with equal fervor, he believed in everything and nothing. With émigrés, he hated Bolsheviks; with Bolsheviks, he hated émigrés. He was the same in France, Germany, and pre- and postrevolutionary Russia.

It galled and fascinated Bunin that Alexei Tolstoy got away with murder: Stiva Oblonsky in *Anna Karenina* come to life. To one and all, he was "Alyosha." He was never alone; he was always the life of the party. No matter how he used and abused people, he was everyone's partner and friend. He played his cards well: a swindler of the first order. For the higher classes, he lisped. For the lower ones, he grunted. He also lived life to the fullest, relishing good food and drink and dressing his strapping figure in expensive suits and shoes. His mind brimmed with projects and plans, many of which he realized. For all his complaints, he never lacked money.

Bunin begrudged Alexei Tolstoy the fact that he spoke, read, told, and wrote stories well. He knew Russia, Russians, and Russian in a way that few did. More personally, Tolstoy was Bunin's guardian angel. Wherever he was, he enticed with pictures of the good life and, more important, with promises of safe havens where Bunin could resume writing. He was as good as his word. For Bunin and others, he offered food, funds, shelter, patrons, and publishers. Indeed, if Bunin was ambivalent about Tolstoy, it was because the man had often insured his survival.

Although Bunin sought to discredit Alexei Tolstoy by any and all means—he doubted the man's aristocratic origins, questioned his revolutionary sympathies, condemned his return to Russia, and censured his pro-Soviet and anti-émigré writings—he knew that such efforts were in vain. Even Bunin's parting with Tolstoy in Paris in 1936 was sweet sorrow. No matter what the issue or problem, Alexei Tolstoy was for Bunin exemplar of the wide Russian soul: restless, resilient, irascible, anarchic, charming, profligate, perverse, and, above all, prone to flashes of brilliance, which ensured Russian literature east and west.

In all of *Recollections*, one thing is clear: Bunin was the lead character, the star of the show. At times in his work, Bunin acted in a way he never did in fiction or life. Interspersed throughout his sojourns to the past were touches of playfulness, humanity, and humor. Never in their wildest imagination would friends and colleagues, readers and reviewers have imagined Bunin as looking on the world with starry-eyed idealism or, more prosaically, as imbibing too much, often at gatherings in his honor. Even less could such individuals have come to terms with Bunin's obsession with Leo Tolstoy or his own youthful misadventures as a Tolstoyan. Even with suspended disbelief, they never would have accepted Bunin galloping about with Gorky's son on his shoulders or being carried in turn by Chaliapin up several flights of stairs.

More often in *Recollections*, though, Bunin seethed with anger and revolt. On one hand, the rage was personal. Beyond a war with the avant-gardists, Bunin censured, rightly, critics who had pigeonholed him as a Chekhov-light, as a second singer of dying gentry nests. He also took to task friends and colleagues who, he believed, in actions or words, had bowed to Soviet pressure and power: Konstantin Stanislavsky, Vladimir Nemirovich-Danchenko, and Maria Chekhova. He chided émigrés for applauding as prodigals such Soviet writers as Esenin and Mayakovsky.

On the other hand, his wrath was political, the bulk of his fury served for the Bolsheviks. The writer of *Recollections* could never accept the events of 1917 and its aftermath as a rational and logical development in accord with the teachings of Georg Hegel or Karl Marx. Rather, what had transpired in Russia was for him a biblical plague, a political, social, and aesthetic apocalypse. In Bunin's view, Lenin and company had unleashed only murder and misfortune, turning his compatriots into degenerates, psychopaths, and sadists. Particularly galling was the moral schizophrenia: the more the Bolsheviks promised heaven on earth, the more they brought hell to the world, taking satisfaction in senseless savagery, in lip-licking delight over spilled blood and guts.

To Bunin, the death and destruction that the Bolsheviks had rained down on Russia was not so much the traditional horror and gore of all revolutions, but, once again, the everyday episodes of anguish and angst that, like the incessant dripping of Chinese water torture, eroded humanness and humanity. The smaller the pictures of revolutionary distress and disorder that Bunin drew in *Recollections*, the more they exceeded a thousand words. An officer thrown alive into the furnace of a locomotive; a state official cannibalized by peasants; a suicide holding a note proclaiming Lenin's kingdom as immortal; and, most poignantly, brothers Yuly and Yevgeny Bunin and sister Maria Bunina-Laskarshevskaya perishing from cold, hunger, and fatigue—in these vignettes Ivan Bunin laced *Recollections* with anger, bitterness, and regret.

Equally painful was the aesthetic damage. In Bunin's mind, the Bolsheviks had things backward. If together with Chekhov, Tolstoy, and Ertel, he plumbed life for ideas, Lenin and company imposed ideas on life. Literature and art had to conform to the theories and theses of a handful of individuals, Anyone or anything that challenged or contradicted state platforms and positions on literature and art, culture, and civilization became the enemy, with fatal results to their beings and to the national creative expression. Soviet writers and artists disavowed the time-honored consensus on writers in Russia. They were no longer priests, prophets, or seers. Rather, in a nod to Stalin, they were engineers of souls in service to the state. Even more distressing to Bunin was that Soviet writers and artists were no longer men, but, with apologies to Dostoevsky, men-gods. In the political myth and hype, Gorky became a Cossack and a martyr. Mayakovsky designated ships and tanks, villages and mountains.

Bunin took Soviet writers and artists to task for other flaws. Socialist realists, he said, saw aesthetic freedom as aristocratic or bourgeois, demanding that poetry and prose look to the future, not to the present or the past. They insisted that national art depict life as it could, would, and/or should be, not as it is or was. Fiction and other aesthetic creations, state-sponsored writers, reviewers, and readers also agreed, should champion grand visions, not paltry events. They should be stark blacks and whites, not shades of gray; they should promise communist utopias, not mythic Edens; they should depict materialist struggles, not spiritual communities, in zero-sum games.

Even after all was said and done, Bunin held his head high. Like any good Russian writer, he countered anger and angst with faith and hope. Like the victims of tornadoes and hurricanes who, sifting through the rubble, find new value and meaning in people, places, and things they once deemed worthless or trifling, Bunin searched through the waste and wreckage of revolution and war for individuals and items to champion the goodness of creation and the tenacity of its citizens. A ruined prince in Russia wrote about ethics. Another exiled royal maintained his dignity, even sanity, with stories of a folk who forsook revolution for Christ, the Gospels, and brotherly love.

Bunin also claimed his rightful due. His was the ultimate story of rags to riches. After several hair-raising adventures in his first months abroad—he was almost lost at sea; he was robbed of everything he had in Sofia, Bulgaria; he was almost blown to bits at a lecture—Bunin arrived in the West, destitute and distressed. It was a miracle that he picked up a pen again. If it were not for the patronage and protection of friends—Alexei Tolstoy, Mark Aldanov, Boris Zaitsev, and Mikhail and Maria Tseitlin were key protectors and patrons—Bunin might have perished completely.

It is perhaps one of the greatest ironies in Bunin's life that he was esteemed more highly in Europe than in Russia. If indigenous readers and reviewers endured Bunin before the revolution only to throw him overboard from the ship of modernity afterward, their counterparts in England, France, and Germany saw him as a guardian of political, social, and aesthetic values and truths. Within a year of his arrival in France, Bunin was presented with a calling card from Alexandre Millerand, president of France. Publishers in London, Paris, Berlin, Prague, and Belgrade were so enthralled by "The Gentleman from San Francisco" that they used it as the starting point for Western editions of his works. D. H. Lawrence and Leonard Woolf translated 'The Gentleman" and other stories for an edition of Bunin's works in 1922 and 1923. French and German translations of the story appeared that same year. (Bunin's "The Gentleman" first appeared in the United States also in 1923.)

Bunin received rave reviews from the critics. "Bunin," a French critic wrote circa December 1922, "is a genuine Russian talent. . . . His anthology, *The Gentleman from San Francisco*, has several stories that are as powerful as anything Dostoevsky wrote." Similarly, a reviewer noted in May 1922: "Bunin's "The Gentleman from San Francisco" . . . [is] a singularly ruthless indictment of modern civilization. . . . Bunin is certainly one of the most important [Russian] writers who have been made accessible to us."[29]

European writers were similarly charmed. "I have just read "The Gentleman from San Francisco," Lawrence wrote to a friend on June 16, 1921. "In spite of its lugubriousness, I grin with joy." Romain Rolland agreed, dismissing Bunin the person, but extolling Bunin the artist. "Bunin is not one of us," he wrote to Louise Cruppi on May 20, 1922. "He is frantically, bitterly anti-revolutionary, anti-democratic, anti-populist, a pessimist to the marrow of his bones. But what a genuine artist he is! How he gives witness to the rebirth of Russian literature! . . . His very consciousness . . . is permeated with the spirit of boundless, unfathomable Asia!" To Bunin himself, Rolland wrote a month later: "Allow me to tell you about the artistic delight I experienced when I read your collection of stories, titled *The Gentleman from San Francisco*. . . . I am particularly struck by the many sensations that penetrate your works; not only your sights and sounds but an entire orchestra of emotions."[30]

Swelling the chorus of praise was John Middleton Murry, who wrote in a review in June 1922: "When [Bunin's] 'The Gentleman from San Francisco' appeared, our feeling was that a new planet had swum into our ken. . . . The ruthlessness with which Bunin stripped the nakedness of modern civilization was comprehensive and synoptic, not petulantly and spasmodically cynical as are so many modern writers with the same theme. . . . It is, indeed, a masterpiece, without a doubt one of the finest short stories . . . of modern times." Four years later, Thomas Mann was compelled to say: "Bunin's 'The Gentleman from San Francicso' has the moral impact of . . . [Leo] Tolstoy's . . . *The Death of Ivan Ilyich*. This story should be translated into all languages. . . . I also did not have to force myself to be carried away by the profundity of *Mitya's Love* for in it is the incomparably tragic tragedy and culture of his land."[31]

Several Western literati wanted to meet Bunin in person. In August 1922, André Gide invited Bunin to attend an annual conference of European writers and artists. Although Bunin declined, he was sorely missed. "Everyone kept deploring Bunin's absence," Gide wrote in his journal on September 3, 1922.[32] At a gathering in his honor by the International PEN Club in London in 1925, Bunin was sought out by the English writer Jerome Jerome, an encounter that he thought sufficiently important to place as the third vignette in *Recollections*.

Even more noteworthy, perhaps, was the fact that no sooner had Bunin entered into exile than he was nominated for the Nobel Prize in Literature. Around mid-June 1922, Rolland (himself the winner of the award in 1915) proposed, however improbably, the joint candidacy of Bunin and Gorky. On August 15 of that year, Aldanov sought to offset Gorky with a triple crown of Bunin, Merezhkovsky, and Kuprin. By the end of the year, Bunin was running alone, with Rolland again submitting a formal nomination.

The suspense continued until November 9, 1933, when Bunin was awarded the Nobel Prize in Literature, the first Russian writer and the first writer in exile to be accorded such an honor. He was also only the thirty-second author to attain this honor, taking his place among a total of 166 winners who, since 1901, had been lauded for achievements in physics, chemistry, medicine, literature, and peace. The timing was also significant: it was the hundredth anniversary of the birth of Alfred Nobel, the Swedish scholar, philanthropist, and businessman.

When in *Recollections* Bunin reflected initially on the Nobel Prize, he did so without the excitement and joy that had attended the actual conferral of the award. Indeed, the first pages of his "Nobel Days" had a restrained, almost bittersweet cast. It was as if Bunin, given all the tumult of his existence, looked on his status as a Nobel laureate as too little, too late, as a distinction that did not mitigate past or future anguish.

Bunin's claim in *Recollections* that the Nobel Prize split his life in two is flawed both mathematically and emotionally. The seventeen years that followed the honor mirrored the sixty-three years that preceded it, although, in truth, they were worse. Just as it was Bunin's fate to know upheaval in politics and art before the Nobel Prize, it would be his lot to know even greater chaos in both spheres thereafter. Worldwide depression, militant fascism, and triumphant communism had triggered a second world war and promised an ultimate third. Modernism was also alive and well, symbolism and futurism ceding to abstract expressionism and absurdist literature and theater.

Even worse, at age eighty, Bunin was surrendering to his most feared enemies: old age, sickness, and death. Chilled by the coldness of the grave, he knew that he was losing lifelong battles on all fronts. Unsurprisingly, in "Nobel Days," Bunin looked on his distinction as a laureate as one in a series of unwelcome incursions, even a cruel joke of history or fate on someone who, throughout his life, begged only to be left in peace.

For all his condemnation of the posturing of Esenin, Blok, and Mayakovsky, Bunin, in the beginning of "Nobel Days," was not above staging his own spectacle. Not unlike the famed "little man" losers and lunatics of nineteenth-century Russian literature—Yevgeny in Pushkin's 1833 "The Bronze Horseman," Aksenty Poprishchin in Nikolai Gogol's 1835 "Notes of a Madman," and Yakov Golyadkin Senior in Dostoevsky's 1846 *The Double* come to mind—Bunin, in "Nobel Days," cast himself as a "pale madman" at the mercy of people and events.

Unlike his fictional protégés, however, Bunin did not wind up dead or insane. Even more to his credit, he achieved what they did not, if only momentarily.

Unlike Yevgeny, he had beaten the state. Unlike Poprishchin, he was king for a day. Unlike Golyadkin Senior, he was welcome in society. Although bewildered, even stunned by the Nobel Prize, Bunin cast off "littleness" quickly. Even as he protested too much, he relished the lights, cameras, and action. In Grasse, France, he embraced the crush of visitors, reporters, and photographers; he bathed in the stream of international telegrams and letters. In Stockholm, the new laureate delighted in the rites and rituals, the flowers and fanfare, the hob-nobbing with kings and queens, and the applause of literati and glitterati.

Even more contrary to "littleness"—fictional or factual—Bunin seized the spotlight. Although, in "Nobel Days," his replies to reporters were short and sweet—undoubtedly, they were longer and more involved in real life—they conveyed an ample sense of self. In rapid-fire succession, Bunin noted his love of travel, his lack of rights as an émigré, and his wish to remain in exile abroad. Wryly, he pointed out that Leo Tolstoy was never offered the Nobel Prize. Equally cheeky, he claimed that his award was for the entire corpus of his writing, not for a particular work.

Even more revealing in "Nobel Days" were those times when Bunin subsumed himself into a larger picture. His distinction as an honoree, he informed with a mythically national cast. It was the most poignant irony in *Recollections* that when Bunin journeyed to Stockholm to receive his award, he saw from the windows of trains, ships, and hotels not the landscapes of France, Germany, and Sweden, but the terra firma of prerevolutionary Russia. Psycho-spiritually, he walked among storybook men and women in fur coats and hats; he strolled amid the magical sunrises and sunsets of St. Petersburg; he wandered among dense forests, rolling plains, and hidden villages, bathed in pale moonlight and covered in funereally tinged snow. Such journeys to times gone by were soul-saving experiences in which he sensed, with every fi ber of his being, that home was where his heart was and that he still lived in Russia, if he had ever left at all.

En route to Stockholm, Bunin knew that he was not finished as a person and a professional. In a self-renewing way, he sensed that he still had a lot of living to do. That he had seen Russia everywhere he went, that he had walked among its people, that he had strolled its cities and villages, affirmed what was for him a key life principle: *Memoro ergo sum*, or "I remember, therefore I am." As did Natalya in *Dry Valley*, Bunin directed memory to assuage the pain and suffering of the past. More importantly, perhaps, he used memory to affirm the present and future, rejoicing in moments that proved to him that there was a God, that life was worth living, that paradise lay open to the senses, that people trumped politics, and that, however slowly, goodness and love triumphed over evil and hate. In a personal *War and Peace*, Bunin pondered over a thousand pages of life narrative to see that, in the end, everyone and everything were where they should be.

Such memory-inspired insight led Bunin to do something that he was quite lax to do. Momentarily, he, as a Nobel laureate, donned the mantel of a leader—a Moses, a Chrysostom, and a Luther—of the Russian diaspora not only in Europe but also worldwide. In a rare moment of sharing, Bunin realized that the Nobel Prize was not his alone. It also belonged to two groups. First were Leo Tolstoy, Chekhov, and other writers in *Recollections* who, he believed, had given to Russian literature international popularity and prestige. Second, and equally important, were the teeming masses of expatriates who, in the wake of revolution and war, now wandered the world as, again with a nod to Dostoevsky, the "humiliated and injured" of modern life, but with self-styled torahs in hand. "Reverence for our literature," Mikhail Pechkovsky wrote in November 1933, "is [part] of the testament, the tablets that the emigration has preserved carefully until it returns to the Promised Land—to Russia."[33]

Bunin's "Nobel Days," the best vignette in *Recollections*, is like the wine at the wedding feast of Cana, in that it was saved until last to celebrate not only the apex of Bunin's life but also the triumph of prerevolutionary Russian literature, culture, and civilization over the ravages of time, space, and history and, most importantly, against all whom Bunin believed would do it ill.

In both Stockholm in 1933 and *Recollections* in 1950, Bunin made a case for himself and for Russian literature before the whole world. On both occasions, he was a success. In a radio broadcast from Stockholm to Europe and beyond, Bunin was elegant and sublime. A singular moment in the public eye, he behaved. In a speech only several hundred words long, he did not rail against God and fate. He even left Bolsheviks and the avant-gardists in peace. Equally rare, perhaps, Bunin also said thank you—first to France, for his adoptive home, and then to Sweden, whose competent and impartial judges had deemed him worthy of the highest literary honor. Even more revealing, Bunin championed a key image and idea: freedom of thought and conscience, along with independence of the writer and the word, were the cornerstones of civilization, the ultimate defense against falseness and lies.

Bunin realized that as much as the distinction of the Nobel Prize thrilled him and the Russian diaspora, it was a moment that was fleeting and forgotten as quickly as it was celebrated. *Recollections*, though, was for him a different matter. As was the case with *Dry Valley* and *The Life of Arseniev*, it preserved, in indestructible and inviolate prose, a world that had passed from life, never to return. *Recollections* was for Bunin a last hurrah, a final send-off before he left this life. If Bunin was uncomfortable as a leader of Russian expatriates, as a Moses, a Chrysostom, and a Luther, he was not averse to leaving them with words that embraced everyone and everything he saw as right and wrong in pre- and postrevolutionary Russian literature, culture, and civilization. Not unlike Dostoevsky in *The Brothers Karamazov*, Bunin saw his generation as too weak and scarred, vulgar and corrupt to bring about meaningful change in life. It was his hope against hope that new generations would read his *Recollections*, learn its lessons, and carry forth its vision.

Chapter 1

Autobiographical Notes

My life as a writer began rather strangely. It must have begun on our country estate, on an endlessly distant day long ago, when I, as a boy about eight years old in the Oryol Province, happened by chance to come across a book of pictures and was seized suddenly by a passionate and restless desire to make up right away something like a poem or a fairy tale.[1] One picture showed some wild mountains, the white ribbon of a waterfall, and a fat, stocky peasant, a dwarf with an old woman's face and a swollen throat, a goiter, standing under the waterfall with a long stick in his hand and wearing a small, feminine hat with a feather sticking out its side.

In the caption under the picture was a word that struck me and, fortunately, I still did not now know: "Meeting a Cretin in the Mountains." A cretin! Most likely, if this unusual word had not been there, the dwarf, with his goiter, old woman's face, and feminine hat, would only have repulsed me greatly, but nothing more. But a cretin? The word seemed to me something frightening, mysterious, even magical! Suddenly, poetic ecstasy seized me; but on that day, it went for naught. No matter how I tried, I did not write a single line. But was not that day the beginning of my writing?

In any case, the day that I came across that picture was seemingly a prophetic sign since, throughout my long life, I have often met cretins who were rather repulsive (but without goiters). Some of them were not at all magical, but outright terrifying, especially when they joined one or another facet of their cretinism to genuine skill, madness, and hysterical powers. After all, everyone knows that such a thing was, is, and will happen in all realms of human existence. That's just the way life is!

Generally speaking, I have been faced with a most unusual life. I have even been a contemporary of cretins, whose names will endure in world history as the "greatest geniuses of humankind," but who demolished entire kingdoms and destroyed millions of human lives.

I was born in Voronezh, lived there for three years, and once spent an additional night there.[2] But I do not know the city at all since I did not see it on the night I was there. Some association of students invited me to read my works for a charitable event for their group. I arrived in Voronezh in a blizzard, at dark winter dusk. I was met at the station with champagne. I was treated to much more of the stuff at the event itself, and when, at dawn, I was taken to the station to return to Moscow, I was completely smashed.

The three years I spent in Voronezh were my infancy.

My parents moved from Voronezh to the family estate near Oryol; I began to recall my life since that time.[3] There passed my childhood and adolescence.

During those years, the infamous "impoverishment" of the gentry had come to an end. That was the title of a once famous book written by the now forgotten Terpigorev-Atava.[4] After him I was the one who was called the last writer to "extol" dying gentry nests.[5] Then came Chekhov, who "glorified" the ravaged beauty of "cherry orchards," even though he understood gentry landowners, orchards, and estates quite poorly. Even now almost everyone is captivated by the artificial beauty of his "cherry orchard."

I consider Chekhov among the most remarkable Russian writers for the very many and truly splendid things that he gave [to world literature]. But I do not like his plays. I find it even awkward for him and unpleasant for me to recall this famous Uncle Vanya; or Doctor Astrov, who, for no reason at all, keeps harping on the need to plant trees; or Gaev, who presumes to be terribly aristocratic, but whose nobility Stanislavsky portrayed [onstage] by forever cleaning his fingernails with a cambric handkerchief in such a repulsively refined way! I won't even talk about the landowner whose name is straight out of Gogol: Simeonov-Pishchik.[6]

I grew up in just such an "impoverished" nest. It was a remote estate in the steppe, with a big orchard, only not a "cherry" one of course, since, notwithstanding Chekhov, orchards with *only* cherry trees were nowhere in Russia.[7] Some gentry orchards had *sections*, sometimes even quite vast ones, where cherry trees did grow; but, again, Chekhov aside, these orchards were never *right alongside* the manor house. Also, there never was, nor is there, anything wonderful about cherry trees. As everyone knows, they are quite ugly things, with crooked branches and small leaves and flowers (not at all like those cherry trees that grew so largely and lavishly under the windows of the manor house in the Moscow Art Theater).[8] It is also completely unlikely that Lopakhin would have been so foolish and impatient as to order these profitable trees to be cut down without giving the former owner time to leave the estate. But he had to hurry to do so apparently, because Chekhov wanted the audience to hear the sound of axes, to see with their own eyes the demise of gentry life, and to have Firs say as the curtain falls: "They have forgotten the servant. . . ."

This Firs is a rather believable character, but only because writers have portrayed the type of the old servant a hundred times before Chekhov. The other individuals in the play, I repeat, are simply unbearable. Gaev, like other characters in Chekhov's drama, mumbles nonsense constantly in his conversations. As if playing billiards, he says, "Yellow ball in the middle. . . . Doublet in the corner. . . ." Ranevskaya, allegedly a landowner and a Parisian, both laughs and cries hysterically: "What a wonderful orchard! White masses of flowers, the blue sky! The nursery! My dear, wonderful room!" (She cries.) "My dear little wardrobe!" (She kisses the thing.) "My little table! Oh, my childhood, my innocence!" (She laughs from joy.) "My white, all white orchard!"

Later, as if right out of *Uncle Vanya*, are hysterics from Anya: "Mama! Mama, are you crying? My dear, kind, good Mama, my wonderful Mama, I love you . . . I adore you! The cherry orchard has been sold, but do not cry, Mama! We will plant a new orchard, more splendid than this one, and happiness, deep, serene happiness will descend upon your soul, just like the sun does during twilight, and you will smile, Mama!"

Standing alongside all of thisis the student Trofimov, a type of "stormy petrel."[9] "Forward!" he exclaims. "We staunchly march to the bright star shining there, in the distance. Do not fall behind, friends!"

Ranevskaya, Nina Zarechnaya. . . . Truly, only provincial actresses could come up with such names![10]

In my youth, new writers were almost always urbanites, who said many stupid things. One well-known poet—he is still alive, I do not wish to cite his name—wrote in his verse that he walked along "with my hands making my way through ears of wheat," even though such a plant does not exist in nature. As everyone knows, millet and wheat sprout not "ears" but grains (more accurately, panicles), which grow so low that it would be impossible to grab hold of them while walking. Another poet (Balmont) wrote fervently that "passion leaves like a harrier in flight," but a harrier, an evening bird from the owl family, is gray, slow, mysteriously quiet, and completely noiseless in the air. Balmont also rhapsodized over a flowering plantain—"the plantain is all in bloom!"—he writes—but such a plant grows along field roads, sprouts only small green leaves, and never flowers. And what about the many gentry estates and their owners that Gumilyov portrayed so wretchedly. Such places have

Slanting, two-storied homes
And *also* a farmyard and barn,

Even more surprising, gentry men, it turns out, are "proud of their new light tight-fitting coats" and, loving tyranny and the *Domostroi*, cede nothing to any old-fashioned Tit Titych.[11] Their daughters dare not utter a sound in their presence, but, forced to marry hateful and repulsive men, dream of "becoming mermaids," of drowning themselves in some stream or pond. And it was not all that long ago that one famous Soviet poet described a hunter walking "on *turf*" in the woods and "carrying a *golden fox in his game bag*." He might as well have carried his dog in his pocket.[12]

By the way, why did Stanislavsky and Nemirovich name their theater the Moscow "Art" Theater—as if to distinguish it from all other dramatic institutions? Surely, must not artistry be found in any theater—just as in all forms of art? Has not every actor aspired and continued to aspire to be an artist in the theater? Surely have there been so few actor-artists in Russia and in all other countries of the world?

Incidentally, the Art Theater is now called the Gorky Art Theater. First and foremost, this theater was made famous by Chekhov. Even to this day a seagull is on its curtain.[13] But when it was ordered that the theater bear the name of Gorky, the author of the pulp-like and absolutely artificial *Depths*, both Stanislavsky and Nemirovich accepted the directive humbly, even though the latter once declared to Chekhov for all of Russia to hear: "This is your theater, Anton."[14]

How the Kremlin can scare people! Before me is a book, *Chekhov as Remembered by His Contemporaries*, published in Moscow in 1947.[15] Among the memoirists is M. P. Chekhova, who writes: "Anton Pavlovich was surrounded by people from literature, politics, sciences, and the arts: Alexei Maximovich Gorky, L. N. Tolstoy, V. Korolenko, Levitan, and Kuprin visited our home. . . ."[16]

During the last years of Chekhov's life, I not only visited him every day at his home in Yalta but also sometimes stayed with him for weeks on end.[17] I was almost like a brother to M. P. Chekhova; but, now a very old woman, she did not even dare to mention me when, in a cowardly, servile piece, titled, "Alexei Maximovich Gorky and Vyacheslav Mikhailovich Molotov," she wrote:

"Vyacheslav Mikhailovich Molotov apparently expressed not only his opinion but also that of the entire Soviet intelligentsia, when he wrote to me in 1936: 'The little house of A. Chekhov calls to mind this glorious writer of our land, and many of our citizens should visit this abode. V. Molotov, a Chekhov admirer.' What wise and gracious words!"[18]

The "Gorky Art Theater." How do you like that? But it is only the beginning. All of Russia, now renamed the USSR, has agreed humbly to the most brazen and idiotic insults to Russian historical life. The city of Peter the Great now bears the name of Lenin.[19] Königsberg, the city of Kant, is now Kaliningrad; ancient Nizhniy Novgorod is now Gorky City; and time-honored Tver is now Kalinin (after a most insignificant typesetter).[20]

Even the entire Russian emigration accepted such changes with utmost indifference. It also attached no significance when a curly haired drunk, having charmed it with hawkish, heart-tweaking lyrics "to the tune of an accordion"—and about whom Blok said very rightly: *"Esenin has a talent for vulgarity and blasphemy"*—once promised to change the name of his homeland from "Kitezh" to "Inoniya."[21] Tearing into his accordion, he cried out:

I hate the breath of Kitezh!
I bestow Inoniya with fame!
I will pluck out God's very beard!
I will curse His very name!

In Inoniya I will transcend the dunces,
I will sometimes be drunk from wine,
Clearly will I see it all and then
With eyes that rage and shine,
I will proclaim that.
This new era is no small change,
Lenin's name be the world's and mine![22]

Why did the Russian emigration forgive Esenin for everything he had done? Was it because he, as a reckless Russian type, often bemoaned his bitter fate in such an artificial way?[23] Such goings-on are not all that new, since did not another "brat," on his way from Odessa to Sakhalin, also moan and groan with the greatest self-delight:

I stuck my mother with a knife,
I killed my father then and there,
And my sweet little sister
I raped without a care. . . .[24]

The emigration forgave Esenin, this "uneducated genius," even though there were so many of these "naturally talented types" in Russia that Don Aminado wrote:

I'm so bored with uneducated geniuses
Their plows, cows, and moos,
I'm sick of their native dress and drink
And poetry that stinks of booze!

To be a poet is easy now
There's no need to be forlorn:
Just shake your locks and give off cries
And with pen in hand, cover God with scorn. . . . [25]

Esenin's first steps onto the poetic scene are well known. His contemporary, the poet G. V. Adamovich, who knew Esenin personally, was more than accurate when he wrote: "Esenin appeared in Petersburg during the first world war and was accepted in literary circles with mocking surprise. Felt boots, a light-blue belted shirt, blond hair cut in a fringe, eyes that were cast downward, and modest sighs: 'Where's our place now, we bumpkins from the village!'[26]

"But beneath this masquerade were frenzied careerism, stark boldness, insatiable pride, and love for glory, which, at any moment, were ready to burst forth in the most daring ways. What Sologub said about Esenin is impossible to say in print. Kuzmin made a wry face, and Gumilyov shrugged his shoulders. Gippius looked at Esenin's felt boots through a lorgnette and asked: 'What kind of leg warmers are those?'[27]

"All this forced Esenin to move to Moscow, where, having attached himself to the 'imagists,' he became popular quickly. Then began his scandals and uproars, 'God, deliver the calf,' outbursts of mania for greatness, Isadora Duncan, his tours with her throughout Europe and America, his frenzied assaults on her person, return to Russia, new marriages, scandals, drunkenness—and suicide. . . ."[28]

Esenin also talked about himself in a very precise way—how he taught his friend Mariengof that one had to barge into society and to live at its expense. Mariengof was no less a scoundrel than Esenin. He was a most repulsive villain who once wrote a line about the Mother of God that was vile beyond imagination, but equal to what Babel once wrote about her.[29] Here is what Esenin taught Mariengof:

"One cannot climb into literature in just any old way, Tolya. One has to take up the most precise politics. Just look at Bely: his hair is already gray, and he has a bald spot, but even with his cook, he goes about inspired.[30] It is still quite all right to play the fool. People in Russia are quick to love fools.

"Do you want to know how I climbed Parnassus? I did it in a light, tight-fitting man's coat, a shirt embroidered like a towel, and crumpled-up boot tops. Everyone looked at me through lorgnettes. Oh, how splendid! Oh, how like a genius!' But I blushed like a girl and did not look up from shyness. . . . Then I was dragged from salon to salon and sang tavern ditties with an accordion. . . . [31]

"Klyuev did the same thing. He pretended to be a painter. He once entered the back door to Gorodetsky's house to ask if, perhaps, he could paint something. He started to read his poems to the cook. She immediately went to the master, who invited the poet-painter into his room. But the poet stayed where he was. 'Why do we need the bedroom?' he said. 'I'll dirty the master's chair and track mud onto the newly waxed floor. . . .' The master again asked him to sit down, Klyuev again refused, saying that he would stand. . . ."

Also interesting are the recollections of Rodion Beryozov, a former friend of Esenin's, published in *New Russian Word* in New York.[32] Tenderly, he wrote about Esenin:

"Fellows from the village where Esenin was born visited him now and then and would ask him:

'Seryozha, do you remember how we used to drag nets with so many golden carp in them? And how we used to pasture the horses and eat baked potatoes at night?'

"Esenin answered:

"'I remember everything, my brothers. The banquets in my honor in New York, these I have forgotten, but everything that is ours and native to us, that I remember.'"

But Beryozov also recalled that Esenin wore only silk shirts and the very latest ties and shoes, even as he proclaimed publicly in his verse that he was "very much his own fellow," shaking his curly head, lilting the ends of his lines, and, of course, recalling, off the cuff, that he was hooligan, a scandalmonger, "reckless Russia":

A blue fire rushed through the land,
The forgotten haunts now lie low,
I remember the first time I sang about love,
The first time I refused a row. . . . [33]

What should one supposedly admire here? The lyrics of a scoundrel who long turned his hooliganism into a profitable profession, into eternal bragging and other similar shortcomings?

May is blue. The weather glows warm.
The garden bell does not sound well,

A berry tree sleeps inside its white cloak,
The wormwood flutters with sticky smell. . . .

The action here takes place in a garden in May. But where did Esenin get hold of wormwood, which, as everyone knows, is dry and sharp, not sticky. Furthermore, even if it smelled in a sticky way, how could it "waft" in the process?

Later in the poem, despite the sleeping berry tree,

The garden bursts forth, like a frothy fire,
And the moon, with all its might above,
Seeks that one and all tremble
From the aching words "my love."

One can understand the wish of the moon. After all, Balmont once insisted that even "every lizard seeks aching sensations."[34] But again: where in this glowing warmth did he get such a frenzied moon and a fiery, exploding garden?

Esenin ends his poem with these lines:

Only in this solace and quiet,
Under the accordion of a merry May,
I sit alone and want for nothing,
Accepting all, come what may,[35]

Here May turns out to be already merry and even accordion-like. But there is nothing wrong in this: people admire such things. . . .

Beryozov continues that Esenin loved spring. "I often met Esenin at the editorial offices for *Red Virgin Soil*.[36] Always and everywhere, he listened to songs. Picture it: Esenin, leaning against a bookcase, a cane in his left hand, in a black bowler hat, patent leather shoes, and a stylish light overcoat with raglan sleeves, and listening to us singing. . . ."

Beryozov also recalls other "pictures": how Esenin lived and "created" (playing roles other than hooligan ones):

"Esenin lived on Bryussovsky Lane in a large apartment on the eighth floor. The windows of the room looked out onto the Kremlin. The place belonged to Galya Benislavskaya, who later became his wife.[37] There were elegant engravings and bright and pleasant wallpaper. The desk had an orderly look. The dining room had a couch with red pillows on one side and a bed covered with a silk bedspread from Samarkand on the other and, in the middle, a table with a dark tablecloth and a vase of fruit. . . .[38]

"Esenin wrote on Sundays, and in the morning, Galya, not wishing to disturb him, went to the country for the entire day. There she walked alone through fields and woods, thinking that, at that very moment, inspired lines flowed from Esenin's pen. . . .

"We were sitting at the dining-room table. Esenin told us about his trip to America, about the terrible angst he experienced on the other side of the ocean, and about the tears he shed whenever he found himself at home and saw graceful birch trees bending in the wind. He then went into the corridor, and we, rising from our chairs, heard him order in a whisper: 'Grusha, go get some flowers, the prettiest ones that you can buy.'[39]

"I always knew when a wave of inspiration had seized Esenin's heart. He put flowers on the table and got all dressed up, as if he were going to church. Creative forces had already consumed his entire being. We would leave, meeting Grusha with the flowers, and Galya would wander the countryside alone and pray to the skies, flowers, forests, and sky-blue lakes for God's servant, Sergei, for his inspired art. . . ."[40]

I got sick when I read such a thing. Even Mayakovsky was better! When he talked about his own trip to America, he just "swore" at it, without vile words about his "tormenting angst" beyond the ocean or about his tears at the sight of birch trees. . . . [41]

About Esenin, also Khodasevich once wrote in an article in *Contemporary Annals* that among the way Esenin seduced girls was to offer to take them to places where the people were shot by the Cheka.[42] "I can arrange such a thing for you easily," he told them. Khodasevich continued: "The powers that be and the Cheka protected the gang that surrounded Esenin. . . . They were useful to the Bolsheviks because they brought confusion and ugliness into Russian literature. . . ."[43]

I began to publish at the end of the '80s, The so-called decadents and symbolists, having arrived on the scene several years later, insisted that Russian literature had "come to a dead end"; that it had begun to turn gray and wither way; and that it did not know anything except realism, an "accepted" description of reality. . . . But right before they appeared, was there not, for example, *The Brothers Karamazov*, "Klara Milich," and "The Song of Love Triumphant"?[44] Were Fet's *Evening Fires* or the poetry of Vladimir Solovyov so realistic? Could one call gray the best things of Leskov, not to mention the wondrous, incomparable "folk" tales of Tolstoy, his *Kreutzer Sonata*, and *The Death of Ivan Ilyich*?[45] Were not new the spirit and form of Garshin and Chekhov, who were just entering literature?

I entered literature in the mid-'90s. Unfortunately, I did not meet Polonsky or Fet. I also did not make the acquaintance of Garshin, whose wonderful humanity coincided with his talent, and who, if he had not committed suicide, would have, undoubtedly, become one of our greatest Russian writers.[46] I did meet not only Tolstoy himself but also Chekhov. I crossed paths with Ertel, another remarkable individual and the author of the novel *The Gardenins*, which will always be a part of Russian literature.[47] I encountered Korolenko, the author of the amazing "Makar's Dream."[48] I also once ran into the legendary Grigorovich, seeing him in Suvorin's bookstore. I also came face-to-face with the poet Zhemchuzhnikov, one of the authors of "Kozma Prutkov," whom I often visited at his home and who called me his young friend. . . . [49]

But in those years, Russia was also host to a cruel, full-flamed war between the Populists and the Marxists, who affirmed that the down-and-out proletariat was the bulwark of the coming revolution.[50] Gorky, one of this group, reigned supreme in literature, having seized deftly on Marxist hopes for the barefoot tramp, the author of "Chelkash" and "The Old Woman Izergiil."[51] In the latter story, some Danko, an "ardent fighter for freedom and a bright future"—such fighters are always ardent—tears a flaming heart from his chest as a torch to rush somewhere forward, enticing humankind to follow him to disperse gloomy reaction.

Another group hailed the famous Merezhkovsky, Gippius, Balmont, Bryusov, and Sologub. . . . In these years, the all-Russian glory of Nadson had already come to an end. But it was not all that long ago that his close friend Minsky summoned the storm of the revolution:

Let the storm hit where I live,
Let me even be food for its fury![52]

Minsky, though, never became fodder for the storm but rather restrung his lyre in the same way they did.

I also met Balmont, Bryusov, and Sologub when they were passionate fans not only of the French decadents but also of Verlaine, Przybyszewski, Ibsen, Hamsun, and Maeterlinck. At that time, they were not at all interested in the proletariat. It was only much later that many of them began to sing à la Minsky:

Proletariat of all lands, unite!
Our will, our strength, our might![53]

Or like Balmont or Bryusov, who, necessarily, began as a decadent; then, during the first world war, became a monarchist, a Slavophile, and a patriot; and ended his career in a passionate wail:

Lenin is no more!!
O grief, O sorrow!
There he lies, cold and decayed,
Never to see tomorrow![54]

Shortly after we had become acquainted, Bryusov, barking through his nose, read me this terrible nonsense:

Spring joyful tears
And let out a hearty cry!
For high above the mast
A sailor passes by![55]

He also yapped out another absolutely amazing piece, about the rise of a sphere, which, as everyone knows, is still called the moon:

There rises a naked celestial sphere
In the light of an azure moon so dear![56]

Later, for several years running, Bryusov began to write things that were so much more intelligible and that developed his poetic talent so resolutely that he attained great skill and diversity in verse. At the same time, though, he often rushed off into wild verbal awkwardness, even complete swinery:

The alcove is locked,
The shadows quake,
You may slump and slouch,
But we two are at stake . . . [57]

Invariably, Bryusov was no less pompous than Kozma Prutkov.[58] He posed as a demon, a wizard, a merciless "*maître*," and a "captain of a ship. . . ." Steadfastly, he also began to decline as a poet, to become an absolutely ludicrous, if insane, versemonger who conjured up these unusual rhythms:

In the long-famed years of Cook,
You smashed the ribs of freights,
So that their chief would know you and
Your singular experiences and fates . . . [59]

Then there was Balmont, who exasperated even Gippius with his poetic flourishes. I was once at his literary "Fridays" at the home of the poet Sluchevsky.[60] A huge crowd had gathered. Balmont was in rare form. He read his first poem with such self-ecstasy that he even licked his lips:

Lilacs, lilies, lilting love. . . . [61]

He then read a second poem, rapping out with machinelike precision:

A black canoe, caught in a storm
Headed for the bank

But it lacked the sorcerer's touch
And beat the shore and sank. . . . [62]

Gippius kept giving Balmont sleepy looks through her lorgnette, and when he had finished and everyone was silent, she said slowly:

"Your first poem is very vulgar, your second is incomprehensible."

Balmont's face turned bloodred:

"I detest your insolence; but I'd like to know, what exactly didn't you understand about my poem?"

"I don't understand what this canoe is all about and why and how it lacks a sorcerer's touch," Gippius replied distinctly.

Balmont became like a cobra:

"A poet should not be surprised when a philistine asks him to explain his poetic images. But when another poet pesters him with bourgeois questions, he cannot restrain his anger. So you don't understand my image? Well, I can't put my head on your body so that you can understand what I am saying!"

"But I'm terribly happy that you cannot," Gippius replied, "because I'd find it a genuine misfortune to have your head."

Balmont was a truly amazing person. Many people sometimes admired him for his "childishness," as well as for his laughter, which, often unexpected and naive, always had a certain devilish cunning. By nature, he spoke with a great deal of feigned tenderness and "sweetness," but he often acted completely differently with much wild rowdiness, beastly pugnacity, and street-like impudence. Balmont was a man who, throughout his life, truly exhausted himself by his own narcissism. He was intoxicated with self. He was so self-confident that once, in a completely simpleminded way, he published a story about how during a visit to Tolstoy, the great writer, rocking in a swing, died from laugher when Balmont read his verse to him. Not at all distressed by Tolstoy's chuckling, he ended his story:

"The old man pretended skillfully not to like my poems!"[63]

With stunning naivete, Balmont talked a great deal about others, for example, when he visited Maeterlinck:

"The people at the Art Theater were preparing to stage *The Blue Bird* and, knowing that I was about to go abroad, asked me to see Maeterlinck to find out his thoughts about staging the play.[64] I agreed with pleasure, but something strange happened when I met him. First, I rang his doorbell for almost an entire hour. Second, I was met by some shrew, who barricaded the entrance with her body. Third, when I finally crossed the threshold, I saw an empty room with a lone chair in the middle. A huge dog was sitting on it, with Maeterlinck standing alongside. I bowed and gave my name, assured fully that my host would know who I was. Maeterlinck just looked at me in silence, but the cursed dog began howling. I had a sudden passionate urge to pitch the monster onto the floor and to berate its master for his lack of hospitality.

"But, restraining my anger, I told him the purpose of my visit. Maeterlinck continued to remain silent, but the dog now began choking from its howling. Rather sharply, I said: 'Would you kindly deign to tell me your thoughts about the staging of your play?' Finally, Maeterlinck opened his lips and said: 'I don't think anything about it at all. Good-bye.' I raced out of there like a speeding bullet, like a raging, demented demon. . . ."

Balmont also talked about his adventures at the Cape of Good Hope.[65]

"When our vessel dropped anchor in the harbor"—Balmont could never simply say "ship"—"I descended onto dry land and immersed myself in the country." (Again he simply could not say that he walked out of town.) "I came across a type of wigwam, took a look inside, and saw an old woman who was so strikingly primitive and old that I wanted right away to express my closeness to her. But though I speak many of the world's languages, I do not know 'Zulu.' The old witch rushed at me with a big stick. I had to run to save myself."[66]

"I speak many of the world's languages. . . ." Balmont was not the only one to lie so shamelessly about his knowledge of foreign tongues. Bryusov did the same thing, based on how he went on about himself and as noted by some Myasnikov in an article titled "The Poetry of Bryusov," in a book published in Moscow in 1945: "Bryusov spoke French and Latin fluently, and, without a dictionary, he could read English, Italian, German, Greek, and some Spanish and Swedish. He also had a working knowledge of Sanskrit, Polish, Czech, Bulgarian, Serbian, biblical Hebrew, classical Egyptian, Arabic, classical Persian, and Japanese. . . ."[67]

Not far behind him was S. A. Polyakov, his colleague at the "Scorpion" publishing house. His colleague M. N. Semyonov said about him recently in the newspaper *Russian Thought* that this Polyakov "knew all the European languages and about a dozen Eastern ones. . . ." Just think: all the European languages and about a dozen Eastern ones![68]

Bryusov "spoke many of the world's languages" so poorly that he found it difficult to carry on even the simplest conversation in French. One time, when we were émigrés in Paris, I introduced Balmont to my literary agent, an American by the name of Bradley. When this man addressed him in English, Balmont blushed, became confused, and switched to French. But here, too, he lost his way and kept making crude mistakes.[69]

How then could Balmont do so many translations from various languages, including Georgian and Armenian? Most likely, often from word-for-word translations. And beyond words is how he rendered them in his own way. Here, for example, is a sonnet by Shelley. His first line is not very complex: "In the desert, in the sands, lies a great statue." That is all that Shelley said. But what did Balmont do with it? "In the bare sands, where eternity keeps watch over the silence of the desert."[70]

Further, as regards Balmont's ignorance of "Zulu" and the regrettable consequences of such unfamiliarity, there were so many other sad situations when he spoke in languages that he knew more or less, even if only in forcefully passionate exclamations. I know that the police in London often beat him mercilessly for such fervor and that one night the patrolmen in Paris did the same thing. Balmont was walking along with some woman behind two policemen. He was screaming at her in a frenzied way, emphasizing the Russian word "*vash*," or "your" ("your sly glance, your sly mind!"). The officers thought that Balmont was screaming at them in the Parisian jargon of thieves and hoodlums, in which the word "*vache*," or "cow," is an extremely derogatory term for officers of the law, even more stupid than "pharaoh," the label that insults them in Russia.[71]

One summer, the writer Fyodorov and I were visiting Balmont in a German settlement around Odessa and went for a swim. We got undressed and wanted to go into the water, when, unfortunately, out of the waves came Fyodorov's brother, a huge man, a tramp from Odessa's port, and a convict who was always in trouble with the law. When Balmont saw him, he fell into a tragic rage for some reason, rushed toward the man, and said in a theatrical voice:

"Hey, you, barbarian, I challenge you to a fistfight."

The "barbarian" gave him a blank, lazy look, grabbed him with his terrible paw-like hands, and threw him against the sharp thickets along the shore. Balmont crawled out all banged up and bloody.

Balmont was a surprising type of individual. Throughout his long life, he never uttered a simple word. In his poems, he often described the secret delights of his lovers with an extremely vile image: "The Enchanted Grotto."[72]

He was also a rather calculating type. One time, he sought to please Bryusov by writing in his journal, *The Scales*, that I was "a tiny brook that could only babble."[73] Later, when times had changed, he suddenly became kinder to me. Having read "The Gentleman from San Francisco," he told me:

"Bunin, you have the sense of a ship."[74]

Still later, at a gathering in Paris after I had been awarded the Nobel Prize, Balmont compared me not to a tiny brook but to a lion. In my honor, he read a sonnet that, not forgetting himself, of course, began:

I am a tiger, but you are—a lion!

Balmont was also calculating politically.

The first volume of the *Literary Encyclopedia*, published in Moscow in 1930, said about him:

"Balmont was one of the leaders of Russian symbolism.[75] After completing high school, he entered Moscow University, where he was expelled for participating in a student movement.[76] Very quickly, though, his social interests ceded to individualism and aestheticism. The abrupt end of revolutionary currents in 1905, together with the publication in Paris of his anthology of revolutionary verse, titled *Songs of an Avenger*, turned Balmont into a political émigré.[77]

"After the tsar's manifesto, Balmont returned to Russia in 1913. To the imperialistic war, he responded like a chauvinist. But, in a journal for the 'People's Committee on Education' in 1920, he published a poem titled 'Prophesy,' in which he greeted the October Revolution with enthusiasm.[78]

"Having gone abroad on a mission for the Soviet government, Balmont crossed into the camp of the White Guard emigration. . . . [79] Having exchanged his admiration for the harmonious pantheism of Shelley for the repulsively demonic vision of Baudelaire, he, as Bryusov said about him, 'wanted to sing of passion and crime.' In his sonnet titled 'Freaks,' Balmont glorified 'crooked cactuses, shoots of henbane, snakes, lizards, outcasts, plagues, leprosy, darkness, murder, misfortune, Sodom and Gomorrah.'[80] He enthusiastically hailed Nero as his 'brother.' . . ."

I do not know what this "Prophesy" is all about, but with it, undoubtedly, Balmont met the Bolsheviks just as "excitedly" as he met "plague, leprosy, darkness, murder, and misfortune." I do know several other pieces with which he greeted 1905. In the fall of that year, Balmont published a poem in the Bolshevik newspaper *New Life*, for example, with these lines:

One who does rejects the victory of brave and bright workers,
Is a shameful card sharp who plays a dishonest game![81]

Such a thing could not be any more stupid, groveling, and coarse. Why "shameful"? Why a "card sharp"? What is this "playing a dishonest game"?

But this was just the beginning. *Songs of an Avenger* features gems that are simply beyond description. In a poem titled "To the Russian Officer," written in response to the rout of the Moscow uprising at the end of 1905, one reads:

Vulgar soldier! You still don't get it,
Whom do you serve as a slave?
You've joined forces—and not for the minute!
With the base, the lying, the knave!
In the flower of your youth,
You were such a handsome man.
But, scoundrel, how you've fallen!
In quagmires, backwoods, and sand!

Your uniform is covered with blood,
You scum, cursed one, hired killer
May your corpse lie in worm-filled mud![82]

But that's nothing. Here are "songs" about the tsar:

Our tsar is a blind, wretched slob,
If not jail, the knout, or the gallows,
Then the firing squad will do his job . . .
Our tsar is a coward who doesn't feel a thing,
But just wait, your majesty,
The hour of reckoning will ring! . . .
Our tsar is a paltry little geek,
And now a really dirty bird.
Who only mumbles, and does not speak. . . .
Most vile of vile! Collapse, the stink of gauze,
Get a knife, the pus-filled abscess has swollen,
Close ranks, comrades, and rally for the cause!
We'll stick the prickly pig,
We'll kill the wolf with his bushy tail,
And whose jaws are really big.
Our tsar wants to strut and lie,
He calls the people to peace,
But then robs them on the sly,
Our tsar whines like a pup who's hot,
He's a troll, a drunk, a creep,
Who should be taken out and shot![83]

All this was published in 1907 in Paris, where Balmont fled after the events in Moscow. In no way, though, did such pieces prevent him from returning to Russia fully safe and sound.

Even before Russia's first revolution, Grzhebin began to publish an illustrated satirical journal, decorating the cover of the first issue with a full-page picture of a naked human ass topped by an imperial crown; but he never fled anywhere, and no one laid a finger on him. Gorky fled first to America, and then to Italy. . . . [84]

Korolenko, that noble soul, dreamed about revolution by recalling these lines from another poet:

The roosters sing in Holy Russia
Soon they will see the light of day![85]

In all the pathos, Andreev lied through his skin when he wrote to Veresaev about the revolution: "I fear the Kadets somewhat, since I see them as the future powers that be. They are builders more of improved prisons than of life. Either the revolution and the socialists will win or there will be a constitution of sauerkraut. If there is a revolution, it will be something stupendously joyous, great, and unprecedented. There will be not only a new Russia but also a new world!"[86]

"But still one more messenger came to Job and told him: 'Your sons and daughters were eating and drinking wine at the home of your firstborn brother. But a great wind came from the desert and shook the four corners of the house. And the house fell on them and they died. . . .'"[87]

"Something stupendously joyous" finally came to be. Even E. D. Kuskova once said:

"The Russian revolution was accomplished in a zoological way."[88]

This was said in 1922, but it is not at all just. The zoological world never has had such senseless savagery—savagery for the sake of savagery—that the human world does and especially during revolutions. A wild animal or reptile always acts rationally, with a practical goal. It devours another wild animal or reptile only because it must eat; or, it simply destroys its prey when the predator interferes with its existence. It is content to do only these two things. It does not lick its lips in murder, or get drunk on killing, or mock or ridicule its sacrificial victim—as a human being does, especially when he knows he can do so with impunity; or when for a period of time (like during a revolution), his savagery is seen as "holy anger" and heroism and is rewarded with power, material blessings, and such honors as the Order of some Lenin or the Order of the "Red Banner."[89] The zoological world does not curse, destroy, or spit like swine on the past; it does not have a "bright future"; it does not have professional planners of universal happiness on earth; and, for the sake of this happiness, it does not allow legendary murders to go on for entire decades with the help of a million-man army of professional killers, hangmen, and the most terrible degenerates, psychopaths, and sadists who were selected and organized with truly demonic art—as did that army that began to take shape in Russia in the first days of the kingdom of Lenin, Trotsky, and Dzerzhinsky and that became famous with so many changing names as the Cheka, the GPU, and the NKVD. . . .[90]

By the end of the '90s, the "great desert wind" had not yet arrived, but one could sense it coming. Indeed, it had already been causing rot in the "new" literature that had suddenly replaced the old. The new people of this new literature had already moved into the forefront, but they were not at all like their very recent predecessors, "masters of thought and feeling," as they were called at the time. Several of the earliest members of this group still reigned supreme, but the number of their followers kept declining. The fame of the newer ones, though, kept growing. Not for nothing, obviously, did Akim Volynsky announce: "The world has given birth to a new cerebral line!"[91]

Almost all of the new people in the forefront of this new literature, everyone from Gorky to Sologub, were individuals who were naturally gifted, as well as extremely energetic and forceful. But was what extremely remarkable about these days as the "desert wind" drew near was that the force and the capability of almost all of these innovators were of rather poor quality. They were innately depraved and tied up with things that were vulgar, speculative, and false; catered to the street; and thirsted shamelessly for scandals and success.

Leo Tolstoy ascertained a bit later:

"How incredibly cheeky and stupid today's new writers are!" . . . [92]

It was a time of an already sharp decline in literature, mores, honor, conscience, measure, taste, intelligence, and tact. . . . Very aptly (and proudly) did Rozanov announce: "Literature is like my pants. I do what I want in them. . . ."[93]

Blok wrote in his diary:[94]

"Literary circles smell vilely. . . ."

"Bryusov has still not grown tired of acting, clowning around, and playing small dirty tricks. . . ."

"The Merezhkovskys—Khlystovstvo. . . ."[95]

"Vyacheslav Ivanov's article is stifling and obtuse. . . ."[96]

"All my closest friends are borderline decrepit, sick, and insane. . . . I myself am tired and ill. . . . This evening I drank myself into a stupor. . . . Remizov, Gershenzon . . . everyone is sick. . . . The modernists have only curls framing emptiness. . . ."

"Gorodetsky tries to prophesy about some Rus. . . ."

"Esenin has a talent for vulgarity and blasphemy."

"Bely has yet to reach manhood. He is always rapturous, nothing about existence, everything not from life."

"Everything with Alexei Tolstoy is ruined by hooliganism and a lack of aesthetic restraint. One would only think that life is a barren fig tree and stunts. . . ."

"Art exhibits. 'Wandering Dogs'. . . ."[97]

Blok also wrote about the revolution, for instance, in May 1917:

"Old Russian power was rooted so deeply in the idiosyncrasies of Russian life which are, a rather large part of Russians that it is pleasant to think in a revolutionary way. . . . But Russians could not become a revolutionary people right away. The collapse of the old power was for them an unexpected 'miracle.'

Revolution presupposes a will. But was there a will? No, only in handfuls of people off to the side. . . ."[98]

In July of that year, he continued:

"German money and propaganda are everywhere in sight. . . . It is night, with noise and laughter in the streets. . . ."

As everyone knows, Blok eventually went somewhat wild over Bolshevism, but in no way did this exclude the truth of what he had written about the revolution earlier. I have cited his views not for political reasons, but to say that the "revolution" that began in Russian literature in the 1890s was also a kind of "unexpected miracle." From the very beginning, this literary revolution smacked of that hooliganism, that lack of moderation and restraint, and those stunts that Blok in vain was ascribing only to Alexei Tolstoy. Indeed, there were also "curls framing emptiness."

In his time, Blok himself was also guilty of such "curls," and what curls they were!

Andrei Bely used a capital letter for each word when, in his writings, he called Bryusov the "Mysterious Knight of the Wife, Vested with the Sun."[99] Even before Bely, though, Blok himself presented a 1904 book of his poems to Bryusov with the inscription:

To the Lawmaker of Russian Verse,
To the Helmsman in the Dark Cape
To the Guiding Green Star.[100]

One should note that this "Helmsman," this "Green Star," and this "Mysterious Knight of a Wife, Vested with the Sun" was the son of a petty Muscovite merchant, a dealer in corks, who lived in his father's house on Flower Boulevard. The house was a genuinely provincial place typical for a third-guild merchant, with a wicket fence and gates that were always under lock and key, and guarded by a dog on a chain in the yard.

I met Bryusov when he was still a student. He had black eyes, high Asiatic cheekbones, and a body that was fat and packed like a shopkeeper's.

This merchant, though, spoke in a very refined, edifying, and high-blown way, fragmented and nasally precise, as if he were barking into his reedlike nose. He always talked in maxims, in an instructive tone that did not tolerate objections. Everything he said (about art) was extremely revolutionary: long live the new and down with the old. He even proposed that all old books be burned in bonfires "just as Homer did to the Alexandrine Library!"—he exclaimed. But along with such things, so that everything be new, this "daring man, this destroyer" had the most harsh and rigid rules, regulations, and statutes, for the slightest infraction of which he, apparently, was also ready to burn people at the stake. Even the meticulousness in his low-ceiling room on the mezzanine of his house was remarkable.[101]

"The Mysterious Knight, the Helmsman, the Green Star. . . ." But the titles of all the books of these knights and helmsmen were no less amazing. There was *The Snow Mask*, *The Goblet of Blizzards*, and *Serpentine Flowers*. . . . [102] At the time, moreover, these people also had the habit of placing the names of their books in the very top left-hand corner of the cover. I remember that Chekhov once looked at one such cover and burst out suddenly with a happy laugh, saying:

"This is for the squint-eyed!"

Here is still one more piece of evidence of this type:

About three years ago, it was in 1947, a book titled *A. P. Chekhov as His Colleagues Remember Him* was published in Moscow.[103] In it were the recollections of A. N. Tikhonov (A. Serebrov). This Tikhonov spent his entire life around Gorky. In his youth Tikhonov studied at the Mining Institute, and in summer 1902, he prospected for coal at the estate of Savva Morozov. This Morozov once visited his estate together with Chekhov. "It was here," Tikhonov says, "that I spent several days in Chekhov's company and once even talked to him about Gorky and Andreev. I had heard how Chekhov loved and esteemed Gorky, how he did not stint on praise for the author of 'The Stormy Petrel' and how he almost suffocated from enthusiastic interjections and exclamation points [over him].

"'Excuse me . . . I don't understand,' Chekhov interrupted me with the strained politeness of someone who has stepped on another's foot: 'I don't understand why you and all of Russian youth have gone so crazy over Gorky. You all love his "Stormy Petrel" and "Song of the Falcon." . . . But this is not literature, but merely a bunch of shrill words. . . .'[104]

"I was so surprised that, sipping my tea, I burned my tongue.

"'The sea laughed,' Chekhov continued, as he fidgeted nervously with the string about his pince-nez. 'You, of course, are in ecstasy [over such a phrase]! How wonderful! But it's only cheap stuff, pulp fiction. You read the "sea laughed" and you stop. You think that you have done so because it is good and artistic. No way! You stop because you simply did not understand right then and there how it is so—the sea—and that it bursts out laughing suddenly. The sea neither laughs nor cries; it rustles, it splashes, it shines. . . . Take a look at Tolstoy: The sun rises, the sun sets. . . . No one laughs or sobs. . . .'

"With his long fingers, Chekhov kept touching the ashtray, the saucer, and the milk bottle. Suddenly, in disgust, he pushed everything away from him.

"'You've been quoting from *Foma Gordeev*,' he continued, tightening the thick crow's feet around about his eyes. 'Again it's unsuccessful! It's built on a straight line, on one hero; like shish-kebab on a skewer. And all the characters in it speak the same way, in *okanie*. . . .'[105]

"Obviously, I wasn't doing well with Gorky. So I tried to remedy things by switching to the Moscow Art Theater.

"'It's nothing. A theater is a theater,' Chekhov again dampened my enthusiasm. 'At least [there], the actors know their roles. Moskvin is even a talented individual. But, generally speaking, our actors are a very boorish lot. . . .'

"Like a drowning man clutching a straw, I made a dash for the 'decadents,' whom I saw as a new trend in literature.

"'There are no, nor have there ever been, any decadents,' Chekhov finished me off mercilessly, 'Where did you get such a thing? They are not decadents, but swindlers and thieves. You cannot believe them. And their legs are not at all "pale," but hairy like everyone else's. . . .'[106]

"I mentioned Andreev. Chekhov looked at me askance with an unkind smile:

"'What Leonid Andreev—the writer? He's simply a paralegal, one of those who loves to talk terribly, in a pretty way. . . .'"

Chekhov talked to me about "decadents" in a different way than he did to Tikhonov—not only as swindlers and thieves.

"What kind of decadents are they!" he said. "They are the most robust peasants who should be arrested!"

It is true—almost all of them were "swindlers and thieves" and the "most robust peasants," but one cannot say that they were healthy or normal. The strengths (and literary talents) of the "decadents" of Chekhov's times, and of those who swelled their ranks and achieved fame thereafter, were no longer called decadents or symbolists, but futurists, mystical anarchists, and argonauts, who, just like the others—Gorky and Andreev, and later the frail and sickly Artsybashev, or the sodomite Kuzmin with his half-naked skull and grave-like face that always flushed like the corpse of a prostitute—were all indeed great but in the same way that "holy fools" and hysterical and crazy people are. Who among them could be called healthy in the usual sense of this word?[107] They were all cunning and knew well how to attract attention to themselves, but most holy fools and crazy and hysterical people also possess such qualities.

What an astonishing horde of sick and abnormal types in one or another form, to one and another degree, there still were in Chekhov's time and how they increased in the years after! There was the consumptive-looking Gippius, who, not for nothing, wrote under a masculine name.[108] There was Bryusov, who was obsessed with a mania for fame. There was the silent and stonelike Sologub—a "brick in a suit coat," Rozanov called him—the singer of death, the "father" of his own devil, and the author first of "Quiet Boys" and then of *The Petty Demon*, with the pathological Peredonov.[109] There was the stormy "mystical anarchist" Chulkov, the frenzied Volynsky, and the stunted and terrible-looking Minsky, with his huge head and lifeless black eyes.

Gorky had a sickly passion for faulty speech—"I drug this small book over to you, violet devils"—as well as for pseudonyms, which he used in his youth, names that were pompously rare, with some kind of third-rate, caustic irony: Iegudiil Khlamida, A Certain Someone, X, Antinom the Outgoing, and the Garrulous Self-Critic. . . . Gorky also left behind an incredible number of portraits of his entire life right down to his old age that were simply striking in their numerous theatrical poses and expressions: first naive and pensive, then insolent, next sullen and convict-like, the frenzied stance of a street agitator with a neck and shoulders that were tense and raised as far they could go. He was also an absolutely tireless chatterer, with countless diverse grimaces that again were first terrible and gloomy, then joyous and idiot-like, with furrows under his hairy eyebrows and huge folds on his forehead like an old wide-cheeked Mongol.

Not for a minute could Gorky be among people without posing and phrase-mongering, first purposely coarse and extreme, then romantically exalted; without absurdly profuse ecstasies—"I'm so happy, Prishvin, to live on the same planet as you!"; and without any and all other kinds of homeric lies.

He was abnormally stupid in his exposés: "This is a city, this is New York. From afar it seems like a huge jaw with crooked black teeth. It breathes clouds of smoke into the sky; it wheezes likes a glutton suffering from obesity. Entering it, you feel as though you have fallen into a stomach of iron and stone. Its streets are slippery, scarlet-colored throats through which slide dark pieces of food—living people. Train cars are huge worms; locomotives are greasy ducks. . . ."[110]

He was a prolific hack. In a huge book written by some Balukhatov, titled *The Literary Work of Gorky* and published immediately after his death in Moscow, the author writes: "We still do not have an accurate idea of the full extent of all of Gorky's written activity: so far, we have registered 1,145 fictional and publicist works. . . ."[111]

Not long ago, I read in the Moscow *Beacon*: "Gorky, one of the greatest proletarian writers in the world, intended to gift us with still many, many more works, and without a doubt, he would have done so, if base enemies of our people, supporters of Trotsky and Bukharin, had not cut short his remarkable life. About *eight thousand* of Gorky's treasured manuscripts and materials are being preserved carefully in his archive in the Institute of World Literature of the Academy of Sciences of the USSR. . . ."[112]

Such was Gorky.

But there were still so many abnormal others! Tsvetaeva, with her endless lifelong stream of barbaric words and sounds in verse, ending her existence in a noose after her return to Soviet Russia; the very tempestuous drunkard Balmont, who fell into a violent and erotic madness right before his death; the morphine addict and sadistic sexual maniac Bryusov; the drunken tragic actor Andreev. . . . [113]

There is nothing to say about the monkey-like frenzies of Bely. The same also goes for the unhappy Blok. Blok's paternal grandfather died in a psychiatric hospital; his father had "peculiarities bordering on spiritual sickness"; his mother "underwent treatment regularly in a hospital for the spiritually sick." From youth on, Blok himself suffered from a vicious scurvy. His diaries are rife with complaints not only about his illness but also about his distress with women and wine and, later, a "profound neurosis and right before his death, inflamed heart valves and the loss of his rational faculties. . . ."[114] There was also intellectual and spiritual imbalance, and a rare flightiness: "In his own words, school repulsed him by its terrible plebeianism, which was at odds with his thoughts, manners, and feelings."[115] Here he studied to be an actor. In his first years at the university, he imitated Zhukovsky and Fet and wrote about love "amid rosy mornings, scarlet sunrises, golden valleys, and flowering meadows."[116] He then mimicked V. Solovyov and became a friend and comrade in arms of Bely, who "headed the mystical circle of argonauts."[117] In 1905, he "joined the mob, red banner in hand, but quickly became completely cold to the revolution. . . ."

During the First World War, Blok managed to get to the front, as something like a hussar. Arriving in Petersburg, he told Gippius first that "he had had a good time" during the war, but then something completely different: it was boring and repulsive there. He sometimes assured her that "all Jews should be hanged. . . ."[118]

(I have taken the last few lines from Gippius's *Blue Book* and from her Petersburg diaries and everything else on Blok from biographical and autobiographical information on him.)[119]

Blok also had sickly seizures of blasphemy. At the end of the '20s in so-called Leningrad, there existed a journal, titled *Russian Contemporary*, "with the very close collaboration of Gorky, Zamyatin, and Chukovsky" and, as was said in its program, pursuing "only cultural goals."[120] In the third issue of this cultural journal were some "priceless literary materials," one of which was something particularly valuable, namely:

"The Thoughts, Musings, and Comments of Alexander Alexandrovich Blok, Excerpted from His Posthumous Manuscripts."

Amid these "thoughts" are several remarkable things, especially one piece about Christ.

Gorky himself had a not very respectful stance toward Christ, calling him, smirkingly, a "great pedant."[121] But, in this regard, where could Gorky go after Demyan Bednyi, Mayakovsky, and, alas, Blok! It turns out that Blok took it into his head to write nothing more, but nothing less, than a "play from the life of Christ." Here is an outline of this "play":

"Heat. Thick cactuses. The fool, Simon-Peter, with a hanging lip, is catching fish."

"Christ enters. He is neither man nor woman."

"Thomas (the doubter!)—is checking out things."

"He has had to believe: he has been forced and duped into doing so."

"He puts his fingers in and becomes an apostle."

"But others are forced to spread the inquisition, the papacy, hiccuping priests, and the Constituent Assembly. . . ."[122]

Will the fans of this "great poet" believe all these monstrous atrocities? But I am writing them out word for word. Here are some more:

"Andrei the First-Called. He loiters about, not remaining in place."

"The apostles steal cherries and wheat for Christ."

"Mother tells son: It is indecent. The marriage in Cana of Galilee."

"An apostle will blurt out something, and Jesus will elaborate."

"The Sermon on the Mount: a political mass-meeting."

"The powers that be are worried. They arrest Jesus. His disciples, of course, slip away. . . ."

Here is the conclusion of the outline of this "play":

"Lyuba must read a thing or two by Renan and, on a map, point to the small place where he walked. . . ."[123]

"He," of course, is written in small letters. . . .

This absurdity ("hiccuping priests and the forced-to-spread Constituent Assembly") and the purely clinical blasphemy (that one line alone about the apostle Peter—the "fool Simon with a hanging lip")—were, it seems, something of the poisonous air at this time. Blasphemy and sacrilege are key features of revolutionary times. They began with the very first wafting of the "desert wind." Sologub had already written "A Liturgy to Me," that is, to his very self, praying to the devil—"My Father, Devil!"—and himself pretending to be one. In the "Wandering Dog" in Saint Petersburg, Akhmatova said: "We are all sinners, we are all whores!"[124] There also was once staged "The Flight of the Mother of God and Child into Egypt," some kind of "liturgical act," with Kuzmin writing the words, Sats composing the music, and Sudeikin coming up with decorations and costumes. In the "act," the poet Potyomkin played the ass, bent at a right angle, leaning on two crutches, and carrying on his back Sudeikin's spouse as the Mother of God.[125]

In this "Dog" were already quite a few future "Bolsheviks": Alexei Tolstoy, still young, large, and fleshy faced, often appearing there as an important gentry man, a baron, in a raccoon fur coat, a beaver or top hat, and hair cut à la peasant; Blok, with the stonelike, impenetrable face of a handsome man and poet; and Mayakovsky, in a yellow jacket, with eyes that were so very dark and provokingly impudent and gloomy, with lips that were sinuous, toadlike, and compressed. . . . By the way, one should note here that Kuzmin died—already under the Bolsheviks—supposedly with the Gospels in one hand and, in the other, the *Decameron* by Boccaccio.[126]

Under the Bolsheviks, any kind of blasphemous obscenity bloomed with pornographic flowers. About thirty years ago, someone wrote to me from Moscow:

"I'm standing in a crowded streetcar, surrounded by smiling mugs, Dostoevsky's 'God-bearing folk' loves to look at pictures in *The Atheist*: in one, stupid old women 'take Communion'—they eat the intestines of Christ—in another, Lord Saboath is in a pince-nez, reading something by Demyan Bednyi in a gloomy way. . . ."[127]

Mostly likely, this was *A Flawless New Testament by the Evangelist Demyan Bednyi*, [whose author], for many years, was one of the most celebrated grandees, wealthy men, and swine-like lackeys of Soviet Moscow.[128]

Babel was among the most abominable blasphemers. One time, the émigré Social Revolutionary newspaper, *Days*, critiqued a collection of his stories and found that "his works were uneven": "Babel possesses an interesting everyday style. Freely, he sometimes stylizes entire pages—for example, his story 'Sasha the Christ.'[129] Further, there are things without a trace of revolution or revolutionary life, for example, his story 'The Sin of Jesus.' . . ."[130] Unfortunately, the paper continues—but I do not understand what is there to regret here—the most characteristic parts of the piece cannot be cited here because of its extreme vulgar expressions. It also seems that the story, in its offensive tone and vile content, has no equal even in anti-religious Soviet literature. Its characters—God, an angel, and a woman, Arina, who works in a hotel and who crushes in bed the angel given to her by God in place of a husband so that she will not become pregnant often. . . . [131] This verdict was rather severe, although also somewhat unjust, for its "revolutionary" tinge is, of course, its vileness.[132]

I remember still another story by Babel at the time, which describes a statue of the Mother of God in a Catholic church, but which I have tried right away to repress. The vileness describing Her breasts deserves the executioner's block, all the more so since Babel was seemingly both completely healthy and normal in the usual sense of these words.[133]

Among abnormal individuals, one must also remember one Khlebnikov. Khlebnikov's first name was Viktor, but he changed it to "Velimir." I met him sometimes before the revolution (the February one).[134] He was a rather quiet and gloomy type, either hungover or pretending to be so. Now, not only in Russia, but sometimes here in emigration, people talk about his genius. Such a thing, of course, is also very stupid, although Khlebnikov did have the rudimentary beginnings of a wild artistic talent. He had a reputation as a well-known futurist, but also a truly insane one at that. But was he really insane?[135] Of course, in no way was he normal. Rather, he always played the role of a madman who speculated off his insanity.[136] In the twenties, amid all the literary and everyday news that came out of Moscow, I once received a letter about him. Here's what it said:

When Khlebnikov died, people in Moscow wrote about him endlessly, gave lectures about him, and called him a genius. At one gathering, dedicated to his memory, his friend P. read recollections about him. He said that he had long regarded Khlebnikov as a most great individual and that he had always wanted to meet him, to know his noble soul a bit more closely, and even to help him financially: Khlebnikov, "thanks to his indifference to the things of this world," was severely in need. Alas, all attempts to become friends with Khlebnikov were in vain: "Khlebnikov remained inaccessible."

Once, though, P. succeeded in reaching Khlebnikov by phone. "I would like to invite you to my place, Khlebnikov answered that he would come, but only somewhat later, since now he was wandering among mountains, in the eternal snows, between Lubyanka and Nikolskaya.[137] But suddenly I heard a knock on the door. I opened it and saw: Khlebnikov!"

The next day, P. moved Khlebnikov into his place. Immediately, Khlebnikov began to pull the blanket, pillows, sheets, and mattress from the bed in his room and to put everything on the desk. He then crawled on top of it completely naked and began writing his book *The Tables of Fate*, with its main feature being the "mystical number 317."[138] Khlebnikov was so filthy and slovenly that his room soon became a pigsty, and the landlady chased both him and P. from the apartment.

Khlebnikov was again fortunate. He found refuge with a grain merchant, who came to be extremely interested in *The Tables of Fate*. Having lived with the man for about two weeks, Khlebnikov began saying that for this book he had to spend some time in the steppes of Astrakhan.[139] The grain merchant gave him money for a ticket, and, ecstatic, Khlebnikov rushed to the train station. At the train station, though, he was allegedly robbed. The grain merchant again had to loosen his purse strings and, finally, Khlebnikov left.

After some time, P. received a letter from a woman in Astrakhan who begged him to come for Khlebnikov right away; otherwise, she wrote, Khlebnikov would perish.

So, it seems, P. flew to Astrakhan on the first train out of town. Having arrived there at night, he found Khlebnikov, who took him immediately outside the city into the steppe. There he began saying that that he had "succeeded in communicating with all 317 "Presidents" and that such a thing was of great importance for the entire world. He then struck P. so hard on the head with his fist that the man lost consciousness.

When P. regained his senses, he, with difficulty, wandered back into town. Once there, extremely late at night, and after several long searches, he again found Khlebnikov in some café. Having caught sight of P., Khlebnikov again rushed at him with his fists—"Villain! How dare you resurrect yourself! You're supposed to be dead! With my worldwide radio, I've just contacted all the Presidents [of the universe] and have been chosen by them to be President of the Earthly Sphere!"

"From that time on," P. continued, "my relationship with Khlebnikov went downhill and we went our separate ways." Khlebnikov was no fool, though. Having returned to Moscow, he soon found a new patron, the well-known baker Filippov, who began to support him and to meet all his needs.[140] According to P., Khlebnikov resided in a luxurious room at the hotel "Deluxe" on Tverskaya Street and adorned the door with a colorful poster that he had made himself: a picture of a sun standing on small paws and beneath it the inscription:

"President of the Terrestrial Globe. Office Hours from Twelve Noon to Eleven-Thirty A.M."

The very pulp-like play of a madman. But then to please the Bolsheviks, this madman burst forth with verse that was fully rational and profitable:

There's no living with the masters!
They devour us without care
Grand old ladies, respected old men,
We'll strip their asses bare!
These gentry cows, these Ukie pigs,
They're all part of one barnyard,
Young and thin, fat and gray,
We'll kick their asses hard!

Amid thundering heavens, with whistling whips,
No mercy will we show,
This noble herd, this exalted flock,
We'll beat their bottoms low!
In fields we'll be like shepherds,
And brandish a cocked gun,
We'll tie a lord to a bull
And drop their derrières for fun!

Further from a laundress:

I'd go to a knacker's yard
And lead all gents to ropes
Then take them by the throat
And rob them of all hopes.
I'd rinse out my undies
Rinse them out, I would,
And these poor gents,
I'd slash their throats for good!
Pools of blood I'd spill
It would make any head spin!
So that these poor gents without their heads
Could no longer raise a din![141]

Blok, in his "The Twelve," also had this:

How the time will pass,
I will watch and watch. . . .
And my head and brow
I will scratch and scratch. . . .
And with my trusty knife,
I will slash and slash![142]

Is this very much like Khlebnikov? But, after all, all these revolutions, all these "slogans" are monotonously vulgar. One key theme—slash the priests, slash the lords! Ryleev also wrote:

The first knife is for the boyars, the nobles,
The second is for the priests, the holy ones![143]

One should also note: what "high style" there was in the speeches of the politicians, in the revolutionary appeals of the poets during the first revolution and then before the beginning of the second! In Moscow, for example, the poet Sergei Sokolov, who, of course, not content with such a bird as a falcon, called himself Krechetov, and who named his publishing house "Vulture," wrote in this vein:

Arise! Punish the enemies of our land,
Like a sharp sickle cuts down wheat!
Forward! To where noise and screams,
And red banners dance in the heat!
And when waves of boiling red blood
Nurse fields far and wide,
Then our country will resurrect anew,
And flower in earthly pride![144]

Of course, in such verse, blood and virgin soil are indispensable. Still another example: the revolutionary verse of Maximilian Voloshin:

To the Russian people: I am the Angel of Vengeance!
Into dark wounds and upturned earth I spread my seeds.
Gone are the times of patience and remorse.
My banner is bloodred! My voice-alarm tells my deeds!—[145]

When the revolution came to be, "high style" gave way to the very lowest—take only what I copied from *Songs of an Avenger*. With the ascent of the Bolsheviks to the throne, poets began to sound their lyres in an absolutely boorish way:

We have torn the crown
From old Kremlin bowed low,
And behind low-growing fences
With fiery oars we row![146]

Is this not a miracle: low-growing fences. And further:

We took Christ to the cross
But Barabbas to Tversky Way,
We sat wearing hats, our knees apart,
And tore off legs, come what may.[147]

The last time I was in Petersburg—the very last time in my life!—was in early April 1917, when Lenin arrived in town. I was at an opening of an exhibit of Finnish artists.[148] Gathered there was "all of Petersburg," headed by our then ministers of the Provisional Government, well-known deputies of the Duma, with hysterically servile speeches to the Finns.[149] Later I was at a banquet honoring these artists. Good Lord, how very fine and significant was everything I saw in Petersburg at that time, the homeric chaos that poured forth from that banquet! Everyone had gathered there, all the "flower of the Russian intelligentsia": famous artists, actors, writers, social figures, ministers, deputies, and one tall foreign individual, namely, the ambassador of France.[150] But above it all reigned Mayakovsky.

At dinner I sat with Gorky and the Finnish artist Gallen.[151] Mayakovsky began by moving up suddenly, shoving a chair between us, and starting to eat from our plates and drinking from our glasses. Gallen looked at him with eyes as big as almonds—as though someone had brought a horse into the banquet hall. Gorky laughed loudly. I moved aside.

"Do you hate me all that much?" Mayakovsky asked me merrily. I answered: "No, that would be too great an honor for you!" Mayakovsky opened his trough-like mouth to say something else, when Milyukov, our then minister of foreign affairs, rose for an official toast. Mayakovsky rushed over to him, to the middle of his table. He jumped up on a chair and began to howl so obscenely that Milyukov was taken aback. After a second, he got a hold of himself and again proclaimed: "Ladies and gentlemen!" But Mayakovsky began to howl even more than previously. Milyukov parted his hands and sat down. Then the French ambassador rose to speak. Apparently, he felt fully assured that, in his presence, the Russian hooligan would stop. Or so he thought! Right away, Mayakovsky began to drown him out with an even shriller roar.

A savage and senseless frenzy broke out in the hall. Mayakovsky's comrades in arms also began to yell and began banging their fists on the table and their shoes on the floor. They started to laugh, howl, scream, and grunt. Suddenly everything was drowned out by the truly tragic wail of some Finnish artist who looked like a shaved walrus. Already drunk and mortally pale, he apparently had been shaken to the depths of his soul by the excessive swinery. With whatever strength he had and literally with tears in his eyes, he began to cry out one of the few Russian words he knew:

"Too much! Too-o much! Too-o-o much!"

The one-eyed caveman Polyphemus wanted to devour the wandering Odysseus.[152] Even when Mayakovsky was in high school, he was called, prophetically, Idiot Polyphemovich.[153] Mayakovsky and others were also rather voracious and extremely powerful in their one-eyedness. For a time, the Mayakovskys of this world seemed to be only street clowns. But not for nothing did Mayakovsky call himself a futurist, a man of the future. He already felt that the polyphemic future belonged undoubtedly to them, the Mayakovskys, who would shut soon and forever the mouths of all other tribunes even more splendidly than they had done at the banquet to honor Finland. . . .

"Too much!" Yes, fate gave us way too much of "great, historical" events. I was born too late. If I had entered this world earlier, I would not have the literary memories I do now. I would not have had to live through all that has been so inseparable from them: 1905, the first world war, 1917 and its continuation, Lenin, Stalin, Hitler. . . . Indeed, how one can envy our ancestor Noah! In all, only *one* flood was his lot. What a warm, solid, and comfortable ark did he have and what rich provisions: an entire seven pairs of clean and two pairs of unclean, but otherwise very edible, animals. The herald of peace, a dove with an olive branch in its beak, did not deceive him—not like today's doves (of "comrade" Picasso).[154] Superbly did Noah land on Ararat and splendidly did he eat, drink, and sleep the sleep of the righteous man, warmed by the bright sun, in the primordially pure air of a new universal spring, in a world devoid of all pre-flood ~~Flood~~ foulness—not like our world, which has returned to pre-flood times. True, Noah had an unhappy episode with his son. He really was a Ham.[155] But the main thing: all the world had one, if a sole, Ham. But now?

In spring of that '17, I also met Prince Kropotkin, who perished so terribly in the polyphemic kingdom of Lenin.

Kropotkin belonged to the famous Russian aristocracy. As a youth, he was one of the closest courtiers of Emperor Alexander II. Later he fled to England, where he lived until the Russian February revolution, before spring 1917.[156] It was then that I met him in Moscow and was extremely surprised and moved by this acquaintance. Here was a man who was so very famous throughout all of Europe—a well-known theoretician of anarchism and author of *Notes of a Revolutionary* and a well-known geographer, traveler, and explorer of eastern Siberia and the polar regions.[157] He was a little old man with rosy blushing cheeks and white downy hair and, in both manner and speech, lively and somehow so completely enchanting, childishly naive, and dear. Clear, lively eyes; a kindly, trusting look; and a societal, soft, and rapid speech—and this touching childishness. . . .

At that time, Kropotkin enjoyed universal respect and great concern. He, a revolutionary—although an extremely peaceful one—returned to the homeland after having been separated from it for many years, the pride of the February revolution, which finally "freed Russia from tsarism." He had been settled in a nobleman's residence—I do not remember exactly whose—on one of the best streets in the gentry section of Moscow. At the end of that year, his apartment was the site for "discussions for a League of Federalists."[158] The end of that year—but what was there then in Russia? But here Russian intellectuals gathered and were creating a "League" in that bloody madhouse, which, at that time, all of Russia had become.

So much for the "League"! But there is more:

In March 1918, the Bolsheviks chased him from his home and took the place for themselves. Kropotkin moved quietly to another apartment—and began seeking a meeting with Lenin in the extremely naive hope of forcing him to repent the monstrous terror that was sweeping through Russia. Finally, he gained an interview. Somehow he was on "good terms" with Bonch-Bruevich, one of Lenin's closest associates, and it was at his place in the Kremlin that the encounter took place.[159] It is completely incomprehensible: how could Kropotkin be on "good terms" with this villain, one who was exceptional even for the Bolsheviks.[160] But, it turned out, he was. And even more incredible: Kropotkin sought to turn Lenin onto a "humanitarian path." But having failed to do so, he was "disappointed" and bewildered, saying:

"I found that it was utterly useless to convince this man of anything. I reproached him for having allowed two and half thousand people to be murdered for the attempt on his life.[161] But I realized that such a thing made no impression on him. . . ."[162]

When the Bolsheviks chased the anarchist prince from his second apartment, "it turned out" that he had to leave Moscow for the provincial city of Dmitrov and to live there in primitive conditions, the likes of which no anarchist had ever dreamed of. There he ended his days, enduring truly a million deprivations: torment from hunger, torment from scurvy, torment from cold, torments for the old princess, his wife, who had become disabled from constant worries and struggles for a piece of moldy bread. . . . The little old unhappy prince longed for a pair of felt boots, but did not get them. He wasted several months in vain—months!—to get a coupon for the things.[163] He spent his evenings by the light of a splint, finishing his posthumous work *Ethics*.[164]

Can one imagine anything more terrible? Nearly his entire life, the life of a man who once had been especially close to Alexander II, and who had been destroyed because of revolutionary dreams, of reveries of an anarchical paradise—this among ourselves, individuals who still have not learned to walk firmly on hind legs—a life that ended in cold, in hunger, by the light of a smoking splint *over a manuscript on human ethics*, amid a revolution that had finally come to be.

Chapter 2

Rachmaninov

When I first met him in Yalta, what took place between us was something that could happen only in the romantic youths of Turgenev and Herzen, when people could spend entire nights talking about the splendid, the eternal, and high art. Until his final departure for America, we met from time to time in a very friendly way, but our times together were not like that first encounter, when, having talked almost the entire night on the beach, he put his arms around me and said: "Let's be friends forever!" Our life paths were already very different, fate kept us apart, our meetings were always accidental, mostly short. It also seemed that my noble friend had grown very reserved with time.[1]

But on that night, we were still young and anything but reserved. Somehow we felt close to each other, almost from the first very words we exchanged amid a large crowd that had gathered—I do not remember why—for a grand dinner at the "Russia," the best hotel in Yalta.[2] We sat next to each other, drank Abrau-Durso champagne, and then went out onto the terrace, continuing to talk about the decline in poetry and prose in Russian literature. Stealthily, we went down to the courtyard of the hotel, then to the embankment and out onto the pier—it was already late, not a soul could be seen—and we sat on some cables, breathing in their tarry smell and that completely special freshness that belongs only to the Black Sea. We talked and talked ever more passionately and happily about all the marvelous things that we remembered from

Pushkin, Lermontov, Tyutchev, Fet, Maykov. . . . Excitedly and slowly, he began to recite a poem by Maykov that he, perhaps, had put to music at the time or only dreamed about doing so:

At the grotto I waited for you at the set hour,
But the day grew dark, eerie, and thin,
The poplars hung their heads in sleep:
In vain! The moon rose, silver and dim;
Kefal's lover leaned her elbows,
On the glowing gates of a new day,
From her braids dropping golden seeds of opals and pearls
On blue valleys and forests on her way . . . [3]

Chapter 3

Repin

I have known such painters as the Vasnetsovs, Nesterov, and Repin. . . . Because I was so thin, Nesterov wanted to paint me as a saint, as he had done with others. I was flattered but refused—not everyone would agree to see himself as a saint. Repin honored me as well. Once, when I was in Petersburg with my friend, the painter Nilus, he invited me to sit for a portrait at his dacha in Finland. "I hear from my fellow painters," he wrote, "the happy news that our splendid painter Nilus has arrived—ah, if only I could be as skilled with colors—and that with him is you, splendid writer, whose portrait I dream of painting. Come, dear one, we'll talk it over and sit down to work."

Happily, I hurried off to his place: after all, what an honor to be painted by Repin.[1] I arrived there on a splendid sunny and very frosty morning, the yard of Repin's dacha laid out for a vegetarian, in clean air, in deep snow, with all the windows of the house thrown wide open.

Repin met me in high felt boots, a fur coat, and a fur hat. He kissed and embraced me and then led me to his studio, which was as cold inside as it was out. He said:

"Here's where I'll paint you every morning, then we'll have that kind of lunch that the Good Lord has ordained: herbs, my dear fellow, herbs. You'll see how it cleanses body and soul, and soon you'll even give up that damn tobacco of yours."

I began bowing low, thanking him fervently and mumbling that I would come tomorrow, but that I had to return to the station right away—I had terribly urgent business in Petersburg. I exchanged kisses immediately with my host and ran to the station as fast as my legs could carry me. There I made a dash for the buffet, downed a glass of vodka, began puffing deeply on a cigarette, and jumped into a train car. The next day I sent a telegram from Petersburg: "Dear Ilya Yefimovich, I'm in complete despair. I've received an urgent summons from Moscow and am now leaving right away on the next train. . . ."

Chapter 4

Jerome Jerome

Is there a Russian who does not know his name, who has not read his works? I doubt, though, that many Russians can boast of having met him.[1] Two or three, perhaps—myself included. Until 1926, I had never been to England. But that year the people of the London office of the PEN Club took it into their heads to invite me to London for several days.[2] They arranged a literary banquet to introduce me to English writers and members of English society. All the trouble for visas and expenses they took upon themselves—so here I was in London.

I was taken to all kinds of places, but in every one of them, I invariably endured something worthy of a story by Jerome. What some of those dinners must have cost, one side singeing me with a fireplace burning like a flaming hyena, and on the other, polar cold!

Right before I left London, I was in a home with an especially large group of people. It was a rather pleasant and lively affair, but so crowded that it had become too hot, and the kind hosts threw open all the windows, not realizing that it was snowing out. Jokingly, I cried out in alarm and saved myself by rushing up to the upper floor, where there were also many guests. Bounding up the stairs, I heard someone calling me happily: suddenly there appeared Jerome Jerome.

He walked up the stairs slowly and entered the middle of the room, the crowd making way for him respectfully. Greeting people he knew, he glanced about the room inquiringly. It turned out that he had come only to meet me, and we were introduced.

In a somewhat old-fashioned and folksy way, he stretched out his large thick hand and looked at me fixedly with small blue eyes shining, alive with a playful, merry spark.

"I'm so very glad to meet you," he said. "I live like a child now. I never go out at night and am in bed by ten o'clock. But tonight I'm breaking the rules and came here for a minute to see what you were like and to shake your hand. . . ."

He was a thickset, very strong, and stocky old man with a face that was ruddy, wide, and clean-shaven, in a long and full black frock coat, a starched shirt with a turned-down collar, and a modestly narrow black ribbon bow tie—a genuine old-world shopkeeper or clergyman. After several minutes, he made a decisive exit and left me with a lasting impression of a very pleasant person, but certainly not of a humorist or a writer of world renown.

Chapter 5

Tolstoy

I admired him almost from childhood.

As a boy, I already had some idea of what he was like, not from reading his books, but from conversations at home. I remember how my father often laughed telling us about how some of our gentry neighbors read *War and Peace*: one read only *War*, the other only *Peace*.[1] The first skipped everything to do with peace, and the second—just the opposite.

As a youth, my feelings for Tolstoy were already not simple.

My father used to say:

"I knew him somewhat. I met him during the Sevastopol campaign. I played cards with him during the siege of Sevastopol. . . ."[2]

I remember looking at him in amazed surprise: he had seen Tolstoy in person!

From that time on, writers were some special kind of being for whom I had an ineffable feeling, one that I cannot define even to this day, just as I cannot say how, when, and why I myself became a writer. I find these questions as impossible to answer as to say when and how I became the man I am. When I decided (somehow by myself) that I was meant to be exclusively a writer, life in the world of poetry and prose became my second existence. I also do not remember exactly when I began reading Tolstoy or how I distinguished him from others. It often turns out that someone discovers something that he finds splendid and dear suddenly, by surprise.

But that did not happen to me with Tolstoy. I do not remember such a moment. The splendid things that I encountered as a child, an adolescent seemingly never surprised me. On the contrary, I felt that I had known them for a long time, so that all that remained was for me to rejoice on meeting them again.[3]

But then came long years when I was truly in love with him, with the image that I had created of him, and which tormented me with a dream to meet him in person. Such a wish never left me, but how was I going to make it come true? Go to Yasnaya Polyana?[4] But what excuse would I have? What would I say to him when I got there?

Finally, I could bear it no longer. One fine summer morning, I saddled my Kirghiz suddenly and made for Yefremov, in the direction of Yasnaya Polyana, which was no more than seventy miles from me.[5] But having galloped all the way to Yefremov, I got cold feet and decided to spend the night there and to think things out more soberly. But all night long I could not sleep from excitement, constantly unable to make up my mind as to whether I should go or not. I roamed the town for hours and became so tired that, finding myself at the public garden at dawn, I fell dead asleep on the very first bench that came my way. When I awoke and sobered up completely, I thought a bit more and galloped back home, where the workers said to me:

"Hey, master, how did you manage to get your Kirghiz all worked up in one night? Whom were you chasing after?"[6]

In vain I "chased" after Tolstoy for several years more.[7]

In my youth, I was captivated by dreams of a pure, healthy, and gentle life amid nature, in personal chores, in simple clothes, and in brotherly friendship not only with the poor and oppressed but also with the entire vegetable and animal world. Again mainly from my love for Tolstoy as an artist, I became a Tolstoyan—of course, not without the secret hope that such a thing would, at last, give me a legitimate reason to meet him and even, perhaps, to enter into the circle of people closest to him. So began my Tolstoyan "obedience."[8]

At the time, I lived in Poltava, which for some reason turned out to have quite a number of Tolstoyans, with whom I became acquainted very soon.[9] On the whole, they were an absolutely insufferable lot, but I put up with them. The first one I came to know was a certain Klopsky, who was fairly well known in some circles and who was even cast by Karonin as the hero in his sensational story "The Teacher of Life."[10] He was a tall, lean man in high boots and a Russian blouse, with a thin, gray face and turquoise eyes, a clever scoundrel and crook, an incessant chatterbox eternally teaching and preaching to all. He loved to surprise people with sudden stunts and rudeness, as well as with an entire demeanor that helped him to flit from town to town in a rather happy and well-fed way.

Among the Tolstoyans in Poltava was also a doctor Alexander Alexandrovich Volkenshtein, who, by background and bearing, was a gentleman in the grand style, somewhat like Stiva Oblonsky.[11] The first thing that Klopsky did when he arrived at Poltava was to make for Volkenshtein and, through him, the salons, where Volkenshtein introduced him as a man with an "ideological" bent, a preacher, and simply to amuse others, a curious type.

Klopsky often said such things as:

"Yes, yes, I see how you live here. You lie, you suck on candies, you offer prayers, you worship idols in your churches that should have been blown up ages ago. When will all this end, these absurdities and abominations into which the world has sunk?

"Here I was, traveling from Kharkov.[12] In comes a man who, for some reason, is called a conductor and says: 'Your ticket.'

"I ask him: 'What exactly do you mean by a ticket?'

"He answers: 'The ticket that you're traveling on.'

"But I tell him: 'I'm traveling not on a ticket but on train rails.'

"'You mean to say you don't have a ticket?'

"'Of course, I don't have one,' I say.

"'Well, in that case, we'll leave you off at the next station.'

"'That's splendid,' I reply. 'That's your business, but mine's to keep on going.'

"At the next station, people actually showed up. 'Please get off the train,' they said.

"'Why should I?' I say, 'I'm fine as is.'

"'You don't wish to get off?'

"'It would seem that I don't.'

"'Then we'll make you.'

"'But I won't go.'

"'Then we'll drag you off and carry you out.'

"'Well, then, drag me off, that's your business.'

"And that's what they did. To an astonished respectable crowd, two strapping good-for-nothings, two peasants who would have been better off plowing a field, carried me off in their arms. . . ."

That was the famous Klopsky.

Others were not so famous, but also good. There were the brothers D., who had settled on land near Poltava, people who, though very humble initially, were remarkably boring, dim-witted, and proud.[13] There was a certain Leontiev, a small, puny, and sickly young man, but with a face of rare beauty, a former page in the tsar's court, who tortured himself by laboring as a peasant and lying to himself and everyone else that such work made him happy. There was also an enormous Jew who looked like a genuine Russian peasant and who later became known as Teneromo, an individual who always carried himself with utmost importance and who looked on simple mortals condescendingly, an insufferable rhetorician and sophist who busied himself with making barrels. It was under him that I began as a Tolstoyan. He was my main instructor both in the "teaching" and in manual labor. I was his apprentice and learned to make hoops. What did I need these hoops for? Again because they somehow united me to Tolstoy and gave me the secret hope that someday I might see and draw close to him.

To my great joy, this hope came about completely unexpectedly. Very quickly, the entire brotherhood accepted me as one of their own, and Volkenshtein—it was at the very end of ninety-three—invited me suddenly to go with him first to the "brotherhood" of the Kharkov District, to the peasants in the village of Khilkovo—which belonged to the well-known Tolstoyan Prince Khilkov—and then to Moscow, to Tolstoy himself.[14]

The journey was a difficult one. We traveled third-class and changed trains several times, always riding in carriages with the common folk and eating "unslaughtered things," that is, the devil knows what, although Volkenshtein sometimes could stand it no longer and rushed to the refreshment stand, where, in a terribly greedy way, he gulped down two or three glasses of vodka and burned his mouth on hot meat-pies, after which he said to me in all seriousness:[15]

"I've again ceded to lust, and I suffer greatly for what I have done. But still I must struggle with self, since I know that meat-pies do not control me, but I, them. I'm not their slave. If I want to, I eat them, if I don't, I don't. . . ."

What made the journey even more difficult was that I was burning with impatience to get to Moscow as soon as possible. But we had to travel on wretched trains, to stay a while with the Khilkovo "brotherhood," and to establish a tie with them so as to "strengthen" both ourselves and them in this search for paths of the "good" life. And so we did—we lived with the Khilkovo peasants, it seemed for three or four days, and, during this time, I hated these rich, pious, and saintly looking people, their pies with potato stuffing, their psalm singing, their tales about their incessant and relentless struggles with "bosses and priests," and their pedantic arguments on the Scriptures with truly all the force of their souls.

Finally, on January first, we moved on. I remember waking upon that morning with such happiness that I forgot myself completely and blurted out: "Happy New Year, Alexander Alexandrovich!"—for which I received from Alexander Alexandrovich a most cruel rebuke: What did this mean—a new year—did I not understand what old-fashioned nonsense I was repeating? But I did not let it bother me. I listened and thought: fine, fine, all this is genuine garbage. But tomorrow evening we will be in Moscow, and the day after that, I will see Tolstoy. . . .

So it came to be.

Volkenshtein, though, dealt me a moral blow: the minute we arrived at our Moscow hotel, he went off but did not take me with him. "It's not possible, it's not possible." I have to give Lev Nikolaevich some warning. I have to let him know in advance—and off he went. He returned home late that evening but said nothing about his visit. He only nodded to me hurriedly: "Truly I have drunk my fill of holy water!"—though I saw quite accurately, by the smell coming from him, that after holy water, he also had had some Chambertin to prove that he was not the slave of Chambertin, but the other way around.

The only good out of all of this was that Volkenshtein had notified Tolstoy, although I held out little hope for a meeting: he was a highly flighty individual, a slightly feminine, portly, handsome, dark-haired man. The next evening, though, quite beside myself, I finally rushed off to Khamovniki.[16]

How to tell you what followed?

It was a frosty, moonlit night. I ran all the way, and when I arrived, I could hardly catch my breath. Everything was quiet and desolate, an empty, moonlit side street. Facing me were gates, an open wicket fence, and a snow-covered yard. In the distance on the left was a wooden house with a reddish light coming from several of the windows. Further to the left, behind the house, was a garden and above it wintry stars, charming and fairy tale–like, with softly shimmering, multicolored lights. Indeed, everything was like a fairy tale. What an unusual garden, what an extraordinary home, how mysterious and meaningful were those lighted windows: for behind all these—He, He! His Very Self! It was so quiet that I could hear my heart pounding—from joy but also from a terrible thought: Would it not be better for me to glance once more at the home and then to run away?

In despair, I at last rushed into the yard and onto the porch and rang the bell. The doors opened right away, and I saw a footman dressed in a shabby tailcoat and a warm, bright, and comfortable foyer, with many fur coats on hangers, and, in striking contrast to them, an old sheepskin coat. Right before me also was a steep staircase with a red carpet. More to the right was a locked door, behind which I heard guitars and happy young voices, surprisingly heedless of how their voices rang out in such a completely unusual home.

"Whom should I say is calling?"

"Bunin."

"How's that again, sir?"

"Bunin."

"Very well, sir."

The servant ran upstairs and immediately, to my surprise, came skipping down, sideways, holding on to the banister.

"Will you kindly wait upstairs, in the hall. . . ."

There I was in for another surprise. Hardly had I entered, when all of a sudden, a small door opened at the end, to the left, and out came an individual flinging his feet out awkwardly, but adeptly—behind the door were two or three steps leading into the corridor—a large, gray-bearded, and slightly bowlegged man, in a wide, baggy blouse of gray flannel, trousers akin to harem pants, and square-toed shoes. [He was] swift, light, terrible, sharp-eyed, with pronounced eyebrows.[17] He moved toward me quickly. Right away (and curtsying somewhat), he extended or, more accurately, threw out a large hand, palm turned upward, taking all of my hand into his, pressing it softly, with a sudden smile that was enchanting and tender, but also somehow sad and even slightly mournful. I saw that his small eyes were not at all sharp or terrible, but alert, like an animal's. The downy and thin remnants of his gray hair curled slightly at the ends and were parted in the middle, peasant-style; the tufts of his arched brows hung over his eyes; his beard, dry, wispy, uneven, and transparent, showed his slightly pronounced lower jaw.

"Bunin? Was it your father I knew in the Crimea? Have you come to Moscow for a long time? What for? To see me? You're a young writer? Well, write, if you feel like it, but remember that it can never be the goal of life. . . . Please sit down and tell me about yourself. . . ."

He began speaking as hastily as he had entered the room, pretending momentarily not to notice my complete confusion and rushing to put me at ease.

What else did he talk about? He kept asking:

"Single? Married? One can live with a woman but only as a wife and never leave her. . . . You wish to live a simple, working life? That's good, but don't force yourself to do so and don't wear it on your sleeve, one can be a good person in any way of life. . . ."

We sat at a small table. A rather tall ancient porcelain lamp shone softly from under a pink lampshade. His face was shadowed softly behind the lamp, and all I could see was the very soft gray flannel of his blouse and his large hand, to which I longed to press my lips with ecstatic, truly filial tenderness. I also heard his aged, slightly alto-like voice and the characteristic sound coming from his somewhat protruding jaw. . . .

Suddenly there was a rustle of silk. I looked up, shuddered, and jumped to my feet—a large and well-dressed woman in a shining black silk dress, with beautifully set hair, and extremely dark lively eyes, glided in from the drawing room.

"Leon," she said, "you've forgotten that people are waiting for you."[18]

Tolstoy also rose. With raised eyebrows, an apologetic, almost guilty smile, and small and somehow darkly sad eyes, he looked straight at me and again took my hand:

"Well, good-bye, good-bye. God willing, come and see me when you're again in Moscow. . . . Don't expect much from life. You won't have a better time of it than what you have now. . . . There's no happiness of life, only occasional flashes of it. . . . Appreciate them, live for them. . . ."

I left and ran home quite beside myself, and I spent a completely insane night, seeing him constantly in my dreams with such striking clarity and in such wild confusion that even now I find it painful to recall how I got hold of myself, and woke up rambling and jabbering about something.[19]

Having returned to Poltava, I wrote to Tolstoy and received several kind letters in reply.[20] In one of them he again made it clear that it was not worth my while to be a Tolstoyan, but I was not to be stopped: I had given up making hoops, but I had begun to sell books published by "Mediator," illegally, without the necessary license to sell them at markets and fairs, for which I was arrested and sentenced to prison—but was saved, to my great distress, by a manifesto by the tsar. After that, I opened a bookshop, a Poltava branch of "Mediator," but so messed up accounts that at times I felt like hanging myself.[21] Finally, I simply abandoned the bookstore and headed to Moscow, where I continued trying to convince myself that I was a brother and soulmate of the leading lights of this "Mediator," as well as of those individuals who hung around the place constantly, instructing each other in the "good" life.

I saw Tolstoy there several times. He sometimes dropped by or, more accurately, rushed in (he moved in an extraordinary light and quick way) in the evenings and, without taking off his sheepskin coat, stayed for an hour or two, surrounded on all sides by the "brotherhood," who often asked him in a serious way:

"Lev Nikolaevich, what should I do if I were attacked by a tiger?"[22]

He smiled confusedly and said:

"What kind of tiger? Where would this tiger come from? I've never seen a tiger in my life. . . ."

I also remember saying to him, attempting to utter something pleasant and to get in his good graces:

"Temperance societies are now springing up everywhere."[23]

He frowned slightly.

"What kind of societies?"

"Temperance societies. . . ."

"You mean to tell me that people get together not to drink vodka? Nonsense. Why should people gather if not to drink? And if they do get together, they should drink. Everything is nonsense, lies, talk, not action."

I was at his home once more. I was led first across the hall where I had first sat with him by that dear pink lamp, then through a little door and down the steps into a narrow passage. Timidly, I knocked on the door to my right.

"Come in," answered the aged, alto-like voice.

I entered and saw a small, low room, drowning in twilight darkness, with an iron shield with two burning candles in an antique candlestick, a leather couch by a table, and finally Tolstoy himself, with a book in his hands. As I entered, he rose quickly and awkwardly, or so it seemed to me, throwing the book confusedly into a corner of the sofa. With my sharp eyes, I saw that he had been reading or, more accurately, rereading (and truly, not for first time, as we authors, sinners that we are, always do) his own work that had just come into print—"Master and Man."[24] In my excitement over this piece, I uttered a cry of delight tactlessly. But he blushed and waved his hands:

"Oh, please! It's terrible, so worthless that I'm ashamed to go out into the street!"

That evening his face was drawn, dark and stern, as though cast in bronze. He was also suffering greatly—his seven-year-old son, Vanya, had died only a short time before.[25] He began talking about the child:

"Yes, yes, he was a sweet, charming boy. But what does it mean—he's dead? There is no death, he's not dead, because we love him, we live for him!"

We soon left the house and went to the offices of "Mediator." It was a dark night in March, a spring wind was blowing, fanning the lights of the streetlamps. We ran diagonally across the snowy white Maiden's Field.[26] He jumped over ditches so quickly that I could hardly keep up, he again saying abruptly, sternly, and sharply:

"There is no death! There is no death!"

I saw him for the last time about ten years later. On a terribly cold evening, walking along the Arbat amid the lights behind dazzling ice-covered shop windows, I bumped into him running straight at me with his springing, bouncy step. I stopped and took off my hat. He also stopped and recognized me right away.[27]

"Oh, it's you. Hello! Put your hat back on, please. . . . Well, how and where do you live, and what are you doing?"[28]

His aged face was so stiff and blue, with an absolutely unhappy look. The knitted pale-blue thing perched on his head was like an old woman's shawl. The large hand that he had pulled out from his arctic fur glove was completely frozen. Having spoken to me for a while, he pressed my hand several times firmly and tenderly, and, with uplifted brows, he again looked sadly into my eyes:

"Well, Christ be with you. Christ be with you. Good-bye. . . ."

Chapter 6

Chekhov

I met him in Moscow at the end of '95, and I still remember several characteristic phrases.

"Do you write a lot?" he asked me for some reason.

I answered that I wrote little.

"A mistake," he said glumly, in a deep husky voice. "You have to work, you know . . . without stopping . . . your entire life."

Having fallen silent, he added without any apparent connection:

"As I see it, once one has written a story, he should cross out the beginning and the end. It is here that we writers lie most of all. . . . One should be brief, as brief as possible."

We did not see each other again until the spring of '99. Having gone to Yalta for several days, I ran into him one evening on the embankment.

"Why haven't you visited me?" he asked. "Come tomorrow without fail."

"When?" I asked.

"In the morning, around seven."

Most likely, seeing the surprise on my face, he explained:

"We get up early. Do you?

"Me, too," I said.

"Well then come as soon as you get up. We'll have coffee. Do you drink coffee? One should drink coffee in the morning, not tea. It's a wonderful thing.

When I work, I have nothing but coffee and bouillon until evening. Coffee in the morning, bouillon at noon."

We walked along the embankment silently and sat down on a bench in the square.

"Do you like the sea?" I asked.

"Yes," he answered, "only it's so empty."

"That's why it's good," I said.

"I don't know," he answered, gazing off into the distance and apparently lost in his own thoughts. "As I see it, it would be nice to be an officer or a young student. . . . To sit in some crowded place and to listen to some lively music. . . ."

As was his manner, he fell silent and added without any visible connection:

"The sea is very difficult to describe. Do you know what I recently read in a schoolboy's notebook? 'The sea was big.' That was it. I thought it was wonderful."

In Moscow, I had seen a middle-aged man, tall, well built, and agile, who greeted me in a friendly way, but also so simply that I took it for coldness. In Yalta, I saw that he had changed greatly: he had grown thin, his face had darkened, his movements were slower, his voice was more hollow. But on the whole, he was almost the same: friendly, but reserved. He spoke in a rather lively way, but still even more simply and briefly, and still lost in his own thoughts, leaving it to his companion to connect the quick flow of his thoughts as he kept gazing on the sea through the pince-nez on his slightly raised face.

The next morning, I went to his dacha. I remember well the sunny morning we spent in his small garden. From then on, I began to visit him more often and soon became a member of the family. His stance toward me changed accordingly—it became more heartfelt, simpler. . . .

The white stone dacha in Autka; the small garden where he, with such care, raised the trees and the flowers he always so loved; his study, decorated only with two or three pictures by Levitan; and the large semicircular window looking out on the gardens that overran the valley of the Uchan-Su and the blue triangle of the Black Sea; the hours, days, and sometimes even weeks that I spent there will remain in my memory forever. . . . [1]

Alone with him, he often laughed infectiously. He loved to joke, to come up with all kinds of things, absurd nicknames. As soon as he felt the least bit better, there was no end to them. He loved conversations about literature. He often went into raves over Maupassant, Tolstoy. He often talked especially about them and also about Lermontov's "Taman."

"I cannot understand," he said, "how he, while still a boy, could do such a thing![2] If one could write such a piece and a good vaudeville to boot, he would die in peace!"

He often said:

"Writers should never read their things before they are published. They should never listen to other people's advice. So, if you make a mistake or go offtrack—let the mistake be yours alone. One must be bold in his work. There are big dogs and little dogs, but the little ones must not be put off by the big ones. All must bark—with the voices that God gave them."

When people talk about deceased writers, they say that such individuals rejoiced in another's success, that they were free of pride. But Chekhov delighted truly in any kind of talent and could not help but do so: the word "untalented," it seemed, was, on his lips, the highest kind of abuse. He regarded his own literary success with inner bitterness.

"Well, Anton Pavlovich, soon we'll be celebrating your jubilee!"

"Oh, I know all about these jubilees," he replied. "For twenty-five years they tear a writer to pieces, and then they give him an aluminum quill pen and spend the entire day showering him with kisses, tears, and ecstatic nonsense."

"Have you read it, Anton Pavlovich?" you would ask, having seen an article about him somewhere.

He would only squint slyly from above his pince-nez:

"I thank you humbly," he replied. "They'll write a thousand lines about someone and then add at the bottom: 'There's also this writer Chekhov: a groaner-moaner. . . .' But what kind of groaner-moaner am I? How am I a 'gloomy person,' how am I a 'cold-blooded individual,' as the critics call me? After all, of all my things, my most favorite story is 'The Student.'[3] A disgusting word: 'pessimist.'"

Occasionally, he added:

"When, my dear sir, when people abuse you somewhere, you'll remember us sinners a bit more often: as if in a seminary, the critics rip you to shreds for the slightest slipup. One predicted that I would die under a fence: he imagined me as a young man kicked out of school for drunkenness."[4]

He once said: "One should sit down and write only when he feels as cold as ice."

"'Scorpion' is publishing my work in a slipshod way," he wrote to me after the first issue of *Northern Flowers* appeared. "They put me first, and after I read their advertisement in *Russian News*, I swore I'd have nothing more to do with scorpions or crocodiles or grass snakes."

At my insistence, he gave one of his humorous stories ("On the Sea") to one of the almanacs by 'Scorpion.'[5] He regretted it later.

"All this new Moscow art is rubbish," he said. "I remember I once saw a sign in Taganrog: 'Plant for *Artificial* Mineral Waters.' The very same thing here. What is new is only that which is talented. What's talented is new."

One of my last remembrances of him dates back to early spring 1903. Yalta, the hotel "Russia." It was already late evening. Suddenly I was called to the telephone. I went over to it and heard:

"Dear sir, get hold of a good cab and come and get me. Let's go for a ride."

"A ride? Tonight? What's with you, Anton Pavlovich?"

"I'm in love."

"That's good, but it's nine o'clock. And besides—you might catch cold. . . ."

"Young man, don't argue!"

Ten minutes later I was in Autka. The home where he lived alone with his mother in the winter was, as always, quiet and dark. Two small candles burned dimly in the study. Also as always was the case, my heart ached at the sight of this room where he spent so many lonely winter evenings.

"A marvelous night!" he said, greeting me with unusual tenderness and a somewhat melancholic joy. "It's so boring at home! The only joy I have is when the phone begins ringing and someone asks what I'm doing and I answer: 'I'm catching mice.' Let's go to Oreanda."[6]

The night was warm, quiet, with a clear moon and light white clouds. The carriage drove along a white road. We were quiet, looking at the shining plane of the sea. Then came the forest, with light patterned shadows; after that, darkening clusters of cypress trees rising to the stars. We stopped the carriage and walked quietly under them, past a ruined palace, pale blue in the moonlight. Suddenly he stopped and said:

"Do you know how many years people will keep reading me? Seven."

"Why seven?" I asked.

"Well, seven and a half."

"You're sad today, Anton Pavlovich," I said, looking into his face, pale in the moonlight.

Thoughtfully, with lowered eyes, he dug up some gravel with the end of his walking stick. But when I told him that he was sad, he glanced at me mischievously:

"It's you who are sad," he answered. "Because you've spent money on a cab."

He added in a serious tone:

"No, people will read me only for seven years, and I have even less to live: six years. Only don't tell the reporters in Odessa. . . ."[7]

He lived not for six years, but just over a year.

In January, when I was in Nice, I received one of his last letters:

"Greetings, dear I.A.! I wish you a Happy New Year, new happiness. I got your letter, thank you. Everything with us in Moscow is fine, but (except for the New Year) there is nothing new in sight. My play has still not been staged, and I don't know when it will appear. . . . [8] Very possibly, I'll come to Nice in February. . . . Give my regards to the dear warm sun, the quiet sea. Enjoy yourself, take heart, write a bit more often to your friends. . . . Keep well, cheerful, and happy and don't forget your stormy, northern countrymen who suffer from indigestion and bad moods. I kiss and hug you."[9]

One time (as usual, unexpectedly), he said:

"Do you know what once happened to me?"

Peering into my face through his pince-nez for some time, he burst out laughing:

"For some reason I was going up the main stairs at the Moscow Nobility Club, where Yuzhin-Sumbatov was standing by a mirror, his back toward me.[10] He was holding Potapenko by his coat button and insistently, even through his teeth, telling him: 'Yes, you understand, you're now the first, the very first writer in Russia!'

"But suddenly, he saw me in the mirror, blushed, and, pointing to me over his shoulder, added quickly: 'He, too. . . .'"

To many it will seem strange, but true: He disliked actors and actresses, saying:

"They're seventy-five years behind the rest of society. They are vulgar people, consumed with pride. I remember Solovtsov. . . ."

"Wait," I said, "don't you remember the telegram you sent to the Solovtsov Theater after his death?"[11]

"What doesn't one have to write in letters and telegrams? Or have to say so as not to offend. . . ."[12]

Having fallen silent, he said with a new burst of laughter:

"Just look at the Moscow Art Theater. . . ."

His notebook has a thing or two that I heard from him myself. He asked me several times (each time forgetting that he had already done so and laughing heartily):

"Do you know that type of lady who, when you look at her, you always think she has gills under her bodice?"

More than once, he said:

"In nature, a repulsive caterpillar turns into a charming butterfly; but with people, it is just the reverse. . . ."

"It's terrible to dine daily with someone who stutters and talks rubbish. . . ."

"When a bad actress eats a partridge, I feel sorry for the partridge, which was a hundred times more clever and talented than she. . . ."

"No matter how much people rave about her, Savina as an actress is the same as Viktor Krylov as a playwright. . . ."[13]

Sometimes he said:

"A writer should be destitute. He must be in a situation where he knows he will die from hunger if does not write, if he gives in to laziness. Writers should be put in prison and there forced to write in solitary confinement, with floggings, beatings. . . . Oh, how grateful I am to fate to have been so poor when I was young!

"How I admired Davydova![14] It so happened that Mamin-Sibiryak would come to her and say:

"'Alexandra Arkadievna, I don't have a kopeck to my name. Give me at least fifty rubles as an advance.'

"She answered: 'Even if you're dying, my dear, I won't. I'll give you some only if you agree that I can lock you up right away in my study; furnish you with ink, pen, paper, and three bottles of beer; and let you out only when you knock on the door and tell me that you have a story ready.'"

But sometimes he said something just the opposite:

"A writer must be fabulously rich, so rich that, at any moment, he can travel around the world in his own yacht; arrange an expedition to the sources of the Nile, to the South Pole, to Tibet and Arabia; and buy all of the Caucasus or the Himalayas. . . . Tolstoy says that an individual needs only six feet of land.[15] Rubbish—a corpse needs six feet of land, but a living person needs the entire earthly sphere. Especially—a writer."

Speaking of Tolstoy, he once said:

"What particularly strikes me about him is the contempt he has for all of us other writers, or, more exactly, not contempt, but simply that he sees all of us as complete nothings. Sometimes, he praises Maupassant, Kuprin, Semyonov, and me. . . . Why? Because he sees us as children. Our stories, novels, and tales are for him child's play; that's why he puts Maupassant and Semyonov in the same heap. Shakespeare is quite another matter. Shakespeare is an adult who irritates him because he does not write like Tolstoy does. . . ."

One time, reading the newspaper, he looked up and said unhurriedly, without any intonation:

"It's always like that: Korolenko and Chekhov, Potapenko and Chekhov, Gorky and Chekhov. . . ."

Now he has been set apart [from others]. But I still think that he has not yet been understood as he should: He was too original and complex a man, a hidden soul.

His notebook has this remarkable line:

"Just as I will lie alone in the grave, so am I truly living alone now."

In the same notebook he jotted down:

"How willingly do people deceive themselves, how they love prophets and pontificators, how they are like a herd!"

"For every one intelligent individual, there are a thousand stupid ones; for one intelligent word, there are a thousand stupid ones and they stifle everything."

He was stifled for a long time. Before the "The Peasants," by no means one of his best things, the general public read him willingly, but only as an engaging storyteller, the author of "A Game of Vint" and "The Complaint Book." . . . [16]

People with "ideas" had little interest in him. They recognized his talent, but they did not take him seriously. I remember several of them laughing genuinely at me when I, as a youth, dared compare him with Garshin, Korolenko. Some even said that they would never begin reading a writer [like Chekhov] who began under the name Chekhonte: "One cannot imagine," they said, "Tolstoy or Turgenev choosing such a vulgar nickname."[17]

Real fame came to him only when the Art Theater staged his plays. Most likely, this must have hurt him as much as when people began talking about him only after "The Peasants." After all, his plays were far from the best things he wrote, and their success also meant that it was the theater that attracted attention to him, that his name was seen a thousand times on posters, and that one remembered "twenty-two misfortunes," "dearly esteemed wardrobe," "they have forgotten the servant."[18]

Chekhov often said:

"What kind of dramatists are we! The only real dramatist is Naidyonov: a born playwright with the most dramatic spring inside him. He now must write ten more plays. If nine should fail, the tenth will be so successful that you will shout with delight!"

[Once] having fallen silent, he broke out into merry laughter:

"You know, not long ago I was at Tolstoy's place in Gaspra.[19] He was still in bed, but he talked a great deal about everything, including me. Finally, I got up and said good-bye. But he held me by the hand and said, 'Kiss me,' and after I kissed him, he leaned suddenly close to my ear and said in a lively, old-man's patter: 'But just the same I can't stand your plays. Shakespeare wrote badly, but you're even worse!'"[20]

For a long time, Chekhov was seen only as a "gloomy" writer, "the singer of twilight moods," a "sick talent," as an individual who looked at everything in a hopeless and indifferent way.

Now they have swung to the other extreme: "Chekhov's tenderness, sadness, and warmth," "Chekhov's love for humanity. . . ." I can imagine how he himself would feel, reading about his "tenderness"! He would be even more repulsed by his "warmth," "sadness."

Even talented people strike the wrong note about him. Yelpatievsky: "In Chekhov's home, I met people who were gentle and kind, unassuming and unexacting. . . . He was attracted to such types. . . . He was always drawn to quiet, misty valleys, to hazy dreams, and to quiet tears. . . ." Korolenko characterizes his talent with such pitiful words as "simplicity and soulfulness," his "sorrow for specters." One of the best articles about him belongs to Shestov, who called him a "merciless talent."[21]

Even in everyday life, Chekhov was both sparse and precise with words. He valued them extremely highly. Words that were pompous, false, and bookish affected him sharply. He himself spoke splendidly—always in his own way, clearly, correctly. When he talked, one never heard the writer in him. He used metaphors and epithets rarely, and when he did, they were, more often than not, everyday. He never flaunted or relished a successfully uttered word.

He hated "high-flown" words. A memoir has this wonderful excerpt about him: "I once complained to Anton Pavlovich: 'Anton Pavlovich! What am I to do? I'm so consumed by introspection.' Anton Pavlovich replied: 'Drink a little less vodka.'"

Truly, his hatred of "high-flown" words, the way many poets, particularly contemporary ones, used words carelessly, was why verse dissatisfied him so sharply. Lermontov's "The Sail," he once said, "was worth all of Urenius."[22]

"What Urenius?"

"Why, isn't there such a poet?"

"No."

"Well, then Uprudius," he said seriously.[23]

"When Tolstoy dies, everything will go to the devil," he often said.

"Literature?"

"Literature, too."

About the Moscow "decadents," as they were then called, he once said:

"What decadents? They're big strapping peasants. They ought to be arrested."

He was also unflattering about Andreev:

"I read one page from Andreev—and then have to walk for two hours in the fresh air."

When something particularly amused him, he always howled with pleasure.

People of the most diverse ranks gathered at his home: He was the same with everyone. He never showed preferences; he never injured anyone's pride or made them feel forgotten or unwanted. But invariably, he kept everyone at a formal distance.

He had a great sense of personal dignity, independence.

"I fear only Tolstoy. Just think: after all, it was he who wrote how Anna felt, how she saw her eyes shining in the darkness! Seriously, I'm afraid of him," he said, laughing, as though he enjoyed his fear.[24]

Once Chekhov spent nearly an hour deciding on which trousers to wear for a visit to Tolstoy. Having taken off his pince-nez, he looked younger, and as was his custom, mixing the sublime with the ridiculous, he kept coming out of the bedroom with different pairs of pants on.

"No, these are obscenely narrow! He'll think: hack!"

He would then go out, put on another pair, and again come out laughing:

"But these are as wide as the Black Sea! He'll think: scoundrel!"

Once, accompanied by a few close friends, he went to Alupka for lunch in a restaurant.[25] He was in a merry and very joking mood. Suddenly, at an adjoining table, a gentleman rose with a champagne glass in his hand:

"Ladies and gentlemen! I propose a toast to Anton Pavlovich, who is here with us, the pride of our literature, the singer of twilight moods. . . ."

Having turned pale, he got up and left.

I stayed in Odessa for long periods and spent nearly all my time with him. I often left late at night, but he would say:

"Come by early tomorrow."

Chekhov lisped certain sounds, his voice was somewhat hollow, and he often spoke without any intonation, as if muttering: at times it was hard to tell if he was speaking seriously or not.

Every now and then, I would decline an invitation. He would take off his pince-nez, press his hands to his heart, and, with a barely perceptible smile on his pale lips, repeat in a clear, distinct way:

"I beg you most earnestly to come, monsieur le Marquis Bouquichon![26] If you get bored with this old forgotten writer, go sit with Masha, with Mama, who is in love with you, and with my wife, Knipshits the Hungarian. . . . [27] We'll talk about literature. . . ."

When I visited Chekhov, we sometimes spent the entire morning in his study in silence, looking through newspapers, of which he had a great many. He would say: "Let's read the newspapers and dig up something from a provincial column for plots for dramas or vaudevilles." Occasionally, we would come across a thing or two about me—most often, something very stupid—and he hastened to soften the sting:

"They've said even dumber, much crueler things about me, or they've forgotten me altogether. . . ."

It also happened that they found a "Chekhovian mood" in me. Becoming animated, even upset, he exclaimed with restrained excitement:

"Oh, how stupid this is! Oh, how stupid! They went after me for 'Turgenevian notes.' . . . You and I are as much alike as a borzoi and a bloodhound. You are much sharper than I. You write: 'The sea smelled like a watermelon.' . . . That is wonderful, but I would not have said such a thing. About that girl student—that's a different matter!"

"What girl student?"

"You remember, we were making up a story: a hot day, the steppe beyond Kharkov, a very long moving mail train. . . . You added: a girl student with a leather belt is standing by the window of a third-class car, shaking out from a teapot wet leaves, which the wind carries off into the face of a fat man leaning out from another window. . . ."[28]

Sometimes he put down the paper, took off his pince-nez, and laughed loudly in a lighthearted way.

"Something you read?"

"A merchant from Samara named Babkin," he said in a weak voice, laughing, "has bequeathed his entire fortune for a monument of Hegel."[29]

"You've got to be kidding."

"Cross my heart. To Hegel."

Having put down the newspaper, he asked suddenly:

"What will you write about me in your memoirs?"

"It's you who'll be writing about me. You'll outlive me."

"You could be my son."[30]

"All the same. You have peasant blood."

"And you have gentry blood. Peasants and merchants degenerate terribly quickly. Read my 'Three Years.'[31] You're also a most healthy individual, even though you're quite thin, like a fine borzoi. Take some drops for your appetite, and you'll live to be a hundred. I'll write a prescription for you. I'm a doctor, after all. Nikodim Palych Kondakov himself came to me, and I cured him of piles.[32] But in your memoirs about me, don't write that I was a 'sympathetic talent of crystal purity.'"

"That's what they've written about me," I said, "that I had a sympathetic gift."

He began to laugh loudly, with the excruciating pleasure he showed whenever he particularly liked something.

"Wait, what was it that Korolenko said about you?"

"Not Korolenko, but Zlatovratsky. About one of my first stories. He wrote that my piece 'would have done credit even to a greater writer.'"[33]

He doubled up in laughter. Then he put on his pince-nez and, looking at me sharply and cheerfully, said:

"Still, it is better than what they wrote about me. As if in a seminary, the critics flog us every Saturday. It serves us right. I began writing as the poorest son of a bitch. I'm a proletarian, after all. As a child, I sold tallow candles in our shop in Taganrog. Oh, how devilishly cold it was there! But with pleasure I wrapped the ice-cold candle in a scrap of cotton paper. Our latrine was on a vacant lot about half a mile from our house. Sometimes, I'd run in at night and find a bum there. We'd scare the hell out of each other!

"Here's my advice to you. Stop being a dilettante and become a craftsman, if only for a while. It's awful to write as I did—for a piece of bread—but in any case, one has to be a craftsman and not wait for inspiration all the time."

Then, after a pause:

"Without fail, Korolenko should cheat on his wife to begin to write a bit better. Otherwise, he's way too decent. Do you remember telling me how he once wept uncontrollably over a poem in *Russian Wealth* by some Verbov or Vetkov about how the 'wolves of reaction' surrounded a bard, a native poet, in a field in a terrible snowstorm, and how this poet struck such a melodious tune on the strings of his lyre that the wolves ran away in fear? Was it you who told me that? Was that true?"[34]

"Word of honor, it's true."

"Oh, by the way, do you know that all the cabdrivers in Perm' look like Dobrolyubov?"[35]

"You don't like Dobrolyubov?"

"No, I like him. They're all decent people. Not like Skabichevsky, who once wrote that I would die under a fence from drinking because I didn't possess a 'divine spark.'"[36]

"Do you know," I said, "that Skabichevsky once told me that he had never seen how rye grows and that he had never spoken to a single peasant?"

"There you are, but all his life he wrote about the folk and stories of peasant life. . . . Yes, it is terrible to recall what people wrote about me! My blood was cold, they said—do you remember my story 'Cold Blood'?—and that I could truly care less about what I depicted—a dog or a drowned man, a train or a first love. . . . *Gloomy People* saved me somewhat, all the stories there were seen as worthwhile because they depicted the reaction of the eighties.[37] Also my story 'An Attack of Nerves'—an 'honest' student goes mad thinking about prostitution. But I cannot stand Russian students—they're good-for-nothings."[38]

Once, when he again began joking about what precisely I would write in my memoirs about him, I replied:

"I'll write, first of all, about how and why I met you in Moscow. It was in '95, in December. I did not know that you had come there. I was with a poet in the Great Moscow Tavern; we were drinking red wine and listening to the player piano.[39] The poet kept declaiming his verse, getting more and more passionate about himself. We left very late, but the poet had gotten so carried away that he continued to recite his verse on the staircase. Still exclaiming, he began looking for his coat on the hanger. The porter said sweetly:

"'Allow me, sir, I'll find it for you. . . .'

"The poet turned on him like a wild beast:

"'Quiet! I can find it!'

"'But, if you'll allow me, sir, this isn't your coat. . . .'

"'What's that, you scoundrel? You mean I'm taking someone else's coat?'

"'Exactly so, someone else's, sir.'

"'Quiet, you scoundrel, it's my coat!'

"'No it's not, sir, it's not yours!'

"'Then tell me this instant, whose is it?'

"'Anton Pavlovich Chekhov's.'

"'You're lying. For that I'll kill you on the spot!'

"'If that's what you wish to do, but the coat is Anton Pavlovich Chekhov's.'

"'You mean he's here?'

"'He always stays here.'

"We almost rushed to meet you at three o'clock in the morning. But, fortunately, we got hold of ourselves and called on you the next day. The first time you were not there—we saw only your room, which the maid was straightening up, and a manuscript on the table. It was the beginning of 'A Woman's Kingdom.' . . ."[40]

Chekhov died from laughter and said:

"'I can guess who the poet was. Balmont, of course. But how did you know what manuscript was lying on the table? That means you peeked?"

"Forgive us, dear one, we couldn't resist."

"Pity that you did not stop by that night. It's nice to go off somewhere suddenly at night. I love restaurants."

He once became unusually cheerful when I told him that our village deacon, on my father's name day, somehow ate two pounds of caviar right down to the last grain. He used the story to begin his work "In the Ravine."[41]

He loved to repeat that if an individual does not work and live constantly in the world of art, he, even if be Solomon the Wise, will feel empty and devoid of talent.

Sometimes he took a notebook out of his desk and, raising his face, his pince-nez sparkling, waved it in the air:

"Exactly one hundred plots. Yes, my dear sir, exactly one hundred plots! You're no match for me, young man! I'm a worker! Want me to sell you a couple?"

Sometimes he allowed himself to go on evening walks. One time we were coming back late. He was very tired and could barely keep up—the past few days he had stained many handkerchiefs with blood—he was silent and had closed his eyes.[42] We were going past a lighted balcony with the silhouette of a woman behind a canvas curtain, when suddenly he opened his eyes and said very loudly:

"Have you heard? What a terrible thing! Bunin has been murdered! In Autka, in the home of a Tartar woman!"

Bewildered, I stopped, amazed, but he whispered quietly:

"Silence! Tomorrow all of Yalta will be talking about Bunin's murder!"

A writer once complained: "When I recall how weak and poor my first writings were, I could cry from shame."

"Oh, how can you say such a thing!" he exclaimed. "It's wonderful to begin badly! Understand that with a beginning writer, if it all comes out the way it should, he's finished, he might as well give up!"

He began to argue passionately that merely competent people, that is, individuals who lack originality and talent, mature early and quickly because they adapt to circumstances and "live lightheartedly," whereas talent torments, seeking to come to the fore.

Many Turks and people from the Caucasus worked on the shores of the Black Sea. Knowing the mix of suspicion and contempt that Russians have for foreigners, he never missed an opportunity to say enthusiastically what an honest, hardworking people these individuals were.

He ate little, slept little, and loved order greatly. His rooms were remarkably clean, his bedroom was like a young girl's. No matter how ill he felt sometimes, he never allowed himself the slightest leeway in his dress.

His hands were large, rough, and pleasant.

Like almost everyone who thinks a great deal, he often forgot that he said something more than once.

I remember his silence, his cough, his closed eyes, the thoughts on his face, peaceful and sad, almost weighty. But it was not "sadness" or "warmth."

A winter day in the Crimea, gray, cool; thick, sleepy clouds over the Yaila.[43] It is quiet in the Chekhov home; the alarm clock in Yevgeniya Chekhova's room ticks regularly. He, without his pince-nez, is sitting in his study, at his desk, and jotting down something slowly, carefully. Then he gets up, puts on his coat, hat, and low leather galoshes, and heads out somewhere where a mousetrap has been set. He returns, holding a live mouse by the end of its tail, goes out onto the porch, walks slowly through the garden right up to the fence, beyond which a Tartar cemetery lies on a stony knoll. He throws the mouse there carefully and, looking attentively at the young trees, heads for a small bench in the middle of the garden. A crane runs after him, then two small dogs. Having sat down, he, with a small cane, plays gently with one of them, which has rolled on its back at his feet. He grins: fleas are crawling over its pink belly. . . . Then, leaning back on the bench, he looks into the distance, at the Yaila, his face raised, thinking about something. He sits like that for an hour, an hour and a half. . . .

Did he have at least one great love in his life? I do not think so.

"Love," he wrote in his notebook, "is either the remains of something that was once enormous, but is deteriorating, or it is a part of something that is going to become something huge in the future but that in the present does not satisfy and gives much less than one expects."

What did he think about death?

He often said firmly and deliberately that immortality, life after death in whatever form—is complete nonsense.

"It's superstition. Any kind of superstition is a terrible thing. One should think clearly and courageously. We'll talk about it thoroughly sometime. I'll prove to you that just as two times two equals four, immortality is absurd."

But then more than once he said the opposite even more firmly:

"There's no way we can disappear without a trace. Immortality is a fact. Just wait, I'll prove it to you. . . ."

In the last years of his life, he often dreamed aloud:

"To become a tramp, a pilgrim, to go to the holy places, to live in a monastery in a forest, by a lake, to sit on a little bench by some monastery gates during summer evenings. . . ."

His "Archbishop" passed unnoticed—unlike *The Cherry Orchard*, with its big paper flowers, glowing thickly white behind the windows on stage. But who knows what would have become of his fame if it were not for such works as "A Game of Vint," "The Peasants," and the Moscow Art Theater![44]

"A month later a new vicar-archbishop was appointed, and no one remembered the Right Reverend Pyotr. Soon he was forgotten altogether. Only the old woman, the dead man's mother, who is now living in a remote local little town, when she goes out at sunset to bring in her cow, meets other women down in the pasture and begins to talk about her children, about her grandchildren, saying that she had a son who was an archbishop, speaking timidly, afraid that people will not believe her. . . . And indeed, not everyone did. . . ."

The last letter I received from him from abroad was in mid-June 1904, when I was living in the country.[45] He wrote that he was feeling fine, that he had ordered a white suit, and that he feared for Japan, a "wondrous country," which, of course, would be beaten and crushed by Russia.[46] On July fourth, I rode on horseback to the village post office, collected my mail and newspapers, and headed over to the blacksmith to reshod my horse. It was a hot sultry steppe day, with a dimly lit sky and a hot southern wind. Sitting on the doorstep of the blacksmith's shop, I opened the newspaper—and suddenly, it was just as if an icy razor had slashed my heart. . . .

A cold had hastened his death. Before leaving Moscow for abroad, he went to the baths; having finished there, he got dressed and went out too soon. He met Sergeenko in the dressing room and ran away from him, from his persistent chatter.[47]

This was the very same Sergeenko who wore out Tolstoy many years before (*How Tolstoy Lives and Works*) and whom, for his thin and lanky figure, invariably black suit and black hair, Chekhov called:

"A funeral hearse on legs."[48]

A year and a half ago, I was giving a public reading of my literary memoirs in Paris and, as an aside, said that I did not like his plays, that they were, in my opinion, all very poor, and that he should not have written dramas about a gentry life that he did not know.

Many people were incensed, indignant. E. D. Kuskova wrote two lengthy feuilletons about my memoirs in *New Russian Word*. "In Geneva," she wrote, "both young and old were offended by Bunin on Chekhov, Balmont, and Gorky. . . . These writers are loved even now, and Chekhov is being read even though, it would seem, that old mournful Russia with its moaners and groaners has receded into the past. . . ."[49]

This is genuinely insulting to Chekhov—to debase him as a portrayer of "old, mournful Russia." It is Kuskova who has every reason to be offended, and the "old boys" in Geneva should not forget when Gorky, with loathsome coarseness, called them, Russian intellectuals, a "pantry with rotten food."

One should also be affronted by the famous actress Yermolova. Among her published letters is one to her friend, a doctor Seredin in Yalta: "You ask why I don't like Chekhov's story 'In the Ravine'? Because all this *chekhovshchina* is for me a symbol of relentless darkness, of all imaginable sorrow and disease." Further, she regards Gorky as a "dear, enlightened soul" and asks Seredin: "You're close to Gorky. Don't let him turn his back on that bright note that sounds so forcefully in his works. . . ."[50]

Reading such a thing, one cannot believe one's eyes! "In the Ravine" is, in all respects, one of the most splendid creations of Russian literature, but for Yermolova, it is "*chekhovshchina*, a symbol of relentless darkness," and Gorky—a "dear enlightened soul," who has written so very many purposely dirty, vile, and gloomy things, and a "bright note," it seems, that has sounded "forcefully"!

CHAPTER 7

Chaliapin

It was often said in Moscow that Chaliapin made friends with writers to spite Sobinov, his rival in fame, and that what attracted him to such individuals was not a love of literature, but a wish to further his reputation not only as a famous singer but also as a "progressive with ideas."[1] So that part of the public who always and everywhere goes crazy over tenors, does so over Sobinov. But it seems to me that Chaliapin's attraction for us writers was not always self-serving. I remember how passionately he wanted to meet Chekhov, how many times he spoke to me about it. Finally, I asked him:

"But what's stopping you?"

"Chekhov doesn't appear in public," he answered, "so there's never a chance to be introduced to him."

"Good Lord, as if you need a reason. Grab a cab and go."

"But I don't want to look like a boor! Besides, I know that I'd be so shy with him that I'd also come off as a complete fool. But if sometime you'd take me to him. . . ."

I hurried to do as he wished and saw that he was right: entering Chekhov's room, he blushed to his ears and began mumbling something. . . . But he left completely enchanted.

"You won't believe how happy I am that I finally have met him, how charmed I was by him! What a man, what a writer! Now everyone else will seem like camels to me."

"Thanks a lot," I said, smiling.[2]

He howled all the way down the street.

There is a famous photograph—famous because it appeared on postcards in hundreds of thousands of copies—of Andreev, Gorky, Chaliapin, Skitalets, Chirikov, Teleshov, and me. We had gathered for lunch at a German restaurant in Moscow called the "Alpine Rose." Having made merry for a long time, we decided suddenly to have our picture taken. But Skitalets and I got into a bit of an argument. I said:

"Again pictures! Always pictures! A doggie wedding that never ends!"

Skitalets took offense.

"Why a wedding and a doggie one, to boot?" he answered in a coarsely forced voice. "No way do I see myself as a dog. But I don't know about the others."

"And what else would you call it?" I said. "We're having a splendid banquet, a holiday. But then you go and say 'the people are dying of hunger,' Russia is perishing, home to 'all kinds of disasters, below the power of darkness, above the darkness of power,' over it 'roars the stormy herald like black lightning.' But what's going on in Moscow and Saint Petersburg? Day and night a holiday, one all-Russian event after another: a new anthology by Knowledge, a new play by Hamsun, a premier at the Art Theater, one at the Bolshoi, girl students fainting at the sight of Stanislavsky and Kachalov, cabs rushing off to the Strelna and Ravine. . . ."[3]

Such words could have led to an argument, but laughter reigned supreme. Chaliapin exclaimed:

"Bravo, rightly said! But nonetheless, brothers, let's go and immortalize a doggie wedding! We often have our pictures taken, true, but we have to leave something for posterity. First a person sings and sings, but then he dies and a lid is put over him."

"Yes," Gorky chimed in, "a person writes and writes, but then he dies like a dog."

"I, for example," Andreev said somberly. "I'll be the first one to go."

He often said such a thing, and everyone laughed at him. But that's the way things turned out.[4]

Everyone considered Chaliapin very left-wing and roared with delight when he sang "The Marseillaise" or "The Flea," which was seen as something revolutionary, a satanic mocking of kings:

There one lived a king,
And with him lived a flea. . . . [5]

But what happened suddenly? Satan fell on his knees before the king—a rumor swept over all Russia: Chaliapin had knelt before the tsar. To Chaliapin's ire, there was no end to what people said about him. How many times did he try to vindicate himself for his sin!

"But how could I not kneel?" he said. "It was a benefit performance for the Imperial Opera Choir, who decided to use the tsar's presence to ask for a raise in salary by falling on their knees before him. And that is what they did. And as I was singing with them, what was I supposed to do? In no way did I expect people to genuflect, and suddenly I see the entire choir falling on their knees, as if mowed down by a scythe, their hands stretched out toward the royal box! So again, what could I do? Stick out like a telegraph pole amid the entire choir? That would have caused a real scandal!"[6]

The last time I saw Chaliapin in Russia was in early April 1917, when Lenin had just arrived in Petersburg. I was also in Petersburg at the time, and, together with Chaliapin, I received an invitation from Gorky to attend a solemn gathering at the Mikhailovsky Theater, where Gorky was to deliver a speech about some "Academy of Free Sciences" that he had just founded.[7] I do not understand or remember why Chaliapin and I were invited to this extremely stupid gathering. Gorky gave an exceedingly long and pretentious speech and then announced:

"Comrades, with us are Chaliapin and Bunin! I ask you to welcome them!"

The hall broke out into frenzied applause, with people stomping their feet and calling us to appear onstage. We hid behind the curtains, when someone came running after us suddenly, saying that the audience wanted Chaliapin to sing. It seemed that Chaliapin would have to "fall on his knees" again. But he told the individual firmly:

"I'm not a fireman to climb on the roof at the first command. Tell that to the audience."

The person disappeared; but Chaliapin said to me, spreading his hands bewilderingly:

"Well, pal, I'm in one hell of a fix. I can't sing and I can't not sing—after all, these devils will remember this someday and hang me on a streetlamp. But all the same, I'm not going to sing."

And he did not.

Chaliapin, though, was not so brave under the Bolsheviks. But, in the end, he managed to run away from them. . . . [8]

The last time I heard Chaliapin sing was in June 1937 in Paris. He was giving a concert, then with Afonsky's choir. I think that even then he was seriously ill.[9] He was unusually nervous. Of course, he was always nervous whenever he performed—that is usual for singers. I saw how Yermolova shook all over and crossed herself right before she went out on the stage. I also saw how Rossi himself, after playing the role of Lensky, went into his dressing room.[10] They all fainted dead away. The same thing probably happened to Chaliapin, only the public never saw such a thing. But at the final concert, people did, Chaliapin saving himself only with his talent for gestures and intonations.

Offstage, Chaliapin sent me a note, asking me to see him. I went. He was pale, sweating, and holding a cigarette in his trembling hand. Right away he asked (something that, of course, he never would have done earlier):

"Well, how was I?"

"Splendid, of course," I answered. Then I joked: "You were so good that I joined in and disturbed everyone around me greatly."

"Thank you, dear one, please join in any time," he said with a faint smile. "But, you know, I'm not feeling very well, and tomorrow I'm leaving for a rest in the mountains, in Austria. The mountains, pal, are great. And where are you going for the summer?"

Again I joked:

"Anywhere but the mountains, I'm always there: first Montmartre, then Montparnasse."

He again smiled, but in a very distracted way.

Why did Chaliapin give that final concert?[11] Probably because he felt that his days were numbered and wanted to say good-bye to the stage. He did not do it for money, though he loved money greatly. He almost never sang for charity or benefits. He loved to say:

"Only birds sing for free."

I last saw Chaliapin six weeks or so before he died, when M. A. Aldanov and I visited him.[12] He was already very sick, but with still a great deal of energy for acting and life. He was sitting on a chair in the corner of his dining room alongside a lit lamp with a yellow lampshade, wearing a wide black silk robe and red slippers, with a shock of hair raised high over his forehead, splendid and huge, like an aging lion. Never had I seen him looking so magnificent, so like a thoroughbred. What kind of blood did he have? That very special northern Russian blood that flowed through the veins of Lomonosov or the Vasnetsov brothers? As a youth he had an extremely plebeian cast, but, with the years, he kept changing and changing. . . .

When Tolstoy first heard him sing, he said:

"No, he sings too loudly."[13]

Even now there are still many intelligent people who are convinced sincerely that Tolstoy understood absolutely nothing about art, his "abuse of Shakespeare and Beethoven."[14] Leaving them aside, how can we explain such a view of Chaliapin? Was he completely indifferent to all the merits of Chaliapin's voice, his talent? Of course not. Tolstoy simply kept silent about these strengths.[15] He talked only about what he saw as defects, pointing out what Chaliapin always had, particularly at this time—he was only about twenty-five years old—a certain excessive intemperance, an emphasis on all his talents. Chaliapin had way too much of a "Herculean sweep," both innate and acquired onstage, which, from early youth, had become his entire life and was inflamed by the constant ravings of the public everywhere and anywhere, throughout the entire world, wherever they saw him: the opera stage, the concert platform, a famous beach, the salon of a millionaire. Moderation is difficult for one who has tasted fame!

"Fame is like seawater," Chekhov joked, "the more you drink, the thirstier you get."

Chaliapin drank this water incessantly but was thirsty constantly. But can one condemn him because he loved to vaunt his talent, his daring, his going "from mud to monarch"?

He once showed me a picture of his father:

"See what a parent I had. He beat me mercilessly!"

But the picture showed an extremely decent-looking individual, about fifty years old, wearing a starched shirt with a turned-down collar, a black tie, and a raccoon coat. I had my doubts: Did he really thrash his son?[16] Why is it that all these "self-educated types" are invariably "beaten mercifully when they were children and youths"?

"Gorky and Chaliapin rose from the bottom of the native sea. . . ." But was it really "from the bottom"? Goodness knows, a parent who worked in a local zemstvo office and went about in a raccoon fur coat and a starched shirt cannot be from the bottom.[17] As I see it, Chaliapin's memoirs of his childhood and youth, generally speaking, have been somewhat embellished, along with his accounts of friends and comrades of the time—for example, some smithy who told Chaliapin so poetically:

"Sing, Fedya, and your soul will rejoice! A song is like a bird. Free it and it will fly!"[18]

Nonetheless, the fate of this individual was truly like a fairy tale—it is a long way from friendship with a smithy to pleasant dinners with great princes and crowned heirs. His life was immeasurably happy in all respects: truly, God gave him all that was earthy in the worldly realm, as well as great physical strength, which began to decline only after forty years of wandering all over the world and ceding to all kinds of earthly temptations.

I once stayed next door to Battistini in a hotel in Odessa. At that time, he was touring in Russia, and although seventy-four years old at the time, he amazed everyone not only with the resonant freshness of his voice but also with his overall sprightliness.[19] What was the secret of his youthfulness? In part, he took care of himself. After every performance, he returned home immediately, drank some hot milk mixed with seltzer water, and went to bed. But Chaliapin? I knew him for many years, and I remember that most of our meetings took place in restaurants. I do not recall where and when we met. I do remember, though, that we addressed each other in the familiar "you" one night at the Great Moscow Tavern, in a huge building opposite the Iversky Chapel.[20] Besides the tavern, there was also a hotel inside the building, where I stayed for long periods of time when I came to Moscow. The word "tavern" no longer suited the expensive and spacious restaurant that it had gradually become over the years and all the more so when I lived above it at the hotel. At the time, it had just been enlarged with several new rooms, richly furnished and decorated, and designed for the particularly grand dinners and nightly carousals of well-known Moscow merchants of the more Europeanized kind. That night, I remember the most notable individual among the merrymakers was a Moscow Frenchman by the name of Sue who came with his ladies and friends, including myself. As they say, the champagne at Sue's table flowed like water, and he kept sending hundred-ruble tips to the Neapolitan musicians, who, dressed in red jackets, played and sang on a stage lit brilliantly by a chandelier.

Suddenly, Chaliapin's enormous blond-haired figure appeared at the door. He cast a so-called eagle eye on the orchestra and, with a sudden wave of his hand, joined in the playing and singing. Needless to say, such an unexpected "royal" favor sent the Neapolitans and all the merrymakers into frenzied ecstasy! We drank the entire night, almost until morning. Then, leaving the restaurant, Chaliapin and I stopped to say good-bye to each other on the staircase to the hotel. Suddenly, he said to me in his Volga tenor voice:

"I think, Vanyusha, that you are very drunk, and because the elevator is turned off, I've decided to carry you to your room on my back."

"Don't forget," I said, "that I'm staying on the fifth floor, and am not that light."

"No matter, dear one," he replied, "I'll get you there!"

And truly he did, no matter how hard I struggled. When we got there, he played his "Hercules" role to the end, ordering a bottle of "hundred-year" burgundy and paying an entire hundred rubles for it (which, it turned out, tasted like raspberry water).

One should not exaggerate things, but one should not minimize them either: he lived life without counting the cost. He talked constantly, never allowing anyone to get a word in edgewise. Tirelessly, he went on about one thing, then another, with all kinds of facial expressions, and pouring forth humorous catchphrases and words—more often than not, the most obscene kind. He lit one cigarette after another, acting always like "Hercules" in a truly passionate way.

One cold winter night in Moscow, we were tearing along in a cab from the Prague to the Strelna.[21] It was terribly cold; the cab was going at full speed, but he sat upright, his fur coat thrown open, talking and laughing to the top of his lungs and smoking in such a way that sparks flew into the wind. I could not stand it any longer and shouted:

"What are you doing?! Settle down, button your coat, and throw away that cigarette!"

"You're the smart one, Vanya," he answered in a sweet-sounding voice, "but you're getting worked up over nothing. I've got this special Russian constitution; it can stand anything."

"I'm fed up with this Rus of yours!" I said.

"Now there you go, scolding me again. I'm afraid of getting scolded: such a thing can drive one to an early grave. You always tell me: 'Go easy, young man.' Why, Vanya?"

"So you won't strut about in peasant coats, lacquered boot-tops, and flaming silk shirts with crimson belts and collars; so you won't dress up looking like a populist along with Gorky, Andreev, and Skitalets; and so you won't have your picture taken with them in those phony, pensive poses—remember who you are and who they are.

"But how am I really different from them?"

"Because while Gorky and Andreev are very capable people, their writings are only 'fictional' and often cater to the street. But your voice is not 'fictional.'"

"Drunks, Vanya, are always prone to flatter people."

"But it's true," I said laughing. "In any case, keep still and button up your coat."

"Well, have it your way."

Having buttoned up his coat, Chaliapin burst into a round of "Karl has enemies" so suddenly that the horse bolted into the night. . . .[22]

At that time in Moscow, there existed a literary group called "Wednesday" that gathered every week at the home of the writer Teleshov, a rich and hospitable man.[23] There we read our writings, offered critiques of each other's works, and had dinner. Chaliapin was a frequent guest. He listened to readings—though he lacked the patience to do so. Sometimes he sat down at the piano and sang—Russian folk songs, French chansonnettes, "The Flea" or "The Marseillaise" or "Volga Boatmen"—everything "took our breath away."

One time, having arrived at "Wednesday," he immediately announced:

"Brothers, I want to sing!"

He telephoned Rachmaninov and told him the same thing:

"I've a terrible urge to sing! Take a cab and come down right away. We'll sing all night long."

Of course, there was posturing in all this, but one can easily imagine what that evening was like. That night, Chaliapin said quite justly:

"This is not your Bolshoi Theater. People should not hear me there, but at evenings like these, with Seryozha."[24]

He also sang like that once in Capri, at the Hotel Quisisana, where my wife and I spent three consecutive winters. We had hosted a dinner in his honor and had invited Gorky and several other people from the Russian colony there. After dinner, Chaliapin offered to sing—and another absolutely wonderful evening followed. All the hotel guests and many of the locals crowded into the dining room and all the drawing rooms of the hotel and listened breathlessly, with shining eyes. . . .[25]

When, later on, I once had lunch at his house in Paris, he himself recalled that evening:

"Do you remember how I sang at your place in Capri?" he asked.

He started the gramophone, began putting on some records that he had made earlier, and listened to himself with tears in his eyes, muttering:

"I sang not badly! Others should be so lucky!"

Chapter 8

Gorky

The strange relationship between Gorky and me—strange because for almost two decades we were seen as good friends, but, in reality, we were not—began in 1899.[1] It ended in 1917. It so happened that the man, who for twenty years had not a single personal reason for his hostility toward me, suddenly became my enemy, evoking in me horror and indignation for a long time. With the years these feelings have ceased; he has ceased simply to exist for me.[2]

But here is something completely unexpected:

L'écrivain Maxime Gorki est décedé. . . . Alexis Péchkoff connu en littérature sous le nom Gorki, était né en 1868 a Nijni-Novgorod d'une famille de cosaques. . . .

Here is still one more legend about him. First, a barefoot tramp, then a Cossack. . . . No matter how surprising, no one, to this day, understands precisely many things about Gorky's life. Who knows his true biography? Why haven't the Bolsheviks, who have proclaimed him a most great genius and who publish his countless writings in millions of copies, yet to furnish an account of his life?

The fate of this individual is like a fairy tale. How many years of worldly fame have there been for its bearer, one undeserved beyond all parallel, based not only on an extremely fortunate confluence of political events but also on a great many other circumstances—for example, the public's complete ignorance of his biography. Of course, this talent, still to this day so unlike anyone else's—who could say finally, boldly, and sensibly, what it consists of—this talent who has given birth to such a thing as "The Song of the Falcon"—a song in which, for some completely unknown reason, this bird "crawled high into the mountains and lays there" before it meets a terribly proud raven that has flown its way.[3]

Everyone repeats: "A barefoot tramp rose from the depths of the sea. . . ." But no one knows the rather famous lines from the Brockhaus dictionary: "Gorky-Peshkov, Alexei Maximovich. He was born in 1869 in a completely bourgeois milieu: his father was a manager of a large shipping company; his mother—a daughter of a rich dye merchant. . . ."[4]

All the rest—no one knows precisely, based only on Gorky's autobiography, an extremely suspicious thing if only from his style alone: "I learned to read and write first from my grandfather and the Psalter and then as a galley boy aboard a ship, from the cook Smuryi, a man of legendary strength, coarseness and—tenderness. . . ." Such a sugary eternal image from Gorky![5]

"Until then I hated any printed page passionately, but Smuryi fostered in me a fierce love for reading, and, almost insanely, I become engrossed in Nekrasov, the journal *Spark*, the Uspenskys and Dumas. . . . [6]

"Moving from cooks to gardeners, I devoured both the classics and pulp fiction. At age fifteen, I was seized by a ferocious desire to study and went to Kazan, assuming naively that education was free to anyone who wanted it. But such a thing was not the case, the result being that I found work in a pretzel factory and became acquainted with students.[7] . . . At age nineteen, I took a bullet and, having been laid up for some time, came back to life, buying and selling apples. . . . [8] When I came of age, I was drafted, but when I learned that people who put holes in themselves were not taken for military service, I set out as a copier for a lawyer named Lanin, but I soon felt out of place among intellectuals and left to wander throughout southern Russia. . . ."[9]

In 1892, Gorky, in the newspaper *The Caucasus*, published his first story, "Makar Chudra," which begins extremely vulgarly.[10] "The wind wafted through the steppe in the pensive melody of a lapping wave rushing toward the shore. . . . The gloom of an autumn night shuddered and withdrew from us in fright amid the sparks of a fire that loomed over the massive figure of the old gypsy, Makar Chudra. Half lying in a pose that was handsome, free, and strong, he drew on his large pipe methodically, emitting thick clouds of smoke from his mouth and nose, and said: 'Does the slave know freedom? Does he understand the vastness of the steppe? Does his heart rejoice over the talk of the sea? No way! For he, pal, is a slave!'"

Gorky's famous "Chelkash" appeared three years later. He was already the talk of the intelligentsia, since many people had become engrossed in "Makar Chudra" and other creations of his pen: "Yemelyan Pilyai" and "Grandfather

Arkhip and Lenka." . . . [11] Gorky also had become famous for his satires—for example, "About the Siskin, Who Lied and the Woodpecker, a Lover of Truth"—and well known as a feuilletonist who wrote pieces (in the *Samara Gazette*) under the name "Iegudiil Khlamida." But then "Chelkash" appeared. . . .

It was during this period that I first heard of him: in Poltava, where I lived for a while, a rumor spread suddenly throughout the town: "A young writer by the name of Maxim Gorky has taken up residence near Kobelyaki.[12] He is a wondrously picturesque figure. A passionate hefty chap in the widest cape, a hat that is all brim, and a heavy knotted truncheon in his hand. . . ."

I met Gorky in the spring of '99. I was in Yalta, walking along the embankment for some reason, and saw: Chekhov coming toward me, hiding behind a newspaper, if not from the sun, then from someone who, walking with him, was saying something in a deep bass voice and waving his hands constantly high from under his cape.[13] When I greeted Chekhov, he said, "Meet Gorky." I introduced myself, taking a good look at him and convinced that what people had been saying about him in Poltava was correct only partially: the cape, that brimmed hat, and the truncheon were all there. Under the cape was a yellow silk peasant blouse, belted with a thick long silk, cream-colored braid and embroidered with multicolored silks along the collar and hem. But he was not hefty or passionate, but just a tall and somewhat round-shouldered, ginger-haired fellow with eyes that were small, greenish, quick, and shifty, a nose that was freckled and duckish, and a mustache that was blond and that he smoothed constantly with his large hands, coughing and spitting on them a bit before he did. We walked a bit and he began to smoke, inhaling deeply but immediately resuming droning on and waving his hands. Having finished his cigarette quickly, he put it out with spit on his cigarette holder and threw it away, continuing to talk and looking occasionally at Chekhov quickly and trying to figure out what kind of impression he was making on him. He talked loudly, as if from his entire soul, with passion, and all in heroic exclamations that were somewhat vulgar and primitive. It was an endlessly long and endlessly boring story about some rich merchants and peasants from the Volga—boring primarily because of its hyperbolic monotony—all these rich men were completely byliny-type giants—with unrestrained imagery and pathos. Chekhov hardly listened. But Gorky kept talking and talking. . . . [14]

Almost from that day on there arose between us something like a friendly intimacy, for his part, something sentimental with a certain timid admiration:

"You're the last writer of the gentry," he said, "of that culture that gave to the world Pushkin and Tolstoy!"[15]

As soon as Chekhov had called a cab and had gone home to Autka, Gorky invited me to go with him to Vinogradskaya Street, where he had rented a room. There, wrinkling his nose and smiling an awkward, happy, and comically stupid smile, he showed me first a photograph of his wife holding a hefty baby with lively eyes, then a piece of pale-blue silk, saying with the same grimace:

"You see, I bought this for a blouse for her . . . for her very self . . . it's a present I'm taking to her. . . ."[16]

He was now a completely different individual from the one on the embankment with Chekhov: kind, laughably affected, and modest to the point of self-effacement, speaking not in a bass voice with deliberate coarseness, but all the time in a seemingly apologetic, dramatically soulful Volga speech with stressed "o's" everywhere. He played both sides—with the same pleasure, in the same untiring way. Later I saw that he could carry on monologues from morning till night with the same smoothness, entering into one or another role in tender moments when he tried to be particularly convincing, even calling forth easily tears to his greenish eyes. Here he revealed several other traits, which I noticed constantly in him in later years. The first was that Gorky was different in public than when he was alone with me and not with strangers. With people, he often spoke in a deep voice and went pale from vanity and pride and from public raptures over him. Gorky always talked about something that was coarse, sublime, or important. He loved preaching to his admirers, speaking to them first sternly, casually, then dryly and didactically. But when he was alone with me or among close friends, he became pleasant, as if naively happy, modest, and shy, even too much so. The second trait I noticed in him was his adoration of culture and literature, conversations about which were his genuine hobby. Things he told me a hundred times later, he first said then in Yalta.

"You understand that you're a genuine writer, first because you have culture in your blood, the legacy of the noble art of Russian literature. Our brother, the writer for the new reader, must learn to become cultured untiringly. He must value it with all the forces of his soul. Only then will something worthwhile come out of us!"

Undoubtedly, there was pretense in this, there was also self-abasement, which is stronger than pride. But there was also sincerity—how else could Gorky have affirmed the same thing for so many years, often with tears in his eyes?

He was lean and rather broad in the shoulders, which he always held high and hunched over his thin chest. He walked in long strides, toes pointed out, with a certain—you will forgive me for the word—thievish foppishness, ease, and grace—how often have I seen that kind of gait in the port of Odessa! His hands were large and gentle, like a priest's. When he greeted you, he kept your hand in his for a long time, squeezing it pleasantly, and kissed you with his soft lips firmly in a drawn-out way. His cheekbones protruded like a Tartar's. His hair, rather black and brushed back, grew low and wildly over a small forehead, wrinkled like a monkey's—the skin of his forehead and eyebrows kept going up in folds toward his hair. The expressions of his face (at that time rather fair-colored, as happens with red-headed individuals) sometimes flashed something clownish, but very lively and very comic—and would later appear in his son Maxim, whom, as a child, I used to sit on my shoulders, hold him by his feet, and gallop around the room until he squealed in delight.[17]

When we first met, his fame was spreading throughout all of Russia. It only continued to grow. The Russian intelligentsia lost its heads over him, and one can understand why. Not only was it a time of a great upsurge in Russian revolutionary activity, to which Gorky responded so readily, but it was also a period of struggle between the "Populists" and the newly arrived Marxists. Gorky was annihilating the peasant and singing hymns to the "Chelkashes," whom the Marxists, in their revolutionary hopes and plans, were counting on so heavily. As a result, every new work of Gorky's immediately became an all-Russian event.[18] He himself kept changing and changing—in his way of life, in his manner with people. He was now renting an entire house in Nizhniy Novgorod, had a large apartment in Petersburg, and often appeared in Moscow and the Crimea. He ran the journal *New Life* and founded the publishing firm Knowledge. He had already started writing for the Art Theater, and for the actress Knipper, he wrote in her books such dedications as:

"I'd like to bind this book for you, Olga Leonardovna, to the skin of my heart!"[19]

He had already introduced to the public first Andreev, then Skitalets, and became very close to them.[20] From time to time, he did the same with other writers, but in most cases the intimacy was brief: having charmed the fortunate individual with his attention, he withdrew his favors suddenly. It was painful to see him with guests, in society. Wherever he appeared, he was surrounded by so many people, their eyes riveted on him, that it was impossible to break through. He became increasingly awkward and false, not looking at anyone, but sitting in a circle of two or three celebrities. He frowned fiercely, coughed like a soldier (on purpose), smoked one cigarette after another, and drank red wine—he always downed a full glass in one gulp. Every now and then, he proclaimed loudly, for general consumption, some maxim or political prophecy in a loud voice, and again, pretending not to notice anyone around him, he sometimes frowned and drummed his long fingers on the table; other times, with mock indifference, he raised his eyebrows and the folds on his forehead, speaking only with his friends, and even with them in an abrupt, offhand way. The changing expressions on his face, they repeated on their own, intoxicated publicly and proudly by their closeness to him and time and again moving to address him by his first name in a seemingly nonchalant and independent way:

"How very true, Alexei. . . . No, you're wrong there, Alexei. . . . You see, Alexei. . . . The fact of the matter is, Alexei. . . ."

Everything youthful had already disappeared in him—it happened very quickly—his complexion became coarser and darker, drier; his mustache, thicker and bigger—people called him the corporal—many wrinkles appeared on his face, and his glance had something evil and arrogant about it. When we met privately, he was almost the same as before, only more serious and confident. But with the public (whose ecstasies he simply could not live without), he was often rude.

At a large party in Yalta, I saw the actress Yermolova—her very self and already old at the time—go up to him to present him with a gift—a beautiful cigarette case made of whalebone. She was so shy, so confused, and blushed so deeply that tears burst forth in her eyes.

"Here, Maxim Alexeevich . . . I mean Alexei Maximovich. . . . Here I . . . for you. . . ."

He stood by a table, squashing the end of his cigarette in an ashtray and not even raising his eyes to her.

"I wanted to express to you, Alexei Maximovich. . . ."

He, sneering grimly at the table and, as was his habit, jerking back his head and tossing his hair from his forehead, muttered thickly, as if to himself, a verse from the book of Job:

"How long wilt thou not turn your glance from me, nor depart from me until I can swallow my own spittle?"[21]

But what if he had been "left alone"?

He now always walked about in a dark blouse, with a Caucasian belt with silver plate, and special boots with short tops tucked into his black trousers. Everybody knows how Andreev, Skitalets, and other "Maximovites" imitated Gorky's "folk" dress and also started wearing boots with short tops, peasant blouses, and tight-waisted peasant coats. It was insufferable.

We met in Petersburg, in Moscow, in Nizhniy Novgorod, and in the Crimea. We also did business together: first, I contributed to his journal *New Life*, then I began to publish my first books with his publishing house, Knowledge, and also took part in Knowledge anthologies.[22] His books sold almost into the hundreds of thousands, others—mostly under the trademark of Knowledge—also did quite well. Knowledge raised the fees of writers considerably. With the Knowledge anthologies, we received—one, 300 rubles, another 400 rubles, still another, 500 rubles per sheet; he—a 1,000 rubles. He always loved lots of money. He also began collecting: rare old coins, medals, gems, precious stones. Restraining a contented smile, he handled them deftly and gently, turning them over in his hands, examining them and showing them to others. He drank wine in the same way: with relish and taste. (At home he drank only French wine, even though there was excellent Russian wine in great supply.)

I always marveled—how he had enough of everything. Day in, day out, in public—at a gathering in his home or at someone else's—he sometimes spoke for hours on end, without stopping, drinking incessantly, smoking a hundred cigarettes a day, sleeping five or six hours at the most, and writing novel after novel, play after play in his firm, round script! It is a widespread belief that he was completely illiterate and that someone corrected his manuscripts. But he wrote completely correctly (and with unusual literary competence, even when he had just begun to write). And how much did he read, this eternal semi-intellectual, this dogmatist!

People have always spoken about his rare knowledge of Russia.[23] It turns out that he acquired it in the short period of time when, leaving Lanin, he "wandered in the south of Russia." When I met him, he was no longer wandering. Nor did he ever wander anywhere later: he lived in Crimea, in Moscow, in Nizhniy Novgorod, in Petersburg. . . . In 1905, after the December uprising in Moscow, he emigrated abroad through Finland. He visited America and spent seven years in Capri—until 1914.[24] Finally, having returned to Russia, he entrenched himself firmly in Petersburg. . . . The rest is well known.

For five years in a row, my wife and I went to Capri and spent three entire winters there.[25] At that time, I met Gorky every day, we spent almost every evening together, and we became very close. This was the time when I found him to be most pleasant.[26]

In the beginning of April 1917, we parted forever. On the day I was leaving Petersburg, he organized a huge meeting at the Mikhailovsky Theater where he issued a "cultural" appeal for some kind of "Academy of Free Sciences," dragging me and Chaliapin there. As he mounted the platform, he said: "Comrades, among us are so-and-so and so-and-so. . . ."[27] The audience greeted us with stormy applause, but I was not greatly taken with the type of people there. Then Gorky, Chaliapin, Alexander Benois, and I went to the Bear restaurant. There was a small bucket of caviar and lots of champagne. . . . When I got up to leave, he followed me into the corridor, embraced me warmly many times, and kissed me firmly. . . .

Soon after the Bolsheviks seized power, he went to Moscow and stayed with his [former] wife, Yekaterina Pavlovna [Peshkova]. She called me on the phone to say: "Alexei Maximovich wants to speak with you." I answered that we now had nothing to say and that I considered our friendship over once and for all.[28]

Chapter 9

His Imperial Highness

One day when I was going through my papers, I came across a package marked "Pyotr Alexandrov."

In it was a bundle of letters from Pyotr Alexandrovich; the manuscript of his sketch titled "Solitude"; a small book of short stories (*The Dream* by Pyotr Alexandrovich, Paris, 1921); and, finally, a cutting from the Paris Socialist newspaper *Days*—an article written by Mark Aldanov after his death: he had spent the last years of his life in exile and died of rapid consumption at the age of fifty-five.[1]

He was a remarkable man.

Aldanov called him a man of "absolutely extraordinary kindness and spiritual nobility." But he was outstanding also in many other ways. He would have been marvelous even if he had been an ordinary mortal.[2] But royal blood flowed in him, he having chosen for his literary work so modest a pen name: Pyotr Alexandrov. In real life, he bore an infinitely more impressive nomer: Prince Pyotr Alexandrovich of Oldenburg. He hailed from a family that is considered one of the oldest in Europe—the last of the Russian branch of the Princes of Oldenburg, which merged with the Romanovs—a great-grandson of Emperor Paul I, married to a daughter of Alexander III (Olga Alexandrovna).[3]

He astounded me the first time we met. It was several years ago in Paris. I had stopped in at "Zemgor" for some reason.[4] The reception room was crowded, but standing by the doors, alone behind everyone else, was an elderly man, very tall and strikingly thin, leggy like a uniformed soldier. I passed him quickly, but he caught my attention right away. He was waiting for something patiently and standing quietly and modestly but, at the same time, also so freely, easily, and straightforwardly that I thought right away: "Some kind of former general. . . ." Giving him a cursory glance, I experienced momentarily that sharp pang that one now often feels at the sight of certain poor, elderly people who once knew wealth, power, and fame. He was well scrubbed and spotlessly clean (in a military way). His simple and cheap clothes were also clean and neat: a light raincoat of nondescript color, a paper collar, and heavy, English army–type shoes. . . . I was struck by his height and thinness—distinctive, ancient, knightly, and museum-like. His skull was small, completely bald and aristocratic, with striking signs of degeneracy.[5] The thin, dry skin on his small bony face had a reddish tinge, as though it had been scorched slightly. His little clipped mustache was also reddish yellow, and his faded eyes under his thinning triangularly raised eyebrows (more accurately, what was left of his eyebrows) were mournful, quiet, and very serious.

What happened next was even more surprising. An acquaintance of mine came up to me and, smiling for some reason, said:

"His Highness asks your permission to introduce himself to you."

I thought he was joking. Who has ever heard of a Highness asking permission for such a thing?

"What Highness?"

"Prince Pyotr Alexandrovich of Oldenburg. Surely you saw him? There he is, standing by the door."

"But what's this—'asks my permission to introduce himself?'"

"Well, as you see, he is a most unusual man. . . ."

Later I learned that he wrote short stories about the life of the people à la Tolstoy's folktales. Soon after we met he came to see me, bringing with him the very book that was the reason why he had visited "Zemgor," to publish at the printing press there at his own expense. It consisted of three short stories under the general title *The Dream*.

Speaking of these stories, Aldanov wrote: "Medieval chroniclers speak with horror about the bloody deeds of the Oldenburg clan. . . . One of this group, Egilmar, was particularly known for his cruelty.[6] A descendant of his and a great-grandson of Tsar Paul Petrovich, he wrote stories about the lives of workers and peasants and, shortly before his death, wished to join the Populist-Socialist party! Russia has had all kinds of great princes. Some, in 1917, turned out to be ardent republicans, unnerving the late Rodzyanko with a red ribbon in their buttonholes. The Prince of Oldenburg did not wear such a ribbon. A close friendship, forged in childhood on March 1, 1881—the day Alexander II was murdered—bound him to Nicholas II. No one loved the late emperor more selflessly than he. But he always considered the tsar's policies to be insane. He even tried to 'influence' the tsar and, mistrusting the power of his own convictions, wanted Nicholas to draw close to Tolstoy. This alone gives an idea of the mental and spiritual makeup of the Prince of Oldenburg. There was nothing in him of the 'red prince,' of the Philippe Égalité obligatory in every dynasty.[7] He never chased, nor could he have chased, after the popularity that, in his position, would have been so easy to acquire."

Of course, his stories are interesting only insofar as they give an insight into his spiritual cast. He wrote about the "golden hearts" of the folk who awakened suddenly from the intoxication of revolution to give themselves to Christ, to His Gospel of brotherly love—"the only salvation for the world in all its sufferings." He wrote passionately, lyrically, but also so clumsily and naively. But he himself was aware of his literary failings, and when we became friends, he often said to me with all his moving, immeasurable modesty:

"Forgive me, for God's sake, for pestering you with my writings. I know that it's impertinent on my part, I know that I write like a child. . . . But after all, this is my entire life now. More and more, I only dream about it, I only prepare myself to write. I dream day and night, but nonetheless I keep hoping that I'll finally write something worthwhile. . . ."

His "Solitude" is quite remarkable for a prince of royal blood:

"The end of September. A fine day. All around are strips of emerald greenery, yellow stubble, and black earth. Threads of silvery cobweb waft about gently. The woods grow dark, still not bare of leaves. Far off, among the forest islands, churches gleam whitely. I am on horseback. Two borzois—a white dog and a red-colored bitch—run at a trot under the very horse's hooves. The Kabardin, swaying slightly, steps softy on the smooth verdure. Gradually, I sink into a kind of semi-slumber. The reins fall out of my hands and hang down the horse's neck. I do not pick them up, afraid to move so as not to end the blissful torpor that has seized my entire being. . . ."

"A hare darts out from under the horse's legs, the horse flinches, and, instinctively, I seize the reins. 'After him! After him!' I shout at the top of my voice, galloping after the dogs. The white dog catches up to the hare and knocks it down on the young shoots of the winter crop. . . ."

"I drive through a lane. The dogs, their tongues hanging out and panting heavily, walk behind the horse. Gradually, the excitement of the chase passes. I recall the sweet stupor that seized me, and I try to return myself to that state, but in vain. . . . Why don't I hear Her ringing laughter? Why don't I see Her large kind eyes, Her gentle smile? Will the separation, the solitude, be forever, for my entire life?"

"I enter the village. The threshing machines hum merrily, their flails thumping on the ground. . . . In the pasture, not far from the church, I stand near a sooty forge. "Semyon, hey Semyon,' I call out several times, getting off my horse. A short, stocky peasant comes out of the shed, walks up to the horse, says hello, looks at me tenderly from top to bottom, and smiles:

"'Good day, Semyon. Won't you come over to my place tonight and sit and talk?' I say shyly, almost pleadingly, afraid that he might refuse. 'Why not? I'll stop by, thank you,' he answers simply, pulling at the hare strapped to my saddle. . . ."

"My estate is not far from the village. The white house, with its columns and attic, stands sadly, its windows all boarded up. The stables are on the right; on the left is the little wing where I live. An old worker comes out to meet me. I get off my horse, he takes the bridle and leads it to the stable. I enter my wing. I drink several glasses of vodka, eat quickly. I sit down in my armchair, try to read, but cannot even finish a page. . . . I go up to the window, look across the yards at the boarded-up house, return to the table, pour another glass of vodka, and drink it down in one gulp. . . ."

Knowing that there is not a single false word in these lines, I found it difficult to read them without shaking my head: what a strange man! As for the truth of it all, he told me about all this himself. Having written "Solitude," he pleaded with me especially to help him publish it somewhere, saying with his usual childlike simple-heartedness and shyness:

"I'll not hide it from you that such a thing would make me very happy. The sketch is very dear to me because, forgive my indiscretion, all of it is true—I experienced it all personally, suffering greatly when . . . that is, when I and Olya—Olga Alexandrovna—separated. . . ."

Rereading these lines, I again ask myself that very same question that comes to mind every time I think of him: In the final analysis, who was this prince who, timidly, implored a blacksmith to spend an evening with him, a man, who, with the simplicity of a genuine saint, even with others, referred to Nicholas II as Kolya? (Yes, on one occasion, at a gathering of a friend of ours, with most of the guests being old revolutionaries, he, listening to their lively conversation, exclaimed completely sincerely: "Oh, what dear, charming people you all are! How sad that Kolya never spent an evening like this! Everything, everything would have been different if you and he had known each other!")

To the question—what kind of man was he?—I could never find a precise answer. I cannot even now. Several people simply called him "abnormal." Maybe so, but, after all, saints and other blessed individuals were "abnormal." . . .

His letters to me also evoke a picture of him:

"I've settled down in the countryside, on my own little farm around Bayonne. I've taken up farming. I've got a cow, some chickens, and rabbits. I dig in the garden. . . . On Saturdays I visit my parents, who live nearby in the area around St.-Jean-de-Luz. . . . [8] I've not written anything for a long time; I cannot even finish a story I began last summer; when I do finish it, I'll send it to you with a request for your severest criticism. . . . I miss my Parisian friends very much. . . . My mind goes back to your apartment there: how cozy it was and how easy it was to talk to you! I'll never forget your kindness to me . . ." (1921).

"Many thanks for your dear, kind, and affectionate letter! I rejoice with all my soul that you again have sat down to work. You say that you're thinking of heading south, that Paris is expensive and cold. . . . Come down here; it is warmer and cheaper. Last summer, before I came to live on the farm, I stayed twice at a little boardinghouse on the outskirts of St.-Jean-de-Luz. I paid twenty francs for everything. The food was excellent; the rooms, of course, were far from luxurious, but pleasant and clean. The landladies, a mother and two daughters, were Basque, descendants of a famous whaler. They were nice and old-fashioned, and I felt quite at home with them . . ." (1921).

"It has been very cold. Now it's the rainy season, the sea is seething. . . . My mood is not good and I want spring to come quickly to chase away my anguish. Today I started writing, but nothing came of it. I cannot find the words to express my thoughts, to draw pictures . . ." (1922).

"Your letter has made me indescribably happy. Thank you so much for everything that you've done for me. I've started on a story that I've had in my mind, but it is hard going. The weather is terrible, storms and rains. Perhaps, the spring and sun will ease my soul, but now angst and terrible loneliness. . . . I ask earnestly that you let me know when my story will be published in *Northern Lights* and where can I buy this journal. I look forward impatiently to seeing you in Paris . . ." (1923).[9]

To tell the truth, I did not know him well. We did not meet often . . . we always lived in different places. I never saw him before the revolution, and I have little information about his life in Russia. Before the war, he was a major general who commanded the imperial fusiliers. . . . In 1917, he retired and settled in the country, in the Voronezh Province, where the peasants—also a strange story—asked that he represent them in the Constituent Assembly. . . . When the terror began, he escaped to France and lived near his father, Alexander Petrovich of Oldenburg, in that farm near Bayonne (which, incidentally, he bequeathed to his former personal servant, who had left Russia with him and who remained with him as a servant and a friend almost to his death). . . . I also do not know his character fully. God knows, perhaps he had traits other than the ones I knew. I was familiar only with his splendid qualities: a "truly exceptional kindness," a "spiritual nobility," the likes of which one searches high and low, an unusual simplicity and delicacy with people, a rare tenderness in friendship, and a passionate and untiring striving for everything that gives to the human heart peace, love, light, and joy. . . .

At first he lived around Paris—and it was here that we met most often. Then, as I have already noted, he moved to the vicinity of Bayonne. Quite unexpectedly, to our great surprise, he married a second time. One day I met him in our consulate (this was before France had recognized the Bolsheviks, when the embassy on rue de Grenelle was still at the disposal of émigrés), and suddenly he embraced me particularly affectionately and said: "Don't be surprised, I'm going to introduce you to my fiancée. . . . [10] We've come here on business, to go through the various formalities that are necessary for marriage. . . ." Again his married life was brief. He also did not live long after that. A year later, my wife and I went to Vance (near Nice) to look for a dacha, when suddenly we met him: he was sitting alone in a café on the square. As soon as he caught sight of us, he jumped up in surprise and hurried over to us:

"My God, how glad I am to see you! I never would have expected such a thing!"

"But why are you here yourself?"

He waved his hand and burst into tears:

"You see, I dare not even embrace you or kiss Vera Nikolaevna's hand. They've discovered suddenly that I have consumption and sent me here for treatment, hoping that the south would save me. . . ."

But the south did not help. He moved to Paris and spent his last winter in a sanatorium. But the sanatorium was also of no avail. In the spring, he was taken back to the Riviera, where he soon died in poverty and completely alone.

That winter he paid me a final visit. In a letter, he asked for permission to come. "I beg you, if it is possible for you to set up a meeting about a very important matter for me. . . ." Soon, one evening, he arrived—barely alive, gasping for breath, and soaking wet from the rain. His business was such that even now it hurts me to remember it. He was going to be placed under guardianship and declared insane (all because he had signed his farm in Bayonne over to his personal servant), and he had come to ask that I write some kind of certificate, saying that I considered him to be of sound mind and body. . . .

"But for God's sake, dear one, what good is a certificate from me?"

"Ah, as if you don't know: a great deal of good! Please, if you can, write it!"

I wrote it, of course. But very soon death freed him from all our certificates.

His coffin is still standing in the vault of the Russian church in Cannes, awaiting return to Russia, to rest in peace in his native earth.[11]

Chapter 10

Kuprin

It was very long ago when I first learned of his existence and saw his name in *Russian Wealth*, a name that in those days everyone stressed on the first syllable. As I saw later, such a thing so irritated him for some reason that he, as he always did in angry moments, screwed up his small eyes like a wild beast and muttered suddenly and fiercely in the staccato-like patter of an army officer:

"I am Kuprin and I ask everyone to remember that. I'd advise you not to sit on a hedgehog without your pants."

How much of the wild beast was there about him in those days—his sense of smell was truly remarkable! And how much of the Tartar was in him!

He was so secretive about many things of his personal life that, despite our long and close friendship, I do not know much about his past. I know that he studied in Moscow, first at the Cadet School, then at the Alexander Military Institute. For a short time, he was an officer on the Russo-Austrian border. After that, what all did he not do? He studied dentistry, worked first in various offices, then in a factory; he was also a surveyor, an actor, and a minor journalist. . . . What did his father do? It seems that he was an army doctor—why Alexander Ivanovich landed in the Cadet School. I also know that Kuprin's father died early and that his widow was so destitute that she had to live in the "Widows' Home" in Moscow. I also know that she was a princess with a Tartar name, and I always saw that Alexander Ivanovich was very proud of his Tartar blood.[1] At one time (during the height of his fame), he even wore a brightly colored skull-cap, which he sported in the homes of friends and in restaurants, where he sat so stolidly and importantly, as befitted a genuine khan, screwing up his eyes in an especially narrow way.[2] It was the time when editors of newspapers, journals, and anthologies chased after him in cabs from one restaurant to another, where he spent days and nights with chance acquaintances and regular friends, and begged him humbly to accept a thousand or two thousand rubles in advance if only for the promise that he would graciously not forget them.[3] Massive and broad-faced, he merely screwed up his eyes and fell silent. Then suddenly, he hissed—"To hell with you this very minute!"—in so sinister a whisper that timid people acted as if they had been swallowed by the earth.

But even then, the worst period of his life, there was much in him that was completely different, but just as characteristic: together with great pride, there was much unexpected modesty; along with a quick temper, there was a great deal of kindness, goodwill, and shyness, which was often even pathetic. There was also naivete, simple-heartedness that was sometimes insincere, boyish gaiety, and the endearing sameness with which he always proclaimed his enduring love for dogs, fishermen, the circus, the famous animal-trainer Durov, the wrestler Poddubny—and for Pushkin, Tolstoy—he always spoke of Vronsky's horse as the "extremely enchanting, divine Frou-Frou"—and also Kipling.[4]

In recent years, critics have often compared Kuprin to Kipling. The comparison, of course, is ill chosen. In several of his works, Kipling reached the heights of genuine genius, and, as a poet, he was so great, so original, who could be compared to him? That Kuprin could love him is perfectly understandable.[5]

I had supported Kuprin right away when he first appeared in *Russian Wealth*, and so I was very glad to hear when I was living with the writer Fyodorov in Lustdorf, near Odessa, that he had come to come to stay with the Karyshevs, who were sharing Fyodorov's house.[6] Fyodorov and I went immediately to meet him. It was pouring down rain, but we did not find him at home. "He's probably gone for a swim," we were told. We ran down to the beach and saw a man crawling clumsily out of the water. He was about thirty, short, slightly stout, and pink, with with close-cropped chestnut-colored hair and narrow eyes that looked at us shortsightedly.

"Are you Kuprin?"

"I am, and who are you?"

We introduced ourselves, and he beamed a friendly smile instantly and shook our hands energetically with his small hand (about which Chekhov once said to me: "A talented hand!").

We became friends surprisingly quickly. At that time he was so very cheerful and good-hearted that he answered every question about him, except those that touched on his family and childhood, with the exceptional haste and readiness that was typical of his staccato-like patter.

"Where did I come from just now? From Kiev. . . . I served in the army on the Austrian border, then I left the military, although I consider the rank of officer to be the highest of them all. . . . I lived and hunted in Polesye—no one can even imagine what it is like to shoot grouse right before dawn! Next I wrote all kinds of muck for kopecks for a little Kievan newspaper and lived in the slums with the worst bastards around.[7] . . . What am I writing now? Absolutely nothing I cannot think of anything, and so I'm in a terrible fix. . . . Look at these boots: they're so worn out that I can't go to Odessa in them. . . . Thank God, the Karyshevs are putting me up, otherwise I'd have to take up stealing. . . ."

During that wonderful summer, we spent many warm, starry southern nights together, roaming about or sitting on the cliffs overlooking the pale, lethargic sea. I kept trying to persuade him to write, if only for money alone.

"No one will publish me anywhere," he always groaned pitifully in reply.

"But you've already published!"

"Yes, but now I feel I'll write such nonsense that no one will want it."

"I know Davydova, the editor of *God's World*, quite well. I guarantee she'll take you."

"Thank you, but what shall I write? I can't think of anything!"

"Well, you know soldiers. Write something about them. Something about a young private who walks about on watch at night and who suffers, homesick and thinking of his village. . . ."

"But I don't know the village!"

"No problem, I do. Let's think up something together. . . ."

So he wrote his "Night Relief," which we sent to *God's World*, and then another little story, which I took immediately to Odessa, to *Odessa News*—for some reason, he was "too frightened" to do it himself—and for which I managed to get twenty-five rubles for him in advance.[8] He was waiting for me on the street, and when I emerged from the editorial offices with a twenty-five ruble note, he could not believe his eyes from happiness. He rushed out to buy himself a pair of shoes, then hired a cab and hurried me off to the "Arcadia," a seaside restaurant, to treat me to fried mackerel and white Bessarabian wine. . . . But how many times, for how many years, did he, when he was drunk, shout at me in that frenzied staccato-like patter:

"I'll never forgive you for having dared to be my benefactor, to provide me with shoes, a beggar, and a barefooted one at that!"

Our friendship, which lasted for several decades, was altogether strange. Sometimes he was tender, calling me lovingly Richard, Albert, and Vasya, but, all of sudden, when sober, he would be angry, resentful: "I hate the way you write; your pictures strain my eyes. The only thing I value in you is your excellent style—and your equally superb horsemanship. Do you remember how we used to ride off into the mountains in the Crimea?"[9]

His drunken states were beyond description. Despite his remarkable health, he, after one glass of vodka, would pick a fight with almost anyone who came his way. His rash, savage nature was as completely astonishing as his unpredictable moods. The more I got to know him, the more I became convinced that he had no hope for a normal, everyday life, or for sitting down to regular literary work. He squandered his health, his strengths, and his gifts with incredible extravagance. He lived any old way, like a reckless man who could care less about anything in the world.

In the first years of our friendship, we met mostly in Odessa. There I saw him sink lower and lower. He spent his days in port, in the foulest taverns and pubs; his nights, in the most terrible flophouses. He read nothing and was interested in no one other than fishermen, circus wrestlers, and clowns. . . . In this period, he said, more often than not, that he had become a writer by sheer accident, but in meetings with me, he indulged in his love for all kinds of aesthetic observations with great passion, even sensuality. He also had sharp spiritual inclinations—he loved to poke fun at people. "Take any blockhead, he talks often with rapture; take any arrogant talentless individual and make a fool of him with the most shameless praise, to 'unhinge' him in every way possible—what could be sweeter?"

Suddenly, his life changed greatly. He came to Petersburg, entered the literary scene, married unexpectedly the daughter of Davydova, whom I had introduced him to, and became the owner of *God's World*, since Davydova died a few days after his sudden proposal to her daughter.[10] He began to live a comfortable life, with the manners of a gentleman. More and more, he became his own man in the highest literary circles. Most important, he began to write a great deal and achieved greater and greater success with each new work. At that time, he wrote his best stories: "The Horse Thieves," "The Swamp," "The Coward," "The River of Life," "Gambrinus." When *The Duel* appeared, his fame became especially great. . . . [11]

Eighteen years ago, in Paris, when we, Kuprin, and his second wife were living as extremely close neighbors in the same building, he was drinking particularly heavily, and the doctor who examined him told us firmly: "If he doesn't stop drinking, he has no more than six months to live."[12] But he did not even think about stopping and lived for fifteen more years—"a fine fellow in all respects," as several people said about him. There is a limit to everything, though, and so the exceptional powers of my friend came to an end. About three years ago, having arrived from the south of France, I met him on the street and gasped inwardly: not a trace remained of the old Kuprin! He walked with feeble and pitiful steps; he plodded along so thinly and weakly that it seemed that the first puff of wind would knock him off his feet. He did not recognize me right away, but when he did, he embraced me with such touching tenderness, with such mournful meekness that tears came to my eyes.[13]

I received a postcard from him—two or three lines written in such huge, shaky curlicues and with such absurd omissions of letters that they seemed done by a child. . . . All of this was why during his last two years I never saw or visited him. God forgive me—but I did not have the strength to see him in such a state.

Last summer, on my way back from Italy, I woke up as my train was nearing Paris and, having opened the newspaper brought by an attendant, was stunned by news for which I was not prepared at all:

"Alexander Kuprin has returned to the USSR. . . ."

Of course, I experienced no political feelings about his "return." He did not leave for Russia—he was taken there, already quite ill, having become like a child. I felt only deep sadness that I would never see him again.[14]

Rereading Kuprin, I thought about the days of his fame and his stance to it. Others—Gorky, Andreev, Chaliapin—lived in permanent intoxication over their triumphs, in constant awareness [of their renown] not only among people, at various public gatherings, but also when they visited each other in private rooms of restaurants. They sat, talked, and smoked in a terribly unnatural way, forever stressing their exclusive company, as well as their supposed friendship [to all], adding to every word: "thou, Alexei; thou, Leonid; thou, Fyodor. . . ."

But Kuprin, even in those years when his fame inside Russia was hardly less than that of Gorky and Andreev, bore it as if nothing new had happened in his life. He seemed not to attach the slightest significance to his renown. He did not part with old and new friends, with drinking companions like the tramp and drunkard Manych.[15] Money and fame, it seemed, had given him one thing—the complete freedom to do exactly as he pleased in life, to burn his candle at both ends, to send everybody and everything to the devil.

"I'm proud, but not ambitious," I once told him.

"And me?" he replied quickly. At that moment, he seemed lost in thought, screwing up his eyes, as was his custom, and staring intently into the distance. Then he began in his army-like patter: "Yes, me too. I'm wildly proud, and that's why sometimes I'm so abjectly shy. But as to ambition, I don't even have the right to such a thing. I became a writer by accident; for a long time I kept going any old way, then I began to feed myself with little stories—that's my entire writer's history. . . ."

He often repeated—"I became a writer by accident." Of course, that is not true, as refuted by his autobiographical confessions in "Junkers."[16] But what was true was that when he left the army and kept going any old way, he did so with a small Kievan newspaper, not only with journalistic work but also with his "poor little stories." He told me that he sold these things for a "few kopecks but very easily" and that he wrote them "on the run, whistling while he worked," his talent satisfying easily the tastes of editors and readers. Then just as skillfully, he continued to write not only for the little Kievan newspaper but also for "thick" journals.

I said: "because of his talent." I should have said more forcefully—"his great talent." Everyone knows the circumstances in which he grew up, where and how he spent his youth, and the kind of people he associated with later in life. But what did he read? Where and when? In his autobiographical letter to the critic Izmailov, he wrote:

"When I left the army, the worst thing was that I had no knowledge whatsoever, scientific or practical. With an avid fervor unsatisfied to this day, I threw myself on life and books. . . ."[17]

But did he hurl himself on books for long (and did he really "throw himself" at all)? At any rate, the words "to this day" are extremely doubtful. All his development, all his education took place "on the run," having him assume easily by virtue of his talent—how should I put it?—an intellectuality, so to speak—a level of writing that was completely average. One also has to remember that he drank all his life, so it is surprising that he was able to write at all, and still more often, so vividly, strongly, and sanely, in complete contrast to the way he lived his life.

Critics have spoken endlessly about the unusual "elemental" and "spontaneous" aspects of Kuprin's works, about the "captivating primordial experiences" of his writing. Even now one reads: "What prevented Kuprin from becoming a great writer was the elemental nature of his gifts, his truly Russian improvidence, his extremely great confidence in 'instinct' at the expense of finishing and polishing his thoughts . . . that he 'did not graduate from the conservatory' as the symbolists used to say about the naturalists. . . . Kuprin was, by nature, not a bookish type, he was not inspired by literary subjects. . . . Neither he nor his heroes are ambivalent. . . ."

All this demands great reservation. Is it true to say that he was not ambivalent? Did he truly live in a way that was "elemental," "spontaneous," and "instinctive"? Truly, any sea was for him knee-deep; he did not take care of his body, mind, and heart; his reputation was, and for a long time will be, cause for gossip. But what kind of writer was he? No, he did not graduate from the "conservatory" (which one is another matter). Even with the force of his talent, the speed by which he wrote, he was *far from profiting from everything*.

There are also little things—even in his mid-career, stories had such vulgar expressions as "a chic woman," "a posh restaurant," and "the iron law of struggle for existence"; "his tender, almost feminine nature shuddered at the vulgar touches of reality with its stormy but severe needs"; and "Nina's shapely, graceful figure, her small face framed by locks of ash-colored curls, wafted before his intelligent gaze in a persistent way. . . ."

None of these is very serious—but the misfortune is that Kuprin's talent, his great giftedness, became infected not only by small, external clichés but also by big, external ones. Did the little Kievan newspaper want something suitable? Sure thing—I'll do it in five minutes flat, and I won't be squeamish about writing something like "the setting sun lit up the treetops with its slanting rays." You need a story for *Russian Wealth*? Nothing to it. Here for you is *Moloch*:

"The factory whistle wailed in a long drawn-out way, announcing the beginning of the working day. The thick, wheezing sound, it seemed, was coming from under the earth and spreading over all its surface. . . ."[18]

In a literary sense, is this really bad for an introduction? Everything is in its place—right down to the cheap rhythm of the two sentences, which keeps apace rhythmically with the setting sun with its slanting rays. Everything is *as it should be* and as was demanded in *models of the time*. Everything that was supposed to be in a story about Moloch is there: "The tender, almost feminine nature" of the sickly nervous intellectual, the engineer Bobrov, who, in his "suffering" service to capitalism, surrenders to morphine; the capitalistic "shark" Kvashin, who joins his employee, a base careerist, to the "slim and gracious" Nina, the daughter of another factory worker whom Bobrov loves, with the goal of making Nina Kvashin his mistress; the revolt of the workers, driven to despair by hunger and cold; the fire at the factory. . . .

I always remember the many great strengths in "The Horse Thieves," "The Swamp," "At Rest," "The Forest Backwoods," "The River of Life," "The Coward," "Staff Captain Rybnikov," "Gambrinus," the wonderful stories about the Balaklava fishermen, even *The Duel* and the beginning of "The Pit."[19] But there were always many things that irritated me even in these works. For instance, in "The River of Life," there is the last letter of the student who shoots himself in the Hotel "Serbia": "I am not the only one to perish from moral infection. . . . The entire past generation has grown up in a spirit of pious silence, of compulsory respect for elders, of the absence of personality and voice. May this vile time be cursed, this time of silence and beggary, this prosperous and peaceful existence under the silent shelter of pious reaction!" Is this not "literature" at its worst?

I did not reread him for a long time, and when I decided to do so again, I became upset immediately. At first I began only to leaf through his books and saw my many pencil marks made long ago in the margins:

"It was a terrible and gripping scene. . . . Here in the factory human labor boiled like a huge and solid machine. From various corners of the world, a thousand people had gathered here, submitting to the iron law of struggle for existence, to relinquish their power, health, intelligence, and energy for only one step forward of industrial progress . . ." (*Moloch*).

"The entire opposite corner of the hut was occupied by a large stove, and from it looked out two heads, hung downward, hair bleached by the sun. . . . An empty table stood in the corner before the icon, and a wretched lamp with glass black from soot hung on a metal hook from the ceiling. The student sat down by the table and immediately became bored and depressed, as if he had spent many, many hours here in tormenting, forced idleness. . . .

"Having finished his tea, the peasant crossed himself, turned the cup upside down, and put the remaining crumb of sugar carefully back into the little tin. . . .

"A fly buzzed and beat persistently against the windowpane, as if repeating one and the same tiresome, endless complaint. . . .

"'What is the meaning of life?' the student said with passionate tears in his eyes. 'Who needs this pitiful, inhuman vegetative existence? What sense is there in the sicknesses and deaths of children guilty of nothing, whose blood is sucked by a hideous swamp-like nightmare?'" ("The Swamp").

"A strange sound broke the deep night silence suddenly. . . . It echoed through the forest, low over the very earth and died away . . ." ("The Forest Backwoods"),

"He would open his eyes and the fantastic sounds would turn into the simple creak of sledge runners, the sound of a small bell on the shaft; and as before, white fields extended to the right and left; and as before, the black, bent back of the daily driver stuck out before him; and as before, the crops of the horses swung regularly as they swished their knotted tails. . . .

"Allow me to introduce myself: the local police officer and, so to speak, the Thunderer, Irisov, Pavel Afinogenovich . . ." ("The Jewess").[20]

Truly, it would have been difficult not to notice all these hackneyed phrases, used and reused a thousand times—these children's heads invariably "hanging over the top of the stove," the eternal bitten-off piece of sugar, the fly "repeating its wearisome complaint in a precise way," the Chekhovian student from "The Swamp," the Turgenevian "strange sound, resounding suddenly through the forest," the Tolstoyan slumber in the sleigh ("and as before, the crops of the horses swung in a regular way . . ."), and this Thunderer Inspector whose last name is, inevitably, Irisov or Hyacintov but whose patronymic is Afinogenovich or Ardalyonovich. . . . Then again, in "Small Fry," the conversations, as Chekhovian as can be, between the teacher and the medical assistant, lost somewhere in the northern snows.[21]

"Sometimes it began to seem to the teacher that from the time he could first remember, he had never left Kursha . . . that it existed only in a forgotten fairy tale or in a dream that he had heard of in another life, where there were flowers, kind, courteous people, intelligent books, tender women's voices, and smiles. . . . [22]

"'I've always thought, Sergei Firsych,' the teacher said to the medical assistant, 'that it's a good thing to be of some, even of the slightest, use. I look at some most splendid building, palace, or cathedral, and I think: let the name of the architect remain immortal forever and ever. I rejoice in his fame, I don't envy him at all. But then couldn't a simple bricklayer also lay a brick and cover it with lime and love—couldn't he, too, feel happy and proud? And I often think that you and I are tiny people, small fry, but that if one day humanity becomes splendid and free'. . . ."

In the story "Narcissus," I marked the description of a societal salon, some baroness and her friend Betsy—yes, inevitably Betsy!—and the thundery evening—in which "the approaching storm could be felt in the thick, scorching air"—and the first kiss of lovers, which writers have tied to the "approaching storm" a thousand times. . . . [23]

In "The Pit," I marked a passage where "little flames lit up in the long green Egyptian eyes of the artist," whose singing so stunned the young ladies of the brothel that the author himself exclaims completely seriously: "Such is the power of genius!"

I read on. I grabbed hold of the first volume that came my way, read the first story, and became even more upset. The book opens with a story titled "At the Railway Siding," with the following plot: three people meet by chance, traveling in the same train compartment—a young man, a young woman "with a very slim, elegant figure and ash-blond hair streaming in the wind," and her husband, a repulsive old civil servant depicted extremely caustically: "Mr. Yavorsky could not and would not speak about anything other than his own self, his own rheumatism and hemorrhoids, and regarded his wife as his lawful property. . . ."[24]

This old man lectures and nags his unhappy "property" day and night. He becomes jealous of the young man and is rude to him as well. In so doing, he fans the love that has begun to kindle between the two people, and which, at long last, they confess to each other at a siding, where their train has stopped alongside another train going in the opposite direction. They run over to the other train, having decided to abandon the old man and to join their lives together forever. The young man exclaims passionately: "Forever? For our entire lives?" But the young woman, "instead of an answer, buries her face in his chest."

Then I reread things that I had forgotten most of all: "Solitude," "Sacred Love," "Night Lodging," and his military tales, "Night Relief," "The Campaign," "The Inquest," and "The Wedding." . . . [25] The first three stories again turned out to be weak: their unconvincing narratives and execution—written in the style of Maupassant and Chekhov and again too neatly, too smoothly, and too deftly. . . .

"Vera Lvovna was seized by a sudden overwhelming desire to cling to her husband as tightly as possible, to bury her head into the strong chest of this man who was so close to her, to feel his warmth. . . . Little white clouds kept passing across the bright and round moon and burst forth suddenly with a fantastic golden glow. . . . For the first time in her life, Vera Lvovna encountered the terrible knowledge that, sooner or later, comes to the mind of every sensitive and thoughtful individual—the knowledge of that pitiless, impenetrable barrier that stands forever between two close people. . . ."[26]

In this story, as in the others, everything is vulgar and cheap. But his military tales are very different, and, reading them, I began saying to myself: "This is excellent!" Here, too, everything is again excessively neat, smooth, and deft, but it also embraces genuine craftsmanship. Everything adheres to a different standard, especially "The Wedding," a story that, unlike the other stories, does not make you think: "Oh, how much of Chekhov and Tolstoy is in here!"—a work that is very cruel and prone to wicked caricature—but brilliant just the same. When I got to the stories written at the height of his great talent—"The Horse Thieves," "The Swamp," and so forth—I thought no longer about their defects, some major: the cheap ideology, the desire to keep up with the spirit of the times with denunciation and civic nobility, and the premeditated effort to impress readers with a dramatic plot and almost brutal realism. . . . I delighted only in the various qualities of his stories: the freedom, power, and vividness of his narratives, his precise and tempered style. . . .

Here is an article about him—the lines of the well-known critic Pilsky, who, for many years, was a close friend of Kuprin:

"Kuprin was frank, direct, and quick in his replies. He had a joyous and open passion and artlessness, a warm kindness for all about him. . . . At times, his gray-blue eyes flashed with a wondrous light, the winds of talent shone and fluttered in them. . . . To the very last years of his life, he dreamed of complete independence, of heroic daring. He delighted in 'iron times, eagles, and giants.' . . ."[27]

Much more will be written in this foolish vein. People will speak again and again about how much "elemental, animal" there was in Kuprin, about how much he loved nature, horses, dogs, cats, and birds. . . . Of course, there is a great deal of truth in such things, but talking about the difference between Kuprin the writer and Kuprin the man—whom almost everyone characterized in the same way—I do not at all wish to say that the man never revealed himself in the writer. He revealed himself, of course, and the longer he lived, the more he did so. "Kuprin's warm kindness toward all living things" or, as another critic put it, "Kuprin's blessing upon the entire world"—that existed as well. But one should remember that it did so only in the last period of his life and work.[28]

CHAPTER 11

Semyonovs and Bunins

"A country cannot be anything in use and glory if it does not have people who have known the flow of heavenly forces and of time, shipbuilding, the geography of the entire world . . ." (*Regulation of the Imperial Russian Academy of Sciences*, 1747).

To "such" people belonged and continues to belong Pyotr Petrovich Semyonov-Tyan-Shansky, of the famous Semyonov family.[1]

I first learned the many domestic details about the man from his son V. P. Semyonov-Tyan-Shansky, who lived as an émigré in Finland and who, for a while, corresponded with me in an intimate way. (The Semyonovs are relatives of the Buninas.)[2]

From him I learned of the sad fate of the extensive memoirs left by his father. Only the first volume was published (only one copy exists outside of Russia). V. P. sent it to me and told me the story of the second volume, the publication of which coincided with the revolution, and by the time of the October cataclysm, only eleven sheets were published in all.[3]

As is well known, when the Bolsheviks seized power, they introduced their own spelling and ordered that all the typography of letters they had banned from the alphabet be destroyed.[4] V. P., who was supervising the publication of the memoirs, had either to stop the typesetting of the second volume or to finish it in the new spelling, thereby issuing the book in a rather strange format. Trying to avoid such a thing, V. P. found another printing house, which disobeyed the Bolshevik order secretly and had still not destroyed the condemned letters. The manager of the printing house, afraid of winding up with the Cheka, agreed to finish typesetting the book in the old spelling only on the condition that V. P. obtain a written authorization from the Bolsheviks. V. P. attempted to do so but, of course, was refused. He was told: "No, you will have to publish your memoirs in our spelling: let everyone see from the twelfth sheet on the exact moment of our victory. Besides, even if we gave you permission, it would not help: the letters of the old regime have been destroyed in all publishing houses. Also, if in the unlikely case you have found a firm that has still kept them, we ask you to tell us immediately so that we can dispatch its manager to a suitable place. . . ."

So, I repeat, the book got stuck on the eleventh sheet, and what happened to it, even V. P. himself (who left Russia soon afterward) did not seem to know. He wrote to me only what I have said here, adding: "This second volume consists of my father's expedition to Central Asia. It has a great deal of valuable scholarly material, as well as interesting pages for the general public—for example, the story of his meeting in Siberia with Dostoevsky, whom he had known in his early youth.[5] Likewise, the third and fourth volumes contain sharply vivid pictures of the various classes of Russian society, not only in the late 1850s but also in the epoch of the great reforms of Alexander II and his collaborators. . . ."[6]

Dostoevsky is mentioned also in the first volume, which I have had in my possession for some time, the pages about the writer preceded by a description of the Petrashevsky Circle and of Petrashevsky himself.[7]

"We met at Petrashevsky's home regularly every Friday," P. P. [Semyonov-Tyan-Shansky] writes. "We went there willingly, most of all because he had a home of his own and could arrange pleasant gatherings. He himself seemed to all of us to be eccentric, if not mad. He was an interpreter at the Ministry of Foreign Affairs. His only duty was to attend the trials of foreigners and to inventory property seized by the state, particularly libraries. He chose for himself all the forbidden foreign books, putting authorized ones in their place, and, in so doing, built a library of his own, which he put at the disposal of all his friends and acquaintances.

"Being an extreme liberal, atheist, republican, and socialist, he was a striking example of a born agitator. Everywhere, wherever he could, he preached a jumble of ideas with extraordinary passion, but without any order or logic. For his propagandistic goals, he sought to become a teacher at military-academic institutions, declaring that he could teach all eleven subjects [in the curriculum]. When he was called upon for a test on one of them, he began his public lecture thus: 'This subject can be approached from twenty different points of view,' . . . and he actually did so from all twenty, but he did not get the job.

"In his dress, Petrashevsky showed the same extreme originality: he wore everything that was frowned on at the time, that is, long hair, a mustache, a beard; he walked about in a kind of Spanish *almaviva* and a four-cornered top hat. . . . One time he arrived at the Kazan Cathedral in a woman's dress, stood among the ladies, pretending to pray devoutly.[8] His somewhat robber-like face and black beard, which he had not concealed carefully enough, aroused the astonished attention of his neighbors. Finally, a local inspector came up to him and said: 'My dear madam, you seem to be dressed like a woman'; but he replied boldly: 'My dear sir, you seem to be a woman dressed like a man.' The inspector was so taken aback that Petrashevsky, taking advantage of the situation, disappeared safely from the cathedral. . . .

"Our circle did not take him seriously," the memoirist continues. "But his parties continued to flourish, and new faces kept appearing at them. They were spent in animated conversations in which writers unburdened their souls, complaining about the cruel restrictions by the censors. There were literary readings and papers on the most diverse literary and scientific subjects, all of them obviously with interpretations that, at that time, could not find themselves in print. There also flowed fiery speeches about the emancipation of the serfs, which seemed to us to be such an unattainable ideal. N. Ya. Danilevsky gave an entire series of lectures on socialism and on Fourierism, with which, at the time, he was particularly taken. Dostoevsky read excerpts from his stories *Poor Folk* and *Netochka Nezvanova* and indicted passionately landowners for their abuse of the serfs . . ."[9]

Speaking of Dostoevsky, the author says that he first met the writer when Dostoevsky had just gained fame for his novel *Poor Folk*, had quarreled with Belinsky and Turgenev, had broken off completely from their literary circle, and had begun to frequent the circles of Petrashevsky and Durasov.[10]

"Generally speaking, I knew Dostoevsky for a long time and was on close terms with him," he writes, "and, incidentally, in no way can I agree with the claims of many people who say that Dostoevsky was a very well-read but not educated individual. He was not only well-read, but also educated. In his childhood, in his father's home, he acquired an excellent foundation. He had a complete command of French and German, which he read quite fluently. In the Engineering Academy, he studied systematically and diligently, in addition to general subjects, higher mathematics, physics, and mechanics.[11] His wide erudition added amply to his specialized education. One can dare say that he was much more educated that many other Russian writers of his time. He also knew better than others the Russian people and the village, where he lived in his childhood and youth. He was much closer to the peasants, to their way of life than many well-to-do gentry writers. Such intimacy, though, did not prevent him very much from seeing himself as the nobleman he was truly, and from sometimes displaying lordly habits to an excess.

"Much has been said and written about the poverty that Dostoevsky purportedly experienced as a youth. But this poverty was extremely relative. In my opinion, what Dostoevsky suffered from was not genuine poverty, so much as the difference between his means and wants. I remember our life in camp and the financial demands he made on his father for daily expenses.[12] I lived almost next to him, in a canvas tent exactly like his own. Like him, I also went without tea, boots, and a trunk for books to call my own. I received only ten rubles for the entire time there. Although I studied in an expensive, aristocratic school, I was at peace. But for Dostoevsky, all this was a calamity. In no way did he wish to be left behind our friends who had their own tea, boots, and trunks for books, and whose expenses for camp varied between hundreds and thousands of rubles. . . ."[13]

In the first volume of his memoirs, Semyonov often talks about our Bunin clan, to which the Semyonovs are related, and particularly about Anna Petrovna Bunina, who died just over a hundred years ago.[14] No one remembered the anniversary, but it deserved to be so. Taking into account the time in which Bunina lived, one cannot but agree with those who regarded her as one of the most remarkable women in Russia. Besides Semyonov's memoirs, one can find some information about her in an article written a long time ago by Alexander Pavlovich Chekhov.[15] He says that nowadays Bunina's name is found only in histories of literature and even then, perhaps, only because her portrait still hangs on the walls of the Academy of Sciences.[16] In her time, though, she was known very widely, her poetry was read and enjoyed greatly by the educated public, [and] it sold out quickly and received enthusiastic reviews.[17] It was praised by Derzhavin, read by Krylov in public, and enraptured Dmitriev, who was one of her closest friends. Grech said that Bunina "occupies an honored place among contemporary writers and first place among Russian women writers," and Karamzin added: "There is not a single woman among us who can write as forcefully as Bunina does."[18] Empress Yelizaveta Alekseevna presented her with a brooch shaped like a golden lyre and studded with diamonds to "wear on festive occasions." Alexander the Blessed granted her a large pension, and the Russian Academy of Sciences published a collection of her works. Her fame ended with her death; yet even Belinsky himself remembered her flatteringly in his reviews.[19]

Anna Petrovna's father owned the well-known village of Urusovo, in the province of Ryazan. Anna was born there in 1774. P. P. Semyonov says that her father gave to her three brothers what was an extremely good education in those days.[20] The oldest brother was a most educated man of his time. He knew many foreign languages perfectly and belonged to a Masonic lodge.[21] The younger brothers served in the navy, where one of them, during the war of Catherine II against the Swedes, was taken prisoner and sent by the king of Sweden to the university in Uppsala, where he received his degree.[22] As for Anna, a great honor was her lot—she became a member of the Russian Academy of Sciences, though as a child her education had been scanty, since at that time the education of young ladies was seen as an unnecessary luxury.[23] She became learned through her own efforts and determination, when her older brother began taking her to Moscow and introduced her to the circle of his literary and, generally speaking, enlightened colleagues.[24] Here she met and became friends with Merzlyakov, Kapnist, Prince A. A. Shakovskoy, Voeikov, V. A. Zhukovsky, and V. L. Pushkin. In later years, she was influenced greatly by N. P. Novikov and Karamzin, "to whom, more than anyone, she owed her correct and elegant literary style." She poured over the pages of the *Moscow Journal*, of which he was the editor.[25] Then she met him in person in a group called "Conversation of the Lovers of the Russian Word." This group was founded in Petersburg in 1811. It had twenty-four regular and thirty-two honorary members including Anna Petrovna. The founder of "Conversation" was Shishkov, and members included Krylov, Shakovskoy, Kapnist, Ozerov, and even Speransky himself.[26] Its purpose was "to counteract the innovations introduced by Karamzin into the Russian language, to implement in life imitations of models of the Slavic tongue." It was extremely curious that Karamzin was one of its members.[27]

The death of Anna's father changed her life considerably. After his passing, she went to live with her sister, Maria Petrovna Semyonova, having received an inheritance that gave her a yearly income of 600 rubles. She was now independent and free. Taking advantage of her good fortune, she did not stay with Semyonova for long. In 1802, her brother-in-law, Semyonov, went to Petersburg. Anna Petrovna begged him to take her with him, and, once there, she refused to return to the country. Her brother-in-law was "extremely shocked" at her behavior and tried to change her mind, but she stood firm. She had come to Petersburg allegedly only to see her brother who was a sailor there. When she decided to stay in Petersburg, her brother also began to persuade her to return home, but also in vain. Then Semyonov returned to the country, her brother soon left on a campaign, and she found herself completely alone in the capital. Such a situation was as highly unusual in those times. But it did not bother her in the least.[28] She even went further and rented a completely separate apartment for herself on Vasilievsky Island, "availing herself of the services of a respectable woman."[29]

Having gotten what she wanted, and despite the fact that she was already twenty-seven years old, she began to educate herself with remarkable energy and activity. She began to study French, German, English, physics, mathematics, and, most of all, Russian literature. She made rapid progress. When her brother returned from his campaign, he was struck by the scope and solidity of her knowledge. Although this newly gained erudition had enriched her mind, it ruined her materially. Living in Petersburg, she spent her entire inheritance. Her situation was becoming worse, and she ran into debt. At this point, her brother hastened to introduce her to writers in Petersburg, to whom she showed her first writings. They applauded her works and helped her to publish them. Her first poem, "From the Seashore," came out in 1806. This was followed by an entire series of new works, which made her so successful with the public that she ventured to publish them in a separate edition under the title *The Inexperienced Muse.*[30] The book was presented to Empress Yelizaveta Alekseevna and was rewarded first with the already-mentioned "diamond-studded lyre," then with a pension of 400 rubles a year.[31] That was the beginning of Bunina's fame. In 1811, she brought out another book of verse, titled *Village Evenings*, which also sold out very quickly. Then she published a second edition of *The Inexperienced Muse* in two volumes, which was also a great success. The year 1812 brought her "highest honors": she issued patriotic hymns, "winning for herself even greater goodwill and a host of new favors from the monarch." But this was to be her last joy. Soon afterward she developed breast cancer, which turned the rest of her life into an endless chain of suffering and which finally brought about her death.

Everything was done to save her or at least to alleviate her suffering. The court and society, who valued her not only for her poetic merits but also for her high intellectual and moral virtues, took a great interest in her. The emperor wanted that the most celebrated physicians be called to her home, and he personally saw to it that she received the best possible treatment. At the expense of the court, dachas were rented for her, and medicines "from the main pharmacy" were dispensed to her free of charge. Court doctors also visited her for free. It was also decided to take up a most popular measure at the time: a trip to England, with physicians particularly hailed for their expertise. The emperor himself again assumed all the expenses for the journey, and "all of Petersburg saw her off with great ceremony and triumph."

But even England did not help. A. P. lived abroad for two years but returned just as ill as when she had left. She lived for another twelve years but wrote almost nothing in that time. She only brought out in 1821 a complete collection of her works in three volumes, which was again rewarded by the court, this time with a life pension of 2,000 rubles a year. She lived her final years partly with relatives in the country, partly in Lipetsk and in Caucasian spas, everywhere seeking relief from her suffering.[32] The cancer in her chest had done its destructive work to such an extent that, unable to lie down anymore, she spent most of her time in the only position she could bear—"on her knees." So, on her knees, she wrote:

To love me or not,
To pity me or not
You, my kith and kin!
Now do as you want . . .

She spent the last days of her life translating the sermons of Blair and constantly reading the Bible. She died on December 4, 1829, in the village of Denisovka, in the district of Ryazan, at the home of her nephew D. M. Bunin, and was buried in Urusovo, the village in which she was born.[33] The modest tombstone, which was once restored by P. P. Semyonov-Tyan-Shansky, may still be standing on her grave. In his memoirs, he quotes the charming dedication that Anna Petrovna wrote on a little book bound in red morocco—a copy of her translation of Blair's sermons:

"To dear Petinka Semyonov in the hope of an illustrious manhood."

CHAPTER 12

Ertel

He is now almost forgotten and, for most readers, completely unknown. His life, though, was as remarkable as his oblivion. Who has forgotten his friends and contemporaries—Garshin, Uspensky, Korolenko, and Chekhov? Yet, on the whole, with the exception of Chekhov, of course, he was no less a writer than they and, in some ways, even greater.

Twenty years ago, on a fine, frosty day in Moscow, I was sitting in his study in a sun-filled apartment on Vozdvizhenka Street and, as I always did in meetings with him, thought:

"What an intelligent man, what talent there is in every word, in every smile! What a mixture of virility and tenderness, of firmness and tact—a thoroughbred Englishman and a Voronezh cattle dealer all in one! How dear was everything in and about him: his lean, tall figure in a splendid English suit, without a single bit of down; the snow-white linen, his large, reddish-haired hands, the drooping light-brown mustache, the melancholic light-blue eyes, the amber cigarette holder with an expensive cigarette giving off fragrant smoke, and the entire study, sparkling with sunlight, cleanliness, and comfort! Who would believe that, as a youth, this man could not tie two words together in the most modest provincial society, did not know how to use a napkin, and wrote with the most ridiculous spelling mistakes?"

Soon afterward, in this very same apartment, he died—of heart failure.

A year later, his collected works (short stories, novelettes, and novels) were published in seven volumes, along with an additional tome of his writing. His novel *The Gardenins* was prefaced by Tolstoy; his correspondence, by his autobiography and an article titled "The Worldview of Ertel," written by Gershenzon.[1]

Tolstoy wrote about *The Gardenins*: "Having begun reading this book, I could not tear myself from it until I had finished it in its entirety and reread some passages several times."

He continued:

"The key merit of the book, besides its serious approach and its knowledge of the life of the people, the likes of which I have not encountered with any other writer—the inimitable, unprecedented merit of this novel is its remarkably accurate, beautiful, varied, and vigorous folk language. Such language one cannot find in either old or new writers. His folk language is not only forceful, beautiful, and true, but it is also varied infinitely. The old servant speaks in one way, the workman in another, the young lad in a third, the women in a fourth, the girls in yet another. Someone once counted the number of words used by a writer. I think that in Ertel's works, the number of words, especially folk words, would be the greatest among all Russian writers. What true, good, and vigorous words they are, too—words used by the people alone. Nowhere are these words overstressed, their exceptional quality overexaggerated. One never gets the feeling that, as often happens with other writers, he wants to show off or surprise his readers with a word he has overheard somewhere. . . ."[2]

This knowledge of the people becomes completely understandable when one looks through Ertel's autobiography:

"I was born," he wrote, "on July 7, 1855. My grandfather came from a burgher family in Berlin. As a youth he wound up in Napoleon's army, was captured near Smolensk, and was taken by a Russian officer to a village near Voronezh.[3] He soon converted to Orthodoxy, married a serf, and registered as a petty citizen of Voronezh. He spent the rest of his life there, working as a bailiff on various gentry estates. My father inherited this post and also married a serf. He had very little education, but he loved to read—mostly historical works—and was also familiar with so-called questions of politics and even, to a certain extent, philosophy. His splendid character included a great kindness behind a stern exterior, a rather precise sense of fairness, and an extremely sober mind that mirrored almost completely the views of the Great Russian peasantry. Unlike my father, my mother—the illegitimate daughter of a landowner beyond the Don—was inclined to sentimentality and even to dreamy romanticism."

"She taught me to read, but I myself learned to write, at first copying out printed letters from books. Then my godfather, Saveliev, the landowner for whom my father had long worked as a bailiff, offered to take me into his home. Saveliev's wife was French, an actress in some boulevard theater in Paris. She hardly spoke any Russian, was quite bored, and treated me like a toy, dressing me up and feeding me sweets. . . . All this did not last long. My father quarreled with Saveliev and lost his job, and I returned to my 'original state.' We spent almost a year in poverty in the apartment of a peasant whom we knew, until my father leased a farm. . . ."

"I was completely free to do as I pleased: to play with village children, to read whatever I wished. When I was thirteen years old, my father 'schooled me in farming.' By that time I knew the four rules of arithmetic and had read *The History of Napoleon*, *Koshchei the Immortal*, *The Travels of Pythagoras*, Kostomarov's *Stenka Razin*, the second volume of *The Museum of Foreign Literature*, Koltsov's *Songs*, the *Works of Pushkin*, an ancient manual for the care of horses, an illustrated book of sacred Scripture, and a comedy by Chaadaev, titled *Don Pedro Prokodurante*.[4] I then taught myself to read Old Church Slavonic and reread several times the *Kiev Paterikon* and several volumes of *The Monthly Readings*. . . . [5] Around the age of sixteen, I met a merchant from Usman by the name of Bogomolov, who furnished me with the works of Darwin, including *The Descent of Man*, and issues from *Russian Word*, [from which I read] articles by Pisarev with great fascination. . . ."[6]

"My father made me his assistant in running the farm, but I was on such familiar terms with the simple folk that he sometimes threatened to beat me, and actually did so two or three times. . . . I was one of them in the servants' quarters, at tables, in the stables, 'on the street' in the village, at parties and weddings, wherever young village folk gathered. . . . Finally, my father decided that my friendly and familial ties to the villagers prevented me from exercising all authority as a bailiff, so he agreed to let me seek a position elsewhere. Soon I got a job as a clerk on one of the neighboring estates. . . . I saw a railway for the first time when I was sixteen; Moscow and Petersburg, when I was twenty-three. . . ."

What followed was, in those days, typical for a self-taught person "who tore off for the world, for progress": a new friendship with another eccentric merchant, who, "amid the filth and vulgarity of tradespeople," was possessed by a genuine passion for this "progress" and for reading; a relationship with his daughter, who undertook the development of a young "barbarian" in a "bookish" romance, ending in marriage; an attempt to set up farming on a small piece of land rented with his wife's tiny dowry and the collapse of this venture—"I, who was seen as an efficient manager on the estates of rich people, proved to be no good whatsoever on my own small one," and, finally, arrival in Petersburg (thanks to a chance meeting with the writer Zasodimsky, who, for some reason, was visiting Usman) and the beginning of a typical writer's life among the "foremost" representatives of the literature of the time, a life of such poverty that the young writer soon showed the first symptoms of consumption, along with such enthusiasm for "advanced" ideas that he even had to spend some time in the Peter and Paul Fortress and then to live in exile in Tver'.[7]

Here, though, the typical ends. What was altogether atypical was how quickly this "barbarian" developed into a genuinely cultured individual, his unusual spiritual and artistic growth, and, the main thing, the independence of his tastes, views, and strivings, which, even at that time, differed greatly from all those Zasodimskys and Zlatovratskys. "Even in the days of my infatuation with Zasodimsky," Ertel said, "I never abandoned a trait from my father: common sense. I felt that I knew life better and deeper than he, and especially the everyday existence of the folk, for which Zasodimsky believed himself to be its painter. I also understood people better than he did—courtesy of farming activities, my business dealings with merchants, peasants, kulaks, innkeepers, and speculators, in a word, everything that went alongside my love for the people, my laments for their needs and sorrows, my passion for hazy ideals of education, progress, freedom, equality, and brotherhood. . . ."

This "common sense" (if one can use such an exceedingly modest expression) was what made Ertel such a major and original figure in both literature and life. Gershenzon was completely correct when he said that "one cannot imagine a more striking contrast between the figure of Ertel and the flabby, anemic Russian intelligentsia of the eighties." His life, I repeat, was only for a short time more or less typical of the life of an intellectual from the *raznochintsy*.[8] Very soon it again became extremely atypical (even externally). After his exile in Tver', Ertel lived only for short times in the capitals and abroad. He again returned to the country, to farming, to which, almost to the very end of his life, he devoted half of his energy first by caring for a small piece of land that he had rented for himself, then by managing extremely huge and enormously wealthy estates of landowners (at one point, he looked after several estates at a time, scattered over nine provinces, that is, an "entire kingdom," as he himself once wrote to me).

Gershenzon also thinks that Ertel was even a "remarkable" thinker and that his worldview put forth an "extremely original and valuable system of ideas." The power of Ertel's thought, he says, lay in that field of life reserved by Kant as "practical reason."[9] Ertel was, above all, a man of action. Endowed by nature with exceptional vitality, he was a remarkable man of action. He had a passionate desire to be in the endless change of actions and events. And this is what determined his philosophy of life.

His entire worldview answers a twofold question: What does life allow one to do and what does it demand? But he never sought to answer the question about the fundamental force that moves the world, as well as about the final goal of this movement.

He was not a rationalist, though. On the contrary, his intuitive grasp of reality taught him that beneath all that is seen is an element that is invisible, but no less real, and that not to study it in practical calculations means to risk errors in all reckonings. That is why positivism seemed to him to be insufferable nonsense.[10]

He thought that life is divided sharply into two distinct categories: that which depends on the will of the "Great Unknown whom we call God," to which we must submit unconditionally, and that which depends on our will, is alterable, and deems struggle with existence as proper and necessary. He believed in the existence of an absolute truth, but he stood for relativity in its application. He loved to say: "In moderation, friend, in moderation!"—that is, do not accelerate the forward march of history by force. The absolute understanding of good and evil, and the relative activity toward realizing the former and struggling against the latter—that is what is needed for any type of action, including any kind of protest.

Does this mean, though, that he preached "moderation and accuracy"? Rarely was there anyone who was less moderate and tidy than he. His entire life was passionately immoderate, a "perpetual burning in affairs spiritual, social, and practical, in exhaustive searches for external and internal harmony." He himself often complained: "I still have not yet succeeded in balancing my life. . . . Everything that I see and read around me wrings my heart unbearably with such pity toward one and anger toward another that I simply cannot bear it. . . ."

Speaking about his part in the relief work during the famine of the nineties (to which he devoted an entire two years of his life with such passion that he neglected his own affairs completely and wound up genuinely destitute), he said: "Once again I discovered that I could get so carried away by so-called social activity as to forget myself and exhaust all my energies. . . ."[11]

He criticized the Russian intelligentsia severely, especially from a practical point of view. He used to say that its endless protesting, brought about by "nervous irritation" or a "lyrical approach to things," was impotent and goalless because pathos, in and of itself, was a form and not the essence of expression, and because the fundamental quality of any struggle is found, first, in the personal religious and philosophical conviction of the protester and, second, in an understanding of historical reality.

The first thing the Russian intellectual needs, he used to say, is to absorb the teachings of Christ—"a bone in the throat of all those Mikhailovskys"—without which a religious culture of the personality is impossible.[12] The second thing is a profound and serious intellectual and artistic consciousness, as well as a historical sense. He said: "We forget all kinds of 'dated words' so often and easily that we perceive them only with our nerves. . . . The misfortune of our generation is that it lacks all interest in religion, philosophy, and art and that, to this day, it does not think freely or feel in an openly developed way. . . . Besides political forms and institutions, people need 'spirit,' faith, truth, and God. . . .

"You will say: 'But they know how to die for an idea.' Ah, but it is easier to die for an idea than to realize it in life! Even in the event of victory, a society that only protests can do more harm than good. . . . Despotism is bitter, a thousand times bitter, but it is no less bitter if it issues forth from some 'Fedenka' instead of from the Pobedonotsevs of the world.[13] I can well imagine what the 'Fedenkas' would be up to in place of the Pobedonotsevs! As to our attitude toward the folk, here, too, no norm is needed, other than a moral one, which, generally speaking, must determine relations between people, that is, the law of love laid down by Christ."

"It seems to me," he wrote in his notebook, refuting Tolstoy, many of whose views he shared, "that to distribute my estate among beggars is not the entire truth. I should also preserve all that is good in myself and in my children: knowledge, education, an entire number of truly valuable habits, most of which require a hereditary transmission, not a theoretical one. Having given away my estate, will I truly give everything I owe to people? No, thanks to others, I have still many other things that I must also share with close ones and not bury in the ground. . . ."

An absolute understanding of the truth and its relative application were one of his cherished beliefs. With all his being, he believed that a rigid pursuit of principle is cold and deadly, that the warmth of life lies in compromise, and that complete self-denial is as absurd as any absolute realization of truth. "It is unnatural to love another's child as much as one's own. It is enough that one's personal feeling does not stifle a personal sense of justice that does not allow one to murder another's child for the convenience of his own. The norm is in that middle where the shoots of personal life flower and grow in full force, without crushing the love for all living things. . . ."

This man, amazing in his intense internal and external activity, in the freedom and clarity of his thought, and in the breadth of his heart—died too early—he was only fifty-two years old. But before his passing, he believed profoundly that "the meaning of all early suffering will be revealed there." In his adolescence, he underwent a period of passionate religious feeling. Such emotions gave way to "doubts, to attempts to affirm, in place of all my growing skepticism, a faith in goodness, in revolutionary and populist teachings, in the teaching of Tolstoy. . . . But everything in my nature kept changing and changing. . . ."

In many respects, he always remained "a friend of any and all liberties," an intellectual of his time. At the same, he saw life in a "new and ever-changing light." Goodness? It seemed that the word "sounded extremely hollow" and that one had to "think about such a thing a bit carefully." Populism? It, too, seemed that "populist dreams are essentially dreams and nothing more. . . ."

"But it is a different matter altogether to organize (with no politics whatsoever) some sort of gigantic union of educated people to fulfill various peasant needs. . . . Before they can attempt to establish the 'Kingdom of God,' the Russian people and their intelligentsia must first create the basis for such a kingdom, in thought and word, to form a conscious and firmly rooted cultural life. . . .

"Socialism? But do you not think that socialism can only belong to a people whose country roads are lined with cherry trees—and their fruit left whole? But when all that has been planted is a simple, wretched white willow that gets torn out simply 'just for fun,' and when people in a cart will shorten a journey by five yards by driving through some excellent rye—not that of the master, but of the peasants—then there can be *razovshchina* or *pugachevshchina*, anything you want, but not socialism.[14] But then—what is socialism exactly? Life, my friend, cannot begin to run on shafts. Revolution? But revolution as violence is something I loathe organically. . . . Every revolutionary destruction destroys coarsely not only material things but also sacred ones. . . . But then again what are material things? The destruction of 'Cherry Orchards' by a beast-like crowd is as revolting as murder. . . . After all, even Herzen said that it is incomparably more heartrending to lose certain things rather than certain people. . . . Tolstoy? But driving everyone to Thebaid would mean to castrate and deflower life. . . . [15] One cannot direct everyone to work on a farm, to rabid resistance to evil, and to ruinous self-denial. I do not want to live my entire life as a 'Samaritan.' . . . If there were no shadows, there would be no struggle, and what can be more splendid than struggle! The people? For a long time I shed tears, writing about them. . . ."

But years passed—and what did that lover of the folk say? "No, I have never understood Nekrasov's phrase 'to hate while loving' as well as I do now, plunged into the hell of genuine, not abstract, folk life, into the delights of incredibly cruel Russian existence. . . . [16] The Russian people are a profoundly unhappy people, but they also deeply base, coarse, and, above all, lying, deceitful savages. . . . It has been estimated that several thousand revolutionaries perished during the reign of Alexander II; but if the 'real people' had been let loose, they would have dealt with these thousands in the manner of Ivan the Terrible. . . . Atheism? But the person without religion is a pitiful, unhappy creature. . . . The golden domes and ringing church bells are the forms of a great essence that live in every human soul. . . ."[17]

Here are his last confessions, written shortly before his death:

"The terrible mysteries of God are inaccessible to my rational understanding. . . ."

"I believe that the meaning of human suffering will be revealed there. . . ."

"I believe fervently that our life does not end here and that in the next life all the tormenting riddles and mysteries of human existence will be resolved."

Chapter 13

Voloshin

Maximilian Voloshin was one of the most prominent poets of the prerevolutionary and revolutionary years in Russia, and, in his poetry, he brought together many of the most typical features of most poets at the time: their aestheticism, snobbery, symbolism; their enthusiasm for the European poetry at the end of the last century and at the beginning of the present one; and their political "change of landmarks" (depending on what was more advantageous at one time or another). He also had another failing: extremely literary praise for the most terrible and bestial crimes of the Russian Revolution.[1]

Many articles appeared about him after this death, but they said little that was new and gave few insights about him as both a writer and an individual. Several of these pieces were limited to that type of praise that is now said about almost everyone who mentions the Russian Revolution in poetry and prose: he entered among the prophets, the seers of the "coming Russian cataclysm," even though many of these prophets deemed it sufficient to be only passingly aware of the Russian history found in elementary textbooks.

The most interesting remarks about him were in an article by A. Benois in *Latest News*:

"His poetry did not inspire that confidence without which sincere delight is impossible. I did not at all believe him when he mounted the steps of beautiful and resonant words to the highest peaks of human thought. . . . But such an ascent came to him quite naturally, and it was precisely words that attracted him. . . . I always regarded him with certain irony, permissible even in the closest and most tender friendship. . . . His myopic eyes peering through his pince-nez clashed strangely with his 'Zeus-like' appearance, cast him as something helpless and lost . . . as something extraordinarily dear and appealing. . . .

"With remarkable spiritual simplicity, he acted as a 'Medusa' or entertained proconsuls of the Kremlin when, with naive impudence, he took it into his head to read his most terrible poems, full of accusations and tragic laments before Soviet ideologues and rulers. Most likely, he got away with such antics only because no one chose to take him seriously. . . ."[2]

I had known Voloshin personally for quite a long time, but I had not been close to him until our final meetings in Odessa in the winter and spring of 1919.

I remember his first poems. Judging by them, it was difficult to foresee that his poetic talent would, with the years, develop and mature so greatly, both inwardly and outwardly. Even then, the "attraction to words" was particularly characteristic:

Thoughts wind about sobbing winds,
The train rumbles on, trying to catch the sound:
"Titata, totata, tatara, titata"
Pounding the ear from the ground.

From the land where the light of the sun
Pours forth from the sky, burning and clear,
I brought myself a present
Resonant castanets for all to hear. . . .
Prostrate, face downward,

And covered with nightly blue
Trustfully, my lips searched your nipples,
Rubbed with wormwood, oh mother-earth so true![3]

I remember our first meetings in Moscow. Already at the time, he was a notable contributor to *The Scales* and *Golden Fleece*.[4] Even then he had "worked out" his appearance, his bearing, and he spoke and read with extreme care. He was of medium height, very stocky, with wide and square shoulders, small hands and feet, a short neck, a large head, and dark brown and curly hair and a beard. Despite his pince-nez, he contrived cleverly to be a rather artistic type, akin to a Russian peasant and an ancient Greek, to an ox and a curly horned ram. Having lived for a time in Paris, amid mansard poets and painters, he wore a wide-brimmed hat and a velvet jacket and cape.[5] In his stance toward people, he adopted an old-world French vivaciousness, sociability, good manners, and a kind of comical graciousness, something that was very artificial, exquisite, and "enchanting," all of which he was inclined to naturally.

Like almost all his fellow poets, he always read his verse extremely willingly, everywhere he could, at any length, upon the slightest urging of onlookers. When he began reciting, he drew up his heavy shoulders and chest, with its almost womanly bust from under his shirt. He took on the air of an Olympian, a thunder, and began howling in a powerful and tormented way. When he finished, he threw off this threatening and powerful mask right away. Once again there appeared the enchanting, ingratiating smile, the soft, salon-like bubbling voice, a kind of joyful readiness to lie like a rug under the feet of his companion—and also, if he was at someone's house for supper or tea, his cautious but untiring and voluptuous appetite. . . .

I also remember our meeting in Moscow at the end of 1905. At that time, nearly all the prominent poets of Moscow and St. Petersburg had become passionate revolutionaries suddenly—incidentally, with strong support from Gorky and his newspaper *Struggle*, to which Lenin himself contributed.[6] It was during the first Bolshevik uprising that Gorky had entrenched himself firmly in his apartment on Vozvizhenskaya Street. He never stepped out of the place for a moment. Day and night he surrounded himself with a guard of Georgian students, armed from head to toe, assuring everyone that extreme rightists would make an attempt on his life. Also day and night, he received a huge number of guests—friends, admirers, "comrades," and contributors to *Struggle*, which he was publishing at the expense of one Skirmunt and which captivated immediately the attention first of the poet Bryusov, who, in the summer of that year, was still delivering monarchist speeches and demanding that a cross be erected on the dome of St. Sophia, and then of Minsky, with his anthem "Workers of the World, Unite!" and of many others.[7]

Voloshin's works were not published in *Struggle*, but it was precisely somewhere—in Gorky's or Skirmunt's home—that I first heard him recite songs that were quite new for him:

> To the Russian people: I am the Angel of Vengeance!
> Into dark wounds and upturned earth I spread my seeds.
> Gone are the times of patience and remorse.
> My banner is bloodred! My voice-alarm tells my deeds![8]

I also remember meeting his mother at the home of a writer. I was sitting next to Voloshin at tea, when a woman of about fifty entered the room suddenly. She had short gray hair [and wore] a Russian blouse, baggy velvet trousers, and boots with patent leather tops. I almost asked Voloshin who that ridiculous person was.[9]

I remember all kinds of rumors about him: when he joined his fiancée abroad, he always arranged their first meetings in the belfry of a Gothic cathedral; he went about his house in Crimea in nothing but a "tunic," a long sleeveless shirt that must have looked very funny on his fat figure and short hairy legs. . . . [10] It was also around this time that he wrote an autobiographical note, reproduced in facsimile in *A Book about Russian Poets*, which I still happen to have, and which is also rather funny in spots:

"I do not know what about my life would be interesting to others. So I will cite only things that are important to me.

"I was born in Kiev on May 16, 1877, *on the Day of the Holy Spirit*.

"The events of my life embrace countries, books, and people.

Countries: the first impression—Taganrog and Sevastopol; conscious existence—the suburbs of Moscow, the Vagankovo cemetery, machines and railroad workshops; adolescence—the forests around Zvenigorod; at fifteen—Koktebel in the Crimea—the most important and precious place in my life; at twenty-three—the desert of Middle Asia—the awakening of self-knowledge; then Greece and all the coasts and islands of the Mediterranean—the spiritual homeland I found there; the last phase—Paris—the awareness of rhythm and form.[11]

"Books-as-traveling companions: from the age of five, Pushkin and Lermontov; from the age of seven, Dostoevsky and Edgar Allan Poe; from the age of thirteen, Hugo and Dickens; from the age of sixteen, Schiller, Heine, and Byron; from twenty-four on, the French poets and Anatole France; books of recent years—*Bhagavad-vita*, Mallarmé, Paul Claudel, Henri de Régnier, Villiers de l'Isle-Adam—India and France.[12]

"People: Only in recent years have they come to occupy a greater place in life than countries and books. But I will not name them. . . .

"I began writing poetry around the age of thirteen, to paint at the age of twenty-four. . . ."

At the time, he also read everywhere another one of his celebrated poems, about the French Revolution, which also contained a number of strikingly theatrical lines:

That supple, passionate body of mine,
The mob trampled under its feet. . . .

It was also heard that he was taking part in the construction of an anthroposophical cathedral somewhere in Switzerland.[13] . . .

In the winter of 1919, he arrived in Odessa from Crimea at the invitation of his friends, the Tseitlins, with whom he stayed.[14] As soon as he arrived, he immediately took up his usual activities—he recited his poems at the Literary-Artistic

Circle, then in a private club where almost all the writers from Moscow and Leningrad staying in Odessa at that time also read their works, for a certain fee, to the "bourgeois survivors" who were eating and drinking in the room.[15] There he put forth many new poems about all kinds of terrible deeds and people of both ancient and contemporary, Bolshevik Russia. I was amazed to see how much he had progressed in writing and reading poetry, how powerful and skillful he had become in both. At the same time, though, I listened to him with a certain irritation: a kind of "splendid" self-adoration and, given the circumstances of time and place, a blasphemous explosion of words! As usual, I kept asking myself: Whom, in the end, does he remind me of?[16]

His appearance was also threatening: his pince-nez glistened ominously; his body was swollen and raised upward; his thick hair, parted in the middle, curled up in ringlets at the ends; his beard was wonderfully round. His tiny mouth opened in such a refined way, but also howled and roared with such resonance and power. . . . Was he a hefty peasant from the days of Russian serfdom? Or a Priapus? Or a cachalot?[17]

Later, when we met at a party at the Tseitlins' home, he was again "the very kind and dear Maximilian Alexandrovich." As I examined him more closely, I saw that, with the years, his physical appearance had coarsened and he had grown somewhat heavier, but that his movements were still lively and light; crossing the room, he ran with short and quick steps; he spoke a lot and with great willingness; his entire being radiated sociability, benevolence to all, and contentment with everyone and everything—not only with what surrounded him in the light, warm, crowded dining room but even also with the huge and terrible things in the world at large, and in particular in the dark, terrifying Odessa on the verge of entry by the Bolsheviks.[18] With all that, though, he was dressed very poorly—his brown velvet shirt was already quite threadbare, his black trousers were shiny, and his shoes were beyond repair. . . . He was very much in need.

Here are some condensed extracts of notes I took at the time:

"The French are fleeing Odessa, and the Bolsheviks are approaching. The Tseitlins are boarding a ship for Constantinople. Voloshin is staying here in their apartment in Odessa. He is very excited, for some reason especially cheerful and lighthearted. The other evening I met him on the street: 'I'm turning the Tseitlins' apartment into a hostel for men and women poets. We must act; we mustn't surrender to gloom!'"

"Voloshin often spends evenings with us. As before, he is sweet, lively, and jovial. 'Enough of politics! Let's read poetry to each other!' He reads to us his *Portraits*. His portrait of Savinkov is excellent: he compares Savinkov to an elk."[19]

"As usual, Voloshin chatters nonstop, touching on an infinite variety of topics and only pretending that he is interested in his listeners. Of course, he goes into raves over Blok and Bely, and also Henri de Régnier, whom he is translating.[20]

"He believes in anthroposophy and insists that 'men are angels of the tenth circle' who have assumed the appearance of humans along with all their sins, so that one must always remember that a hidden angel lives even in the worst man. . . ."[21]

"We are trying to save the house of a friend in which we are living from being requisitioned. Odessa is now occupied by the Bolsheviks. Voloshin is taking the liveliest part in it all. He has come up with a 'Neo-Realistic Art School,' to be established at our house. He runs about trying to obtain a permit to open it and, in five minutes, has come up with a sign for it written in rather complicated language. He pours forth maxims: 'I recognize only Gothic and Greek architecture. They are the only ones without adornment.'"

"The artists of Odessa also survive in any way they can, organizing a trade union with house painters. The idea for such a thing comes, of course, from Voloshin. He says enthusiastically: 'We must return to the medieval guilds!'"

"A meeting (at the Artistic Circle) of journalists, writers, poets, also about the 'formation of a trade union.' It is very crowded, full of people and all kinds of writers, 'old' and young. Voloshin shines, runs about, and wants to talk about how writers must unite in a guild. With his cloak over his shoulders and a hat hanging down his back—its band fixed to a loop of the cloak—he comes out onstage quickly, gracefully, with small little steps. 'Comrades!' But suddenly wild cries and whistling break out. A horde of young poets on the entire back of the stage raises a furious row. 'Down with everything! To hell with old, rundown hacks! We vow to die for Soviet power!' Kataev, Bagritsky, and Olesha are especially outrageous.[22] The entire gang, 'as a sign of protest,' abandons the hall. Voloshin runs after them. 'They don't understand us. We must explain ourselves to them.'"

"The hands of the clocks have been set forward two hours and twenty-five minutes, and it is forbidden to go into the streets after nine. Voloshin sometimes spends the night with us. We have a little stock of lard and alcohol. He eats greedily, with relish, and keeps talking and talking about the most exalted and tragic themes. From his speeches on Freemasonry, it is clear that he is a Mason himself.[23] With his curiosity and other qualities, how could he have missed a chance to join such a group?"

"The Bolsheviks are inviting the artists of Odessa to take part in decorating the town for the First of May. Some seize the invitation with glee. One should not shrink from life, you see; besides, 'art is the most important thing in life and outside of politics.' Voloshin is also fired up to decorate the city in fantasies. He sees it as good to spread sheets decorated with rhombuses, cones, pyramids, and poetic citations over the streets and on the facades of houses. . . . I remind him that the town he wishes to adorn has neither bread nor water; that endless raids, searches, arrests, and shootings continue nonstop; and that nights are impenetrably dark, with lootings and horror. . . . In reply, he again insists that each of us, even a murderer or cretin, has a *hidden suffering Seraphim* within him; that nine Seraphims descend to earth and enter people to be burned and crucified; and that from them arise illumined and tempered faces. . . ."

"More than once I warned him: stop running after the Bolsheviks, who, after all, know perfectly well whom you were with yesterday. In reply, he chatters on, as do all artists: 'Art is outside time and politics. I'll take part in decorating the town only as a poet and an artist.' 'But what will you be decorating?' I say, 'your own gallows?' Nevertheless, he went. The next day in *Izvestia*: 'Voloshin comes crawling to us. All kinds of bastards are rushing to attach themselves to us. . . .'[24] Voloshin, filled with noble indignation, wants to write a letter to the editor. . . .

"The letter, of course, did not get published. I told him that it would not. But he would not listen. 'They have to publish it, they promised, I've already been to the editorial office.' But they wrote only that 'Voloshin has been removed from the artistic commission for the First of May.' He complained bitterly: 'This reminds me of the time when all the newspapers, having trampled on me for dethroning Repin publicly, would not give me space to respond to their bullying.'"[25]

"Voloshin is busy planning to escape Odessa to his home in Crimea. He burst in yesterday and announced joyfully that the matter is settled and, as it often happens, with the help of a pretty woman. 'Severnyi, the head of the Cheka, billeted himself in her apartment. Gekker introduced me to her, and she introduced me to Severnyi.' Voloshin is in raptures over him. 'Severnyi has a crystal-pure heart. He saves many people.' 'Approximately one for every hundred murdered?' 'All the same, he's a very pure man. . . .' Not satisfied with that, he even had the cruel naivete to tell me that Severnyi cannot forgive himself for letting Kolchak slip through his fingers, even though he supposedly once had him firmly in his hands. . . ."

"Voloshin is escaping to Crimea also with the help of Nemitz, the 'naval commissar and the commander of the Black Sea Fleet,' who, according to Voloshin, is also a poet who writes 'particularly good rondos and triolets.' They are now concocting a story about a secret Bolshevik mission to Sevastopol. The problem, though, is that there is nothing to take it there: Nemitz's entire fleet seems to consist of one sailboat that cannot be put to sea in any kind of weather. . . ."

"By the new calendar, Voloshin left Odessa (on that very same sailing boat) in the beginning of May.[26] He left with a traveling companion whom he called Tatida.[27] He brought her to our place the evening before he left, the two spending the night with us. In spite of everything, it was sad to see him go. We sat in the half darkness, with a small homemade night lamp—we were not allowed to use electricity—and treated our departing friends to very wretched fare. He was already dressed in traveling clothes—a sailor's jacket and a beret. His pockets were stuffed with various lifesaving pieces of paper for all occasions: one in the event of a Bolshevik search on leaving the port of Odessa, another in case they would meet the French or Volunteers at sea—before the Bolsheviks had entered Odessa, he had struck up acquaintances with both groups.[28] Nonetheless, that evening all of us, including him, were far from calm: God knows, how this voyage on a sailboat to Crimea would turn out. . . . We talked for a long while and, this time, peacefully, agreeably. After midnight we finally parted: our travelers had to be in the sailboat at the break of dawn. Deeply moved, we hugged each other and said good-bye. Then, for some reason, Voloshin recalled suddenly how one time in Robin's Café, he and Alexei Tolstoy decided suddenly to puff up their cheeks, slowly at first and then more and more forcibly—with the most serious, almost savage faces—and then, just as slowly, to let out their breath—and how a bewildered crowd began gathering about them, wondering what they were up to. Then he began doing a very good imitation of a bear cub."

He sent a postcard from Yevpatoria, dated May 16th:

"So far, we have reached Yevpatoria safely and have been waiting for a train for two days. We spent a day on Kinburn Spit, another in Ochakov, waiting for the wind. We were stopped twice by a French torpedo boat, tossed about for a night without wind in a swell, came under machine-gun fire around Ak-Mechet, galloped an entire night, changing horses, across steppes and decaying lakes, and are now stuck in a most filthy hotel, waiting for a train. Things are going slowly, but safely. Have come across a mass of the most fascinating human documents. . . . It is very pleasant to remember our last evening at your place, which finished off the entire unpleasant period in Odessa."[29]

Another letter, from Koktebel, arrived in November. I quote the beginning:

"Many thanks for your letter. Just now, during this time, I've been thinking of you for some reason, and your letter seemingly came as a reply to my thoughts. Leaving Odessa was only the beginning of my adventures. The Bolsheviks I either knew or met on the way ranged from sailor-scouts to an army commander, who, passing me off as an old friend, took me to Simferopol in his private railway carriage.

"I spent some time in my studio under enemy fire. The first landing of the Volunteers took place from the ship *Kagul*. I had become so friendly with the entire crew in Sevastopol that their first visit was to me on my terrace. . . .

"Three days after the liberation of the Crimea, I rushed to Ekaterinodar to save my friend General Marks, who had been accused unjustly of Bolshevism and threatened with execution. Alone, without any connections or friends, I obtained his release—something that the citizens of Feodosia cannot forgive, and now I live with the reputation of being a Bolshevik, my poetry also being seen as Bolshevik.[30]

"By the way: the first edition of *Demons Deaf and Dumb* was distributed in Kharkov by the Bolshevik 'Centrag,' and now (Volunteer) 'Osvag' in Rostov has chosen several poems in it to distribute as leaflets. It was only in July that I finally got home and sat down to peaceful work. . . . [31]

"I'm working exclusively on verse. Everything I wrote last summer I sent to Grossman for publications in Odessa.[32] So ask him about my poems on social themes. In the meantime, I'm sending to you for publication in the *Southern Word* two lyrical poems that I wrote last year and that have not appeared anywhere, as well as two short articles: 'The Paths of Russia' and 'Moonshine of Blood.' For the past two months I've been working on a large poem about Saint Seraphim, all tense and unsure as to whether I can cope with such a grandiose theme. It should form a diptych with 'Avvakum.'[33]

"I'll winter in Koktebel, made necessary both by my personal work and by the insane prices, which no amount of fees can keep up with. Speaking of fees: for my poetry, I now get ten rubles a line for verse and three for my articles. This is the minimum rate, but if *Southern Word* will pay more for verse, I'll not refuse.

"I would very much like for you, I.A., to read all my new poems that are with Grossman. I've tried to make them more realistic to modern times (in the cycle *Masks*, the poems: 'The Sailor,' 'The Red Guard,' 'The Profiteer,' and so forth).[34] I'd very much like to know your opinion of them.

"I'm still filled to overflowing with the impressions of this winter, spring, and summer. Truly I was able to examine Russia from top to bottom, through all its political parties: monarchists, clergy, Social Revolutionaries, Bolsheviks, Volunteers, brigands. . . . With all of them I had the opportunity to spend a few intimate hours in their own surroundings. . . ."

That was the last letter I received from him.

He has not been among the living for a long time now.[35] Of course, he was neither a revolutionary nor a Bolshevik, but, I repeat, he always behaved in a very strange way.

The year was 1919—one of the most terrible for Bolshevik crimes. Throughout all of Russia, the prisons of the Cheka were filled to overflowing. The police suspected everyone as counterrevolutionaries and seized whoever came their way. Every night they chased men, women, and children out of the prisons into the dark streets; stripped them of their shoes, clothes, rings, and crosses; and divided the things among themselves. With lamps in their hands, they chased them naked and shoeless out of the city, along the icy ground, into the wastelands. . . . First they worked their machine guns; then they hurled their victims, often still alive, into pits, which they somehow covered with dirt. . . . Who does one have to be to rattle on about such things on a lyre, to turn it into literature, to roll back one's eyes in a literary-mystical way? After all, Voloshin rattled:

Ripe nails are carried in buckets,
Berries are rolled into the mighty roar . . .
Ah, but youth is chased into the black grindstone
Pressed into wine and ready to pour.[36]

What is this one mournful languid "ah!" worth! But Voloshin pours forth even more sweetly:

Twist and turn, elemental snow,
Cover the ancient graves![37]

Vigils and incense are yours, dear youths, chased "to the black grindstone"! I have pitied you as one human being to another, of course, but what can you do, after all, the murderous Chekhists are the stuff of the "elemental snow":

I believe in the rightness of the supreme forces,
That have unchained the ancient ways,
And from the depths of charred Russia
I say: "How right your judgment of these days!"
One should to its diamond core

Temper all the thickness of life,
And if there is little wood in the foundry,
Then, O Lord, here's my flesh to the knife![38]

Most terrible of all is that these words were uttered not by a monster, but by a rotund and curly haired aesthete, a kind and tireless chatterbox and a great lover of food. Almost every day when he visited me in Odessa in the spring of '19, when the "black grindstone"—or, one can say, the not so curly Cheka on

Catherine Square—was "tempering thick life" in an extremely spirited way, he often read to me first his verse at the expense of that "snowy" and "charred" Russia and next his translations of Henri de Régnier, before he launched again into lively anthroposophical eloquence. At this point, I would immediately say to him:

"Maximilian Alexandrovich, leave all this for someone else. Better we have a bite to eat. I have some salo and spirits."[39]

And one had to see how, instantly, he quit his eloquence, and with what appetite did he, the poor hungry man, wolf down the salo, having forgotten completely about his ardent ereadiness, if need be, to surrender his flesh to the Lord.

Chapter 14

The "Third Tolstoy"

The "Third Tolstoy"—that is what people in Moscow often call the recently deceased author of the novels *Peter the First*, *Road to Calvary*, as well as many comedies, stories, and short novels under the well-known name of Count Alexei Nikolaevich Tolstoy.[1] He is called the third because there are two other Tolstoys in Russian literature—Count Alexei Konstantinovich Tolstoy, a poet and the author of a novel titled *Prince Serebryanny*, about the time of Tsar Ivan the Terrible, and Count Lev Nikolaevich Tolstoy.[2] I knew this Third Tolstoy rather well, both in Russia and in exile. He was remarkable in many respects. But what made him even more noteworthy was how he merged an exceptional lack of morality (which, after his return to Russia, ceded nothing to his most important colleagues serving in the Soviet Kremlin) with his rare native talents and great artistic giftedness.[3] In this "Soviet" Russia, where only Chekhists ask each other for advice, he wrote all kinds of things, beginning with street scenarios about Rasputin and the intimate life of the murdered tsar and the tsaritsa, many that were simply terribly vulgar and base, but, even so, talented.[4]

The Bolsheviks were extremely proud of him not only as the foremost "Soviet" writer, but also because he was, after all, a count and a Tolstoy, to boot.[5] Not for nothing did Molotov "himself" say at some "Extraordinary Eighth Congress of Soviets":

"Comrades! Before me is a writer well known to us all, Alexei Nikolaevich Tolstoy. Who does not know that this was the former Count Tolstoy! But now! Now he is Comrade Tolstoy, one of the best and most popular writers of our Soviet land!"[6]

Molotov's last words were deliberate: after all, somewhere Turgenev called Lev Tolstoy "the great writer of the Russian land."

As an émigré, people called him, first scornfully, Alyoshka, then indulgently and affectionately, Alyosha. Almost everyone found him entertaining. He was a cheerful, interesting conversationalist, a superb storyteller, a splendid reader of his own works, and a delightfully frank cynic. He was endowed with a good and very sharp mind. Although he loved to act as a somewhat eccentric and carefree ne'er-do-well, he was not only an adept opportunist and self-seeker but also a generous spendthrift. He commanded a rich Russian language, knew and felt everything Russian, as very few people do. . . .

As an émigré, he often behaved straightforwardly as "Alyoshka," a hooligan. He was a frequent guest at the home of rich people, whom he called bastards behind their backs, but everyone, knowing that he did such a thing, still forgave him. They would say, that's our Alyoshka!

In appearance, he was thoroughbred: tall, strapping, and thickset. His full, clean-shaven face was feminine. On suitable occasions, the pince-nez on his slightly tilted-back head helped him greatly to assume a haughty air. He always wore expensive and top-notch clothes and shoes. Inside, he walked with his toes turned inward—a sign of his stubborn and persistent nature. He played roles and spoke in diverse ways, always changing his facial expression. He first muttered under his breath, then screamed in a thin base voice. Sometimes, in some "salon," he lisped like a societal dandy. Most often, he laughed loudly, in such sudden, unexpected ways, quacking and letting himself go, his eyes popping out of his head. He ate greedily and drank a great deal. He confessed that, at other people's homes, he quenched his thirst and filled his stomach disgracefully but that, having awakened the next day, he wrapped a wet towel around his head right away and sat down to write. He was a first-class worker.

Was he really a count Tolstoy? The Bolsheviks are a sly bunch: the evidence they give for his genealogy is ambiguous and vague:

"A. N. Tolstoy was born in 1883, in the former Samara Province. He spent his childhood at a small estate of Alexei Bostrom, his mother's second husband, an educated man and a materialist. . . ."[7]

Straightforwardly, they say only: "He was born in 1883, in the former Samara Province. . . ." But where precisely? At the estate of Count Nikolai Tolstoy or Bostrom? Not a word about such a thing, only where he spent his childhood. Complete silence always surrounds Count Nikolai Tolstoy, as if he never existed.

Completely unknown is what kind of man he was, where he lived, what he did for a living, or if he had even seen, at least once in his life, the person who bore his name, but whose title he renounced only when he returned to Russia. For all the years I knew him and for all his frankness with me, he never uttered a single word about Count Nikolai Tolstoy. . . . [8]

As an émigré, he vaunted his title constantly, speculating on it in both literature and life. His passion for all kinds of material blessings was so great that when he returned to Russia, he pleased the Kremlin and the Soviet mob right away by writing not only vile scenarios but also lampoons on these very bourgeois whom he had eaten and drunk out of house and home and from whom he had "borrowed" freely. He also wrote the most absurd fabrications on alleged atrocities by Russian "White Guards" in Paris.[9]

Most likely, the facts as to when he was born and where he spent his childhood are completely accurate. But then what? From his personal testimony, Soviet biographers say:

"In 1905, during the first Russian revolution, Tolstoy wrote revolutionary verse. The following year, when tsarist satraps were turning the entire country into a prison camp, he came out with a booklet of decadent verse, which he later bought up and burned. He felt that there was no return to the past. . . ."[10]

Here begins a very awkward and out-and-out lie. It makes no sense whatsoever that in 1905 he wrote revolutionary verse—and that suddenly a year later, "when the tsarist satraps were turning the entire country into a prison camp," he came out with something so untimely as a "book of decadent verse" that later he allegedly began to buy up and burn!

What follows is even better:

"The first world war raised for Tolstoy a mass of new questions and tormenting riddles. . . ."

Truly only in Moscow can people lie so stupidly! Tolstoy—and a "mass" of questions and "new" ones to boot! That means that, earlier, the poor soul was besieged by a "mass" of some other questions! And suddenly there now appeared new ones, and "tormenting riddles" at that. I often witnessed how these questions and riddles tortured him, when, at someone's home, he would take something "on loan" for the tailor, for dinner in a restaurant, for rent on an apartment.

"Tolstoy was lost in the great October revolution. . . . He left for Odessa, spending the winter there. In spring 1919, he went to Paris. About his life in emigration, he wrote in his autobiography: 'It was the most burdensome period in my life. . . .' In 1921, he left Paris for Berlin and joined a group of *smenovekhovtsy*.[11] When he returned to the homeland, he wrote a series of works on White émigrés, about the complete savagery of the White Guard, about his angst as an émigré in Paris. . . . He was disenchanted with the dying gaiety of Parisian taverns, with the nightmares of White Guard executions and reprisals. . . . In the homeland, he also wrote satirical pictures of the mores of capitalist America, which the great Soviet poet Mayakovsky also penned in a genius-like way. . . ."[12]

When was all this published? And for whose amusement? In *New World* in Moscow, in one of the most important Soviet monthly journals to which the most well-known Soviet writers contribute.[13] Here, sitting in Paris, one reads: "The unchecked running wild of White Guards . . . the nightmares of White Guard executions and reprisals. . . ." Why did the White Guards run wild so terribly, most of all in Paris? Whom did they meet and execute? Why did the French government close their eyes to all these Parisian nightmares? Also rather strange is the "dying" gaiety of Parisian taverns that disenchanted Tolstoy, who, apparently, had been charmed by them previously. After all, so many years have passed since the time when he, disenchanted with White Guard nightmares, decided to flee to Russia, where now no satraps turn the country into a prison camp, where no one is murdered or executed by anyone.

But Paris still exists. It has not died, despite its "dying" gaiety when Tolstoy lived there. It has survived to our days in homerically debauched gaiety and lavishness. So, asserts one Yury Zhukov, a Parisian correspondent from Moscow, who wrote an article titled "In the West after the War," in the journal *October*, a Moscow monthly.[14] This Zhukov reports that, time and again, French monks, reeking of the most expensive perfume from a kilometer away, often walk along the great French boulevards and that, from morning to night, "curled and pomaded young men and women smooch and saunter aimlessly in deranged-looking attire." For some reason, this Zhukov also lied about me. I was seemingly "diminutive, dry-looking, with a squeaky voice and the face of a refined aesthete."[15] At one time, people said in Russia: "He is a bold-faced liar." How naive were those distant times! Now, after thirty years of the constant and daily practice of lying "Soviets," even the most pitiful Soviet Zhukov is a hundred times worse than any bold-faced liar!

Of course, Tolstoy died from laughter when, in his autobiography, he talked about his émigré angst, those nightmares that, allegedly, he had in Paris, the "mass" of all kinds of spiritual and intellectual torments during the "first Russian revolution" and the first world war, and how he "had lost his head" and fled from Moscow to Odessa, and then to Paris. . . . He always was an easy, carefree liar, but in Moscow, perhaps, he was so sometimes in a strained way, but I think, very much like an actor, not allowing himself to descend to that hysterical "sincere lying" that brought Gorky to the point of tears all his life.

I met Tolstoy between the first revolution and the first world war, about which Blok (lamenting the collapse of the "former") declaimed so tragically: "Children of Russia's terrible years, we cannot forget anything!"[16] I was then the fiction editor of the journal *Aurora Borealis*, started by a public figure, Countess Varvara Bobrinskaya.[17] One day a tall, strapping, and rather handsome young man appeared at the offices of the journal and introduced himself solemnly ("Count Alexei Tolstoy") and gave to me a manuscript, titled "Magpie Stories," a series of short and very deft trifles in the then fashionable "Russian style."[18] Of course, I accepted them. They were not only skillful, but with that special unrestrained freedom and ease (which distinguished Tolstoy's writings).

From then on, I began to be interested in him. First I read his "decadent booklet of verse," which, allegedly, he had burned long ago. Then I started to read all his writings. I soon saw how varied they were—how from the very beginning of his career, he showed a talent to put on the literary market only things that sold quickly, to changing tastes and circumstances. I never read his revolutionary poems, nor did I ever hear about them from Tolstoy himself. Perhaps, he attempted to write such things in honor of the "first revolution," but abandoned them quickly—either because he was bored by such writing or for the simple reason that this revolution collapsed rather quickly, even as Russian peasants—"God-bearers"—pillaged and burned many gentry estates.

I read his "decadent" booklet, but, as far as I can remember, I found nothing decadent about it. He was merely following what had entranced everyone at the time: stylizing everything that was old and fairy-tale-like Russian. Then came stories of gentry life, also written in the style of the time: satires, calculated caricatures, and deliberate (and not so deliberate) absurdities. It seems that he also wrote several comedies that were aimed at provincial tastes and therefore very profitable. As I have said already, he always adapted in a very resourceful way. Even his novel *Road to Calvary*, first published in Paris, in emigration, in an émigré journal, he, after his return to Russia, reworked so substantially to Bolshevik tastes that all the "White" heroes and heroines in the work become disillusioned fully with their earlier deeds, feelings, and strivings and become ardent "Reds."[19]

Also well known is his novel *Bread*, written to glorify Stalin, a piece of fantastic nonsense about a sailor who somehow gets to Mars and establishes immediately a commune there, and a lampoon titled "Black Gold," about Parisian "capitalist sharks," Russian émigrés who own oil. . . . [20] What his *Satirical Pictures of Life of Capitalist America* was about, I do not know.[21] Never having been to America, he, most likely, learned about life there from such well-known experts as Gorky and Mayakovsky. . . .

After our meeting at *Aurora Borealis*, I did not see Tolstoy for two or three years. I was either traveling with my second wife to various countries as far south as the tropics or living in the country, visiting Moscow and Petersburg rarely and for short periods of time.[22] But once, unexpectedly, Tolstoy paid us a visit at the Moscow hotel where we were staying, accompanied by a young black-eyed woman, a type of Eastern beauty, Sonia Dymshitz, as everyone called her, but whom, invariably, Tolstoy introduced as "my wife, Countess Tolstoy."[23] She was dressed simply and elegantly, but he, in a top hat and huge bearskin coat, looked like a strange, important landowner from the provinces. I greeted them with a courtesy befitting the situation, bowing to the countess. Then, unable to keep from smiling, I turned to the count and said:

"I'm very happy to renew our acquaintance. Come in, please, and take off your splendid fur coat. . . ."

Offhandedly, he muttered in reply:

"Yes, an heirloom, as they say, the remains of former luxury. . . ."

Perhaps, it was this very fur coat that was the reason for our sudden friendship. The count had a mind that was mocking, humorous, and sharply observing. Most likely, he understood my sudden smile and realized immediately that I was not one to be fooled. Moreover, he became friends quickly with people whom he found suitable. After we met two or three times more, he confessed with a quacking laugh:

"I bought this heirloom by chance, for next to nothing, its entire fur is moth-eaten, with disgusting bald spots. But what a grand impression it makes on everyone!"

Speaking about the importance of clothes, he grimaced, looking at me and saying:

"Nothing will ever come of you in life because you don't know how to sell yourself! You dress so unbecomingly. You're thin and all, and there's something about you that is ancient and portrait-like. You should grow a long narrow beard and a long mustache; wear a waisted frock coat and shirts made of Dutch linen, with artistic open collars tied with large black silk bows; long hair down to your shoulders, parted in the middle. You should grow wondrously long nails; adorn the index finger of your right hand with some kind of mysterious ring; and smoke small Havana cigars, not vulgar cigarettes. . . .

"You think that's hoodwinking? But who doesn't hoodwink now in one way or another? You yourself say such a thing constantly! It's true. One person, you see, is a symbolist; a second, a Marxist; a third, a futurist; and a fourth, allegedly a former tramp. . . . [24] Everyone dresses up: Mayakovsky wears a woman's yellow blouse; Andreev and Chaliapin, peasant caftans, loose Russian shirts, and boots with patent leather tops; Blok, a velvet shirt and curls. . . . Everyone hoodwinks, my dear fellow!"

Having moved to Moscow and rented an apartment on Novinsky Avenue, in the home of Prince Shcherbatov, he hung on the walls a few old, blackened pictures of some important old men. To his guests, he muttered with feigned indifference: "Yes, all this is familial rubbish"; but to me, he said with a laugh: "Bought them at the market by Sukharev Tower."[25]

Until October 1917, when the Bolsheviks seized power, Tolstoy and I were on friendly terms, but then we quarreled twice. Life had become very difficult, famine was beginning, one had to spend a lot of money to eat the least bit decently, and funds were acquired only by being base. One of the Muscovite taverns hosted "A Musical Snuffbox": speculators, card sharps, and prostitutes gorged on pirozhki at a hundred rubles a piece and drank some revolting cognac-like stuff, while poets and prose writers (Tolstoy, Mayakovsky, Bryusov, and others) read their own and other people's works, choosing the most obscene among them and emphasizing all the lewd words fully. Tolstoy suggested that I should also read my works there, but I was offended and we quarreled.[26]

Then there appeared Blok's "The Twelve," which became famous later, when his diaries were published, and when shortly before the "February Revolution," he wrote:

"The mutiny of lilac-purple worlds is dying down. The violins, praising phantoms, reveal their truthful nature. The bitter smell of almond trees fills the rarefied air. A huge catafalque swings in the light-purple twilight of the boundless world. On it lies a dead doll whose face recalls the one shone through the heavenly roses. . . ."

Or just as devilishly poetic:

"Hardly had my wife become my bride, when the lilac measures of the first revolution seized us and drew us into the whirlpool. Having wanted destruction for so long, I was the first to be drawn into the gray purple of the Northern Star, into the mother-of-pearl and amethyst of the snowstorm. After the storm had passed, there opened the iron emptiness of the day, threatening a new blizzard. Now again a squall swoops down—its color and smell I cannot discern."[27]

The "squall" was the February Revolution, and, even for Blok, its color and smell became quite apparent right away, although earlier it did not demand such things. The tsarist period of Russian history had come to an end (courtesy of the Petersburg garrison that did not want to go to the front). Power had passed to the Provisional Government; all the tsarist ministers were arrested and imprisoned in the Peter-Paul Fortress. For some reason, the Provisional Government invited Blok to the "Extraordinary Commission" to investigate the activities of the ministers.[28] Blok received a salary of 600 rubles a month—a considerable sum at the time—to go to interrogations. For a while, he himself took part in the proceedings and, as later became known, ridiculed interrogees in his diary in a revolting way.[29] Next came the "Great October Revolution." The Bolsheviks now put into the same fortress the ministers of the Provisional Government, two of them (Shingaryov and Kokoshkin) killed without any questioning at all.[30] Blok went over to the Bolsheviks and became the personal secretary of Lunacharsky, whereupon he wrote a pamphlet titled "Intelligentsia and Revolution" and began demanding: "Listen, listen to the music of the revolution!"[31] After that he wrote "The Twelve," entering in his diary for posterity a very pitiful trifle: allegedly, how he penned "The Twelve" in a trance, "all the while hearing sounds of the fall of the old world."[32]

Writers in Moscow once organized a gathering to read and discuss "The Twelve" and I attended the event. I do not remember who exactly read the piece, but he was sitting between Ilya Ehrenburg and Tolstoy. The fame of the work, which for some reason people called a *poema*, had become completely beyond dispute; so when the reader finished, there reigned a reverential silence, then muffled exclamations: "Amazing!" "Remarkable!"[33]

I took the text of "The Twelve" and, leafing through it, said roughly the following:

"Ladies and gentlemen! To the shame of all humankind, you know what has been going on in Russia already for an entire year. There is no name for the senseless atrocities that the Russian people have committed since the beginning of February of last year, since the February Revolution, which people, absolutely shamefully, still call a 'bloodless' coup. The number of murdered and tortured people, almost all of them guilty of nothing, has probably reached a million. The tears of widows and orphans saturate the Russian soil. Everyone kills with ease. Soldiers still run from the front in crazed hordes; peasants in the villages, workers and all kinds of other revolutionaries in the cities. Soldiers, who, even last year, were stabbing officers with their bayonets, still continue along their murderous path, running home to seize and divide land not only from landlords but also from rich peasants. They destroy everything they can on the way, slaughtering railway workers and stationmasters and demanding from them trains and locomotives they do not have. . . .

"People from our village write to me such things as peasants, having plundered one gentry estate, amuse themselves by plucking the feathers from living peacocks and then let them go, watching as they, all covered with blood, dash about and, with piercing cries, crash into everything that comes their way. Last April, I was at the estate of a cousin in the Oryol District. One morning the peasants, having torched a nearby manor house and seeing that I had come running over to the blaze, wanted to throw me into the fire, into the flaming cattle shed with all the animals in it. A huge, drunken deserter started yelling that it was I who had set the shed afire so as to burn down the entire village next to it. What saved me was that I also began shouting at the scoundrel, even more obscenely than he had done to me. He was taken aback, as was the entire crowd who had pressed in on me. Gathering all my strength not to turn around, I freed myself from the crowd and walked away.[34]

"And here the other day an individual whom we all know as N.—I said his last name in full—came running in from Simferopol and said that workers and deserters in the city are literally walking up to their knees in blood and that they had burned alive an elderly retired officer in the stove of a locomotive.[35]

"Doesn't it sound strange to you that, in these days, Blok cries out to us 'Listen, listen to the music of the revolution!,' composes 'The Twelve,' and in his pamphlet 'Intelligentsia and Revolution' assures us that the Russian people acted completely correctly, when last October they fired at the cathedrals of the Kremlin, trying to justify such a terrible lie about the Russian clergy, the likes of which I know no equal: 'In these cathedrals,' they said, 'the fat-bellied priest, for entire centuries, has been selling vodka, hiccuping as he does!'

"As for 'The Twelve,' it is indeed an amazing work, but only because it is bad in all respects. Blok is an insufferably poetic poet. Like Balmont, he almost never utters a simple word; everything is beautiful and eloquent beyond all measure. Blok does not know, he does not feel that one can overdo everything in a high style. But after writing a great deal of verse that was purposely enigmatic, almost absolutely incomprehensible to everyone, and literarily fabricated, mystical, and symbolist, he finally has written something that is completely understandable.

"What an extremely cheap and trivial stunt: Blok takes a winter evening in Petersburg, so especially terrible now, where people are perishing from cold and hunger, where even in daytime one cannot go outside for fear of being robbed and stripped naked, and says: Look at what drunken, barbaric soldiers are now doing, but, in the end, all their actions are cleansed by the savage destruction of old Russia and, with Christ leading the way, they are his apostles:

Comrade, take up your gun and be a man!
Shoot bullets into Holy Rus,
Into its ancient,
hut-ridden,
and fat-assed can!

"Why in Blok did Holy Rus turn out to be hut-ridden and fat-assed? Apparently because the Bolsheviks, the fierce enemies of the Populists, have placed all their revolutionary plans and hopes neither on the village nor on the peasantry, but on the dregs of the proletariat, on the tavern poor, on tramps and paupers, on all those who have been seduced by Lenin's absolute decision to 'rob the robbers.'

"Here vulgarly does Blok mock this hut-ridden Rus, the Constituent Assembly (which the Bolsheviks promised the people before October, but dispersed, having seized power), the 'bourgeois,' the average citizen, the priest:

From place to place
A cable has a sign:
"To the Constituent Assembly
All power and fame!"

And here a cassocked man
Why not happy these days,
Comrade priest
With no name?

And here a young miss
In a Persian lamb
Slipped on the ice
And bam!—spread lame!

"'The Twelve' is a collection of rhymed verse, *chastushki*, some seemingly tragic, others dance-like, but pretending to be something Russian, folk-like.[36] All of it is so devilishly boring in its endless chatter and monotony, irritating in its countless ay, ay, ekh, ekh, akh, akh, oy, oy, rat-a-tat-tat, rat-a-tat-tat-tat. . . .

"Blok sought to come up with a folk language, folk emotions, but ended up with something so completely pulp-like, clumsy, and vulgar to the highest degree:

Bourgeois at a crossroads
His nose in collar tucked , , ,
Like a hungry dog, he is mute
Like a question mark—trash.

And the old world, like a mongrel cur
Stands behind, a tail between his legs . . .
Freedom, freedom, ekh, ekh is the cry
Without the cross, rat-a-tat-tat-bash!

Ekh, ekh, without the cross,
Rat-a-tat-tat-tat
And Vanka and Katka in the inn.
In her hose Kerensky cash!

Hey Vanka, you SOB.
Try and kiss me, you bourgeois!
Katka and Vanka are busy, they say?
With what you ask?—just write a dash.

The snow whirls, the driver yells,
Vanka and Katka fly along
'lectric light, on sleddie shafts they go , , ,
Akh, akh, they'll crash!

"This is folk language? *''lectric'*! Try and pronounce that! Also completely ludicrous is tenderness toward sled shafts—'sleddie shafts'—apparently that is folk, too. Here is something still more folk-like:

Hey Katya, my Katya,
You, my fat-mugged girl!
Baggy gray socks you wore.
Gorged on chocolate.
Caroused with cadets,
Now with soldiers you whore?

"Katka's story ends with her murder and the hysterical repentance of the murderer, some Petrukha, the friend of some Andryukha:

Again they fly at full speed.
The driver flies and howls and screams . . .
Stop! Stop! Andryukha, help me, bro,
Petrukha, run to the back, rat-a-tat-tat!

Glad now, Katka—Not a sound!
Lie there, carrion, in the snow!
Ekh ekh, it's no sin to have some fun!
Fly, bourgeois, like a little bird.

For my black-eyed beauty, for my dearest love,
I will drink your sweet little blood.

Rifles on their back, the twelve set out again
The male murderer faceless, below and above!

"The poor murderer, one of Christ's twelve apostles who are going off somewhere, completely unknown where and why, and of the group we know only Andryukha and Petrukha, who howl, sob, and repent—after all, how so always assumed and long known is how much the Russian criminal soul loves to repent:

Okh, native friends.
Loved this girl, I did,
Nights dark and drunken
Did I spend with this kid!

"'You bourgeois, fly like a small sparrow'—again the bourgeois, but no matter how you look at it, it is not his fault that Katka was taken by Vanka. Further, sweet little blood, sweet little love, sweet black-browed beauty, and nights drunken and dark—these hail as Russian style, first coarse, then saccharine, with so many countless exclamation marks as to make one fall ill. Blok has yet to calm down:

Because of her daring boldness
In her fiery eyes
Because of the crimson spot
On her right side,
Stupidly, I ruined her,
Ruined her in a fit of temper, I did . . .
Akh! Took her for a ride!

"In this arch-Russian tragedy, one thing is not completely right: the mix of Katka's thick mug and 'the daring boldness of her fiery eyes.' As I see it, fiery eyes suit a thick mug very little. Also not quite on point is 'the crimson spot'—at least not for such a refined connoisseur of feminine charms as Petrukha!

"From 'behind a curtain' Blok fools the public with complete nonsense. Carried away by Katka, he has forgotten completely his initial idea to shoot a bullet into Holy Rus, but has 'lodged one' into Katka instead, so that the story of her, Vanka, and the reckless drivers becomes the main content of 'The Twelve.'

"Only at the end of his 'poema' does Blok come to his senses to set things right and to get his story on track. Here again is a 'majestic step' and some hungry hound—again a hound!—and pathetic blasphemy: some sweet little Jesus (in a wreath of white roses and with a bloody flag) dances in front of these beasts, robbers, and murderers:

Above the storm, they walk—
With gentle, but majestic step,
Bloody flag in front, hungry hound behind,
And through the soft jewel-like snow
In a wreath of white roses bedecked
Leads Jesus Christ, most kind!"

"How can one not recall," I said as a final word, "what Faust said when Mephistopheles led him to the 'Witches' Kitchen':

Whom does a witch lead by the nose?
as if nonsense herds together
A hundred forty thousand fools!"[37]

When I finished, Tolstoy raised a row. One had to hear how he began screeching at me like a rooster and how theatrically he began yelling that he would never forgive me for my speech about Blok, that he, Tolstoy, was a Bolshevik heart and soul, and that I was a retrograde, a counterrevolutionary, and so forth.

No less strange was another famous work by Blok about the Russian people, titled "The Scythians," written (or "created," as his fans express it invariably) right after "The Twelve." How many contradictory love wails does Blok have there: "O, my Rus, my wife" and the print "patterned kerchief [reaching] to the eyebrows"![38] Here finally are all the Russian people precisely to please the squint-eyed Lenin and hailed by an Asian "with slanting and greedy eyes."[39] Addressing Europeans, Blok speaks in the name of Russia, no less arrogantly than, for example, Esenin ("I'll stick out my tongue like a comet, to Egypt will I spread my legs") or as the Kremlin now does day and night not only to all of Europe but also to America, which helped save these "Scythians" from Hitler:

You are millions; we, darkness unbound,
War with us, just you try!
We are Scythians; yes, we are Asians
With slanting and greedy eyes!

For long you looked eastward,
Our gems readily you sold!
And mocking, you set the time,
Your canons to have and hold,

To love as loves our blood,
Long have you not known such boon,

Forgotten have you loves.
That destroy and burn and ruin

We love flesh—its color, its taste
Its dense and deathly smell
Wrong are we to crush your bones
In our tender-heavy paw-like hell?

Happy are we to seize the reins
Of horses playful and brave,
To break their heavy backs
To subdue the stubborn slave. . . . [40]

In these comic threats, in this literary tommyrot that I have cited in part, several things are completely incomprehensible. What is meant by "our gems readily you sold"? Everything else is really precious: the theme of Asians; the slanting and greedy eyes; the taste and deathly smell of flesh; the tender, heavy paws; the crushed human skeletons; and even the broken backs of horses—although to break the backs of horses is not only stupid and vile but also impossible physically, so in no way can one understand why precisely "we have become accustomed" to such things.

"The Scythians" is a coarse reworking of Pushkin's "To the Slanderers of Russia."[41] The self-boasting of "The Scythians" is also not original. After all, it is an age-old Russian thing: "We toss our hats into the air!" (in other words, for us darkness unbounds). But even more remarkable is the fact that, precisely when "The Scythians" was being "created," there occurred something so decisive and so shameful, as never before in the entire existence of Russia. The Russian army, defending the country from the Germans, collapsed entirely; the truly "darkness-unbound Scythians," allegedly so threatening and terrible—"War with us, just try!"—were abandoning the front as fast as their legs could carry them; and, a month later, the famous "shameful peace" was signed by the Bolsheviks at Brest-Litovsk.[42]

At the end of May that year, my wife and I left Moscow for Odessa rather legally. A year before the February Revolution, I had rendered a great service to a certain freelance university instructor named Friche, an avid Social-Democrat and a writer who was giving lectures somewhere.[43] I saved him by petitioning the mayor of Moscow that he not be expelled from the city because of his underground revolutionary pamphlets. Now, under the Bolsheviks, this Friche had become something akin to a minister of foreign affairs. So I went to him and demanded that he give us a permit to leave Moscow immediately (and go to the station at Orsha, which lay beyond the occupied territories).[44] Bewildered, Friche not only hastened to grant my request but also even suggested that I journey to Orsha in a hospital train that was going there for some reason.

So we left Moscow—forever, as it turned out—and what a terrible, terrible journey it was! The train had an armed guard—in case of attack from the last of the "Scythians" who were abandoning the front. At night, it moved along in darkness with lights out as it passed by stations that were covered with vomit and excrement and filled with cries and songs—wild, drunken, and hysterical—that is, the "music of the revolution!"

That year, the Bolsheviks occupied only a small part of Russia. Everything else was free or occupied by Germans and Austrians and, with their consent and support, functioned independently. At that time also, there began the great exodus from Great Russia of people of all ranks and stations, of all ages, shapes, and sizes. Anyone who could, fled into still free and unstaring Russia.

It turned out that, after some time, Tolstoy was also among those on the run. His second wife, the poet Natasha Krandievskaya, together with their two children, came to Odessa in August; then he himself arrived.[45] There he greeted me as if nothing had happened between us, with full sincerity and passion the likes of which I had never seen him do, shouting:

"You'll not believe," he cried, "how extremely happy I am that I finally escaped those scoundrel villains entrenched in the Kremlin. You understand perfectly, I hope, that the reason why I yelled at you at the meeting regarding that idiot 'Twelve' and that I acted vilely all the time was because I had decided to bolt long ago and, moreover, as conveniently and advantageously as possible. I think that, God willing, we'll be back in Moscow this winter. No matter how bestial the Russian people have become, they have to understand what is happening! At the various stops in cities and stations on my way here, I heard such talk from good, long-bearded peasants, not only about all those Sverdlovs and Trotskys but also even Lenin himself, that it made my flesh crawl! 'Just wait, just you wait,' they said, 'until we get our hands on them!' And they will! As God is my witness, I'd now kiss the shoes of any tsar! My hand would not flinch to poke out Lenin's and Trotsky's eyes with a rusty awl if they fell my way—just as the peasants gouged out the eyes of the factory stallions and mares when they robbed and burned the country estates!"

That fall and, later, winter were very troublesome, the town changing hands and some fighting in the streets. We and the Tolstoys, though, lived in Odessa more or less tolerably, sometimes selling a thing or two to the various publishing firms that appeared in the south of Russia. Tolstoy also received a rather decent salary as the manager of a gambling club. In the beginning of April, however, the Bolsheviks took Odessa finally, panicking into retreat the French and Greek military forces that had been sent to defend the city. The Tolstoys fled swiftly by sea (to Constantinople and farther), but we were not able to leave with them.[46] A year later, having spent five months of unspeakable misery under the Bolsheviks before the city was liberated by Denikin's Volunteers—whose main army, in that second autumn, had already reached Moscow—we escaped first to Turkey, then to Bulgaria, Serbia, and finally to France.[47] At the end of January 1920, we again almost fell into the hands of the Bolsheviks and said farewell to Russia forever.

God alone knows why we did not perish on the Black Sea on our way to Constantinople. On a dark and dirty evening, when the Bolsheviks were already entering the city, we left for the port on foot and barely squeezed ourselves in among the countless swarm of other refugees, jamming into the small, dilapidated Greek ship *Patras*. There were four of us: my wife, I, the famous Russian scholar Kondakov, a massive old man about seventy-five years old, and a young woman, his former secretary and almost his nurse. We then sailed to Constantinople in a snowstorm that lasted two full days. The captain of the *Patras* was a drunkard Albanian who did not know the Black Sea. If it had not been for a Russian sailor on board ship, it would have gone down certainly with all its unfortunate passengers. We arrived in Constantinople in an icy twilight with piercing cold and snow. We docked around Stambul and had to walk to a shower in a stone shed—"for disinfection."[48] At that time, Constantinople was occupied by the Allies, and a French doctor ordered that we do so. But I so started shouting that Kondakov and I were "Immortels" (we were both members of the Russian Imperial Academy) that the doctor replied, "So much the better—the shower won't kill you," but he relented and let us go.[49]

Then, by someone else's order, we, along with our pitiful belongings, were thrown into a huge roaring van and rushed beyond Stambul to the so-called Fields of the Dead and left to spend the night in the completely empty ruins of an enormous Turkish home with broken windows.[50] We slept on the floor in complete darkness, finding out in the morning that the place had recently been a home for lepers guarded by a giant black man. It was only toward evening that we moved to Galata, into a building formerly occupied by the Russian consulate, where we again slept on the floor until our departure for Sofia.[51]

In fall 1919, when I was still in Odessa, under the command of Denikin, I received two letters from Tolstoy from Paris.[52] He wrote very seriously:

"At that time (in April) it was very sad for me to part with you. It was a difficult period, as if we were carried away by a wind and came to our senses only slowly, aboard ship. What we had to endure is beyond words. We slept with the children in a damp hold, alongside people with typhus and with lice crawling all over us. For two months, we sat on a remote island in the Sea of

Marmara.[53] It was a beautiful place, but we had no money. We then sailed for three weeks in a cabin that flooded daily from water from the soldiers' lavatory. But now all of this has been made up for by our arrival here (in France). It is so fine here and would even be better if it were not for thinking about how our relatives and friends are suffering back there."

In another letter, he wrote:

"Dear Ivan Alexeevich, Prince Georgy Yevgenievich Lvov (the former head of the Provisional Government, who is now in Paris) spoke to me about you, asking me where you are and whether you would consider being evacuated to Paris.[54] I replied that you probably would if you could be assured a minimum income for two people. I think, dear Ivan Alexeevich, that you would be well advised to agree right away. You will be guaranteed a minimum income and also have at your disposal the journal *Future Russia* (which has just started coming out in Paris) and another enormous publication, of which I have been invited to be the editor, along with editions of your works in Russian, German, and English.[55] The main thing, though, is that you will live in a plentiful and peaceful land, where the red wine is wonderful, with plenty of everything. If you decide to come or if I hear news of your arrival in advance, I'll rent a villa near Paris, at Saint-Cloud or in Sèvres, so that you and Vera Nikolaevna can live with us. It will be very, very nice. . . ."[56]

The first letter also had these lines:

"Send me, Ivan Alexeevich, your books and permission to translate your stories into French. I'll look after your interests and transfer the money to you honestly, that is, without taking anything for myself. People in Paris want to translate your works very much, but none of your books are here. . . .

"All this time I've been working on a novel, about eighteen to twenty sheets long. A third of it is done.[57] I am also earning money on the side, both honestly and otherwise—scenarios. . . . France is an amazing, splendid country, with stable foundations, a kind past, and comfortable homes. . . . No matter what people say, there can never be any Bolsheviks here. . . . I embrace you warmly and passionately, dear Ivan Alexeevich. . . ."

At that time, Constantinople, Bulgaria, Serbia, Czechoslovakia were full of Russian émigrés. So was Paris, where we arrived at the very end of March and where we were greeted not only by the joyful beauty of its spring but also by exceptional, countless Russians, many of whom were known all throughout not only Russia but also Europe. Here were several surviving great princes, millionaire businessmen, famous political and social figures, deputies of the State Duma, writers, artists, journalists, and musicians. In spite of everything, they were filled with hopes for the revival of Russia and excited by their new life and by the diverse activities that were developing more and more in all fields. Whom did we not meet, almost on a daily basis, in those first years of emigration, at all kinds of meetings and gatherings, and in private homes! Denikin, Kerensky, Prince Lvov, Maklakov, Stakhovich, Milyukov, Struve, Guchkov, Nabokov, Savinkov, and Burtsev. There were also the composer Prokofiev; the artists Yakovlev, Malavin, Sudeikin, Bakst, and Shukhaev; and the writers the Merezhkovskys, Kuprin, Aldanov, Teffi, and Balmont.

Tolstoy was right when he wrote to me in Odessa that one could not perish from inactivity and need in Paris. Quickly, we managed financially fairly well, and the Tolstoys, even better. But how could it have been otherwise? One morning, Tolstoy arrived at my place and said: "Let's make the rounds of the bourgeois and collect some money. We writers must start our own personal publishing house. There are enough Russian journals and newspapers in Paris where we can publish, but it is not enough. We need still more places to publish our works!"

So we took a taxi, visited several "bourgeois," explaining briefly to each one the purpose of our visit, and were received with marked cordiality. Within three or four hours, we had collected 160 thousand ranks, and that was thirty years ago! We soon started a publishing firm, which provided financial help not only for Tolstoy and me but for others as well. But the trouble with Tolstoy was that he never had enough money. He often said to me in Paris:

"Good Lord! How well we live in every way! Never in my life have I lived like this. Only the cursed money disappears terribly quickly in the chaos. . . ."

"What chaos?"

"I don't know what chaos. The main thing is that I absolutely hate empty pockets. To go somewhere in town, to look at all the store windows without being able to buy anything—that for me is genuine torture. I have a passion to buy things that are absolutely unnecessary and absurd! Besides, there are five of us, including an Estonian who looks after the children. So I have to wheel and deal constantly."

One time, though, he said something completely different: "If I were very rich, I would be devilishly bored. . . ."

But in the meantime, he had to wheel and deal, and wheel and deal he did. When he arrived in Paris, he met an old Muscovite friend of the Krandievskys, a well-off gentleman, and, with his help, he not only lived his early time there but also had clothes and shoes in ample supply:

"I'm no fool," he told me, laughing. "Right away I brought up a large quantity of underwear and shoes. I now have a full six pairs of the best shoes and on superb shoe trees. I also ordered three lounging suits, a dinner jacket, and two coats. . . . I also have excellent hats for all seasons. . . ."

In the first years of the emigration, several wealthy Russians and banks in Paris, hoping for a collapse of the Bolsheviks, were buying from exiles various properties they had in Russia. Tolstoy sold for eighteen thousand francs an estate that did not exist, and with his eyes popping out of his head, he told me:

"Understanding how idiotic it was, I laid it all out in a fitting way—how many acres, how much arable land, and other things—when they asked me suddenly: 'But just where is this estate of yours?'

"I was on the verge of making a quick exit like the son of a bitch I am, when luckily I remembered suddenly a comedy titled *Old Times in Kashira* and said quickly: 'It's in the Kashira District, near the village of Small Pants. . . .' And, thank God, I sold it!"[58]

In Paris, we got along with the Tolstoys in an especially friendly way, meeting with them often at the homes of our common friends and acquaintances, or Tolstoy also came to us with Natasha, or else he sent us little notes:

"Tonight we are having bouillabaisse from Prunier and such a Pouilly (ancient!), the likes of which no one has tasted, four kinds of cheese, cutlets from Poutine.[59] Natasha and I are afraid that no one will come. I beg you to be here at seven-thirty."

"Perhaps, you and the Tseitlins can stop by tonight, to drink a glass of good wine and to admire the lights of this wonderful city, which can be seen way into the distance from our sixth floor. For the occasion, Natasha and I will cover the foyer with new wallpaper."

But a year went by, then another, with less and less money, and Tolstoy began to grumble:

"I simply don't know what to do next! I've pocketed some thirty-seven thousand francs from everyone I could—as a loan, of course, as one says among respectable people—and now they turn pale whenever I turn up at someone's house for dinner or spend the evening, since they know that I'll approach someone and sigh in a feigned way: 'a thousand francs until Friday or a bullet in my head!'"

I had known Natasha Tolstaya as early as December 1903, in Moscow. One cold evening, she came to me, all covered in frost—it had trimmed the hat and squirrel collar of her fur coat, her eyebrows, and the corners of her mouth—and I was simply struck by her youthful charm and beauty. I was also delighted by her talented verse, which she brought to me to critique and which she continued to write. For some reason, though, she quit writing entirely in Paris. She also did not like the sparse life, saying:

"In emigration, of course, no one will die of hunger, but we can still walk in rags and beat-up shoes. . . ."

I think that she was highly instrumental in Tolstoy's decision to return to Russia.

In the summer of 1921, though, it seemed that Tolstoy thought about neither Russia nor Berlin. He and Natasha lived near Bordeaux, on a small estate that had been bought by Zemgor with the remains of its social funds.[60] From there, Tolstoy wrote to me:

"Dear friends, Ivan and Vera Nikolaevna, no matter how much you mistrust me, it would be useless to assure that I've been intending to write for a very long time, but I kept putting it off, for the sole reason that I would do it tomorrow. . . .

"How are you getting on? We're living in this hole in a tolerable way. We eat better here than in Paris, and on less than half the money. If we had 'guaranteed' funds, it would be paradise, but a boring one. But we don't have money at all, and if something good doesn't happen by fall, then we're in for a bad time. Write to me, dear Ivan, and tell me how your things are going. God won't send us death yet—so we have to groan on. I've been writing a great deal. I've finished a novel and am reworking the end. It'd be nice if both of you would come here to spend the winter together. The house is comfortable, and we would live splendidly and cheaply. We could go up to Paris. Think about it and write me. . . ."

But autumn came and nothing good happened to the Tolstoys. One autumn evening, returning home, we found his card written in words that were somehow fateful:

"I came to read my novel to you and to say good-bye."

The next letters came from Berlin:

"November 16, 1921. Dear Ivan, We have arrived in Berlin—my God, how different is everything here. It's very like Russia or, at any rate, close to it. Life here is very much the same as in Kharkov under the hetman; the mark is falling, prices are rising, and goods are disappearing. But, of course, there is one essential difference: there all life was built on sand, on politics, on adventure—the revolution was ordered only from on high. Here one feels peace in the masses of people, a willingness to work. The Germans work like no one else. There won't be any Bolshevism here, that's clear. Snow is on the streets, just as in Moscow at the end of November—everything is black. The boardinghouse we live in isn't bad, but you wouldn't like it. There's no wine at all, and this is a very great hardship. The local beer causes you to sleep and urinate right away. . . . We'll stay here for a while and then go—Natasha and the children to Freiburg, and I to Munich. . . . [61] Publishing here is in full swing. Marks are worth next to nothing, but living in Germany, you can earn enough. From everything one can see, local publishers have definite plans to sell books in Russia. The question of the old orthography will be decided positively. Soon, very soon, the times will be a bit easier than now. . . ."

"Saturday, January 21, 1922. Dear Ivan, Forgive me for not answering you for such a long time, but not long ago, I returned from Münster and, as you can understand, having gotten caught in the whirl of social life, kept putting off answers to your letters.[62] I'm surprised—why you wish stubbornly not to go to Germany, for example, on the money that you received from your benefit. The two of you could live for nine months in the best boardinghouse in Berlin: you could live like a gentleman, without worrying about a thing. My family and I, living now in two separate homes, spend between thirteen and fourteen thousand marks a month, that is, less than a thousand francs. If I get something for the performance of my play, I'll be set financially for the summer, that is, for the most difficult time of the year.

"We would have died from hunger in Paris. The fees are such that, it seems, to work for journals alone, it'd be difficult to feed a family—but books keep me going. But you could live comfortably on a per-line basis alone. . . . The market for books here is very large and grows every month. Everything gets sold, even books that would have sat around in prewar Russia. Everyone hopes that the market will expand with books moving into Russia: some have already made their way there—ordinary fiction, not to mention books with an appeasing tone. . . . In a word, there are already in Berlin about thirty publishing firms, all of them up and running in one way or another. . . . I embrace you. Yours, A. Tolstoy."

One line is particularly significant:

"If I receive something for the performance of my play, I'll be set financially for the summer. . . ." That means that he was still not thinking about returning to Russia. But this letter was his last one to me.

I met him for the last time accidentally in Paris, in November 1936. One evening I was sitting in a large crowded café and he also happened to be there. For some reason, he had come to Paris, which he had not visited since departing first to Berlin, then to Moscow. Seeing me from afar, he sent a garcon with a scrap of paper: "Ivan, I'm here. Do you want to see me? A. Tolstoy." I got up and went in the direction where the garcon was pointing. He was also walking toward me. When we came together, he began spurting in that laughter that was so well known to me and muttered—"May I kiss you? You're not afraid of a Bolshevik?"—poking fun at his Bolshevism so openly and directly, in that same rapid speech. He continued:

"I'm so terribly happy to see you, and I hasten to ask how long will you keep sitting here, living out your final days in poverty? In Moscow, you'd be greeted with church bells. You can't imagine how much you are loved, how you are read in Russia. . . ."

I interrupted him, joking:

"With church bells? How with church bells? After all, they're forbidden there."[63]

He began to mutter angrily, but with aroused earnestness:

"Please don't pick at me with words. You cannot imagine how you would live. Do you know the life I have, for example? I have an entire estate at Tsarskoe Selo.[64] I have three automobiles. . . . I have such a better collection of rare English pipes than the king of England himself. . . . Do you really think that your Nobel Prize will last a hundred years?"

I hastened to change the subject. I sat with him for a short while—friends I had come to see were waiting for me—he said that he was flying to London on the following day and that he would call me in the morning to meet me again. But he did not call—"things were in chaos"—so that was our last meeting.[65] In many respects, he was not who he was earlier: his entire massive figure had become leaner, his hair had grown thin, huge horned eyeglasses had replaced his pince-nez, he could not drink—forbidden by the doctors—so sitting at the table, all we had was a small glass of champagne. . . .

Chapter 15

Mayakovsky

I think that Mayakovsky will remain in the history of literature of the Bolshevik years as the most base, cynical, and harmful servant of Soviet cannibalism partly because of his posthumous tributes, partly because of his influence on the Soviet mob. With the sole exception of [the Soviet promotion of] Gorky, the propaganda about his worldwide fame, his great and primitive literary gifts, his immense acting talent, his unrivaled pandering to the mob, and his homeric falseness and unparalleled insatiability has rendered such terrible criminal assistance to Bolshevism to a truly "planetary degree." Soviet Moscow, not only with great generosity, but also to idiotic excess, has repaid Mayakovsky for all his praise of the city, for all his assistance in corrupting the Soviet people, in lowering their mores and tastes.

Mayakovsky is proclaimed in Moscow not only as a great poet. In connection with the recent twentieth anniversary of his suicide, the *Literary Gazette* in Moscow announced that the "name of Mayakovsky *has been stamped* on ships, schools, tanks, streets, theaters, and other activities *of long duration*.[1] Ten ships named *Vladimir Mayakovsky* sail the seas and rivers. 'Vladimir Mayakovsky' is painted on the armor of three tanks. One of these reached Berlin, to the Reichstag itself. Attacking aircraft *Vladimir Mayakovsky* struck the enemy from the sky. The submarine *Vladimir Mayakovsky* downed ships in the Baltic. The poet's name marks a square in Moscow, a metro station, a side street, a library, a museum, a region in Georgia, a village in Armenia, a settlement in the district of Kaluga, a peak in the Pamir Mountains, a club of writers in Leningrad, streets in fifteen cities, five theaters, five municipal parks, schools, collective farms. . . ."[2] (Karl Liebknecht was not so lucky: there is only one "Karl Liebknecht Collective Goose Farm" in all of Soviet Russia.)

Mayakovsky was useful even in his suicide, giving another Soviet poet, Pasternak, reason to address his beyond-the-grave shadow with a hint at something even more exalted:

Your shot was like Etna
in foothills of cowards and weaklings![3]

It would seem that a shot could be compared not to a mountain, but to some kind of movement—an avalanche, a volcanic eruption. . . . But since nowadays Pasternak is considered in Soviet Russia and by too many émigrés also a genius poet, he expresses himself as befits any such contemporary extremely gifted writer. Here is another example:

Poetry, I will swear at you
And die with a wheeze.
You're a suburb, a summer in a third-class seat,
Not a sagging sweet voice or tease.[4]

Mayakovsky was famous to a certain degree even before Lenin, standing out among all those swindlers and hooligans called futurists. His scandalous escapades were very tame, cheap, and like all the shenanigans of Burlyuk, Kruchyonykh, and others. He outdid them all, however, by the force of his vulgarity and daring. Hence his famous yellow jacket and savagely painted mug, and what a gloomy and evil puss it was! According to the recollections of one of his friends, he once went out onstage to read his verse to the public that had gathered for him to entertain. He came out, hands in his pockets, a cigarette hanging from the corner of his disdainfully crooked mouth. He was tall, stately, and strong; his facial features were prominent and sharp. When he read, he raised his voice to a roar or muttered to himself lazily, in a barely audible tone. When he finished, he addressed the public prosaically:

"Anyone wishing a punch in the nose is asked to get in line."

He next opened a book of verse, with the supposedly witty title "A Cloud in Pants."[5] Here, too, was one of his pictures for an exhibit—he was also a painter—something that was done helter-skelter on a piece of linen, with a glued-on everyday wooden spoon, and below was the inscription "The barber has left for the baths. . . ."[6]

If such a picture were hung somewhere in a market in some very remote little town, any petty bourgeois passer-by would have looked at it, shaken his head, and moved on. He would have thought that it was a joke by a complete fool or madman. But this joke amused Moscow and Petersburg; there it was considered "futuristic." And if a carnival clown at some fair cried out to onlookers to get in line for a punch in the nose, he would have been dragged out of the place right away and knocked out unconscious. But the Russian intelligentsia of the capitals is amused by the Mayakovskys of this world, agreeing fully that their escapades are called futurism.

On the day that the first Russian war was declared against the Germans, Mayakovsky crawled up the pedestal of the monument to Skobelev in Moscow and bellowed patriotic verses to the mob.[7] Later, he went about in a top hat, black coat, black gloves, and a black wooden cane so that, in such a getup, he would not be drafted. Finally, Lenin came to the throne, bald, squint-eyed, syphilitic, and mispronouncing his *r*'s and *l*'s, beginning that epoch about which Gorky, not long before his violent death, blurted out: "We are in the country, illumined by the genius of Vladimir Ilyich Lenin; in the country where, tirelessly and miraculously, works the iron will of Joseph Stalin!"[8] Having come to the throne, Lenin, "the greatest genius of all times and peoples," as invariably Moscow now calls him, pronounced:

"The bourgeois writer depends on moneybags, on bribery and corruption. Are you free, ladies and gentlemen writers, from our bourgeois public, who demands from you pornography in frames and pictures, prostitution as a 'supplement' to your sacred art?"

"Moneybags, pornography in frames and pictures, prostitution as a supplement. . . ." What verbal giftedness, what murderous sarcasm! Not for nothing does Moscow also affirm: "Lenin was a most great artist of the word." Even more remarkable, however, is what Lenin said soon thereafter:

"So-called 'freedom of creation' is a gentry anachronism. Without fail, writers must enter party organizations."[9]

So Mayakovsky became an inveterate servant of the RCP (the Russian Communist Party). He began to brawl and row in the same way he did when he was a futurist: to yell that "it was enough to live by the laws of Adam and Eve" and that it was time "to throw Pushkin overboard from the ship of modernity."[10]

Then it was my turn to be pitched into the sea. At some public gathering, he said firmly (according to E. D. Kuskova in her "Before and After" articles published last year in *New Russian Word*, regarding my "Autobiographical Notes"):

"Art for the proletariat is not a toy, but a weapon. Down with *buninovshchina*; long live the circles of progressive workers!"

What precisely was the "weapon" demanded by these circles or, speaking more simply, by Lenin and his RCP, the only party with which he replaced all other "party organizations"? The demand was for the "creation of a people with materialist thought, with materialist feelings." The call for this creation was for something even more cherished by Lenin and all his comrades in arms and successors: to wipe from the face of the earth and to spit on everything that was the past, that was considered splendid in this past; to conjure up accursed blasphemy—Lenin's hatred of religion was pathological—and the most savage class hatred; to transcend all limits of unprecedented obscene boasting and praise of the RCP; to sing tirelessly of the "leaders," their henchmen, their *oprichniki*—in a word, immediately to do everything for which it would be difficult to find a more suitable singer, a "poet," other than Mayakovsky, with his malicious, shameless, convict-like, heartless nature, with his vulgar street-like gullet, with his cart-horse poetics and coarse lack of talent even in those wooden verses that he passed off for some supposed new type of verse, and with his poetry to express everything foul and vile to which he was so devoted, all his false ecstasies before the RCP and its leaders, his devotion to both.[11]

Having become, allegedly, a fierce Communist, Mayakovsky only strengthened and developed to an extreme degree everything with which he had attained glory as a futurist, stunning the public with vulgarity and passion for all kinds of loathsomeness. Stars, he called "little globs of spit."[12] Writing in fractured verse about his trip to the Caucasus, he avowed that he *spat* first into the Terek, then into the Aragvi.[13] He loved words even more repulsive than globs of spit. He wrote to Esenin that his, Esenin's, name had been "*pockmarked* by the public."[14] He also poked fun at America, which he visited later, in the same way:

Mommy
gave her breast to her babe.
Who
With snot from his nose.
sucks
as if
in serious business
on a buck, not a breast.[15]

Mayakovsky loved the word "puke." He wrote (most likely, about himself):

Sheets of paper
Smoothness

The poet *pukes up*
With his pen
With the end of his lip,
Like a two-bit whore.[16]

Like Gorky, who allegedly hated gold terribly—many years ago, fiercely did he call New York the "City of the Yellow Devil," that is, of gold—he, Mayakovsky, also had to hate gold, as any sponger of the RCP is supposed to do. Thus he wrote:

As long as
The dollar
Is more generic than all poems,
Pawing,
Grabbing,
Approaches
Broadway, crystal-clad:
Capital—
Its shamelessness![17]

Gorky visited America in 1906; Mayakovsky, twenty years later, and it was simply horrible for the Americans. Not long ago, I read about it in *Literary Gazette*, published in Moscow, by the esteemed organ of the Union of Soviet Writers, in an article by some Atarov, who had on his table "a remarkable, a genuinely great book," the prose and poetry of Mayakovsky about America, [writing] that this book is the "fruit of Mayakovsky's visit to New York" and that after his arrival there "American businessmen had serious reasons for concern: a great poet of revolution had come into the country!"[18]

With the same force that he frightened and exposed America, he extolled the RCP:

We
Not with mugs, lowered low,
We—in new, future life,
Multiplied by electricity
And communism . . .

I would not be a poet,
If
I could not sing:
Amid five-pointed stars
The endless vaulted sky of the RCP.[19]

What was going on under this sky when these verses were being written? Even in Soviet newspapers one could read:

"On June 3rd, 142 corpses were collected on the streets of Odessa, people who had died of hunger; on June 5th, 187. Citizens! Sign up in your worker cooperative to collect the corpses!"

"A former member of the State Duma, Krylov, a doctor by profession, fell as a sacrifice to cannibalism near Samara. He was summoned to the village to attend to a sick person and on the way there was killed and eaten up."[20]

At this same time, the so-called All-Russian Elder Kalinin visited the south of Russia and also witnessed in a fully open way:

"Here some are dying of hunger, others are burying the dead, having tried to use as food the soft parts of those who have passed on."[21]

And what did they do, the Mayakovskys, Demyanovs, and so many others of their group, having gorged themselves "with full mouths," wearing silk underwear, living in the most famous "Podmoskovye," in the Muscovite dwellings of former millionaires?[22] What business was it of Vladimir Mayakovsky, all that was happening under the sky of the RCP? What sky, other than this one, could he see? Truly, has it not been said that a "pig never sees the sky"? Under the sky of the RCP at the beginning of Lenin's reign, the "revolutionary people" went up to their knees in blood, then there was the bloodletting that occupied Felix Edmundovich Dzerzhinsky and his comrades in arms. In those years, Vladimir Mayakovsky outdid even the most inveterate Soviet villains and scoundrels, writing:

To the youth who has pondered life,
And is deciding—
In whose steps to follow.
I say: do not ponder anymore:
But follow
Comrade Dzerzhinsky![23]

He, calling on Russian youths to become henchmen, reminded them of the words of Dzerzhinsky about himself, complete nonsense from the mouth of a monster who destroyed thousands upon thousands of lives:

"He who loves life so powerfully will, as I do, give his life for others."[24]

Together with such calls, Mayakovsky did not forget to glorify the very creators of the RCP, in a personal way:

The Party and Lenin
Who is more valuable than mother-history?

I want
The pen as a bayonet.
Iron
Factory-made
So that
From the Politburo
Stalin can write reports
About the work of verse.[25]

His glory as a great poet keeps growing and growing. His poetic creations are published in "enormous runs by personal order of the Kremlin." For every line, even for one word, journals pay him royalties that are so high that he travels often to "repulsive" capitalist countries. He has been to America. He also has visited Paris, always staying there for a long time, ordering suits and underwear in the best Parisian houses, and choosing to dine in the most capitalist restaurants. He also "spat" in Paris, announcing with the languid fastidiousness of a sated clown:

I do not love
Parisian love—
Any self-taught woman
Adorn cheeks,
Stretching, I begin to dream,
Having said "hey, Rover"
To dogs of savage passion.[26]

Seemingly, Gorky was the first to christen him a "great poet."[27] He invited Mayakovsky to his dacha in Mustamyaki, to read at his place his poem "The Backbone Flute" to a small and extremely select society. When Mayakovsky finished his *poema*, Gorky, with tears in his eyes, shook his hand and said:

"Wonderful, powerful. . . . A great poet!"[28]

It was only several years ago that I read in *Housewarming*, at the time still published in New York, something that was completely remarkable:

"Over the past few years, attempts to exclude Mayakovsky from Russian and world literature have been consigned to the dark archival past."[29]

This was the beginning of a small article by Mr. Roman Jakobson, a very eminent Slavicist, extremely well known for works on *The Lay of the Host of Igor*, he, a native Russian who once studied in a high school with Mayakovsky in Moscow, who was first a professor in Prague, then in New York, and given a chair at Harvard University, the best school in America.[30]

I do not know who "tried" to dethrone Mayakovsky—it seems no one. But Mr. Roman Jakobson has worried in vain. Regarding world literature, he, of course, has somewhat let his tongue run away with him: together with *The Lay of the Host of Igor*, the works of Mayakovsky will hardly be in it, but in the future, free history of Russian literature, Mayakovsky, without a doubt, will be mentioned in a fitting way.

CHAPTER 16

Hegel, a Tailcoat, a Snowstorm

Revolutionary times are not merciful. People are beaten and ordered not to cry. Anyone who does so is seen as a criminal, an "enemy of the people," and, in the best case, a vulgar philistine, a lowbrow. In Odessa, before the Bolsheviks seized it for a second time, I once talked publicly about what the Russian "revolutionary people" had done already in the spring of 1917, especially in provincial cities and villages.[1] At that time, I had arrived at the estate of my cousin, in the province of Oryol. By the way, I said that at one manorial estate around Yelets, the peasants, robbing the place, plucked out the feathers of all the peacocks and let them go, bloodied, with desperate wails, to fly and rush about wherever they could.[2] For this story, I was scolded severely by Pavel Yushkevich, one of the main contributors to the Odessa newspaper *Worker's Word*, who published these lines for my edification:

"One cannot approach revolution, respected academician Bunin, with the criteria and understanding of a criminal news reporter. To mourn your peacocks is philistinism and lowbrow fare. Not for nothing did Hegel teach about the rationality of all existence!"[3]

I answered him in an Odessa Volunteer newspaper that I was editing at the time, saying that plague, cholera, and anti-Jewish pogroms can also be justified if one believes Hegel in such a sacred way, but that nonetheless I felt sorry for the peacocks at Yelets.[4] After all, they did not suspect that Hegel had existed in the world and in no way could take comfort in him.

I often recalled all this in Constantinople, when, having fled the Bolsheviks who controlled Odessa firmly for a second time, my wife and I finally became émigrés (in the beginning of February 1920) and felt that we also had become peacocks shorn of all our feathers. I had visited Constantinople often in earlier, peaceful years.[5] Now, as if on purpose, I landed there for the thirteenth time, and this fateful number justified me fully.

In complete contrast to the past, everything was extremely sad in Constantinople. Previously, I saw it always in the splendor of its spring-like days, merry, noisy, and cordial. Now it seemed poor, gloomy, and dirty from rain or melting snow. A damp, sharp wind knocked me off my feet at its embankments and at the bridge in Stambul. The Turks were taciturn, oppressed by the occupation of the Allies, their contemptuous power over them. They were sad and tender only with us, Russian refugees, who were even more disenfranchised than they, more unfortunate to the *n*th degree in all respects.[6]

Time and again in those days at Constantinople, I was seized by a feeling of joyous gratitude to God for the spiritual respite with which, at long last, he had delivered me from everything that I had experienced in Russia for the past three years. But our material situation was no cause for joy. N. P. Kondakov, with whom we had abandoned Odessa, and I were inseparable in Constantinople. We had to search for a permanent haven and a means to live in some Slavic country—in Sofia, Belgrade, Prague—where émigrés could somehow settle more easily. Having waited for visas and a first train—at the time both were still extremely rare after all the destruction that the four-year war had brought to Europe and the Balkans—we left Constantinople for Sofia.[7]

I had an official document to inform our ambassador in Belgrade about the state of our affairs both at the front and in Odessa. I was supposed to come to Belgrade—long had I hoped that somehow I could settle there—but on the way, my wife and I lived for almost three months in Sofia. That we did not perish there, just as we did not die on the Black Sea, was a miracle.

At that time, the French who occupied Bulgaria arranged housing for Russian refugees. In Sofia, they settled many of them in one of the large hotels, including the Kondakovs and us.[8] So we began our exile amid a multitude of typhus-ridden people, who could have infected us easily. Several days before our departure from Sofia, I, along with others, was invited to an evening bash at the home of a Bulgarian poet, who also had a tavern. I stayed almost until dawn—as the host and the Bulgarian minister of war, who was also among the guests, were determined to keep me there. In an outburst of friendly feeling, the minister even cried out:

"I'll arrest you if you take it into your head to leave!"

I returned home only at dawn—and not entirely sober—and fell into a deep sleep. Only around eleven that morning did I jump out of bed, recalling in horror that I had been invited to a political lecture by Ryss, a very sensitive individual, and that the lecture was to have begun at nine—in Sofia, public lectures were often in the morning. Seeking to share my distress, I ran into my wife's room, which was right across from mine. Ten minutes later, I returned to my room but could hardly stand. The suitcase that contained all our belongings had been robbed down to the last item.[9] Only things of no value were tossed about the floor. Now we were completely destitute, in a state of total despair. Locks for suitcases were rare; so it was impossible to find keys for them. But when I had awakened that morning, I had unlocked the suitcase to take out a gold watch, to find out the time. Sensibly, I did not take it with me since I knew that I would be coming home late at night through dark and deserted Sofia. Having realized that I had left the suitcase unlocked and that I had left the watch on the nightstand next to the bed, I saw that it seemed also to have disappeared.

Fate, though, turned out to be surprisingly magnanimous: it had exacted a large bribe from me, but it also had saved me from a certain death. Almost immediately after I had fallen into complete poverty, someone, I do not recall who precisely, brought me the terrible news about what had happened where Ryss was supposed to have given his lecture. Less than a minute before he was to appear, some kind of "hellish machine" exploded under the stage, and several people in the first row—most likely where I also would have been sitting—were killed outright.

The person who had robbed us was known fully not only to us but also to all the inhabitants of the hotel. The bellboy was a Russian, "the little Bolshevik," as everyone called him, a yellow-haired chap who wore a small foul frock coat and a dirty shirt with a collar fastened at the side. His girlfriend was a maid, a quiet lass not unlike the cheapest prostitutes in the port of Odessa. She was called "a personality *mystérieuse*" by the detective sent by the Bulgarian police to arrest both her and the Russian. The French, however, interfered in the affair and ordered that the investigation be stopped. The thief could also have been one of the Zouaves who lived on the ground floor of the hotel.[10]

The Bulgarian government offered me complimentary passage as far as Belgrade in a separate third-class train car, which was the safest from typhus-bearing fleas. It also furnished us with a small sum of money until we got there. Once in Belgrade, though, we had to live in this railcar on sidetracks alongside the station—so overcrowded was the city at the time—and in no way could I get settled. I even spent what the Bulgarian government had given to us for food.

The Serbs helped us Russian refugees only to exchange those "little bells" (Denikin-backed thousand-ruble notes) that several of us had in our possession, for nine hundred dinars each; but they exchanged only one "bell" per person.[11] I decided to take up the matter with Prince Grigory Trubetskoy, who was stationed at our embassy. I asked that he make an exception for me—to exchange two or three "bells" at a time because I had been robbed in Sofia. He looked at me and said:

"I was informed of your arrival. Are you an academic?"

"Yes, I am," I answered.

"Precisely with which academy?"

This was an insult. Restraining myself as much as I could, I replied:

"I can't believe that you've never heard of me."

He blushed and pronounced sharply:

"All the same, I'll not make an exception for you. I bid you farewell."

I took my nine hundred dinars, and in my distress, forgetting that I could get an additional nine hundred for my wife, I walked out of the embassy, completely beside myself.

So now what was I to do? To return to Sofia, to that repulsive and terrible hotel? In a daze, I stood on the sidewalk and thought to trudge back to my railcar on the sidetracks, when, suddenly, a window on the ground floor of the embassy opened. Our consul shouted at me:

"Mr. Bunin, we've just received a telegram from Paris from Mrs. Tseitlin concerning you: a visa to Paris and a thousand French francs."[12]

In the first years of the twenties in Paris, we sometimes received letters from Moscow with all kinds of truths and lies. Most often, we heard from my nephew (who died fifteen years ago), the son of my cousin, whom I have already noted and at whose estate, in the village of Vasilievskoe, I had lived for long periods of time for many years, right up to our flight to Yelets and, later, to Moscow, and where at dawn on October 23, 1917, I feared absolutely rightfully that I would be murdered by local peasants, who all, inevitably, had gotten drunk the day before, on the Feast of Our Lady of Kazan, their major holiday.[13]

In chronological order are several excerpts, rather remarkable in their own right:

"I'm going bald. For almost four years now, I've not taken off my hat because of the cold. I even sleep with it on."

"That famous actress about whom I've written has died. Passing from this life, she lay in a shirt, blackened with dirt, terrible looking, like a skeleton, her hair ridden with lice and cut in clumps, surrounded by doctors with burning splints in their hands."

"I was at the home of the old countess Belozerskaya. She was sitting in rags, hungry, in the terrible cold, and smoking shag."

"I was gasping from bronchitis. With great difficulty, I got from a pharmacist I knew some kind of ointment to rub on my chest. One time, I set out for the bathroom, and an old neighbor ran up to me and started to devour the ointment. There he was, his entire body shaking, his fingers digging into the jar and gorging himself."

"The other day one of the tenants in our building went to his neighbor to find out the time. Having knocked, he opened the door and saw the man's face directly in front of him: 'Could you please tell me the time?' But his neighbor remained silent, only grinning in a strange way. The tenant asked again—and again the neighbor remained silent. So he slammed the door and left. How did it end? The neighbor was standing, his head in a noose, his feet barely touching the ground. He had hammered a crutch into the lintel and gotten hold of a whip. . . . The other tenants came running, took him down, and lay him on the floor. His leaden hand pressed a note: 'The kingdom of Lenin will have no end.'"

"Several of the people are resettling in Moscow. Natalya Palchkova is here with all her buckets and tubs. She came 'lock, stock, and barrel.' It is impossible to live in the village, she says, mostly because of young men there: 'genuine pirates, predators.' Masha has also come—remember the lass from the house of Fedka the Red? There are advertisements for Samoyeds and 'Tartar classics,' but railway connections are hellish. Transferring at Tula, Masha sat at the station for a full three days, not moving at all, waiting for the train to Moscow. Zinka, the daughter of the smithy at Vasilievskoe, is also here. She traveled for an endlessly long time, crammed terribly in a crowd of peasants. Sitting all the time, she guarded her basket, woven from branches, on which sat her boy, an idiot with a pumpkin-like head. In Moscow, she took him to the Art Theater—to see *The Blue Bird*."

"Not long ago, one of our acquaintances, a well-known scholar, lost a ruble and, as he told me, did not sleep the entire night from grief. His wife remained in the country. She was given a corner in the vestibule behind some cupboards in their former home, which had long been seized and occupied by peasants and their wives. The floor was dirty, the walls were stripped and smeared with the blood of bedbugs. . . . What a way to live out your life, sitting behind cupboards!"

"Some red-faced old man with a head of gray curly hair, a drunkard, lives in our courtyard, in a basement-like caretaker's lodge. A completely new court uniform, long, large, and covered with gold turned up somewhere at his place. He dragged it around for a long time through the yard and the snow, making the rounds of apartments and wanting to sell it for drink, but no one bought it. Finally, a peasant whom he knew came from the country to Moscow and purchased it. 'Don't worry about it,' he said. 'This uniform's well worth the money! I can plow pleasantly in it, for example. Not a drop of rain will penetrate it. It'll keep me warm, the whole thing is in its clasps. It won't wear out a bit!'"

"Others of our countrymen have begun to show up in Moscow. The other day our former gardener appeared. He came, he said, 'to meet his *barin*,' that is, me. At first, I did not recognize him. Since our separation, a red-haired, forty-year-old peasant, intelligent, tidy, hale and hearty, had become a broken-down old man with a gray-white beard, with a face yellow and swollen from hunger. He kept crying, complaining about his difficult life, asking me to get him a place somewhere, and not fully understanding who I was now. I collected some rags from friends and gave him some rubles for the trip home. Trembling, he shoved the rags into his beggarly sack. With tears, he muttered: 'Now I can go and buy some bread!' Around evening he left with his sack for the station. Saying farewell, he kissed my hand several times with his cold wet lips and mustache."

"I was at a meeting of some young Muscovite writers. The room was cold, the lighting was like that of an out-of-the-way railway station. Everyone was smoking and spitting on the floor jauntily. About you, about émigré writers, they responded: 'Rotten Europeans! Living dead!'"

"The writer, the six-fingered Malashkin, is a petty bourgeois from around Yefremov. He says: 'I've finished a new novel. It consists of 448 pages of printed text and is written in an elementary, temperamental way!'"[14]

"The writer Romanov is a petty bourgeois from around Belevsky. He is yellow-haired, with a sharpish small beard.[15] He goes about in a 'cloche' raincoat, black kidskin gloves, all fastened with buttons, a lacquer cane, and an 'artistic,' misshapen hat. His conceit is hellish, his projects, grandiose. 'I'm writing a trilogy,' titled "Rus," he says, 'it will consist of 2,800 pages!'[16] He looks upon Europe in a fastidious way. 'I won't go, it's boring there. . . .' The writer Leonov, having stayed with Gorky abroad, is also bored.[17] He keeps saying: 'If only I had an accordion. . . .'"

"Do you remember Varya B.? She's now living in Vasilievskoe, in an apartment in the Krasovs' hut. She sweeps and cleans a church for a piece of bread. She dresses like an old peasant woman, wearing bast shoes. The peasants say about her: 'She's joined at the hip to the church. Who'll take her as a wife? What a young lady she was previously, but now she's a tattered, ragged thing with only several teeth in her head. As old as death itself.'"

In a village outside of Yefremov near Tula, my older brother, Yevgeny Alexeevich Bunin lived out his final days in a half-ruined peasant hut. He once had a small estate, but after the 1905 peasant riots, he had to sell it and buy a small farmstead, with a house and garden. News about him came to me in Paris:

"You probably do not know that Yevgeny has been chased out of his home in Yefremov and that he's now living in a village outside of town, in a peasant hut with a collapsed roof. In the winter the hut is covered with snowdrifts, and during storms snow blows through the cracks of its rotten walls. . . . He makes a living doing portraits. Not long ago he did a portrait of Vaska Zhokov, a former bell-ringer and tramp, for roughly sixteen kilos of flour. Vaska forced Yevgeny to portray him in a top hat and tailcoat that he had pillaged from the estate of our relatives, the Trakhachevskys—and also in velveteen baggy trousers. On his shoulders, along his tailcoat, were also military straps with rings. . . ."

Having read such a thing, I was again forced to recall the poet Blok, his extremely poetic lines regarding some mystical snowstorm:

"Hardly had my wife become my bride, when the lilac measures of the first revolution seized us and drew us into the whirlpool. Having wanted destruction for so long, I was the first to be drawn into the gray purple of the Northern Star, into the mother-of-pearl and amethyst of the snowstorm. After the storm had passed, there opened the iron emptiness of the day, threatening a new blizzard. Now again a squall swoops down—its color and smell I cannot discern."[18]

This squall was also the February Revolution, with definite color and smell.

He once wrote this doggerel about a tailcoat:

An ancient image, a black shrine,
Before it a scoundrel in tails.
In ribbons and stars,
And orders he hails. . . . [19]

When the "squall" arrived, Vaska Zhokov was depicted by my brother not only in the claimed tailcoat, but with military straps with rings; but he still did not have ribbons, stars, and orders. Rereading the letter from my nephew and imagining well the rotten hut with its ruined roof in which Yevgeny Alexeevich lived, the racks through which the storm blew the snow, I recalled the mother-of-pearl and amethyst in Blok's splendid poetic "storm." For that much simpler storm in Yefremov and for the portraits of all the other Vaska Zhokovs in the world, Yevgeny Alexeevich paid with his life. He set off for Yefremov—most likely, for rotten flour from some other Vanka—fell on the way there, and gave up his soul to God. But my other brother, Yuly Alexeevich, died in Moscow: impoverished, starving, and hardly alive in body and soul. Lost mentally from the "color and smell of the new squall," he was placed in some madhouse "for very old intellectual workers." One time, he lay down on his bunk and never rose again.[20] Our sister Maria Alexeevna died under the Bolsheviks, from poverty and consumption in Rostov-on-Don. . . . [21]

I also received news from Vasilievskoe:

"Not long ago I was in Vasilievskoe. I was in the house where you once lived and wrote. Of course, like everywhere else, the place is filled with peasant families. Life there is now completely savage and primal, like a cattle yard. All the rooms have rotting hay on the floor on which people sleep, together with horse cloth, greasy pillows, chamber pots, tubs, litter, rubbish, and myriad fleas. . . ."

Then came this bit of news:

"Vasilievskoe and all its neighboring estates have disappeared from the face of the earth. In Vasilievskoe, there is not a single home, garden, or linden tree along the main tree-lined path, nor are there centuries-old birches on the banks or your favorite old maple. . . ."

"Vronsky moves quickly, in a rush, enticing the girls, working his way to meet Karenin, boldly pursuing his wife, and finally achieving his goal. Anna, whom the author introduces with such splendor—how she dresses, how she entices the 'elegant' Vronsky so passionately, how she deceives her husband so impudently and sweetly—becomes an extremely common and vulgar woman, without needing to do so, comforting herself with the thought that both her husband and lover are content since she has served both of them with her body, her 'elegant, cultured' body. . . . Count Tolstoy portrays the vulgar world of Vronsky and Anna in a seductive way. . . . But, you know, Count Tolstoy is a gifted writer. . . ."

What is this? This an example of what lengths several people went to, what they talked about in prerevolutionary and revolutionary times. In the 1860s and even in the '70s, more than one blockhead, hating the "tailcoat type," also uttered such monstrous absurdities. The person who wrote such a thing—isn't he a blockhead, too? What about these lines, which only the most desperate blockhead, scoundrel, and liar could write, and for which he could be hanged easily on the first aspen that comes along, if only for the furtive quotation marks in them?

But the person who wrote this is not a blockhead at all, but Alexei Sergeevich Suvorin, who later became a famous writer in the seventies. Even his most rabid enemies saw him after as a great mind, a huge talent. Even Chekhov wrote to Suvorin about his literary taste in an enthusiastic way:

"Your literary taste is so splendid that I believe in it as I do the sun in the sky."[22]

Chapter 17

Nobel Days

On November 9, 1933, in good, old Provence, in good, old Grasse, where, almost without interruption, I had spent almost ten years of my life, a quiet, warm, grayish day in late fall.[1]

On such days I never felt like working. All the same, I sat at my desk since morning always. Even after breakfast I was still there. But, having looked out the window and seeing that it was going to rain, I felt: No, I cannot. There's an afternoon matinee at the cinema today. I'll go to the cinema.

Walking down the hill from "Belvedere" into the city, I looked at Cannes lying in the distance, at the sea hardly visible on such days, at the misty crests of the Esterel, seized by this thought:

"Perhaps, at this very moment, somewhere on the other side of Europe, my fate is being decided. . . ."[2]

Once in the cinema, though, I again forgot about Stockholm.

After the entr'acte came a lighthearted piece of foolishness, titled "Baby." I watched it with particular interest: in it was the pretty Kisa Kuprina, the daughter of Alexander Kuprin. In the darkness was some muffled noise, then the light of a flashlight, and someone touching me on the shoulder and whispering in a solemn and agitated way:

"A telephone call from Stockholm. . . ."

Suddenly my entire life was torn in two.

I walked home rather quickly, experiencing nothing but regret that I would not see Kuprina to the end, as well as boundless disbelief about what I had been told. But no, I could not help but believe. From afar I could see that my home, always quiet and half dark in this season, and lost among the deserted olive gardens covering the mountain slopes over Grasse, was lit brightly from top to bottom. My heart contracted with a kind of sadness. . . . Some break in my life. . . .

All that evening "Belvedere" resounded with the ringing of the telephone, people shouting at me in various tongues from almost all the capitals of Europe. It chimed with the sound of the doorbell from postmen carrying more and more telegrams from almost all the countries of the world—from everywhere, except Russia!—and announcing the first onslaught of all kinds of visitors, photographers, and journalists coming in such numbers that their faces blurred before my eyes. People on all sides shook my hands, repeating the same thing over and over again in an excited and hurried way.[3] Photographers blinded me with flashbulbs to scatter a picture of some pale madman throughout the whole world. Reporters, journalists, interrupting one another, bombarded me with questions. . . .

"When did you leave Russia?"

"I've been an émigré since early '20."

"Are you thinking of going back?"

"Good God, how can I think of going back now?"

"Is true that you are first Russian writer ever to receive the Nobel Prize?"

"That is true."

"Is it true that the Nobel Prize was once offered to Leo Tolstoy, but he refused it?"[4]

"That is not true. The Noble Prize is never offered to someone. The entire process of judging always take place in complete secrecy."

"Did you have any ties or acquaintances in the Swedish Academy?"

"Never, with anyone."

"For precisely which work were you awarded the prize?"

"I think for my work as a whole."[5]

"Did you ever expect to win the prize?"

"I knew that I was among the candidates for a long time, that my candidacy had been put forth often, that I had read many flattering reviews of my works by such well-known critics as Böök, Österling, and Agrell, and that having heard about their ties to the Swedish Academy, I assumed that they were inclined favorably toward me. But, of course, I was never sure of anything."

"When is the Nobel Prize usually awarded?"

"Every year on the same date: December tenth."

"So you will go to Stockholm on that date?"

"Yes, perhaps even earlier. I would like to experience the pleasure of a distant journey as soon as possible. Because we émigrés have no political rights, we have difficulty in obtaining visas, I have not been abroad for the past thirteen years except for once to England.[6] For me, who, at one time, traveled the world endlessly, such a thing has been one of my worst privations."

"Have you ever been to any of the Scandinavian countries?"

"No, never. I have, I repeat, traveled far and wide, but mainly to the east and south. I kept putting off the north until another time. . . ."

Swept away in the powerful whirl, I lived a somewhat insane existence: not a free or peaceful moment from morning to night. Along with all the usual things swirling yearly around each Nobel laureate, my situation was unusual in that I belonged to that strange Russia that was now scattered throughout the world, something that not a single laureate in the world has ever experienced: for all of this Russia, so injured and insulted in all respects, the decision of Stockholm was an event of truly national importance. . . .

On the night of December third and fourth, I was already far from Paris. The Nord-Express, a separate first-class railway compartment—how many years that I had not experienced the emotions connected with all these things! Far into the night, we were already in Germany. The entire time, I stood on the platform of the last car of the train. Rushing forth in the pale moonlight were things that recalled Russia: flat plains, funereal-multicolored from the snow, snow-covered villages in the distance. . . .

We were in Hanover in the morning. I opened my eyes and raised the shade—everything was frozen and covered with ice. There was even ice on the rails. The people passing on the platform wore fur hats and coats. How long have I not seen such things, but how seemingly I had preserved them all in so lively a way in my heart!

In the evening our train stopped at the dock for the ship *Gustaf V*, and we headed slowly for the shores of Sweden. Again interviews, again the flashes of light bulbs. . . . In Sweden, my train car was besieged literally by photographers and journalists. . . . Only late at night did I finally find myself alone. Outside the windows it was dark and white . . . dense black forests in white heavy snows. All this, along with the warm-hot compartment, was exactly like nights at one time along the Nikolaevsky road. . . .

The conferral of the Nobel Prize to laureates always takes place yearly on December tenth at exactly five o'clock in the evening.

On that day I awoke early to a knock on my bedroom door, since the evening before the order was to wake me no later than eight-thirty. I jumped out of bed and thought about what kind of day it would be: the most important one of my life. At eight the northern sky was barely breaking. Streetlamps were still burning along the embankment of the canal. From my windows, I could see that part of Stockholm lying before me with all its towers, churches, and towers so very much like those of Petersburg, and which still so fairy-tale-like beautiful as happens only during sunrise and sunset. But I now had to begin my day early.

December tenth was the anniversary of the death of Alfred Nobel, and that morning, I had to put on a top hat and go out of town to the cemetery, where I had to lay wreaths both on his grave and on that of his recently deceased nephew, Emanuel Nobel.[7] Yesterday, I again had gone to bed at three and now, getting dressed, I felt very shaky. But the coffee was hot and strong, the day was starting out as clear and cold, and thoughts about the unusual ceremony that awaited me that evening, put me in an excited frame of mind. . . .

The official invitation for the ceremony had gone out only several days in advance and was written (in French) in full accord with that exactness that distinguishes all Swedish rituals:

"The Messieurs Laureates are invited to appear at the Concert Hall for the conferral of the Nobel Prize on December 10, 1933, no later than 4:50 p.m. His Highness, accompanied by the Royal House and the entire Court, will be in the Hall to preside at the ceremony and to award the Prize personally to each designate exactly at 5 p.m., after which the doors to the Hall will be locked and the ceremony will begin."

For any Swedish function, to be late even for only a minute or to be even two minutes earlier than the designated time was absolutely unacceptable. So I began to dress almost around three in the afternoon—from fear that something would happen: What if the stud to my frock shirt would disappear, as do all studs in the world in such situations?[8]

We set off at half past four.

On this evening, the city was particularly ablaze with lights—to honor the laureates and to celebrate the coming of Christmas and the New Year. Our chauffeur, a young giant in a fur hat, had the greatest difficulty making his way through the thick and endless stream of cars moving toward the huge "Music House," where the ceremony for the conferral of the prize always take place.[9] We were saved only by the police, who, seeing the procession of laureates following each other as they always do in such situations, held back all the other cars.

We laureates entered the "Music House" with the rest of the crowd, but in the foyer we were separated and led somewhere down some special passageways. So it was from others that I learned what was going on in the ceremonial hall before we appeared onstage.

This hall was amazingly spacious and high. It was all decorated with flowers and filled to capacity with a dense crowd: hundreds of women in evening dresses, diamonds, and pearls; hundreds of men in tails, stars, orders, multicolored ribbons, and all other kinds of solemn distinctions and decorations.

At ten minutes to five, the entire cabinet of Swedish ministers, the diplomatic corps, the members of the Swedish Academy and of the Nobel Committee, and all the invitees took their places and observed a profound silence. At precisely five o'clock, heralds from the stage raised a fanfare, filling the place with the splendid sounds of the national hymn flowing somewhere from above. The monarch entered the hall, accompanied by the crown prince and all the other members of the royal family, followed by the king's retinue and the members of the court. We four laureates were still in the small hall adjoining the back entrance to the stage.[10]

Then came our entrance. The fanfare resounded again from the stage, and we followed the Swedish academicians who were to introduce us and read summaries about us. Because I had been designated the first to speak at the banquet after the ceremony, I now, according to ritual, was the last to go out onstage.[11] I was accompanied by Per Hallström, the permanent secretary of the academy. I was struck by the elegant, crowded hall, how when the laureates appeared and bowed to the crowd, not only the entire assembly but also the monarch himself with all his court and family rose to their feet.

The stage was also huge and decorated with some kind of fresh small roselike flowers. Chairs for the academicians took up the right side. Above all, the panels of the Swedish national flag, solemn and immobile, hung from the walls. Usually the stage is decorated with flags from the countries of the laureates. But what flag did I have as an émigré? The impossibility of the Soviet flag for me had the organizers of ceremony, for my sake, display only one flag—the Swedish one. A noble thought![12]

The president of the Nobel Foundation began the ceremony. He greeted the king and the laureates. The next speaker dedicated his initial words wholly to the memory of Alfred Nobel—this year was the centenary of his birth. Next were narratives about each laureate, who then had to descend the stage and to accept from the hands of the king a portfolio with the Nobel diploma and a case containing a large gold medal, engraved with a profile of Alfred Nobel on one side and, on the other, with the name of the laureate. During intervals was music by Beethoven and Grieg.

Grieg is one of my most favorite composers, and, with special delight, I heard his sounds before Per Hallström read his address about me.

The last minute moved me deeply. Hallström's address was not only splendid but also genuinely sincere. When he finished, he, with charming ceremoniousness, addressed me in French:

"Ivan Alexeevich Bunin, be so kind as to step down into the hall and accept from the hands of His Majesty the Nobel Prize in Literature for 1933, awarded to you by the Swedish Academy."

In the enveloping deep silence, I walked along the stage and down the steps slowly toward the king, who had risen to meet me. The entire audience rose to their feet and held their breath to hear what he would say to me and how I would respond. He greeted me and, in my name, Russian literature as a whole, pressing my hand especially graciously and firmly. With a low bow, I answered in French:

"Sire, I ask Your Highness to deign to accept my profound and respectful gratitude."

My words drowned in the applause.

On the next day, the king hosted the laureates to dinner at his palace. And, on the evening of December tenth, almost immediately after the ceremony, we were taken to a banquet by the Nobel Committee, presided over by the crown prince.

When we arrived, we met again the members of the academy, the entire royal house and court, the diplomatic corps, the artistic world of Stockholm, and other invited guests.

The crown prince and my wife, who was sitting next to him, were the first couple to go up to the table. . . .

My place was next to Princess Ingrid—she is now the Danish queen—and opposite us was the king's brother, Prince Eugene (and, incidentally, a well-known Swedish artist).

The crown prince gave the initial address. He spoke brilliantly, devoting his words to the memory of Alfred Nobel.

Then the laureates gave their speeches.

The prince spoke from his seat. We were on a special stage, set up way in the back of the banquet hall, which was also unusually large and built in the old Swedish style.

A radio loudspeaker carried our words from this stage to all of Europe.

Here is the text of the speech that I delivered in French:

"Your Highness, Gracious Majesties and Sovereigns,

"On November ninth, far from here, in the far-off distance, in an old provencal town, in a poor village home, I received a telephone call about the choice of the Swedish Academy. I would be insincere if I were to tell you, as people do on such occasions, that this was the most moving moment in my entire life. Justly did a great philosopher say that feelings of joy, even the most poignant ones, mean almost nothing when compared to similar ones of sorrow? In no way do I wish to put a damper on this festive day, which I will keep indelibly forever in my memory. But I will allow myself to say that the sorrows that I have experienced during the past fifteen years have far exceeded my joys. And these sorrows have not been personal ones—far from it!

"But I can assure you most firmly that of all the joys of my literary life, this small miracle of modern technology, this telephone call from Stockholm, gave me the greatest pleasure as a writer. The literary prize founded by your great countryman Alfred Nobel is the highest crowning of a writer's work! Ambition is common to almost every person and writer, and I was extremely proud to receive this award from so many able and impartial judges!

"But do I think that November ninth is only about me? No, that would be extremely egotistical. Overwhelmed by the stream of initial congratulations and telegrams, I, in the silence and solitude of the night, thought about the profound significance of this decision by the Swedish Academy. For the first time since the founding of the Nobel Prize, you have bestowed the award on an exile. For what in truth am I? An exile who enjoys the hospitality of France, for which I will be grateful forever.

"Gentlemen of the academy, leaving aside both me and my works, allow me to say that your gesture is, in and of itself, so splendid a one. Areas of the most complete independence must exist in the world. Doubtless, around this table are representatives of every opinion, of every philosophical and religious view. But one unshakable thing unites us all: the freedom of thought and conscience, for which we are indebted to civilization. This freedom is especially necessary for the writer—it is for him a dogma, an axiom. Your gesture, gentlemen of the academy, proves once more that freedom and love are the national cult of Sweden.

"Still, a few more words to end this short speech. I did not wait for this day to admire highly your royal house, your country, your people, and your literature. Love for arts and letters has always been traditional for the Swedish Royal House, as it has been for your entire noble nation. Founded by an illustrious warrior, the Swedish dynasty is one of the most glorious in the world. His Majesty the King, the chivalrous monarch of a chivalrous people, will deign to allow a foreign and free writer, honored by the Swedish Academy, to express to him his most respectful and heartfelt respects."

Acknowledgments

For their assistance in *Recollections*, I wish to thank Jan Adamczyk, Christopher "Kit" Condill, Annabella Irvine, Joseph Lenkart, and Olga Makarova of the Slavic Reference Service at the University of Illinois, who answered myriad, complicated, and often outrageous questions regarding Bunin and his work and who, as always has been the case in my almost fifty-year association with this group, graced their responses with offers of further assistance.

Here at the University of Notre Dame, I wish to thank Thomas Merluzzi and Alison Rice, former directors of the Institute for Scholarship in the Liberal Arts, for their continued financial support; Therese Bauters, Megan Elsen, Nita Hashil, Laura Sills, and the staffs of Interlibrary Loan and Document Delivery for supplying materials for research, particularly Tracey Morton, Trudie Mullins, and Whitney Young; Matthew Pollard and Randy Yoho of the Office of Information Technology for rescuing my files from clouds, cyber- and manmade; Cheryl Reed, who gave to my chaotic files an elegant and professional cast; and Mary Ribelsky and Jane Lichty for their editing of the manuscript.

I also acknowledge my research assistants—Spencer Andrews, David Brosnan, Ruslan Lucero, Katherine Mansourova, Elizabeth May, Ana Miravete, Kaitlin Spillane, and especially Joshua O'Brien, Charles Sedore, and Katarzyna Swierad-Redwood—whom I drove to the brink (and often beyond) with endless queries on pages and dates; obscure questions on people, places, and events; and tortuous searches through newspapers, journals, books, and cyberspace for citations and claims. Truly, *Recollections* would not have come into being without their loyalty and support.

Special kudos go to the four most loyal colleagues of my scholarly career: Jeffrey Brooks, professor emeritus at John Hopkins University; Irwin Weil, professor emeritus at Northwestern University; Yury Corrigan, professor at Boston University; and especially Kathleen Parthé, professor emerita at the University of Rochester, for her precise editing of the manuscript. A special, if fond, note of thanks is also due to Valentina Kurenshchikova, former Russian

Fulbright Foreign Language Teaching Assistant at Notre Dame, for her meticulous reading of my translation.

Last but not least, I thank my wife, Gloria Gibbs Marullo, for allowing Ivan Bunin, for an eighth and (I swear) final time, to enter, if not consume, our life, and my cats, Francis Xavier (aka Ernie) and Agnes Mary, for competing with Bunin for attention and love. (For those who follow my scholarly adventures, Bernadette Marie left this world in February 2016 at the age of nineteen, Bridget Josephine in March 2017 at nineteen and a half, and Benedict Joseph in September 2020 at eighteen and a half.)

Finally, it is with special warmth and affection that I again cite Jan Adamczyk for his assistance not only in this work but also in many of my previous studies. It is with deep admiration and affection for him as a person and a professional that I dedicate *Recollections* to him.

May you all know happiness, health, and peace.

Thomas Gaiton Marullo

Directory of Names

Adamovich, Georgy Viktorovich (1884–1972), poet and critic.
Afonsky, Nikolai Petrovich (1892–1971), musician and choir director.
Agrell, Alfhild (1849–1923), Swedish writer and playwright.
Akhmatova, Anna Andreevna (1889–1966), poet.
Aldanov, Mark Alexandrovich (1886?–1957), writer and critic.
Alexander I (1777–1825), tsar of Russia from 1801 to 1825.
Alexander II (1818–1881), tsar of Russia from 1855 to 1881.
Alexander III (1845–1894), tsar of Russian from 1881 to 1894.
Alexandra Fyodorovna (1872–1918), empress of Russia from 1894 to 1917.
Alexandrov, Georgy (?–?), teacher and writer.
Alexei Petrovich (1690–1718), son of Peter the Great.
Aminado, Don (1888–1957), poet and memoirist.
Andreev, Leonid Nikolaevich (1871–1919), writer.
Andreeva, Maria Fyodorovna (1868–1953), actress and second wife of Maxim Gorky.
Artsybashev, Mikhail Petrovich (1878–1927), novelist and short-story writer.
Atarov, Nikolai Sergeevich (1907–1978), writer.
Babel, Isaac Emmanuilovich (1894–1941), writer.
Baboreko, Alexander Kuzmich (1913–2000), literary scholar.
Bagritsky, Eduard Georgievich (1895–1934), poet.
Bakhrakh, Alexander Vasilievich (1902–1985), writer.
Bakst, Leon Nikolaevich (1866–1924), painter and designer.
Balashov, Abram Abramovich (1855–1942?), vandalizer of Ilya Repin's *Ivan the Terrible and His Son*.
Balmont, Konstantin Dmitrievich (1867–1942), poet and translator.
Balukhatyi, Sergei Dmitrievich (1893–1945), critic and correspondent.
Battistini, Mattia (1856–1928), operatic baritone.
Batyushkov, Konstantin Nikolaevich (1787–1855), poet, essayist, and translator.
Baudelaire, Charles (1821–1867), French poet.
Bednyi, Demyan (1883–1945), poet and satirist.
Beethoven, Ludwig (1770–1827), German composer and pianist.
Belinsky, Vissarion Grigorievich (1811–1848), literary critic.
Bely, Andrei (1800–1934), poet, novelist, literary critic, polemicist, and theorist.
Benislavskaya, Galina Arturovna (1897–1925), lover of Sergei Esenin.
Benois, Alexander Nikolaevich (1870–1960), artist, critic, preservationist, and historian.
Berg, Nikolai Vasilievich (1823–1884), poet and translator.

Beryozov, Rodion Mikhailovich (1896–1941), writer.
Biryukov, Pavel Ivanovich (1860–1931), writer, social figure, and biographer of Leo Tolstoy.
Blair, Hugh (1718–1800), Scottish minister, author, and rhetorician.
Blok, Alexander Alexandrovich (1880–1921), poet and playwright.
Bobrinskaya, Varvara Nikolaevna (1864–1940), social reformer and editor.
Boccaccio, Giovanni (1313–1375), Italian writer and poet.
Bogomolov, I. I. (?–?), merchant and friend of Alexander Ertel.
Bonch-Bruevich, Vladimir Dmitrievich (1873–1955), revolutionary and ethnographer.
Böök, Martin Fredrik (1883–1961), Swedish professor, writer, and literary critic.
Bostrom, Alexei Apollonovich (1881–1921), politician.
Bradley (?–?), literary agent for Ivan Bunin.
Bryusov, Valery Yakovlevich (1873–1924), poet, novelist, and critic.
Bukharin, Nikolai Ivanovich (1888–1938), revolutionary, politician, and author.
Bunin, Dmitri Maximovich (1765?–1825?), nephew of Anna Bunina.
Bunin, Ivan Alexeevich (1870–1953), writer.
Bunin, Ivan Petrovich (1753–after 1842), brother of Anna Bunina.
Bunin, Pyotr Maximovich (1746–1801), father of Anna Bunina.
Bunin, Vasily Petrovich (?–1805?), brother of Anna Bunina.
Bunin, Yevgeny Alexeevich (1858–1933?), brother of Ivan Bunin.
Bunin, Yuly Alexeevich (1857–1921), brother of Ivan Bunin.
Bunina, Anna Petrovna (1774–1829), poet and relative of Ivan Bunin.
Bunina-Laskarzhevskaya, Maria Alexeevna (1873–1930), sister of Ivan Bunin.
Bunina-Semyonova, Maria Petrovna (1774–1847), sister of Anna Bunina.
Burlyuk, David Davidovich (1881–1967), Ukrainian futurist.
Burtsev, Vladimir Lvovich (1862–1942), revolutionary, scholar, publisher, and editor.
Byron, Lord (1788–1824), English poet and politician.
Carducci, Giosuè (1835–1907), Italian poet, writer, literary critic, and teacher.
Catherine II (1729–1796), empress of Russia from 1762 to 1796.
Cézanne, Paul (1839–1906), French painter.
Chaadaev, Pyotr Yakovlevich (1794–1856), philosopher.
Chaliapin, Fyodor Ivanovich (1871–1938), singer.
Chekhov, Alexander Pavlovich (1855–1913), writer and brother of Anton Chekhov.
Chekhov, Anton Pavlovich (1860–1904), writer.
Chekhova, Maria Pavlovna (1863–1957), sister of Anton Chekhov.
Chekhova, Yevgeniya Yakovlevna (1835–1919), mother of Anton Chekhov.
Chernyavsky, Vladimir Stepanovich (1889–1948), poet.
Chertkov, Vladimir Grigorievich (1854–1936), friend and publisher of Leo Tolstoy.
Chirikov, Yevgeny Nikolaevich (1864–1932), novelist, playwright, and publicist.
Christian II (1481–1523), king of Denmark and Norway from 1513 to 1523 and of Sweden from 1520 to 1521.
Chrysostom, John (349–407), archbishop and church father.
Chukovsky, Kornei Ivanovich (1992–1969), writer, poet, critic, scholar, translator, and editor.
Chulkov, Georgy Ivanovich (1879–1939), writer, essayist, and critic.
Churchill, Winston (1874–1965), English statesman.

Claudel, Paul (1868–1955), poet, dramatist, and diplomat.
Cook, James (1728–1779), English explorer, navigator, and cartographer.
Cruppi, Louise (1862–1925), friend of Romain Rolland.
Danilevsky, Nikolai Yakovlevich (1822–1885), naturalist and Slavophile.
Darwin, Charles (1809–1882), English naturalist and geologist.
Davydova, Alexandra Arkadievna (1848–1902), editor, publisher, and mother-in-law of Alexander Kuprin.
Davydova-Kuprina, Maria (1881–1966), wife of Alexander Kuprin.
Denikin, Anton Ivanovich (1872–1847), general.
Derzhavin, Gavriil (Gavrila) Romanovich (1743–1816), poet and statesman.
Desyatovsky-Zablotsky, Andrei Parfenovich (1807–1881), statesman.
Dickens, Charles (1812–1870), English writer and social critic.
Dimitri of Rostov (1651–1709), monk.
Diocletian (244–311), Roman emperor from 284 to 305.
Dmitriev, Ivan Ivanovich (1760–1837), poet and statesman.
Dobrolyubov, Nikolai Alexandrovich (1826–1861), critic.
Domitian (AD 51–96), Roman emperor from AD 81 to 96.
Dostoevsky, Fyodor Mikhailovich (1821–1881), novelist and short-story writer.
Dudchenko, Mitrofan Semyonovich (1867–1946), Tolstoyan and brother of Tikhon Dudchenko.
Dudchenko, Tikhon Semyonovich (1853–1920), Tolstoyan and brother of Mitrofan Dudchenko.
Dumas, Alexandre, *père* (1802–1870), novelist.
Duncan, Isadora (1878–1927), American dancer and wife of Sergei Esenin.
Durov, Anatoly Pavlovich (1864–1916), circus artist.
Durov, Sergei Fyodorovich (1816–1869), poet, writer, translator, and political activist.
Dymshitz-Tolstaya, Sofya Isaakovna (1884–1963), second wife of Alexei Nikolaevich Tolstoy.
Dzerzhinsky, Felix Edmundovich (1877–1926), founder and first head of the Soviet secret police.
Dzierzynska-Bulhak, Aldona Kojallowicz (1870–1966), sister of Felix Dzerzhinsky.
Égalité, Philippe (1747–1793), French aristocrat.
Egilmar I (1040–1112), patrilineal ancestor of the House of Oldenburg.
Ehrenburg, Ilya Grigorievich (1891–1967), writer, journalist, translator, and cultural figure.
Eliasberg, Alexander Samoilovich (1878–1924), literary historian, writer, translator, and editor.
Ertel, Alexander Ivanovich (1855–1908), novelist and short-story writer.
Esenin, Sergei Alexandrovich (1895–1925), poet and husband of Isadora Duncan.
Eugene (1865–1947), Swedish prince and artist.
Fedotova-Ertel, Maria Ivanovna (?–?), wife of Alexander Ertel.
Fet, Afanasy Afanasievich (1820–1892), poet.
Filippov, Nikolai Dmitrievich (1874–?), baker and patron.
Fonvizin, Denis Ivanovich (1745–1792), writer and playwright.
Fourier, Charles (1772–1837), French philosopher.
France, Anatole (1844–1924), French poet, journalist, and novelist.

Friche, Vladimir Maximovich (1870–1929), literary critic and commissar for foreign affairs.
Fyodorov, Alexander Mitrofanovich (1868–1949), poet.
Gallen-Kallela, Axel (1865–1931), Finnish painter.
Galsworthy, John (1867–1933), English novelist and playwright.
Garshin, Vsevolod Mikhailovich (1855–1888), short-story writer.
Geinrikh, Yelizaveta Moritsovna (1882–1942), mother of Alexander Kuprin.
Gekker, Naum Leontievich (1861–1920), literary critic.
Genghis Khan (1155?–1227), Mongol emperor.
Gerasimov, Mikhail Prokofievich (1889–1939), poet.
Gershenzon, Mikhail Osipovich (1869–1925), philologist, philosopher, and literary historian.
Gide, André (1869–1951), French writer.
Gippius, Zinaida Nikolaevna (1867–1945), poet, critic, novelist, memoirist, and wife of Dmitri Merezhkovsky.
Glazer, Yelena Ottobaldovna (1850–1923), mother of Maximilian Voloshin.
Glebova-Sudeikina, Olga Afanasieva (1885–1945), artist, sculptor, and translator.
Gnedich, Pyotr Petrovich (1855–1925), writer, poet, dramatist, translator, entrepreneur, and scholar.
Goethe, Johann von (1749–1832), German poet, dramatist, novelist, and statesman.
Gogol, Nikolai Vasilievich (1809–1852), dramatist, novelist, and short-story writer.
Golovin, Alexander Yakovlevich (1863–1930), artist and state designer.
Gorky, Maxim (Alexei Maximovich Peshkov) (1868–1936), writer and political activist.
Gorky-Peshkov, Maxim Maximovich (1897–1934), son of Maxim Gorky.
Gorodetsky, Sergei Mitrofanovich (1884–1967), poet.
Grech, Nikolai Ivanovich (1787–1857), journalist, writer, and philologist.
Grieg, Edvard (1843–1907), Norwegian composer and pianist.
Grigorovich, Dmitri Vasilievich (1822–1899), writer.
Grossman, Leonid Petrovich (1888–1965), scholar, writer, and literary critic.
Grot, Yakov Karlovich (1812–1893), philologist.
Gruzdyov, Ilya Alexandrovich (1892–1960), critic and playwright.
Grzhebin, Zinovy Isaevich (1869–1929), artist and publisher.
Guchkov, Alexander Ivanovich (1862–1936), politician.
Gumilyov, Nikolai Stepanovich (1886–1921), poet, literary critic, traveler, military officer, and husband of Anna Akhmatova.
Gustav III (1746–1792), king of Sweden from 1771 to 1792.
Gustav V (1858–1950), king of Sweden from 1907 to 1950.
Gustav VI (1882–1973), king of Sweden from 1950 to 1973.
Hallström, Per (1866–1960), Swedish writer, dramatist, poet, and member of the Swedish Academy.
Hamsun, Knut (1859–1952), Norwegian novelist.
Hegel, Georg Wilhelm Friedrich (1770–1833), German philosopher.
Heine, Heinrich (1797–1856), German poet, journalist, essayist, and literary critic.
Hermant, Jacques (1855–1930), French architect.
Herod (73–4 BC), king of Judea.

Herzen, Alexander Ivanovich (1812–1870), writer, journalist, and editor.
Hitler, Adolf (1889–1945), German dictator.
Hugo, Victor (1802–1885), French poet, novelist, and dramatist.
Humboldt, Alexander von (1769–1859), Prussian polymath, geographer, naturalist, and explorer.
Ibsen, Henrik (1828–1906), Norwegian dramatist.
Ingrid (1910–2000), Swedish princess and queen of Denmark from 1947 to 1972.
Ivan IV, the "Terrible" (1530–1584), tsar of Russia from 1547 to 1584.
Ivanov, Vyacheslav Ivanovich (1866–1949), poet, critic, and scholar.
Izmailov, Alexander Alexeevich (1873–1921), literary critic.
Jakobson, Roman Osipovich (1896–1982), Russian-American linguist and literary theorist.
Järnefelt, Arvid (1861–1932), Finnish judge and writer.
Jerome, Jerome (1859–1927), English humorist.
Kachalov, Vasily Ivanovich (1875–1948), actor.
Kalinin, Mikhail Ivanovich (1875–1946), president of the USSR from 1919 to 1946.
Kandaurova, Margarita Pavlovna (1895–1990), ballerina.
Kant, Immanuel (1724–1804), German philosopher.
Kaplan, Fanny (Fanya) Efimova (1890–1918), attempted assassin of Vladimir Lenin.
Kapnist, Vasily Vasilievich (1758–1823), poet and playwright.
Karamzin, Nikolai Mikhailovich (1766–1826), writer, poet, historian, and critic.
Karonin, Nikolai Yelpidiforovich (1853–1892), writer.
Karyshev. Mikhail Alexeevich (?–?), engineer and friend of Alexander Kuprin.
Kataev, Valentin Petrovich (1897–1986), novelist.
Kedrin, Dmitri Borisovich (1907–1945), poet.
Kerensky, Alexander Fyodorovich (1881–1970), lawyer and political leader.
Khilkov, Dmitri Alexandrovich (1857–1914), prince and Tolstoyan.
Khlebnikov, Velimir (Viktor) Vladimirovich (1885–1922), poet and theorist.
Khodasevich, Vladislav Felitsianovich (1886–1939), poet and critic.
Kipling, Rudyard (1865–1936), English short-story writer, poet, and novelist.
Klopsky, Ivan Mikhailovich (1852–1898), Tolstoyan.
Klyuev, Nikolai Alexeevich (1887–1937), poet.
Knipper, Olga Leonardovna (1868–1959), actress and wife of Anton Chekhov.
Kokoshkin, Fyodor Fyodorovich (1871–1918), lawyer, essayist, and politician.
Kolchak, Alexander Vasilievich (1874–1920), general.
Kollontai, Alexandra Mikhailovna (1872–1952), Soviet revolutionary, theoretician, and ambassador to Sweden from 1930 to 1945.
Koltsov, Alexei Vasilievich (1809–1842), poet.
Komissarzhevskaya, Vera Fyodorovna (1864–1910), actress.
Kondakov, Nikodim Pavlovich (1844–1925), art historian.
Korolenko, Vladimir Galaktionovich (1853–1921), writer.
Kostomarov, Nikolai Ivanovich (1817–1885), historian.
Krandievskaya, Natalia Vasilievna (1888–1963), third wife of Alexei Nikolaevich Tolstoy.
Krechetov. *See* Sokolov, Sergei Alexeevich.
Kropotkin, Pyotr Alexeevich (1842–1921), prince and revolutionary.

Kruchyonykh. Alexei Yeliseevich (1886–1968), poet.
Krylov, Ivan Andreevich (1769–1844), fabulist.
Krylov, Pyotr Petrovich (1859–1922), doctor and member of the Duma.
Krylov, Viktor Alexandrovich (1838–1908), playwright, theater critic, and librettist.
Kulanchikova-Kuprina, Lyubov Alexeevna (1838–1910), mother of Alexander Kuprin.
Kulman, Nikolai Karlovich (1871–1940), critic.
Kuprin, Alexander Ivanovich (1870–1938), writer.
Kuprin, Ivan Ivanovich (1834–1871), father of Alexander Kuprin.
Kuprina, Kisa Alexandrovna (1908–1980), actress and daughter of Alexander Kuprin.
Kuskova, Yekaterina Dmitrievna (1869–1958), publicist, publisher, memoirist, and political activist.
Kuzmin, Mikhail Alexeevich (1875–1936), writer, playwright, and critic.
Kuznetsova, Galina Nikolaevna (1902–1976), poet, prose writer, and memoirist.
Lanin (?–?), lawyer.
Lawrence, David Herbert (1885–1930), English novelist, poet, playwright, essayist, critic, and painter.
Lenin, Vladimir Ilyich (1870–1924), revolutionary leader and writer.
Leonov, Leonid Maximovich (1899–1944), novelist and playwright.
Leontiev, Boris Nikolaevich (1866–1909), Tolstoyan.
Lermontov, Mikhail Yurievich (1814–1841), writer and poet.
Leskov, Nikolai Semyonovich (1831–1895), novelist, journalist, and short-story writer.
Levitan, Isaak Ilyich (1860–1900), painter.
Liberman, Alexander Semyonovich (1912–1999), Russian-American editor, publisher, painter, photographer, and sculptor.
Liebknecht, Karl (1871–1919), German socialist.
Loginova-Muravyova, Tatyana Dmitrievna (1904–1993), artist.
Lomonosov, Mikhailo Vasilievich (1711–1765), writer and scientist.
London, Jack (1876–1916), American novelist, journalist, and social activist.
Louis Philippe (1773–1850), king of France from 1830 to 1848.
Lunacharsky, Anatoly Vasilievich (1875–1933), Bolshevik and first Soviet director of culture.
Luther, Martin (1483–1546), German theologian and reformer.
Lvov, Georgy Yevgenievich (1871–1925), statesman.
Maeterlinck, Maurice (1862–1949), Belgian poet, dramatist, and essayist.
Maklakov, Vasily Alexeevich (1869–1957), lawyer and politician.
Malashkin, Sergei Ivanovich (1888–?), Soviet writer.
Malavin, Filipp Andreevich (1869–1940), painter.
Mallarmé, Stephane (1842–1898), French poet.
Mamin-Sibiryak, Dmitri Narkisovich (1852–1912), novelist, dramatist, and short-story writer.
Mandelshtam, Osip Emelievich (1891–1938), poet.
Mann, Thomas (1875–1955), German novelist, short-story story writer, social critic, philanthropist, and essayist.

Manych, Pyotr Dmitrievich (?–1918), friend of Alexander Kuprin.
Maréchal, Sylvain (1750–1803), French poet, philosopher, essayist, and political theorist.
Maria Fyodorovna (1847–1928), empress of Russia from 1881 to 1894.
Mariengof, Anatoly Borisovich (1897–1962), poet and dramatist.
Marinetti, Filippo (1876–1944), Italian poet, editor, art theorist, and founder of the futurist movement.
Marks, Nikandr Alexandrovich (1860–1921), professor, paleographer, and general.
Marx, Karl (1818–1883), German philosopher, economist, historian, sociologist, theorist, journalist, and revolutionary.
Maupassant, Henri (1850–1893), French writer.
Mayakovsky, Vladimir Vladimirovich (1893–1930), poet.
Maykov, Apollon Nikolaevich (1821–1897), poet.
Merezhkovsky, Dmitri Sergeevich (1865–1941), poet, novelist, critic, philosopher, and husband of Zinaida Gippius.
Merzlyakov, Alexei Fyodorovich (1778–1830), poet, critic, translator, and professor.
Meyerbeer, Giacomo (1791–1864), German composer.
Mikhailovsky, Nikolai Konstantinovich (1842–1904), sociologist, editor, and social and literary critic.
Millerand, Alexandre (1859–1943), politician and president of France from 1920 to 1924.
Milyukov, Paul (Pavel) Nikolaevich (1859–1943), historian and politician.
Milyutin, Dmitri Alexeevich (1816–1912), minister and brother of Nikolai Milyutin.
Milyutin, Nikolai Alexeevich (1818–1872), statesman and brother of Dmitri Milyutin.
Minsky, Nikolai Maximovich (1855–1937), poet and philosopher.
Molotov, Vyacheslav Mikhailovich (1890–1986), Soviet statesman.
Morozov, Savva Timofeevich (1862–1905), businessman and patron of the arts.
Moskvin, Ivan Mikhailovich (1874–1946), actor.
Muromtseva-Bunina, Vera Nikolaevna (1881–1961), second wife of Ivan Bunin.
Murry, John Middleton (1889–1957), English writer.
Mussorgsky, Modest Petrovich (1839–1881), composer.
Myasnikov, Alexander Sergeevich (1913–1982), critic.
Nabokov, Vladimir Nikolaevich (1870–1922), journalist and politician.
Nabokov, Vladimir Vladimirovich (1899–1977), novelist.
Nadson, Sergei Yakovlevich (1862–1887), poet.
Naidyonov, Sergei Alexandrovich (1868–1922), dramatist.
Nekrasov, Nikolai Alexeevich (1828–1878), poet, writer, and publisher.
Nemirovich-Danchenko, Vladimir Ivanovich (1858–1943), theater director, writer, pedagogue, playwright, producer, and theater organizer.
Nemitz, Alexander Vasilievich (1879–1967), vice admiral and naval commander.
Nero (AD 37–68), Roman emperor from AD 54 to 68.
Nesterov, Mikhail Vasilievich (1862–1942), artist.
Nicholas II (1868–1918), tsar of Russia from 1894 to 1917.
Nietzsche, Friedrich (1844–1900), German philosopher, cultural critic, composer, poet, philologist, and scholar.

Nilus, Pyotr Alexandrovich (1869–1943), writer and artist.
Nobel, Alfred (1833–1896), Swedish chemist, engineer, armaments manufacturer, and founder of the Nobel Prize.
Nobel, Emanuel (1859–1932), Swedish-Russian oil baron and nephew of Alfred Nobel.
Novikov, Nikolai Ivanovich (1744–1818), writer, journalist, and philanthropist.
Oldenburg, Alexander Petrovich of (1844–1932), prince, general, and father of Pyotr of Oldenburg.
Oldenburg, Pyotr Alexandrovich of (1868–1924), first husband of Olga Alexandrovna.
Olesha, Yury Karlovich (1899–1960), novelist.
Olga Alexandrovna (1882–1960), duchess, sister of Nicholas II, and wife of Pyotr of Oldenburg.
Oreus, Ivan Ivanovich (Ivan Konevskoy)(1877–1901), poet and critic.
Österling, Anders (1884–1981), Swedish poet and writer.
Ostrovsky, Alexander Nikolaevich (1823–1886), playwright.
Ozerov, Vladislav Alexandrovich (1769–1816), dramatist.
Paléologue, Maurice Georges (1859–1944), French ambassador to Russian from 1914 to 1917.
Panina, Sofya Vladimirovna (1871–1956), landowner.
Pasternak, Boris Leonidovich (1890–1960), Russian poet, novelist, and translator.
Paul I (1754–1801), tsar of Russia from 1796 to 1801.
Pechkovsky, Mikhail Ivanovich (1884–1968), journalist, editor, and lawyer.
Peshkova, Yekaterina Pavlovna (1886–1938), first wife of Maxim Gorky.
Peter the Great (1672–1725), tsar of Russia from 1721 to 1725.
Peter II (1715–1730), tsar of Russia from 1727 to 1730.
Peter III (1728–1762), tsar of Russia for six months in 1762.
Petlyura, Semyon Vasilievich (1879–1926), Ukrainian president, commander, and journalist.
Petrashevsky, Mikhail Vasilievich (1821–1866), thinker and public figure.
Picasso, Pablo (1881–1973), Spanish painter and sculptor.
Pilnyak, Boris Andreevich (1894–1938), writer.
Pilsky, Pyotr Moiseivich (1879–1941), critic.
Pisarev, Dmitri Ivanovich (1840–1868), writer and social critic.
Pobedonostsev, Konstantin Petrovich (1827–1907), jurist, statesman, and tsarist adviser.
Poddubny, Ivan Maximovich (1871–1949), wrestler.
Poe, Edgar Allan (1809–1849), American poet, critic, and short story writer.
Pokrovsky, Fyodor Platonovich (1833–1898), priest.
Polonskaya, Veronika Vitoldovna (1908–1994), actress.
Polonsky, Yakov Petrovich (1819–1898), poet.
Polyakov, Sergei Alexandrovich (1873–1952), factory owner, philanthropist, and translator.
Polycarp (?–?), monk.
Potapenko, Ignaty Nikolaevich (1856–1929), playwright and prose writer.
Potyomkin, Pyotr Petrovich (1886–1926), poet.
Presnyakov, Alexander Yevgenievich (1870–1929), historian.

Prishvin, Mikhail Mikhailovich (1873–1954), writer.
Prokofiev, Sergei Sergeevich (1891–1953), composer, pianist, and conductor.
Przybyszewski, Stanislav (1868–1927), Polish writer.
Pugachyov, Yemelyan Ivanovich (1742–1775), pretender and revolutionary.
Pusheshnikov, Nikolai Alexeevich (1882–1939), translator and nephew of Ivan Bunin.
Pushkin, Alexander Sergeevich (1799–1837), writer and poet.
Pushkin, Vasily Lvovich (1766–1830), poet and uncle of Alexander Pushkin.
Pythagoras (570–495 BC), Greek philosopher and mathematician.
Rachmaninov, Sergei Vasilievich (1873–1943), composer, pianist, and conductor.
Rasputin, Grigory Yefimovich (1869–1916), mystic and intriguer.
Razin, Stepan (Stenka) Timofeevich (1630–1671), revolutionary.
Régnier, Henri de (1864–1936), French poet.
Remizov, Alexei Mikhailovich (1877–1957), novelist, short-story writer, dramatist, poet, and memoirist.
Renan, Joseph Ernest (1821–1892), French writer, philosopher, and scholar.
Repin, Ilya Efimovich (1844–1930), painter.
Rimsky-Korsakov, Nikolai Andreevich (1844–1908), composer.
Ritter, Carl (1779–1859), German geographer.
Rodzyanko, Mikhail Vladimirovich (1859–1924), statesman.
Rolland, Romain (1866–1944), French dramatist, novelist, essayist, art historian, and critic.
Romanov, Mikhail Fyodorovich (1596–1645), tsar of Russia from 1613 to 1645.
Romanov, Panteleimon Sergeevich (1884–1938), writer.
Rossi, Ernesto (1827–1896), Italian actor.
Rostovtsev, Yakov Ivanovich (1803–1860), statesman.
Rousseau, Jean-Jacques (1712–1778), Genevan writer, philosopher, and composer.
Rozanov, Vasily Vasilievich (1856–1919), writer, critic, philosopher, and journalist.
Ryleev, Kondraty Fyodorovich (1795–1826), poet.
Ryss, Pyotr Yakovlevich (?–1948), journalist.
Sanin, Alexander Akimovich (né Schoenberg) (1869–1956), director and teacher.
Sappho (630–570 BC), Greek poet.
Sats, Natayla Ilinichna (1903–1993), writer, actor, and director.
Savina, Maria Gavrilovna (1854–1915), actress.
Savinkov, Boris Viktorovich (1879–1925), writer, revolutionary, and terrorist.
Schiller, Friedrich von (1759–1805), German poet and dramatist.
Sedykh, Andrei (1902–1993), writer, publisher, and editor.
Semyonov, Mikhail Nikolaevich (1873–1952), writer and publisher.
Semyonov, Nikolai Petrovich (1755–1837), military office, husband of Maria Bunina, and brother-in-law of Anna Bunina.
Semyonov, Sergei Terentievich, (1868–1922), writer and playwright.
Semyonov-Tyan-Shansky, Pyotr Petrovich (1827–1914), geographer, statistician, and father of Veniamin Semyonov-Tyan-Shansky.
Semyonov-Tyan-Shansky, Veniamin Petrovich (1870–1942), geographer, statistician, and son of Pyotr Semyonov-Tyan-Shansky.
Serafim of Sarov (1754–1833), monk and saint.

Serafimovich, Alexander Serafimovich (1863–1949), writer.
Seredin, Leonid Valentinovich (1860–1909), doctor.
Sergeenko, Pyotr Alexeevich (1854–1930), Tolstoyan and writer.
Severnyi. *See* Yuzefovich, Boris.
Shakespeare, William (1564–1616), English poet and dramatist.
Shakhovskaya, Zinaida Alekseevna (1906–2001), princess, writer, and editor.
Shakovskoy, Alexander Alexandrovich (1777–1846), dramatist.
Shcherbatov, Nikolai Sergeevich (1853–1929), prince.
Shelley, Percy Bysshe (1792–1822), British writer.
Shestov, Lev Isaakovich (1866–1938), critic and philosopher.
Shingaryov, Andrei Ivanovich (1869–1918), doctor, publicist, and politician.
Shishkov, Alexander Semyonovich (1754–1841), statesman, writer, and admiral.
Shklovsky, Isaak Vladimirovich (Dineo) (1865–1935), writer, editor, publicist, and critic.
Shukhaev, Vasily Ivanovich (1887–1973), artist.
Simon (?–1226), bishop and monk.
Skabichevsky, Alexander Mikhailovich (1838–1910), literary critic and historian.
Skirmunt, Sergei Apollonovich (1862–1932), publisher.
Skitalets, Stepan Gavrilovich (1861–1941), writer.
Skobelev, Mikhail Dmitrievich (1843–1882), general.
Sluchevsky, Konstantin Konstaninovich (1837–1904), poet and prose writer.
Smuryi, Mikhail Antonovich (?–?), corporal.
Sobinov, Leonid Vitalievich (1872–1934), singer.
Socrates (470–399 BC), Greek philosopher.
Sofya Alexeevna (1657–1704), sister of Peter the Great and regent of Russia from 1682 to 1689.
Sokolov, Sergei Alexeevich (Krechetov) (1878–1936), poet, critic, and publisher.
Sologub, Fyodor Kuzmich (1863–1927), poet, dramatist, novelist, and short-story writer.
Solomon (tenth century BC), king of Israel.
Solovtsov, Nikolai Nikolaevich (1857–1902), director, actor, and entrepreneur.
Solovyov, Vladimir Sergeevich (1853–1900), philosopher, mystic, and poet.
Speransky, Mikhail Mikhailovich (1772–1839), statesman.
Stakhovich, Mikhail Alexandrovich (1861–1923), politician.
Stalin, Joseph Vissarionovich (1897–1953), revolutionary and dictator.
Stanislavsky, Konstantin Sergeevich (1863–1938), actor and theater director.
Statius, Publius Papinius (AD 45–circa 96), Roman poet.
Steiner, Rudolf (1861–1925), philosopher, social reformer, and architect.
Stepanova, Praskovya Yevgenieva (1881–1974), writer and memoirist.
Stepun, Fyodor Avgustovich (1884–1965), sociologist and critic.
Stravinsky, Igor Fyodorovich (1882–1971), composer, pianist, and conductor.
Strindberg, Johan August (1849–1912), Swedish playwright, novelist, poet, essayist, and painter.
Struve, Pyotr Berngardovich (1870–1944), political economist, philosopher, and editor.
Sudeikin, Sergei Yurievich (1882–1946), painter and stage designer.

Sukharev, Lavrenty Pankratievich (?–?), colonel.
Sukhomlin, Vasily Vasilievich (1918–1950), journalist and politician.
Sully-Prudhomme, René (1839–1907), French poet and essayist.
Suvorin, Alexei Sergeevich (1834–1912), editor and publisher.
Sverdlov, Yakov Mikhailovich (1885–1919), revolutionary leader.
Svyatopolk-Mirsky, Dmitri Petrovich (1890–1939), historian and critic.
Talin, Vladimir Ivanovich (1881–1944), critic.
Tamerlane (1336–1405), Turco-Mongol conqueror.
Tatlin, Vladimir (1885–1953), painter, architect, and stage designer.
Teffi, Nadezhda Alexandrovna (1872–1952), writer.
Teleshov, Nikolai Dmitrievich (1867–1957), writer.
Telyakovsky, Vladimir Arkadievich (1860–1924), administrator, memoirist, and director.
Teneromo, Isaak Borisovich (1863–1925), Tolstoyan, writer, and critic.
Terpigorev-Atava, Sergei Nikolaevich (1841–1895), writer.
Tikhonov, Alexander Nikolaevich (Serebrov), (1880–1956), writer.
Tolstaya, Sofya Andreevna (1844–1919), wife of Leo Tolstoy.
Tolstaya-Bostrom, Alexandra Leontieva (1854–1906), mother of Alexei Nikolaevich Tolstoy.
Tolstoy, Alexei Konstantinovich (1817–1875), poet, playwright, novelist, and satirist.
Tolstoy, Alexei Nikolaevich (1882–1945), novelist.
Tolstoy, Dmitri Andreevich (1823–1889), statesman.
Tolstoy, Ivan Lvovich (Vanya) (1888–1895), ninth son of Leo Tolstoy.
Tolstoy, Lev (Leo) Nikolaevich (1828–1910), novelist.
Tolstoy, Nikolai Alexandrovich (1849–1900), father of Alexei Nikolaevich Tolstoy.
Trotsky, Leon Davidovich (1879–1940), revolutionary leader and writer.
Trubetskoy, Grigory Nikolaevich (1874–1930), diplomat and publicist.
Tsakni, Anna Nikolaevna, (1879–1963), first wife of Ivan Bunin.
Tseitlin, Mikhail Osipovich (1882–1945), poet and critic.
Tseitlina, Maria Samoilovna (1882–1972), wife of Mikhail Tseitlin.
Tsemakh, Tatyana Davydovna (1890–1943?), poet.
Tsvetaeva, Marina Ivanovna (1892–1941), poet, essayist, and critic.
Turgenev, Ivan Sergeevich (1818–1883), novelist, short-story writer, and playwright.
Tyutchev, Fyodor Ivanovich (1803–1873), poet.
Ulyanov, Alexander Ilyich (1866–1887), revolutionary and brother of Vladimir Lenin.
Uspensky, Gleb Ivanovich (1843–1902), writer, journalist, and cousin of Nikolai Uspensky.
Uspensky, Nikolai Vasilievich (1837–1889), writer and cousin of Gleb Uspensky.
Vasily III (1479–1553), grand prince of Moscow from 1505 to 1533.
Vasnetsov, Apollon Mikhailovich (1856–1933), artist and brother of Viktor Vasnetsov.
Vasnetsov, Viktor Mikhailovich (1848–1926), artist and brother of Apollon Vasnetsov.
Veinbaum, Mark Yefimovich (1890–1973), editor.
Verbov, A. M. (?–?), poet.
Veresaev, Vikenty Vikentievich (1867–1945), writer and scholar.
Verlaine, Paul (1844–1896), French poet.

Viedkov, N. (?–?), poet.

Villiers de l'Isle-Adam, Auguste, comte de (1838–1889), French writer.

Voeikov, Alexander Fyodorovich (1779–1839), poet, critic, journalist, and professor.

Volkenshtein, Alexander Alexandrovich (1852–1925), doctor and Tolstoyan.

Voloshin, Maximilian Alexandrovich (1877–1932), poet, translator, and artist.

Volynsky, Akim Lvovich (1863–1926), literary critic and art historian.

Wirsén, Carl David af (1842–1912), Swedish poet, literary critic, and permanent secretary of the Swedish Academy from 1884 to 1912.

Woolf, Leonard (1880–1969), English theorist, author, publisher, and husband of Virginia Woolf.

Yakovlev, Alexander Yevgenievich (1887–1938), artist.

Yakovleva, Tatyana Alekseevna (1906–1991), fashion designer.

Yelizaveta Alekseevna (1779–1826), wife of Alexander I.

Yelpatievsky, Sergei Yakovlevich (1854–1933), physician and writer.

Yermolova, Maria Nikolaevna (1855–1939), actress.

Yevlogy (1868–1946), bishop and metropolitan.

Yushkevich, Pavel Solomonovich (1873–1945), social democrat and philosopher.

Yuzefovich, Boris Samoilovich (?–?), head of the Cheka in Odessa in 1919.

Yuzhin-Sumbatov, Alexander Ivanovich (1857–1927), dramatist, actor, and writer.

Zaitsev, Boris Konstantinovich (1881–1972), writer and dramatist.

Zamyatin, Yevgeny Ivanovich (1884–1937), writer, critic, dramatist, and editor.

Zasodimsky, Pavel Vladimirovich (1843–1912), writer.

Zhemchuzhnikov, Alexei Mikhailovich (1821–1908), poet.

Zhukov, Yury Alexandrovich (1908–1991), Soviet journalist and politician.

Zhukovsky, Vasily Andreevich (1783–1852), poet and translator.

Zinoviev, Grigory Yevseyevich (1883–1936), revolutionary and politician.

Zlatovratsky, Nikolai Nikolaevich (1845–1911), writer.

Zoshchenko, Mikhail Mikhailovich (1894–1958), writer.

Zweig, Stefan (1881–1942), Austrian novelist, playwright, journalist, and biographer.

Notes

Introduction

1. V. Talin, "Literator I. A. Bunin ob ostal'nykh," *Chisla*, bk. 2–3 (1930): 302.

2. Two months later, a reviewer wrote: "[At] an émigré gathering in Paris [celebrating] the occasion of the anniversary of Pushkin's birth . . . suddenly word went round that Bunin had arrived; he was, in fact, in a far corner of the hall, leaning against the wall—an emaciated man of sixty. His face was gray, his cheeks were sunken, his hair was white; his oblong head was ennobled by cavernous, attentive, kindly eyes.

". . . [Bunin] stared moodily over the hall. . . . Russian émigrés surrounded him and old acquaintances shook his hand. But he spoke little and obviously longed for the refuge of his small, dark room with its table full of manuscripts." E. Bey, "Ivan Bunin," *Saturday Review of Literature* 10, no. 20 (December 2, 1933): 302.

3. Talin, "Literator I. A. Bunin," 303.

4. Talin, "Literator I. A. Bunin," 302. Such fears were valid. As Bunin later told an interviewer from *Soviet Patriot*: "People cannot cut themselves off from the Homeland without a price. I sometimes visit émigré families. Several of the young ones are bored when they read *War and Peace*. . . . They do not understand [the heroine] Natasha Rostova. . . . They look upon her as I would someone from Greenland." V. Kurilov, "U I. A. Bunina," *Sovetskii patriot*, June 28, 1946, 4.

5. Talin, "Literator I. A. Bunin," 302–303.

6. M. Tseitlin, "Ivan Bunin. Roza Ierikhona," *Sovremennye zapiski* 22 (1924): 449–450; Z. Gippius, "Literaturnaia zapis'," *Sovremennye zapiski* 18 (1924): 128.

7. N. Kul'man, "'Tsikady' Bunina," *Vorozhdenie*, December 17, 1925, 4; F. Stepun, "Literaturnye zametki. I. A. Bunin (Po povodu 'Mitinoi liubvi')," *Sovremennye zapiski* 27 (1926): 327; D. Sviatopolk-Mirskii, "Bibliografiia," *Versty*, no. 1 (1926): 209; S. Postnikov, "Russkaia zarubezhnaia literatura v 1925 godu," *Volia Rossii*, no. 2 (1926): 184.

8. Talin, "Literator I. A. Bunin," 304–306.

9. Talin, "Literator I. A. Bunin," 303, 306.

10. Talin, "Literator I. A. Bunin," 303, 305.

11. Talin, "Literator I. A. Bunin," 303.

12. Talin, "Literator I. A. Bunin," 302, 303.

13. Talin, "Literator I. A. Bunin," 303, 304.

14. Talin, "Literator I. A. Bunin," 304.

15. I. Bunin, *Cursed Days*, trans. T. Marullo (London: Phoenix Press, 2000), 240, 241.

16. Bunin, *Cursed Days*, 240, 242, 247.

17. M. Grin, ed., *Ustami Buninykh. Dnevniki Ivana Alekseevicha i Very Nikolaevny i drugie arkhivnye materialy* (Frankfurt am Main: Possev-Verlag, 1982), 3:111; V. Sukhomlin, "Vstrechi s Buninym," *Otchizna*, 1966, 14; A. Baboreko, "Poslednie gody I. A. Bunina," *Voprosy literatury*, no. 3 (1965): 254.

18. T. Loginova-Muravieva, "Zhivoe proshloe. Vospominaniia ob I. A. i V. N. Buninykh," in *Ivan Alekseevich Bunin*, bk. 2, *Stat'i i vospominaniia. Soobshcheniia i obzory*, ed. A. Dubovnik et al. (Moscow: Nauka, 1973), 326–327.

19. A. Sedykh, *Dalekie, blizkie* (New York: Novoe Russkoe Slovo, 1962), 230–231.

20. A first translation of Bunin's *Recollections* appeared in 1951, but it is deficient in several respects. Many of the essays are severely edited or abridged: "Chekhov," "Chaliapin," "Gorky," "Voloshin," "The Third Tolstoy," "Mayakovsky," and "Nobel Days." Some, like the almost sixty-page "Autobiographical Notes," are missing altogether. Also lacking are commentary and notes to explain images and ideas put forth in the work.

21. See M. Grin, "Pis'ma M. A. Aldanova k I. A. i V. I. Buninym," *Novyi zhurnal* 81 (1965): 141.

22. M. Aldanov to I. Bunin, October 9, 1950, in Grin, "Pis'ma M. A. Aldanova," 141, 142; P. Stepanova, "Pisatel' i kretiny," *Vozrozhdenie*, no. 3–4 (1951): 175–176; G. Adamovich, "Po povodu 'Vospominanii,'" in *Odinochestvo i svoboda* (New York: Izdatel'stvo imeni Chekhova, 1955), 109, 111.

23. As Nina Berberova wrote in her memoirs circa 1948: "Bunin's destiny often disturbed him. . . . Some kind of beast ate at him from within, and his increasingly sharp judgments of his contemporaries, together with his even more malicious outbursts at the end of his life—written and oral—bear witness to the fact that he could not forget [modernist] 'idiots and cretins'; that they had tortured him endlessly throughout his life; that in his old age they had become stronger than he; and that, having grown weak, he had sought to defend himself with vulgarity and crudeness." N. Berberova, *Kursiv moi. Avtobiografiia v dvukh tomakh* (New York: Russica Publishers, 1983), 1:293.

24. Implicit in such atavism is Bunin's Buddhistic beliefs. As was the case with many of the characters in his fiction, the avant-gardists were victims of bad karma and regression to lower life-forms in new incarnations in life. For more on Bunin and Buddhism, see T. Marullo, *If You See the Buddha: Studies in the Fiction of Ivan Bunin* (Evanston, IL: Northwestern University Press, 1998).

25. A. Bakhrakh, "Po pamiati, po zapiskam (II) . . . ," *Mosty*, no. 12 (1966): 273.

26. Bunin's remarks on the writer were part of a larger work titled *The Liberation of Tolstoy*, published in Russian in 1937, a dialogue between the two writers on life-questions, with Bunin as student, son, and disciple at the feet of Tolstoy as teacher, father, and guide. For more on *Liberation*, see I. Bunin, *The Liberation of Tolstoy: A Tale of Two Writers*, ed., trans., and with an introduction and notes by T. Marullo and V. Khmelkov (Evanston, IL: Northwestern University Press, 2001).

27. Bunin's comments on the writer were subsumed into an unfinished piece, titled *About Chekhov*, published in 1955, two years after Bunin's death. Through anecdotes and observations, exchanges and reflections, Bunin sought to free Chekhov from limiting political, social, and aesthetic assessments of his life and writing and to present the writer in a more genuine, insightful, and personal way, depicting Chekhov at work, in love, and in ties to such writers as Leo Tolstoy and Gorky. For more on *About*

Chekhov, see I. Bunin, *About Chekhov: The Unfinished Symphony*, ed. and trans. T. Marullo (Evanston, IL: Northwestern University Press, 2007).

28. Bunin's insensitivity here is indeed regrettable.

29. A. Baboreko, *I. A. Bunin. Materialy dlia biografii* (Moscow: Khudozhestvennaia literatura, 1967), 215; review of *The Gentleman from San Francisco and Other Stories*, *London Times*, May 17, 1922, 16.

30. See J. H. Willis Jr., *Leonard and Virginia Woolf as Publishers: The Hogarth Press, 1917–41* (Charlottesville: University Press of Virginia, 1992), 94; A. Baboreko, "Iz pis'ma Romena Rollana k Luize Kruppi," in *Literaturnoe nasledstvo*, ed. V. Shcherbina et al., vol. 84, *Ivan Bunin* (Moscow: Nauka, 1973), bk. 2, 375. Also see Rolland's letter to Bunin, written on June 10, 1922, in R. Rollan, "Pis'mo Romena Rollana k I. Buninu," *Parusa*, no. 1 (1922): 61.

31. J. M. Murry, "Ivan Bunin," *The Nation and the Athenaeum*, June 24, 1922, 444; T. Mann, *Pariser Rechenschaft* (Berlin: S. Fischer, 1926), 7.

32. See A. Gide, *The Journals of André Gide*, trans. J. O'Brien (New York: Knopf, 1948), 3:309.

33. M. Pechkovskii, "Vecher I. A. Bunina," *Novoe russkoe slovo*, November 15, 1933, 3.

1. Autobiographical Notes

1. Oryol is both a city and a province, located two hundred miles southwest of Moscow.

2. Voronezh is located approximately three hundred miles to the southeast of Moscow.

3. Oryol is roughly two hundred miles northwest of Voronezh.

4. Bunin is referring to Sergei Terpigorev-Atava's 1881 work *Impoverishment: Essays of Gentry Ruin.*

After the 1861 Emancipation, gentry landowners faced not only the loss of their serfs, but also undeveloped markets and inadequate capital, technology, and methods for modern farming. As a result, the land possessed by gentry men in Russia fell by nearly a third between 1877 and 1905.

5. As Bunin told an interviewer from the *Odessa Leaflet* on March 12, 1910: "Critics have called my works the 'Lyrics of Fading Away' and 'The Sadness of Desolation' . . . old labels, which, of course, are easier to use than to seek new ones." See A. Ninov, "K avtobiografii I. A. Bunina," *Novyi mir*, no. 10 (1965): 224.

6. Doctor Astrov and Uncle Vanya are characters in Chekhov's 1897 play *Uncle Vanya*; Simeonov-Pishchik and Gaev, in his 1904 work *The Cherry Orchard*. Also, onstage, Gaev was portrayed by Konstantin Stanislavsky as an effeminate dandy who dangled his right hand at the wrist and who wore a tailored double-breasted jacket and a floppy silk bow.

7. Bunin did not know that Chekhov had a cherry orchard of some fifty trees at his estate at Melikhovo. There were also cherry trees in Chekhov's youth in Taganrog, his birthplace on the north shore of the Sea of Azov, about six hundred miles south of Moscow.

8. The Moscow Art Theater was founded in 1898 by Stanislavsky and Vladimir Nemirovich-Danchenko and championed theatrical realism in Russia.

9. Bunin is referring to both Gorky and his 1901 work "The Song of the Stormy Petrel."

10. Nina Zarechnaya is a character in Chekhov's 1896 play *The Seagull*.

11. Tit Titych Bruskin is a merchant in Alexander Ostrovsky's 1856 comedy *Hangover at Another's Feast*.

The *Domostroi*, or *Domestic Order*, was a sixteenth-century codex of rules and regulations, which stressed unquestioning respect and obedience to the heads of family and state, as well as punishment for wives, children, and servants who strayed from patriarchal paths.

12. The citation is from the poet Dmitri Kedrin and his 1937 poem "Fall around Moscow."

13. The Central Committee of the Communist Party ordered that the Moscow Art Theater be renamed the Gorky Moscow Art Theater on September 17, 1932. The seagull is still there.

14. Gorky wrote his play *The Lower Depths* in 1902. Stanislavsky was hardly humble in the acquiescence in renaming the Moscow Art Theater, writing to Gorky on September 29, 1932: "I rejoice that our theater, the close witness of your brilliant literary career for the past forty years, now bears your name. From now on we shall work together for the Soviet theater, which alone can sustain the decaying theater in the rest of the world." See K. Stanislavskii, *Stat'i, besedy, pis'ma* (Moscow: Iskusstvo, 1953), 309–310.

15. L. Kotov, ed., *A. P. Chekhov v vospominaniiakh sovremennikov* (Moscow: Gosudarstvennoe izdatel'stvo khudozhestvennoi literatury, 1947).

16. There are three Tolstoys in Bunin's narrative: Alexei Konstantinovich Tolstoy, poet and novelist; Alexei (Alyoshka) Nikolaevich Tolstoy, émigré (and later Soviet) writer; and Lev Nikolaevich Tolstoy, the author of *War and Peace* and *Anna Karenina*.

17. Yalta is a city in the Crimea, almost a thousand miles from Moscow. Bunin's time with Chekhov there was one of the happiest periods in his life. "My days here in Yalta pass by in a kind of poetic exaltation," he wrote to a friend in mid-February 1901. "We have sun, a joyous, turquoise sky, and the sea below. If only you knew what I see from my windows. . . . I am writing a lot of poetry, and I am beginning many, many stories. I am reading . . . and I dream." See A. Baboreko, "Chekhov i Bunin," in *Literaturnoe nasledstvo*, ed. V. Vinogradov et al., vol. 68, *Anton Chekhov* (Moscow: Izdatel'stvo Akademii nauk SSSR, 1960), 396.

18. The article, if it ever existed, has been lost with time. A 1949 piece titled "A. P. Chekhov in Yalta," published in *Dom-muzei A. P. Chekhova v Ialte. Tekst M. P. Chekhovoi* (Moscow: Iskusstvo, 1951), states that Molotov made his statement about Chekhov on August 17, 1936.

Also, Bunin is not being fair to Maria Chekhova. It is true that, since the revolution, Chekhova had been accommodating the Bolsheviks to preserve the memory of her brother and his work. She had ceded the bulk of Chekhov's archive to Soviet authorities and was also serving as the director of the A. P. Chekhov Home-Museum in Yalta, a position that she held from 1921 until her death in 1957.

What Bunin did not know, though, is that Chekhova, especially in the early years of Soviet power, often feared for her life. In 1920 alone, the Bolsheviks searched her home at least ten times and had even issued an order for her arrest.

It should also be noted that earlier in their time together, Bunin was quite taken with Chekhova. On April 18, 1900, he wrote to Yuly Bunin that he had "paid court" to Chekhov's sister. See A. Baboreko, "Chekhov v perepiske i zapiskakh Bunina," in *A. P. Chekhov. Sbornik statei i materialy* (Simferopol: Krymizdat, 1962), 22–23.

19. The Second All-Union Congress of Soviets, five days after Lenin died and allegedly fulfilling the unanimous request of the workers of the city, renamed Petrograd as Leningrad on January 26, 1924. Apparently, it was Grigory Zinoviev who prompted the change in order to restore the importance of Petrograd-Leningrad after Bolshevik leaders had moved the capital to Moscow.

20. Königsberg, roughly 700 miles west of Moscow, has borne the name Kaliningrad since 1946. Nizhniy Novgorod, situated 250 miles southeast of Moscow, was called Gorky from 1932 to 1990. Tver', located 90 miles northeast of Moscow, was known as Kalinin from 1932 to 1990.

Also, in his pre-party life, Mikhail Kalinin worked not as a type fitter, but as a lathe operator, steam fitter, and patternmaker for cannons. Further, Immanuel Kant was born in Königsberg on April 22, 1724. He lived his entire life there.

21. This quotation, long attributed to Blok, is apparently fiction, not fact. In Russian lore, Kitezh is one of two places: a town that escaped destruction by the Tartars by sinking into Lake Svetloyar, north of Nizhniy Novgorod, or a village located near Suzdal, approximately 125 miles northeast of the Russian capital, that was destroyed by the Tartars, but which, allegedly in calm weather, rents the air with church bells and reveals its ruined buildings at the bottom of a lake. Nikolai Rimsky-Korsakov also used the legend of Kitezh as the basis for his 1907 opera *The Tale of the Invisible Town of Kitezh and the Maid Fevroniya*.

Also, according to Vladimir Chernyavsky, Esenin conceived of Inoniya as "another land" that actually existed in the real world. See V. Cherniavskii, "Tri epokhi vstrech (1919–1925)," in *S. A. Esenin v vospominaniiakh sovremennikov v dvukh tomakh*, ed. A. Kozlovskii (Moscow: Khudozhestvennaia literatura, 1986), 1:220.

22. Bunin is citing from Esenin's 1918 poem "Inoniia."

23. In truth, many émigrés worshipped Esenin in a cultlike way. Some saw him as a child prodigy who hailed from the people. Others regarded the poet as an angelic messenger sent by God. Still others looked on Esenin as a prophet crying in the wilderness, a pilgrim extolling national soul and soil, and a martyr who, like so many Russian writers and artists before him, suffered persecution and death for his beliefs.

24. The "brat" is not a writer, but merely a schoolboy, reciting a naughty children's verse.

The poem in question is "By Both Pen and Ax," published in Paris in 1928. Also, the distance between Odessa, in southern Ukraine, and the island of Sakhalin, in Russia's Far East, is more than forty-six hundred miles.

25. Again, The poem in question is "By Both Pen and Ax."

26. Esenin appeared in St. Petersburg on March 9, 1915. A writer, having met the poet shortly after his arrival in the capital, wrote of one reception: "People . . . listened with growing enthusiasm. . . . Not even knowing Esenin's poetry, these 'intellectuals' felt his wonderful freshness, his unspoiled health, his lack of crudeness, his half-shy and half-insolent youth. They smelled the odor of the faraway village, which seemed so wholesome to them." See Vl. S-kii, "Pervye shagi," *Zvezda*, no. 4 (1926): 214.

27. Fyodor Sologub resented deeply the ease with which Esenin had achieved literary fame in Russia. Even Gorky was smitten with the then twenty-year-old Esenin. He wrote: "Esenin seemed to me to be a boy between 15 and 17, curly haired and light-complexioned, in a light-blue shirt, a long broad coat, and boots with decorative plates. He recalled sickly sweet postcards . . . of princely children . . . [as well as] the image of a lost boy who felt that there was no place for him in huge St. Petersburg." See M. Gor'kii, *Sobranie sochinenii v vosemnadtsati tomakh* (Moscow: Khudozhestvennaia literatura, 1963), 18:202.

28. The Imagists, a literary modernist group that existed from 1919 to 1927, upheld experimental rhythm and rhyme, syntax devoid of adjectives and verbs, and catalogs and chains of images that were unusual, striking, and shockingly blasphemous and obscene.

About Esenin's behavior, Anatoly Mariengof recalled: "One evening, we went out to some bohemian tavern. . . . Esenin was drunk on the first glass of wine. . . . He punched somebody, cursed, smashed dishes, overturned tables, tore up his money, and flung it in the air." A. Mariengof, *Roman bez vran'ia* (Leningrad: Khudozhestvennaia literatura, 1988), 111.

Also, Esenin met Duncan in Moscow in 1921 and married her a year later. He was twenty-seven; she was forty-four. The marriage was a stormy one, if only because each did not speak the other's language (they communicated through gestures), and because the increasingly unbalanced Esenin was wildly jealous of his wife's notoriety, especially in the United States.

Finally, "God, deliver the calf" is from Esenin's 1917 poem "Transformation." The poet committed suicide on December 27, 1925.

29. Bunin noted in his diary on April 12, 1941: "Babel writes . . . about the Mother of God [in his 1924 story 'The End of St. Hypathius']: 'The thin-looking woman sat with her knees spread apart, and with breasts that were long and green like snakes.'" See M. Grin, ed., "Iz dnevnikov i zapisei I. A. Bunina," *Novyi zhurnal*, no. 113 (1973): 151.

30. Esenin was not alone in such a view. Bunin recalled in his 1937 "Notes": "Then there was Bely, who kept 'throwing pineapples in space' and who sang about the coming . . . transformation of the world. He was always in motion. His entire body would twitch. He would first sit down, then run off somewhere, then run back. With an absurdly merry expression, he would continually look all about the room." See I. Bunin, "Iz zapisei," in *Sobranie sochinenii v deviati tomakh* (Moscow: Khudozhestvennaia literatura, 1967), 9:298.

31. Bunin is quoting from Mariengof's 1927 novel, A Novel Without Lies 11–12.

32. The article in question is R. Berezov. "S. Esenin, D. Bednyi, V. Maiakovskii," *Novoe russkoe slovo*, January 30, 1949, 2, 7; February 6, 1949, 2. *New Russian Word*, published between 1910 and 2010, was the daily Russian-language newspaper that chronicled news and events for Russian immigrants and émigrés in North America.

33. Esenin wrote "A Blue Fire Rushed through the Land" in 1923.

34. Consider the "outcast lizards" in Balmont's 1899 poem "Freaks."

35. This stanza, together with the preceding two citations from Esenin's verse, are from his poem "Blue May," written in 1925.

36. *Red Virgin Soil* was a literary journal, published in Moscow from 1921 to 1942.

37. Beryozov's claim is false. Benislavskaya never married Esenin.

38. Samarkand is the second-largest city in Uzbekistan, approximately seventeen hundred miles southeast of Moscow.

39. Esenin and Duncan arrived in New York on October 1, 1922. The visit was a disaster.

40. Many "second wave" émigrés—Russians who came to the West after World War II—were offended deeply by Bunin's remarks on Esenin.

Georgy Alexandrov, in an article titled "To the Memory of Esenin" and published in October 1950, wrote: "Neither in the homeland, nor here abroad will we allow anyone to desecrate Esenin's memory. . . .

"The venerable writer I. A. Bunin, in his *Recollections*, has devoted to Esenin lines that resound sickly and insultingly in the heart of each new émigré who carries with him, among the most cherished remembrances of the homeland, the memory of a poet who perished before his time, and about whom all of Soviet Russia read and sang. . . ."

Alexandrov continued: "We do not know how the older generation of our countrymen, abroad among foreigners, lives and breathes from the homeland. Perhaps, for them, kept in the dark, in the shell of pleasant, prerevolutionary recollections, singing for thirty years the comfortable life of gentry estates, Esenin was only a drunkard." G. Alexandrov, "Pamiati Esenina," *Novoe russkoe slovo*, October 27, 1950, 2.

Bunin stood his ground. In an article titled "We Will Not Allow It," published in January 1951, Bunin wrote: "In the role of a scandalmonger, hooligan, drunkard . . . rascal . . . [and] cynic . . . Esenin truly has no equal."

About allegedly estate-loving émigrés, Bunin continued: "[Alexandrov] does not know . . . the hundreds of thousands of Russians who survived [revolution and war] and who now earn their bread with the most difficult backbreaking work in Bulgaria, Serbia, Czechoslovakia, and France! And it is to these hundreds of thousands of peasant-émigrés that he ascribes dreams of gentry estates!" I. Bunin, "My ne povolim," *Novoe russkoe slovo*, January 7, 1951, 3.

41. Mayakovsky visited the United States from July 30 to October 28, 1925.

42. *Contemporary Annals* was a journal published in France from 1920 to 1940. The article in question, titled "Esenin," appeared in issue no. 27 (1926), 292–322. The Cheka or more formally the All-Russian Extraordinary Commission (Vserossiiskaya chrezvychainaya komissiya) was established on December 5, 1917, as the first in a succession of Soviet secret-police organizations.

43. Vladimir Khodasevich's claim has several sources: (1) the imagists, of which Esenin was a member, had a book published by the Cheka; (2) in October 1925, Felix Dzerzhinsky, head of the Cheka, ordered that the ailing Esenin be cared for in a Soviet hospital; and (3) long-standing rumors among Russian émigrés were that Esenin served the Soviet secret police.

44. Dostoevsky published *The Brothers Karamazov* in 1880; Turgenev, "The Song of Love Triumphant" in 1881 and "Klara Milich" in 1883.

45. Fet wrote *Evening Fires* in 1883. Tolstoy's *The Kreutzer Sonata* appeared in 1889 and *The Death of Ivan Ilyich*, three years earlier.

46. The psychotic thirty-three-year-old Vsevolod Garshin ended his life by throwing himself down a staircase on April 5, 1888.

47. Ertel wrote *The Gardenins, Their Servants, Supporters, and Enemies* in 1889.

48. Vladimir Korolenko's "Makar's Dream" appeared in 1885.

49. Kozma Prutkov was the literary persona of Alexei Konstaninovich Tolstoy and Alexei Zhemchuzhnikov, who attacked evils of the day, particularly bureaucracy.

50. In the 1870s, Russian Populists were intellectuals who advocated popular democracy for peasants and workers, but who were crushed by the authorities in the wake of the assassination of Alexander II. Revived in the 1890s, Russian Populists called themselves social revolutionaries and founded the Social-Revolutionary Party. By contrast, the Marxists insisted that since Russia had entered upon a capitalistic development, it was ripe for revolution by both peasants and workers.

51. Gorky wrote "Chelkash" and "The Old Woman Izergiil" in 1895.

52. Bunin is quoting from Nikolai Minsky's 1888 poem "The Fourth Night."

53. Bunin is citing Minsky's 1905 poem "The Workers' Hymn."

54. The somewhat inaccurate citation is from Bryusov's 1924 piece "Requiem: On the Death of V. I. Lenin."

55. Bryusov wrote the poem, "Oh Cry! Oh Cry!," in 1896.

56. Bunin is citing from Bryusov's 1895 piece "Creation."

57. Bunin is quoting from Bryusov's 1910 "In the Unpeopled Night."

59. The citation is from Bryusov's 1923 poem "In the Pacific Ocean."

60. Konstantin Sluchevsky's "Fridays" took place at his home in St. Petersburg between 1898 and 1903 and included writers, artists, and intellectuals such as Bryusov, Merezhkovsky, Gippius, Sologub, Nemirovich-Danchenko, and Solovyov.

61. Bunin is quoting from Balmont's 1894 verse "Song without Words."

62. The citation is from Balmont's 1894 poem "Canoe of Torment."

63. As a reporter wrote in *Exchange News* in April 1908: "In [the journal] *Scales*, Balmont tells of his visit to L. Tolstoy. 'The old man spoke in a kind, teasing voice. "Do you always write decadent verse?" he asked. "That's not good, not good."

'I read to him "Smell of the Sun," but he laughed quietly and censured it, saying: "Akh, what nonsense. The smell of the sun. What nonsense."

'He . . . then asked me to read something else. I did so. . . . Tolstoy pretended that he did not like it all.'" "Lev Tolstoi pritvoriaetsia," *Birzhevye vedomosti*, April 15, 1908, 2.

64. Maurice Maeterlinck wrote *The Blue Bird* in 1908. It was staged by the Moscow Art Theater that same year. Maeterlinck was also popular among Russian symbolists for his plays of semi-allusions and happenings.

65. Balmont visited the Cape of Good Hope as part of a yearlong trip around the world in 1912.

66. Bunin is quoting from Balmont's 1912 piece "From Southern Distances."

67. Alexander Myasnikov's article was published in V. Briusov, *Izbrannye stikhotvoreniia*, in Moscow in 1945. Also, Balmont studied some forty languages and translated the verse of German, Spanish, French, Georgian, Asian, and East European writers.

68. Scorpion was a publishing house founded in Moscow in 1900 to further European and Russian symbolism. It ceased operations in 1916. *Russian Thought*, a sociopolitical newspaper, was founded in Paris in 1947 to fight totalitarianism, but now connects Russian-speaking communities in Europe with the homeland.

69. Bunin is one to talk, forgetting that he, too, was ill at ease with French.

70. Bunin is referring to Balmont's 1893 translation of Percy Bysshe Shelley's 1817 sonnet "Ozymandias."

71. The story is true. Also, Kornei Chukovsky, in his 1968 memoir "Hospital Notes," recalled being told by Isaak Shklovsky (Dioneo):

"A tipsy Balmont was walking through London at night. The police there had a habit of checking up on drunkards with the help of a baton. If after a light strike, the drunkard did not collapse to the ground, he was allowed to continue on this way. If he did, he was taken to the police station. Balmont did not collapse, but around morning arrived at the boardinghouse all black and blue." See K. Chukovskii, *Dnevnik 1901–1969* (Moscow: Olma-Press, 2003), 2:502.

72. "The Enchanted Grotto" was the title of the fourth chapter in Balmont's 1903 work *Let Us Be like the Sun: A Book of Symbols.*

73. *The Scales*, published between 1904 and 1909, was the leading literary journal of Russian symbolism. Bryusov's review of Bunin appeared in *The Scales* in 1907.

74. Bunin wrote *The Gentleman from San Francisco* in 1915.

75. Russian symbolism was an artistic and literary movement from roughly 1900 to 1910, its adherents advocating trends that were idealist, aesthetic, irrational, and mystical.

76. In 1887, Balmont was expelled from the law faculty of Moscow University for taking part in student disturbances over changes in the school's rules and regulations.

77. Balmont wrote *Songs of an Avenger* in 1907.

78. A Balmont was pardoned in a general amnesty on the occasion of the three hundredth anniversary of the Romanov dynasty. Also, as Balmont wrote to Alexander Eliasberg on March 18, 1907: "Slavs must move forward into first place in Europe and say their own truthful, sonorous, and Slavic word."

The People's Committee on Education was founded in 1917 under the leadership of Anatoly Lunacharsky. Throughout the 1920s and 1930s, it supervised almost all cultural and humanitarian spheres: schools, libraries, museums, theaters, cinemas, clubs, and other institutions of learning, culture, and recreation. See P. Kupriianovskii, *Bal'mont* (Moscow: Molodaia gvardiia, 2014), 220.

79. Having welcomed the revolution, Balmont soon became disillusioned with the Bolsheviks and left Russia permanently for France on May 25, 1920.

80. Bryusov's "Freaks" appeared in 1900.

81. Bunin is referring to Balmont's 1905 poem "Without Equivocation." Also, *New Life* was the first Bolshevik newspaper to be published legally in Russia. It was short-lived, though, appearing in twenty-eight issues in November and December 1905, with a circulation of eighty thousand readers, before being closed down by the Provisional Government on December 16, 1905.

82. The Moscow uprising, the culminating event of the Revolution of 1905, took place between December 7 and 19, 1905. On December 7, Bolsheviks, Mensheviks, and Social Revolutionaries called for a strike, which turned quickly into an armed insurrection against the tsarist government. Although the rebels—a motley assortment of workers, students, and upscale citizens—could have taken the Kremlin, they lacked a unified plan of attack.

By the end of the revolt, more than a thousand people died, including 137 women and 86 children, many of whom were caught in cross fire or burning buildings.

83. Bunin is citing from Balmont's "Our Tsar."

84. The journal in question is *Bugbear*, which came out in only three issues in 1905 and 1906, before it was closed down (and its issues confiscated) by the tsarist police.

The offending picture, done by Zinovy Grzhebin, appeared on page 8 of the first issue, not on the cover. Titled "Eagle Inside Out," the drawing depicted the official two-headed eagle with tail feathers that ended in a crown; but, when turned upside down, it showed the tsar's head and crown, along with his exposed derrière, peering out from under his cape. (A copy of the picture can be found in S. Isakov, *1905 god v satire i karikature* [Leningrad: Priboi, 1928], 48.) Grzhebin did not escape punishment for his deed, though, and was sentenced to more than six months in prison in 1906.

Also, Gorky visited America in 1906, and in that same year, moved to the island of Capri where he lived until 1913.

85. Korolenko, in his 1887 short story "At the Eclipse," is quoting from a poem by Nikolai Berg.

86. Leonid Andreev wrote this letter to Vikenty Veresaev in April 1906.

The Kadets, or Constitutional Democratic Party, formed the most important liberal political party in Russia from October 1905 to the end of the civil war.

87. Bunin is quoting Job 1:18–19.

88. Bunin is paraphrasing from E. Kuskova, "A chto vnutri?," *Volia Rossii*, no. 7 (1922): 38.

89. More accurately, the Order of the Red Banner of Labor was established in 1928 to honor achievements in Soviet industry and culture.

90. GPU or Gosudarstvennoe Politicheskoe Upravlenie (State Political Administration)was the Soviet secret police from 1922 to 1934. NKVD or Narodnyi Komissariat Vnutrennikh Del (People's Commissariat for Internal Affairs) was an organ of the Soviet government that was founded in October 1917.

91. Volynsky did so in an article titled "Literaturnye zametki," in *Severnyi vestnik*, no. 1 (1891), otd. II, 152.

92. Tolstoy made this statement on December 15, 1908. See L. Tolstoi, *Polnoe sobranie sochinenii v devianosta tomakh* (Moscow: Akademiia nauk, 1939), 37–38:531.

93. Bunin is quoting from Vasily Rozanov's 1912 work *Solitaria*.

94. Bunin is citing from P. Medvedev, ed., *Dnevnik Al. Bloka v dvukh tomakh* (Leningrad: Izdatel'stvo pisatelei v Leningrade, 1928).

95. The reference is to Dmitri Merezhkovsky and his wife, Zinaida Gippius. The Khlysty were a mystical sect that, from the mid-seventeenth century on, sought spiritual ecstasy in esoteric (and often bizarre) rituals and rites.

96. Bunin is quoting selectively here. The actual passage in Blok's diary reads: "Vyacheslav Ivanov's article, despite all its profundity, is stifling and obtuse." See A. Blok, *Sobranie sochinenii v vos'mi tomakh* (Moscow: Gosudarstvennoe izdatel'stvo khudozhestvennoi literatury, 1960), 8:387.

97. Bunin is referring to restaurants and nightclubs such as the Bear and the Wandering Dog in St. Petersburg, where, in the years immediately before the revolution, writers and artists, as "wandering dogs" and other self-styled homeless types, met to share their ideas and works.

98. Blok wrote this diary excerpt on May 25, 1917.

99. Conceivably, the reference is to Bryusov's 1908 novel *The Fiery Angel*.

100. The collection in question is *Poems about the Beautiful Lady*, published in 1904.

101. Someone has his facts wrong. Homer lived in the ninth century BC; the Alexandrine Library was founded some six centuries later.

102. Blok published *The Snow Mask* in 1907; Bely, *The Goblet of Blizzards* in 1908; and Balmont, *Serpentine Flowers* in 1910.

103. Bunin is again referring to Kotov, *A. P. Chekhov v vospominaniiakh sovremennikov*.

104. Gorky wrote "The Song of The Falcon" in 1894 and "The Song of the Stormy Petrel" in 1901.

105. Gorky wrote *Foma Gordeev* in 1899. *Okanie* is a northern dialect of Russian, featuring differentiation of the vowels *a* and *o* after hard (non-palatalized) consonants in unstressed syllables.

106. Chekhov is referring to Bryusov's one-line 1895 poem, "O, cover your pale legs. . . ."

107. Mikhail Artsybashev died of tuberculosis in 1927 at the age of forty-eight. Same-sex love was key to Mikhail Kuzmin's life and art. Bunin's homophobia is as regrettable as his racism.

108. Gippius had consumption as a child but was also cured of the disease.

109. Sologub wrote *The Petty Demon* in 1907. Bunin is quoting Rozanov from Z. Gippius, *Zhivye litsa* (Prague: Plamia, 1925), 16.

110. Bunin is quoting from Gorky's 1906 work *In America: The City of the Yellow Devil*.

111. The correct citation is S. Balukhatyi, *The Literary Work of M. Gorky* (Moscow: Akademiia, 1936), xxv.

112. *The Beacon*, first published in 1923, is a literary and sociopolitical journal that continues to this day. Also, many people have discredited claims of Gorky's murder by Leon Trotsky and Nikolai Bukharin, as well as by Stalin himself. The sixty-eight-year-old writer was so exhausted and tubercular at the end of his life that he may very well have died of pneumonia on June 8, 1936, without any criminal intervention whatsoever.

113. Marina Tsvetaeva returned to the Soviet Union in 1939 and committed suicide there two years later.

Balmont had been showing signs of mental illness from about 1932 on. "Balmont is not doing well," Boris Zaitsev wrote to Bunin on July 3, 1935. "He is living in a small wing in a clinic near Paris. He has been having an affair with a 75-year-old crazy woman and has also become friends with a French poet who is laying claim to the French throne. He and Balmont have even founded a political group for this purpose." See M. Grin, "Pis'ma B. K Zaitseva k I. A. i V. N. Buninym," *Novyi zhurnal*, no. 149 (1982): 138–139.

About Bryusov, Khodasevich recalled in 1924: "At the end of 1919 I happened to replace Bryusov at one of his posts. Glancing into an empty desk drawer, I found a hypodermic needle and a scrap of newspaper spotted with blood. In his later years, he was ailing—apparently from a drug addiction." Although Bryusov depicted sexual torture and perversity in his writing, it is most likely the case that he was more libidinous on paper than in life. See V. Khodasevich, "Briusov," in *V. Khodasevich, Nekropol'* (Moscow: Vagrius, 1995), 45.

Even as a student, Andreev was so victimized by alcohol that he often contemplated suicide, and in 1894 he even attempted to take his life.

114. Blok's grandfather was a gentleman of the tsar's chamber and a marshal of the nobility who spent the last two years of his life in a psychiatric hospital. His mother, the daughter of the rector of St. Petersburg University, was also mentally unbalanced: playful and vicarious one moment, but the next, depressed and suicidal.

Blok himself suffered from scurvy in his early twenties. More seriously, the poet was stricken with syphilis, which he had contracted as a schoolboy. Later he was diagnosed with acute endocarditis and psychasthenia.

115. In his 1918 story "Confessions of a Pagan," Blok recalled: "Mama took me to the gymnasium. . . . The smoothly cropped and loudly shouting boys frightened me terribly. I would have run away gladly or hidden somewhere. . . . I felt like a rooster . . . bent over and motionless, not daring to raise my head. . . . Our class was wild . . . great profligates, old smokers, precocious women chasers, cynics, wrestlers, and athletes." See Blok, *Sobranie sochinenii*, vol. 6 (1962), 39, 40, 42.

116. Vasily Zhukovsky was a distant relative of Bunin.

117. The argonauts were a group of young poets, artists, and philosophers who took their name from the legend of Jason and the Golden Fleece and from a 1903 lyrical prose fragment by Bely. Inspired by the poetry of Solovyov and the philosophy of Friedrich Nietzsche, the argonauts awaited the Apocalypse and other cataclysms and wished to reconcile heaven and earth in strivings for the sun.

118. Blok was at the front in southwestern Belarus but, as a supervisor of some two thousand men, was charged with building and repainting lines of communication and defense.

Also, Alexander Presnyakov, in a conversation with the poet in 1913, recalled: "A. A. Blok spoke of the 'mighty poison' that Jews introduced into the Aryan milieu . . . a 'yellow' power [that] poisons everything belittling it, and sucking it with slimy vulgarity and earthliness." See "O 'iudoboiazni' Andreia Belogo," *Novoe literaturnoe obozrenie*, no. 28 (1997): 101–102.

119. See Z. Gippius, *A Blue Book: A Petersburg Diary, 1914–1918*, published in Belgrade in 1929.

120. *Russian Contemporary* appeared in only four issues in 1924.

121. Gorky made such a statement in an article, titled "About Garin-Mikhailovsky," in the journal *Red Virgin Soil*, on April 9, 1927.

122. The Constituent Assembly was a popularly elected group of representatives from throughout the Russian Empire who sought to determine Russian political life after the February and October Revolutions of 1917. The assembly was short-lived, meeting for only thirteen hours before it was closed by the Bolsheviks on January 6, 1918.

123. Ernest Renan was the author of the enormously popular 1863 work *The Life of Jesus*, in which he informed race with personhood and the theology of Jesus: Renan claimed that Jesus had purified himself of his Jewishness and had become an Aryan Christian.

Also, by rejecting Jesus's godhood and miracles, Renan claimed not only that he was restoring Jesus to greater dignity as a human but also that Jesus's life should be written in the same way as any historical individual's. He also insisted that the Bible could and should be subject to the same critical scrutiny as other historical documents. Needless to say, in *The Life of Jesus*, Renan angered many Christians. He also outraged

Jews for depicting Judaism as foolish and illogical and for insisting on the superiority of Christianity over their religious beliefs.

124. Anna Akhmatova did so in the first line of a poem, sometimes titled "The Wandering Dog," written on January 1, 1913.

125. Bunin is referring to Kuzmin's piece "The Birth of Christ," performed only once, on January 6—the Feast of the Epiphany—in 1913.

For the performance, Sergei Sudeikin recast a basement as a cathedral, replete with paintings of angels and devils and blue blunting studded with huge stars. Rows of tables became pews, with more than a hundred candles illuminating moving shadows on the walls.

Mary, played by Olga Glebova-Sudeikina in a gold dress, did, in fact, flee Herod on the back of the poet Pyotr Potyomkin, dressed in a long white robe, and carried a puppet Christ Child that was sewn to her hands.

See L. Tikhvinskaia, *Povsednevnaia zhizn' teatral'noi bogemy Serebrianogo veka. Kabare i teatry miniatiur v Rossii, 1908–1917* (Moscow: Molodaia gvardiia, 2005), 527.

126. Bunin's claim is untrue, but was most likely prompted by the fact that Kuzmin translated Giovanni Boccaccio's *Elegia de Madonna Fiammetta* (written between 1343 and 1345) into Russian in 1913.

127. *The Atheist* appeared in Moscow as a newspaper in December 1922 and as a magazine in March 1925. With Stalin's revival of the Orthodox Church in the wake of the German invasion of Russia in the Second World War, both periodicals ceased publication in June 1941.

128. Bednyi wrote his epic poem *A Flawless New Testament by the Evangelist Demyan Bednyi* in 1925.

129. *Days* was published first in Berlin from 1922 to 1925 and then as a weekly in Paris from 1925 to 1933. Alexander Kerensky was among its editors. Also, Isaac Babel published "Sasha the Christ" in 1924.

130. Babel's "The Sin of Jesus" appeared in 1922.

131. The review appeared in *Days* on October 25, 1925.

132. The fact that Arina rebukes God first for giving her human desires and then for demanding both chastity and virtue was apparently too "revolutionary" for Bunin and the reviewer of *Days* to bear.

133. In his 1923 "Pan Apolek," Babel describes icons with "Josephs with gray hair parted down the middle, pomaded Jesuses, ever-pregnant Marys with knees spread wide."

134. In truth, Viktor Khlebnikov was given the name "Velimir" in 1909, at one of the celebrated "literary Wednesdays," hosted by Vyacheslav Ivanov in 1909. Also, Bunin is referring to the February Revolution of 1917, which ended the Romanov dynasty and established the Provisional Government as prelude to a popularly elected Constituent Assembly.

135. Futurism was a modernist poetic movement founded by Khlebnikov in 1910. An offshoot of Filippo Marinetti's Italian futurism, the Russian futurists rejected the fiction of Pushkin and Leo Tolstoy and affirmed "trans-sense language" and *épater les bourgeois* in literature and life.

136. Claims as to Khlebnikov's insanity were indeed widespread at the time, but the only evidence for such assertions is the fact that Khlebnikov underwent psychiatric testing to escape military service after being drafted in April 1916.

137. Mountains and snows notwithstanding, Khlebnikov was wandering just south of Red Square.

138. In his search for a mathematical understanding of history, Khlebnikov believed that the number 317 had special import. It was the difference between the 365 days in a year and the 48 "forces" he believed to be operative in the universe.

139. Astrakhan is located near the Caspian Sea, roughly eight hundred miles southeast of Moscow.

140. Nikolai Filippov owned the hotel Deluxe in Moscow. It still exists today.

141. Bunin is quoting from Khlebnikov's 1921 poem "The Present Time."

142. Blok wrote "The Twelve" in 1918.

143. Bunin is citing Kondraty Ryleev's 1824–1825 poem "Dinner Songs."

144. Bunin is citing two poems from Sokolov's 1907 collection *The Scarlet Book*. The first four lines are from "The Fugitive"; the last four, from a selection named "The Dragon." Sokolov's publishing house, Vulture, existed from 1903 to 1913. *Krechet*, or "gyrfalcon," is the largest falcon of the species.

145. Bunin is quoting from Voloshin's 1905 poem "Angel of Vengeance."

146. The citation here is from Mikhail Gerasimov's 1921 poem "October."

147. Bunin is quoting with license from Mariengof's 1919 verse "October."

148. Bunin attended the event on April 3, 1917, ironically on the very same day that Lenin, after more than a decade of exile abroad, arrived at Finland Station in St. Petersburg.

149. The Duma came into being in the wake of the 1905 revolution, theoretically as a legislative branch of government but, in reality, with little power or authority. The fourth Duma lasted from 1912 to 1917.

150. The individual in question in Maurice Paléologue, French ambassador to Russia from 1914 to 1917.

151. This was the last meeting between Bunin and Gorky.

152. Polyphemus is the cyclops in Homer's *The Odyssey*.

153. In truth, the young Mayakovsky was called "One-Eyed Polyphemus."

154. Bunin is referring to Pablo Picasso's famous pictures of doves, coupled with messages by the Communists for peace.

155. In Russian, *kham* means "boor" or "lout." In Genesis, Ham laughs at his drunken, naked father and is cursed by the man.

156. Pyotr Kropotkin fled Russia in 1876, the reason being his ties to a revolutionary organization tied to the Populists. He lived first in Switzerland, from where he was expelled in 1881 for publishing revolutionary pamphlets; then in France, from where he was deported in 1886 after spending five years in prison for being a member of the International Workers Association; and finally in London, where he lived until his return to Russia.

157. Kropotkin wrote *Notes of a Revolutionary* in 1902.

158. The League of Federalists consisted of a small group of scholars who shared Kropotkin's views on governmental decentralization.

159. Kropotkin met Lenin sometime between May 8 and 10, 1919.

160. Vladimir Bonch-Bruevich was particularly active in founding newspapers that supported the Bolsheviks, before and after the revolution, most notably *Izvestia* in 1917. He also was key in protecting the Smolny Institute, the headquarters of the Bol-

shevik Party, during the October Revolution. Additionally, he endorsed the so-called Red Terror that broke out after the attempted assassination of Lenin.

161. On August 30, 1918, Fanya Kaplan (also known as Dora Kaplan), a Social Revolutionary, fired two shots into Lenin's neck and shoulder, her motive being to return Russia to the path of revolution. Her attempt at assassination signaled the Red Terror, which, beginning on September 5, freed the police from any legalities to pursue alleged enemies of the Soviet state. (Kaplan herself was executed two days before.) In the first two months alone, the Red Terror claimed between ten thousand and fifteen thousand lives.

162. This is a direct quotation from Kropotkin to Bunin. The purpose of the meeting was twofold: Lenin wished to secure Kropotkin's support for the October Revolution. Kropotkin wished closer ties with the Bolsheviks, having rejected Allied intervention in the Russian Civil War, but also requesting outside humanitarian aid for the country. The two men also discussed ideas on revolution and government, but to no avail.

As an anarchist, Kropotkin believed that government should spring from communes of workers and peasants, with protections for democracy and free thought. Lenin demanded a select, organized, and tightly knit group of party individuals to run national affairs.

Kropotkin also angered the Bolsheviks with attacks on state control of publishing, as well as on official crackdowns on non-Bolshevik literature. More seriously, he objected to the Red Terror unleashed after the attempted assassination of Lenin.

163. Bunin's claim is false. In Dmitrov, located fifty miles north of Moscow, Kropotkin lived in a six-room house with a kitchen and a hall. He and his wife also had special food rations, a cow, a garden, and gifts. Further, the item about the boots is fiction, not fact.

164. Kropotkin wrote the first volume of *Ethics: The Origin and Development of Morality* in 1922. He did not live to finish the work.

2. Rachmaninov

1. Bunin and Rachmaninov first met sometime in April 1900. Rachmaninov and his family left Russia in late 1917.

2. The Russia was the first luxury hotel in Yalta.

3. The citation is from Apollon Maykov's 1840–1841 poem "At the Fixed Hour I Waited for You at the Grotto."

3. Repin

1. A possible date for this encounter is January 18, 1915.

4. Jerome Jerome

1. Jerome Jerome was an English humorist, best known for his 1887 work *Three Men in a Boat*, an amusing travelogue of three individuals and their dog who cruise the river Thames. An instant success, *Three Men* sold over a million copies in the first twenty years of its publication. Still in print today, *Three Men* has been adapted for film,

television, and stage and continues to influence humorists and satirists in England and elsewhere.

Three Men was also a standard textbook for Russian schools. Indeed, it has been said that Russian peasants read only two works in translation: the King James Version of the Bible and *Three Men*.

2. The PEN Club (now PEN International) is an association of writers, established by John Galsworthy. In 1951 Bunin was named the first honorary member.

5. Tolstoy

1. Tolstoy wrote *War and Peace* between 1865 and 1869.

2. The Siege of Sevastopol took place from September 1854 to September 1855 and pitted the forces of Russia against those of France, Britain, Turkey, and Sardinia in the Crimean War of 1853–1856. Tolstoy's experiences there were the backdrop for his 1855 *Sevastopol Sketches*.

3. Bunin is again appealing here to the Buddhist-tinged beliefs in karma, regression, and multiple lives that informed both his worldview and fiction.

4. Yasnaya Polyana was the site of Tolstoy's family estate. It exists today and is located 130 miles south of Moscow.

5. Yefremov is a city roughly 200 miles south of Moscow.

Also, A month or so before his mad dash to see Tolstoy, Bunin had written to the writer on June 12, 1890: "I am one of many who have followed your every word with great interest and respect, and who dare trouble you with my own doubts and thoughts about my life. I know that you are probably tired of listening to the same trite and monotonous questions. So it is doubly awkward for me to ask if I can come and visit you sometime and to talk with you if only for a few minutes. . . . Your thoughts have affected me so deeply."

Tolstoy did not respond to the letter. See A. Baboreko, "Iz perepiski I. A. Bunina," *Novyi mir*, no. 10 (1956): 197–198.

6. At this time, Tolstoy was sixty-two, Bunin was twenty. This was not the first time that Bunin had tried to visit Tolstoy. Sometime earlier that year, he had traveled with the editor of the *Oryol Herald* to visit the writer at Yasnaya Polyana but did not find him at home.

It should also be noted that at Yefremov, Bunin was almost eighty miles from Yasnaya Polyana.

7. It was a full three years more before Bunin summoned sufficient courage to connect with Tolstoy.

When in February 1893 Bunin heard that Tolstoy needed help with his everyday affairs, he volunteered his services, but Tolstoy declined the offer politely.

On June 15, 1893, Bunin again wrote to Tolstoy, enclosing a pamphlet of his own verse. "Perhaps you will find my work completely useless and boring," he wrote to the writer, "but I am sending it to you nonetheless . . . because your work rouses my soul and awakens in me a passionate desire to write (if I dare use this word about myself)."

He continued: "I have wanted to write to you many times about many things, to come and see you. But I was afraid that you would have counted me among those who besiege you from motives of vulgar impetuosity and the like. Please do not take [what I am saying] for impudence or insincerity." Tolstoy did not answer Bunin's letter.

Tolstoy also did not respond to Bunin's 1901 request that he contribute to a literary anthology published by *Odessa News* for victims of famine. See Baboreko, "Iz perepiski I. A. Bunina," 198.

8. As the name implies, Tolstoyans were disciples of the philosophical and religious views of the writer, particularly his ideas on the ministry of Jesus and on the Sermon on the Mount. Espousing pacificism and nonresistance to injustice and evil, Tolstoyans also sought lives that were simple and ascetic, without tobacco, alcohol, and meat.

9. Poltava is a city approximately 175 miles southeast of Kiev and 500 miles south of Moscow.

10. Nikolai Karonin published his story "The Teacher of Life" in 1891, charging that the political and social troubles of the 1880s and early 1890s in Russia were rooted in the failures of intellectuals to offer an alternative to Tolstoyism.

11. Stiva Oblonsky is a character in Tolstoy's 1875–1877 novel *Anna Karenina*.

12. Kharkov is both a city and a region in northeast Ukraine, about 250 miles east of Kiev.

13. Bunin is referring to Mitrofan and Tikhon Dudchenko.

14. The village of Khilkovo was roughly 350 miles north of Kharkov.

15. Volkenshtein is following Tolstoy's practice always to travel third-class and to speak with common people.

16. Khamovniki was the site of a simple, wooden, twenty-room villa that Tolstoy had bought in 1882 in the industrial outskirts of southwest Moscow.

17. Adamovich, in his memoirs, wrote: "Bunin remembered that when he first met the writer . . . 'Tolstoy was so astute, so terrible . . . and his eyes were so frightful, gray, and deeply sunken . . . that I almost . . .' and he ended with words that I cannot print." G. Adamovich, "Bunin. Vospominaniia," *Znamia*, no. 4 (1988): 181.

18. The woman is his wife, Sofya Tolstaya.

19. Bunin was bitterly disappointed by the encounter. Boris Leontiev remarked to Tolstoy on January 30, 1894: "Bunin was very upset that he had spent so little time with you. . . . He loves you very much. . . . He cannot talk about you calmly, without agitation." See L. Tolstoi, *Polnoe sobranie sochinenii v devianosta tomakh* (Moscow: Akademiia nauk, 1955), 67:49.

20. "I've been doing poorly since I returned to Moscow," Bunin wrote to Tolstoy on February 15, 1894. "Although our conversation was brief and our meeting was unsuccessful, your words made a clear and lively impression on me. Something bright and lively shone from them."

He wrote on March 21, 1896: "You are one of the few whose words lift up my soul and bring me to tears. . . . Right now I feel like crying and kissing your hand passionately, as if you were my own father!" See A. Baboreko, *I. A. Bunin. Materialy dlia biografii* (Moscow: Khudozhestvennaia literatura, 1967), 55–57; and Baboreko, "Iz perepiski I. A. Bunina," 199.

21. Mediator was a publishing house founded by Vladimir Chertkov and Pavel Biryukov in 1885 to publish literature for the masses that would serve as an alternative to pulp fiction and expound on the ideals and values of Tolstoy. Bunin opened his

ill-fated bookshop in late December 1894. Also, Bunin is referring to the ascendency of Tsar Nicholas II to the throne on November 1, 1894.

22. Most likely, the individual is asking Tolstoy to defend his ideas on nonviolence and passive resistance to evil.

23. The first Russian Temperance Society was founded in St. Petersburg in 1890.

24. Tolstoy wrote "Master and Man" in 1895.

25. Ivan Tolstoy, the youngest of the writer's thirteen children, died of scarlet fever on February 23, 1895.

26. Maiden's Field is located in southwest Moscow.

27. The Arbat is an old section of Moscow not far from the Kremlin.

28. In other accounts of this meeting, Tolstoy also asked why Bunin had not visited him. As Bunin recalled: "I was as lost as a schoolboy . . . 'I am afraid to visit you,' I confessed sharply. [To which] Lev Nikolaevich repeated insistently and assuredly, 'People should never be afraid, never.'" See V. Shcherbina et al., eds., *Literaturnoe nasledstvo*, vol. 84, *Ivan Bunin* (Moscow: Nauka, 1973), bk. 1, 361.

6. Chekhov

1. Chekhov built his famed "White Dacha" in Autka (renamed Chekhovo in 1944 and located two miles west of Yalta) in 1898. The place became the already-noted museum tended by his sister Maria until her death. It still exists today. The Uchan-Su, from the Crimean Tartar meaning "swift water," is a river in the south Crimea.

2. Mikhail Lermontov wrote "Taman" in 1839, when he was twenty-five years old.

3. Chekhov's habit of screwing up his eyes, throwing back his head, and peering from under this pince-nez was seen by many contemporaries as superciliousness. In truth, the writer had a rash on his cornea, leaving him practically blind in his right eye. Also, Chekhov wrote "The Student" in 1894.

4. More accurately, Alexander Skabichevsky, in a review of Chekhov's anthology *Motley Stories*, compared the writer to a "squeezed-out lemon rotting under a gate." A. Skabichevskii, "Novye knigi. 'Pestrye rasskazy,'" *Severnyi vestnik*, no. 6 (1886): 124.

5. Chekhov wrote "On the Sea" in 1883. *Northern Flowers*, published by Scorpion, was an artistic-literary almanac that appeared in five volumes from 1901 to 1905. *Russian News*, one of the most influential newspapers of its time, was published in Moscow from 1863 to 1918.

6. Oreanda is a town five miles southwest of Yalta. Throughout his life, Chekhov loved to catch mice and then free them on his property.

7. Odessa is in Ukraine, some seven hundred miles southwest of Moscow.

8. *The Cherry Orchard* was first staged on January 14, 1904.

9. Chekhov wrote this letter to Bunin on January 8, 1904, six months before his death.

10. More accurately, it was the Russian Nobility Club, founded in 1782.

11. The Solovtsov Theater—formerly known as the Association of Dramatic Actors—was founded by Nikolai Solovtsov in 1891 and at one time was the main dramatic theater in Kiev. It still exists today, as the Lesya Ukrainka National Academic Theater of Russian Drama.

12. As Chekhov wrote to Olga Knipper on January 20, 1902: "Solovstov's death . . . was a most unpleasant event in my provincial life." See A. Chekhov, *Polnoe sobranie sochinenii i pisem v tridtsati tomakh* (Moscow: Nauka, 1979), 10:174–175.

13. Chekhov was unhappy with Maria Savina's portrayal of the character of Sasha in his 1887 play *Ivanov*. He was also angry when the forty-two-year-old actress, six days before the opening night of *The Seagull* on October 17, 1896, refused to play Masha, the eighteen-year-old daughter of Ilya and Polina Shamraev, believing that the character was too weak and wanting a stronger woman in the work. Also, on the following day, Savina quit the production altogether when the role was given to the thirty-two-year-old Vera Komissarzhevskaya, a more plausible *jeune naïve*.

Viktor Krylov was a hack dramatist who, in the 1870s and with Savina in mind, pumped out three or four plays annually to meet demands of theaters and audiences. It was with Krylov in mind that Chekhov coined the term *krylovshchina*, meaning "bad taste" or "hack work."

14. A woman ahead of her time, Alexandra Davydova was the founder and publisher of the journal *God's World*.

15. Chekhov is referring to Leo Tolstoy's 1886 essay "How Much Land Does a Man Need?"

16. Chekhov wrote "A Game of Vint," ~~and~~ "The Complaint Book" in 1894 and "The Peasants" in 1897.

17. It was a grade-school teacher, a waggish and much-admired priest by the name of Fyodor Pokrovsky, who was the first individual to discern Chekhov's talent and who, when calling on the writer in the classroom, nicknamed him "Chekhonte."

18. Bunin is citing from Chekhov's *The Cherry Orchard*.

19. In 1891, Tolstoy was recovering from an attack of malaria at the estate of Countess Sofya Panina, at Gaspra, roughly ten miles southwest of Yalta.

20. Tolstoy disliked Chekhov's plays for what he saw as both their static quality and their indifference to social issues. "Where is the drama?" he asked Alexander Sanin.

"What does it consist in? It does not go anywhere."

Chekhov took Tolstoy's criticism in stride. Telling Pyotr Gnedich about the writer's dislike of his plays, he "threw back his head and roared so loudly that his pince-nez popped off his nose."

See P. Gnedich, "Iz zapisnoi knizhki," in *L. N. Tolstoi v vospominaniiakh sovremennikov* (Moscow: Gosudarstvennoe izdatel'stvo khudozhestvennoi literatury, 1955), 1:457–458. Also see Sanin's missive to Chekhov, dated March 12, 1900, in "Tolstoi o Chekhove. Neizvestnye vyskazyvaniia," in *Literaturnoe nasledstvo*, ed. V. Vinogradov et al., vol. 68, *Anton Chekhov* (Moscow: Izdatel'stvo Akademiia nauk SSSR, 1960), 873.

21. Bunin is citing from Sergei Yelpatievsky's 1909 work *Nearby Shadows*. The article in question is "Creation from the Void," in L. Shestov, *Nachala i kontsy* (St. Petersburg: M. M. Stasiulevich, 1908).

22. Lermontov wrote "The Sail" in 1831.

23. The poets Urenius and Uprudius either were extremely obscure or did not exist. There is also the possibility that Chekhov might be referring to the poet Ivan Oreus (better known as Ivan Konevskoy).

24. The reference is to Anna Karenina, the heroine of Tolstoy's famous novel written between 1873 and 1877.

25. Alupka is located in the southernmost tip of the Crimea.

26. Chekhov drew his inspiration for "Monsieur Bouquichon," his favorite "tag" for Bunin, either from a foppish manager on a nearby estate or from a French marquis he had seen in a newspaper.

27. The reference here is to Knipper, Chekhov's wife.

28. The city of Kharkov is located four hundred miles south of Moscow.

29. Samara is located some 660 miles southeast of Moscow.

30. Not quite. A difference of only ten years separated the two men.

31. Chekhov's "Three Years" appeared in 1895.

32. As will be seen in Chapter 14, Nikodim Kondakov and his wife will leave Russia with the Bunins.

33. Bunin is paraphrasing Nikolai Zlatovratsky's less than enthusiastic review of his 1901 anthology *To the Edge of the World and Other Stories*, in *Zhurnal dlia vsekh*, no. 12 (1901): 1534.

34. The poets in question are A. M. Verbov and N. Viedkov, individuals who are now so obscure that they do not appear in bibliographical indices and other research materials. The poem in question, though, is Viedkov's 1899 piece titled "Waiting for Morning."

Russian Wealth was a scientific, literary, and political journal that was published first in Moscow and then in Petersburg, from 1876 to 1918.

35. Perm' is located seven hundred miles west by northeast of Moscow.

36. See Skabichevskii, "Novye knigi. 'Pestrye rasskazy,'" 124.

37. Chekhov is referring to the crackdown on revolutionaries, as well as to the pogroms against Jews that took place in the wake of the assassination of Alexander II on March 13, 1881. Also, Chekhov's *Gloomy People* was published in 1890; "Cold Blood," in 1897.

38. Chekhov's "An Attack of Nerves" appeared in 1888.

39. The Great Moscow Tavern was first built in 1879 on the site of the current hotel Moscow. It was later housed in this building.

40. In truth, the piece was Chekhov's 1896 story "House with the Mezzanine: The Story of an Artist."

41. Chekhov's "In the Ravine" appeared in 1900.

42. Chekhov began coughing blood in 1884. He accepted his illness only in 1891, but refused any serious sustained treatment.

43. The Yaila-Dagh is a mountain range in southern Crimea.

44. Chekhov wrote "The Archbishop" in 1902.

45. The letter no longer exists.

46. Of course, in the Russo-Japanese War of 1904 and 1905, just the opposite was the case.

47. Bunin's charge that Pyotr Sergeenko hastened Chekhov's death is false.

48. Sergeenko published *How Count Tolstoy Lives and Works* in 1898.

49. Yekaterina Kuskova published "Before and After (From Memoirs)," in *Novoe russkoe slovo* on February 4 and 7, 1949.

50. Bunin is citing from letters of Maria Yermolova to Leonid Seredin, written on September 16, 1899, and a year later, on February 22, March 5, and April 12. See M. Ermolova, *Pis'ma. Iz literaturnogo nalsediia. Vospominaniia sovremennikov* (Moscow: Iskusstvo, 1955), 154, 171–174.

7. Chaliapin

1. In truth, Chaliapin surpassed Leonid Sobinov as a singer. The two men, though, remained friends throughout their careers.

2. The meeting between Chaliapin and Chekhov took place in the Crimea in 1898.

3. Ravine and Strelna (a favorite place of Grigory Rasputin) were famous restaurants in Moscow, both known for their gypsy choruses.

Knowledge was a publishing association founded in St. Petersburg in 1898, initially printing works for mass readers on natural science, history, and art. In 1900, Gorky joined Knowledge, becoming its director in 1902 and publishing not only his own writings but also the works of writers such as Bunin, Andreev, Chekhov, and Kuprin. With Knowledge, Gorky, by 1914, issued forty anthologies of the fiction of Russian writers.

4. Andreev died on September 12, 1919.

5. Modest Mussorgsky wrote "The Flea" in 1879, with words taken from Johann Goethe's nineteenth-century poem *Faust*. It soon became a popular song among revolutionary youth.

6. On the morning of January 6, 1911, Nicholas II conferred on Chaliapin the highest honor that a singer could aspire to at the time: "Soloist to His Majesty."

On that evening, Chaliapin became an unwitting pawn with members of the chorus of Mussorgsky's *Boris Godunov* who sought to exploit the singer's honor to their own ends. Long unsuccessful in asking the administrators of the Mariinsky Theater in St. Petersburg to raise their pensions, the members of the chorus decided to petition the tsar, who, they knew, would be in the audience.

Immediately before the intermission, the actors in the cast, including Chaliapin, took their bows and were heading to the dressing rooms when, suddenly and loudly, several spectators in the audience demanded that the national anthem be sung. Behind the curtain, members of the chorus began to sing "God Save the Tsar." The musicians rushed back to the orchestra pit; the curtain went up; and the members of the chorus, now down on their knees and stretching their arms out to the imperial box, continued to sing with mounting fervor.

It was a rule of the theater that whenever the national anthem was sung, everyone in the performance had to appear and join in. At the sound of the hymn, Chaliapin and the other soloists appeared onstage, but when the singer saw the chorus on their knees, he began to back away. Several members of the group blocked Chaliapin's exit, though, thereby forcing him to remain in full view.

The director of the Imperial Russian Theaters, Vladimir Telyakovsky, recalled what happened next: "Chaliapin looked in the direction of my box, as though asking what he should do. I shook my head to show that he could see for himself what was happening. Whatever he would do would be wrong. If Chaliapin knelt down, people would ask why he had done so. If he did not, why was he the only one left standing. . . . Such an action could be construed as a political gesture. So Chaliapin knelt on one knee."

Chaliapin recalled: "The entire episode left me with a very unpleasant impression. . . . But I felt neither shame nor humiliation. . . . It did not enter into the remotest cells of my brain that I had done something improper, betrayed something, or departed from my dignity or instinct for liberty. For all my failings, I have never been and will never be a slave or lackey. . . . I was not kneeling *before the Tsar*. On the whole, I did not feel any involvement in the incident." The incident at the Mariinsky Theater caused a national and international sensation. Media had a heyday. "Not a single paper," Telyakovsky added, "reported the story as it really happened. The more that was written, the more entangled the entire thing became. Chaliapin, moreover, utterly weary, harassed, and anxious to justify himself about something of which he was, in actual fact, completely innocent, talked to representatives of the press from various countries about it in such a way that, by omitting some details and muddling up others, he actually laid himself open to further attacks."

Almost everyone censured Chaliapin. Gorky wrote to the singer on July 13, 1911: "You evidently do not realize what a wicked deed you have committed. As you are not ashamed of yourself, we had better not see each other. Do not visit me." Similarly, in spring 1911, Gorky wrote to Bunin: "My dear, wondrous friend, truly one has to have a heart of stone to live in these cursed days when . . . Fyodor Chaliapin, a genius, went down on his knees before Nikolai Romanov, the most untalented of men."

Chaliapin's kneeling before the tsar led to endless rifts, insults, persecutions, and sleepless nights, which brought the singer to a nervous breakdown, thoughts of suicide, and the desire to leave Russia. Assaults were nonstop. Traveling by train from Monte Carlo to Nice, Chaliapin was once accosted by a group of students or shop assistants, who, outraged by his genuflecting at the Mariinsky Theater, crowded into his carriage, yelling "Flunky!! Traitor!"

See F. Chaliapin, *Maska i dusha. Moi sorok let na teatrakh* (Paris: Izdatel'stvo "Sovremennya zapiski," 1932), 323–325; V. Telyakovskii, *Vospominania* (Moscow: Nauka, 1965), 398, 402; and M. Gor'kii, *Pis'ma v dvadtsati tomakh* (Moscow: Nauka, 2002), 9:5, 66.

7. In truth, the event took place on March 12, 1917. The Mikhailovsky Theater, built between 1831 and 1833, attracted spectators primarily from aristocratic and court circles, as well as diplomats and foreigners living in the imperial city. Its repertoire consisted mainly of contemporary and classical works of French drama.

8. Chaliapin long suffered from a consensus by Russian émigrés that he had been a dupe of Gorky, who, allegedly, had nurtured revolutionary hopes and ideas in his friend.

Before 1917, Chaliapin had opposed the tsar. He had refused to sing on the occasion of the three hundredth anniversary of the Romanovs in 1913. He had also opted for the Social Democrats and even wished to join the Bolsheviks but was dissuaded from doing so by Gorky. "You're not fit to do such a thing," Gorky advised the singer. "I beg you, once and for all, do not join any party, but be an artist . . . that is quite enough for you."

It was through Gorky, though, that Chaliapin met Lenin, Stalin, Trotsky, and other high-ranking Bolsheviks.

After 1917, Chaliapin undertook various official duties and worked on numerous committees for artistic affairs. In 1918, he was named the artistic director of the Mariinsky Theater; a year later, he was elected to its managing board. Also at this time, Chaliapin took part in many performances and concerts for the workers and soldiers of the Red Army.

Eventually, Chaliapin became disillusioned with the new Soviet state. Interference by party hacks, the vulgarization of culture, and tempting offers from abroad caused him to leave Russia in 1921.

Even in exile, Chaliapin held his tongue about the Bolsheviks. When, on August 24, 1927, the Soviets stripped Chaliapin of his title of "People's Artist" and were threatening to take away his Russian citizenship, he did not attack the leadership in his homeland. Indeed, it was only in 1932, ten years after he left Russia, that Chaliapin disapproved publicly of Soviet power. "The practice of Bolshevism proved even more dreadful than its theory," he wrote. "Perhaps the most terrible aspect of the regime was that Bolshevism had become saturated with that awful intolerance and bigotry, that obtuse smugness that is Russian philistinism. . . . Indeed, Bolshevism seemed to be like a parade of all the characters in Russian satirical literature, from Fonvizin to Zoshchenko. They all came to offer their best to Vladimir Ilyich Lenin." See Chaliapin, *Maska i dusha*, 181, 290.

9. The event took place on June 18, 1937. Nikolai Afonsky organized and headed the famous Metropolitan Choir of Paris from 1925 to 1947; its members often accompanied Chaliapin in his performances. Also, Chaliapin had been suffering from diabetes since age thirty-five. Toward the end of his life, he was also afflicted with anemia, emphysema, leukemia, and heart disease.

10. Ernesto Rossi toured Russia in 1877, 1878, 1890, 1895, and 1896. Lensky is a character in Pushkin's *Eugene Onegin*, written between 1823 and 1831.

11. Bunin is incorrect. Chaliapin gave his final performance on June 23, 1937, in Eastbourne, England.

12. Chaliapin died on April 12, 1938.

13. Sofya Tolstaya wrote sometime in 1900: "At that time there appeared a new young singer, Fyodor Ivanovich Chaliapin. . . . Wanting to sing for Lev Nikolaevich, he came to see him on January 8th. . . . I do not recall what Chaliapin sang, but his voice, a bass, was much too loud for our parlor and especially offended Lev Nikolaevich." See S. Tolstaia, *Moia zhizn'* (Moscow: Kuchkovo pole, 2011), 2:558.

14. Leo Tolstoy believed that Beethoven's *Ninth Symphony* "brought about disunion among men." He also opined that if peasant children preferred the "Song of the Volga Boatmen" to Beethoven's masterpiece, it was because they were simple and pure, and that culture was abject and base. See L. Tolstoi, *Polnoe sobranie sochinenii v devianosta tomakh* (Moscow: Akademiia nauk, 1951), 30:165–166.

15. In fact, Tolstoy could be so moved by Chaliapin's singing that he once wiped away a tear furtively, lest anyone notice the emotion that the singer had aroused in him. He also told his wife, Sofya: "Chaliapin is the most talented singer I have ever heard in my life." See her diary entry, dated January 18, 1904, in S. Tolstaya, *The Diaries of Sofia Tolstoy*, trans. C. Porter (New York: Harper Perennial, 2009), 339.

16. Chaliapin's father was an alcoholic who often terrorized his family. The singer recalled: "At first the day would pass without quarrelling, . . . but then my father got rougher and rougher with [my mother], until he finally beat her before my very eyes. . . . He once beat her unconscious and I was convinced that he had killed her; she was lying on a trunk, her dress torn, motionless, not breathing and her eyes shut. I burst out crying in despair, and she, regaining consciousness, looked around frantically and then comforted me: 'Don't cry, it's all right.'" See V. Borovsky, *Chaliapin. A Critical Biography* (New York: Knopf, 1988), 39.

17. The zemstvo was a self-governing institution that oversaw economic affairs in Russian districts and provinces from 1864 to 1918. It also often served as a formal vehicle for liberalism in Russia.

18. Bunin is quoting from the singer's memoirs. See Chaliapin, *Maska i dusha*, 36.

19. The Italian baritone Mattia Battistini, after debuting as Hamlet in St. Petersburg in 1893, visited Russia annually until 1914. He never, though, sang in Odessa at age seventy-four.

20. More accurately, the Chapel of the Iversky Icon of the Mother of God by the Gates of the Resurrection dates back to the late seventeenth century. It was torn down in 1922 but rebuilt in 1996.

21. The Prague, an art nouveau masterpiece on the Arbat in Moscow, dates back to the 1870s and was one of the most luxurious restaurants in tsarist times.

22. Chaliapin is singing an aria from Giacomo Meyerbeer's 1836 opera *The Hugenots*.

23. Wednesday was a literary-artistic circle in Moscow that existed from 1899 to 1916 and included such painters as Alexander Golovin, Apollon Vasnetsov, and Isaak Levitan; such singers as Chaliapin, such actors as Vasily Kachalov; and such writers as Boris Pilnyak and Alexander Serafimovich, as well as Bunin, Kuprin, Gorky, Andreev, Bely, and Balmont.

24. Chaliapin's impromptu concert took place in fall 1904.

25. Bunin and company heard Chaliapin sing at the hotel in Capri on February 14, 1912.

8. Gorky

1. Bunin is lying shamefully here. "Life is so willful and capricious," he wrote to Gorky on August 20, 1910, "but there exist moments in human relationships that one never forgets, that exist by themselves and outside of any time—like those moments when I am with you: a present that makes people feel alive and that gives unforgettable happiness." On March 15, 1915, he continued to his erstwhile friend: "Truly you are one of the very few whom I think about in my soul when I write. I value your support very much." See V. Denitskii et al., eds., *Literaturnyi arkhiv*, vol. 2, *M. Gor'kii. Materialy i issledovaniia* (Moscow: Akademiia nauk SSSR, 1936), 419, 447.

2. Again, Bunin is careless with the truth. It was he who initiated the hostilities, the first evidence for a split between the two men occurring eight years after the revolution. "Bunin . . . is hostile to meet me," Gorky wrote to Stefan Zweig on February 22, 1925, "because he thinks I champion tyrants." See N. Zhegalov at al., *Arkhiv A. M. Gor'kogo*, vol. 8, *Perepiska A. M. Gor'kogo s zarubezhnymi literatorami* (Moscow: Akademiia nauk, 1960), 17.

3. About the work, Bunin continued to Georgy Adamovich on January 16, 1947: "Enclosed are some things from my [would-be] anthology, Gems of World Literature. . . . 'It crawled high into the mountains and lay there.' . . . This is how Gorky begins his 'Song about the Snake [*sic*] and the Falcon,' in which the snake, not being a moral reptile, somehow kills a falcon by biting into its heart, right through its feathers and bony chest." See A. Zweers, "Pis'ma I. A. Bunina k G. V. Adamovichu," *Novyi zhurnal*, no. 110 (1973): 161.

4. Both claims are true. More accurately, Bunin is quoting from the *New Encyclopedic Dictionary* (St. Petersburg: Izdatel'stvo F. A. Brokgauza and Efrona, 1913), 14:351.

5. Mikhail Smuryi was a retired corporal who forced the young Gorky to read books to him from his own collection of leather-bound volumes that he kept in his trunk. Smuryi also rescued Gorky from marrying a young prostitute who, after plying him with liquor, locked him in a cabin aboard ship.

6. *The Spark* was a weekly journal, published in St. Petersburg from 1859 to 1873.

7. Kazan, situated approximately 450 miles east of Moscow, was the site of a renowned university, whose students included both Leo Tolstoy and Lenin.

8. In December 1887, a depressed Gorky bought a revolver and aimed it at his heart. Mercifully, the bullet pierced a lung and lodged in his back. Within a month, he was again working, at a bakery.

9. Gorky was twenty years old at the time. Little is known about Lanin, other than the fact that he was a lawyer in Nizhniy Novgorod for whom Gorky worked as a courier and that he had access to the man's extensive library. From Lanin, Gorky also gained a solid knowledge of the tsarist legal system, information that he used in his works. Years later, Gorky often assisted Lanin's widow financially.

Also, the youthful Gorky disliked intellectuals for what he saw as their truculence, cynicism, dogmatism, sophistry, pretense, and concerns for personal well-being and gratification. He also resented being seen by this group as a "son of the people."

10. *The Caucasus* was a political and literary newspaper published in Tiflis from 1846 to 1894.

11. Gorky published "Yemelyan Pilyai" in 1915 and "Grandfather Arkhip and Lenka" in 1893.

12. Kobelyaki is roughly ten miles southwest of Poltava.

13. In truth, Chekhov was quite taken with Gorky. "You are an unquestionable talent," he wrote to the young writer on December 3, 1898. "You express yourself with so much power that I am seized with envy. . . . You feel keenly, you are plastic. When you picture a thing, you see it and probe it with your hands." A. Chekhov, *Polnoe sobranie sochinenii i pisem v tridtsati tomakh* (Moscow: Nauka, 1979), 7:51.

Maria Chekhova recalled: "When A. M. Gorky visited, the two conversed for hours on a bench . . . [so much so] that we called it 'Gorky's bench.'" M. Chekhova, *Iz dalekogo proshlogo* (Moscow: Gosudarstevennoe izdatel'stvo khudozhestvennoi literatury, 1960), 38.

14. Byliny are East Slavic oral epic poetic narratives about the lives of such folk heroes as Dobrynya Nikitch, Ilya Muromets, and Alyosha Popovich.

15. Gorky's praise of Bunin bordered on worship. He wrote to the writer on October 31, 1912: "Your great heart knows not only the sadness of Russian life but also the 'sadness of all lands and of all times'—a great creative sadness about that happiness that keeps moving the world forward. . . .

"Your work . . . is full of earnest love for our native tongue—the beauty of which you have always felt. . . . Your writing gives us the joyful right to proclaim that you are the worthy heir of those poets who linked Russian literature to European writing and who have made it one of the most remarkable phenomena of the nineteenth century.

"Fondly and respectfully, we, your readers, convey our best wishes to a poet who has 'given his life to creating'—long live the 'blessed sweet anguish of your labors.'" See V. Mikhailovskii, ed., *Gor'kovskie chteniia, 1958–1958* (Moscow: Institut mirovoi literarury imeni A.M. Gor'kogo, 1961), 69–70.

16. The woman in question is Yekaterina Peshkova, whom Gorky married in 1896 and who, a year later, gave birth to a son, also named Maxim. Although the two separated in 1903, they remained legally married even after Gorky took several common-law wives.

Also, Bunin wrote to his brother Yuly on April 14, 1899: "When I was in the Crimea, I saw Chekhov and Gorky. (Gorky and I became fast friends—in many respects, he is a remarkable and splendid invididual)." See A. Ninov, *M. Gor'kii i Iv. Bunin: Istoriia otnoshenii, problemy tvorchestva* (Moscow: Sovetskii pisatel', 1984), 24–25.

17. Having joined the Bolsheviks, the twenty-year-old Maxim Peshkov fought in the battle for the Kremlin in October 1917. Close to Lenin, he worked for *Pravda*, the Cheka, and the NKVD. Peshkov died suddenly on May 11, 1934, allegedly after catching a cold on a fishing trip. People believed, though, that he was murdered as the result of a lover's quarrel or from official orders to intimidate his father.

18. This is not true. Gorky expressed fear and abhorrence of Russian peasants much later, most notably in his 1922 work *On the Russian Peasantry*.

19. Not quite. "The skin of my heart is similar to the blood of my heart," Gorky wrote to Knipper on December 5, 1900. "It is red—and very suitable for binding books." See M. Gor'kii, *Polnoe sobranie sochinenii. Pis'ma v dvadtsati chetyrekh tomakh* (Moscow: Nauka, 1997), 2:77.

Also, Bunin is mistaken on two counts. The journal in question is *Life*, which began in 1897 and, because of its Marxist direction, was closed by the tsarist government in 1901. Also, Gorky never ran the journal but, in it, published such pieces as *Foma Gordeev* and "Song of the Stormy Petrel."

Gorky's early plays included *The Petty Bourgeois* (1901), *The Lower Depths* (1902), *Summerfolk* (1904), *Children of the Sun* (1905), and *The Barbarians* (1905).

20. After reading Andreev's 1898 story "Bargamot and Garashka," Gorky launched him into Muscovite literary society and helped him to publish a collection of short stories in 1901.

21. Gorky is quoting from Job 7:19.

22. As already noted, the journal was *Life*, not *New Life*. In it, Bunin published not only his 1900 poem *Leaf-Fall*, which he dedicated to Gorky, but also three short stories: "Antonov Apples," also in 1900, and, a year later, "The New Road" and "The Fog."

23. Bunin included. "Alexei Maximovich has spent all his time in Russia," he told an interviewer for *Odessa News* on December 16, 1910. "He has absorbed a wealth of impressions and knowledge about his homeland." See V. Shcherbina et al., eds., *Literaturnoe nasledstvo*, vol. 84, *Ivan Bunin* (Moscow: Nauka, 1973), bk. 1, 368.

24. Gorky and Maria Andreeva departed for New York in April 1906. In October 1907, the two left first for Naples, then Capri, where they stayed until December 27, 1913. Four days later, the couple returned to St. Petersburg, courtesy of the partial political amnesty issued by Nicholas II on the occasion of the three hundredth anniversary of the Romanov dynasty.

In truth, Gorky feared arrest upon entry to the homeland, but was encouraged by Lenin and others to return. Despite rejoicing from all sectors of society, particularly students and workers, he kept a low profile, retreating to the Finnish village of Mustamyaki (now called Yakovlevo and located in Russia), roughly forty miles north of St. Petersburg.

25. The Bunins were on Capri from 1909 to 1913.

26. As Vera Muromtseva-Bunina wrote in her diary on March 26, 1909: "Gorky has roused Ian [her name for Bunin] powerfully. They look at things differently, but . . . they love sincerely." See M. Grin, ed., *Ustami Buninykh. Dnevniki Ivana Alekseevicha i Very Nikolaevny i drugie arkhivnye materialy* (Frankfurt am Main: Possev-Verlag, 1977), 1:83–84.

27. Bunin noted this event earlier, in his piece on Chaliapin.

28. The conversation between Bunin and Yekaterina Peshkova took place in late November 1917. Consider also this exchange between Bunin and Muromtseva-Bunina on January 19, 1920:

"I: 'What if you would meet Gorky sometime?'

"Ian: 'First, I will spit at him. Then, anything I can get my hands on, I'll throw at his head.'

"I: 'Really?'

"Ian: 'How can I forgive him that . . . he first brought Russia to disaster and that he is now with the Bolsheviks? No, for such a person, there can be no forgiveness.'" Grin, *Ustami Buninykh*, vol. 2 (1981), 333.

9. His Imperial Highness

1. Aldanov wrote this obituary on March 23, 1924.

2. Pyotr was quite mortal. Bunin, either from ignorance or discretion, leaves out many salacious details about the man. Known as "Petya," Pyotr Alexandrovich of Oldenburg had surprised Olga Alexandrovna, the youngest sister of Nicholas II, with a proposal of marriage. "I was so taken aback that all I could say was 'thank you,'" she recalled. Nonetheless, Pyotr was accepted not only because Olga wanted independence from her mother, Empress Maria Fyodorovna, but also because she feared marriage to a foreigner.

Olga was not the only one to be nonplussed. The entire court was abuzz, since Pyotr had shown no interest in women and was suspected of being pushed into the union by his ambitious mother, a granddaughter of Nicholas I.

Circa December 1900, Nicholas II wrote to his mother, Maria, musing: "I cannot believe that Olga is actually ENGAGED to Petya. . . . Probably they were both drunk yesterday. . . . Alexandra and I laughed so much . . . that we have yet to recover."

Indeed, the misgivings were so great that a prenuptial agreement promised Olga an annuity of one hundred thousand rubles from the tsar, as well as a fund of a million rubles more from which she could draw interest.

The qualms were justified. Pyotr was both a hypochondriac and a gambler, often losing large sums of Olga's money. His indifference to women continued unabated. The marriage unconsummated, Pyotr was believed by family and friends to be homosexual.

Unsurprisingly, the union between Pyotr and Olga did not last. After living separately for fifteen years, the marriage was annulled by Nicholas in October 1916. A month later, Olga married an officer with whom she had fallen in love.

After the revolution, Pyotr escaped to France, where, in 1922, he married again, but the couple remained childless. In 1924, Prince Pyotr of Oldenburg died in Antibes, France, at the age of fifty-five. See E. Bing, ed., *The Letters of Tsar Nicholas and Empress Marie* (London: Ivor Nicholson and Watson, 1937), 148.

3. The House of Oldenburg is of North German origin and includes royal branches not only in Russia but also in Denmark, Greece, and Norway. After the dynastic crisis brought about by the death of Peter II in 1730—the direct line of the Romanovs had come to an end—the House of Holstein-Gottorp, a cadet branch of the House of Old-

enburg, ascended to the throne with Peter III, a grandson of Peter I. All the Romanovs from the eighteenth century to 1917 came from this group.

4. Zemgor—the Russian acronym stands for the United Committee of the Union of Zemstvos and Towns—was an organization founded in 1915 and headed by Georgy Lvov to assist the tsarist government during the First World War. It was disbanded by the Bolsheviks in 1919. Reestablished by émigrés as the Russian Land-City Committee for Assistance to Russian Citizens Abroad, Zemgor was, in 1921, registered officially in Paris, with Lvov as its first chair.

5. The "degeneracy" of the Russian gentry-aristocracy, if not of all of humankind, was a common theme in Bunin's fiction, courtesy of his attraction to ideas of Buddhist regression and rebirth.

6. The real monster of the Oldenburg clan was Christian II, king of Denmark and Norway, who was dethroned in 1523, but not before capturing Stockholm in 1520 and, despite a promise of amnesty, slaughtering nearly a hundred leading nobility and clergy in what is now known as the Stockholm massacre.

7. The person in question is Louis Philippe Joseph d'Orléans, an aristocrat who championed the French Revolution, but who was guillotined during the Reign of Terror. His son Louis Philippe became king of France after the July Revolution of 1830.

8. Bayonne is some four hundred miles southwest of Paris. Saint-Jean-de-Luz is twelve miles southwest of Bayonne.

9. *Northern Lights* was an émigré journal, which, from 1921 to 1923, published in Berlin the fiction of such writers as Balmont, Voloshin, Khodasevich, Bunin, and Alexei Tolstoy, as well as articles and reviews on literary, artistic, and social matters.

10. Following Estonia and Finland in 1920, Poland in 1921, and Germany in 1922, and for reasons that were more economic than political, France—together with Great Britain, Italy, Sweden, Denmark, Austria, Norway, and Greece—recognized the Soviet Union in 1924. "France has recognized the Soviets," Muromtseva-Bunina wrote on October 29, 1924. "I cannot think without shuddering that a red flag will fly over the [Russian] embassy." See M. Grin, ed., *Ustami Buninykh. Dnevniki Ivana Alekseevicha i Very Nikolaevny i drugie arkhivnye materialy* (Frankfurt am Main: Possev-Verlag, 1981), 2:131.

11. Prince Pyotr Alexandrovich of Oldenburg is buried in the Russian Orthodox Church of St. Michael in Cannes.

10. Kuprin

1. Kuprin's father, Ivan Kuprin, was a minor government official who died of cholera at age thirty-seven. Kuprin's mother, Lyubov Kulanchakova-Kuprina, hailed from an ancient line of Tartar princes who played a large role in the so-called Kasimovsky kingdom, founded by Prince Vasily III in his struggle against the khanate of Kazan.

2. Kuprin also claimed, outrageously, to have descended from Genghis Khan and Tamerlane. As has been the cases several times in this memoir, Bunin's racial insensitivity is again in view.

3. Bunin has in mind Kuprin's enormous popularity with the publication of his 1905 work *The Duel*, which in that year alone sold over forty thousand copies. "Kuprin was renowned throughout Russia," he told Alexander Bakhrakh circa 1943. "Editors would

seek him out . . . and give him 2,500 rubles per page." See A. Bakhrakh, "Po pamiati, po zapisiam: Razgovory s Buninym," *Novyi zhurnal*, no. 130 (1978): 180.

4. In a 1916 article titled "About Anatoly Durov," Kuprin wrote about the man's passing: "We have lost a man with a seething temperament, gifted with a native comic talent, a great sensivity, and an ability to understand art." Also, Kuprin so admired Poddubny for his physical and spiritual strength that he advised the man on styles of wrestling and even corresponded with him. See A. Kuprin, *Polnoe sobranie sochinenii v desiati tomakh* (Moscow: Voskresenie, 2007), 8:411. The reference to Frou-Frou is again to Tolstoy's *Anna Karenina*.

5. Nabokov is often cited as one such critic, although evidence for the claim is lacking. Kuprin wrote about Rudyard Kipling in 1918: "Kipling possesses the most colossal and diverse knowledge. He is familiar with the most prosaic, everyday details in the lives of officers, administrators, soldiers, doctors, surveyors, and sailors; he knows the most complex details of hundreds of professions and trades; he is familiar with the subtleties of every sport; he impresses with his scientific and technical learning.

"But with all this baggage, he never tires. On the contrary, he uses such measure and skill that one is ready to believe that Kipling himself caught cod with fishermen in the North Atlantic, stood guard at a lighthouse, tossed about with a cruel Indian fever, took part in bloody punitive expeditions, built bridges, and drove iron trains as a machinist. . . .

"This confidence is one of the mysteries of the striking charm of his stories, and of his great and deserved fame." See A. Kuprin, "Rediard Kipling," in *Polnoe sobranie sochinenii*, 8:460.

6. Kuprin's work first appeared in *Russian Wealth* in 1893. Lustdorf is almost forty miles east of Odessa.

7. Kuprin was in the army on the Austrian border from 1890 to 1894. Polesye is a natural and historical region, stretching from parts of eastern Poland and crossing the border between Belarus and Ukraine into western Russia. Kuprin worked for newspapers in Kiev between 1894 and 1901.

8. Kuprin wrote "Night Relief" in 1899. *Odessa News* was a daily literary, political, and commercial magazine published from 1894 to 1920.

9. Bunin could be equally gracious. "My dear friend," he wrote to Kuprin on January 15, 1909. "Even if a thousand black cats would come between us, I loved you, I love you, and I will always love you. You and your talent are one, and your gifts have afforded [me] many joys." See A. Baboreko, "Neopublikovannye pis'ma I. A. Bunina," *Russkaia literatura*, no. 2 (1963): 177, 182.

10. Kuprin married Maria Davydova in February 1902. After the death of Alexandra Davydova, her mother, Maria took over *God's World*, with Kuprin assuming responsibility for the fiction in the journal. Incidentally, Bunin also enjoyed a long courtship with Maria. See A. Bakhrakh, *Bunin v khalate* (Bayville, NJ: Tovarishchestvo zarubezhnykh pisatelei, 1979), 76.

11. Kuprin's "The Swamp" appeared in 1902; "The Horse Thieves" and "The Coward," in 1903; and "The River of Life" and "Gambrinus" in 1906. Also, Kuprin published his highly successful *The Duel* in 1905.

12. Bunin recalled to Bakhrakh circa 1943: "During his last years in Paris, Kuprin started to seem more sympathetic and complaisant, although he was always morbidly

rancorous. . . . 'Once, at a gathering, Kuprin got drunk and began taking out after me with insults, snickering, and double entendres. I endured the abuse for a long time, but then I got angry and said loud enough for everyone to hear: "Look here, you damned platypus, if you don't shut your mouth, I'm going to crash this bottle over your Tartar head. . . ."

"' I thought that there would be a fight . . . but nothing happened. Kuprin looked at me with surprise. He quieted down immediately . . . then he burst out crying. "So I'm a platypus!" he said. "Brothers, see how I'm being insulted!"'" See Bakhrakh, *Bunin v khalate*, 77.

Also, the individual in question is Yelizaveta Moritsovna Geinrikh, the sister-in-law of the writer Dmitri Mamin-Sibiryak. Kuprin arrived in France in July 1920.

13. Kuprin benefited from Bunin's largesse also as an émigré. "You cannot imagine how, in this moment of sharp and bitter need," he wrote to the writer in 1934, "your wondrous five thousand francs, your brotherly help, have come to the rescue." See U. Assadullaeva, "Poslednii poedinok Ivana Bunina," *Vremia i my*, no. 40 (April 1979): 31.

14. Rumors were rife that Kuprin, long mired in poverty, sinking morale, and poor health, did not know what was happening when he left Paris for Russia.

15. P. D. Manych was a minor literary figure in St. Petersburg who appears in Kuprin's 1904 short story "Off the Street," as the character Andrei, a man of social standing who has fallen on hard times.

16. Kuprin wrote "Junkers" between 1928 and 1931. "It has long been the dream of Alexander," Kuprin wrote in the work, "to be a poet or a novelist."

17. Kuprin wrote this letter to Alexander Izmailov on March 16, 1913.

18. Kuprin wrote *Moloch* in 1896.

19. Kuprin's "The Forest Backwoods" appeared in 1898; "At Peace," in 1902; "Staff Captain Rybnikov," in 1906; and "The Pit," in 1915. "The Listrigons," written between 1907 and 1911, was a cycle of eight stories about the fishermen of Balaklava, now part of Sevastopol in the Crimea.

20. Kuprin's "The Jewess" was written in 1904.

21. Kuprin wrote "Small Fry" in 1907.

22. Kursha is located 145 miles southeast of Moscow.

23. Kuprin's "Narcissus" appeared in 1897. The reference is to Betsy Tverskaya in Tolstoy's *Anna Karenina*.

24. Kuprin published "At the Railway Siding" in 1894.

25. Kuprin wrote "Solitude" in 1898; "Sacred Love" and "Night Lodging," in 1895; "Night Relief," in 1899; "The Campaign," in 1901; "The Inquest," in 1894; and "The Wedding," in 1908.

26. Bunin is quoting from Kuprin's "Solitude."

27. Bunin is citing P. Pilsky, *Critical Essays*, published in 1910.

28. Bunin was well aware that his comments about Kuprin were received poorly by émigré readers. "Not long ago, I wrote an article about Kuprin for *Contemporary Notes*," Bunin told Bakhrakh circa 1943. "Many people were very unhappy with what I wrote. But I wrote what I thought . . . so I cannot help it if it did not turn out to be a 'posthumous panegyric.'" See Bakhrakh, *Bunin v khalate*, 76.

11. Semyonovs and Bunins

1. Pyotr Semyonov-Tyan-Shansky was a Russian geographer and statistician. Among his claims to fame was that as a youth, he was, along with Fyodor Dostoevsky, a member of the Petrashevsky Circle in St. Petersburg, a group of progressive individuals, many of whom were arrested in 1849 and exiled for alleged anti-government activity.

In Berlin in the 1850s, Semyonov-Tyan-Shansky studied natural science with Alexander von Humboldt and Carl Ritter (whose research he later translated into Russian).

Encouraged by Humboldt, Semyonov-Tyan-Shansky, in 1856–1857, explored the largely unknown Tyan Shan, a large system of mountain ranges in Central Asia. He was quite successful in his quest, being the first European to see much of the terrain there, as well as rejecting Humbodlt's assertion about volcanic beginnings in the region. Also, the popularity of his 1858 monograph *Traveling to Tyan-Shan*—the first systematic description of the area—was so great that half a century later, Nicholas II authorized that "Tyan-Shansky" be added to his family name.

Semyonov-Tyan-Shansky was also instrumental in advancing the study and practice of statistics in Russia. In fact, he was instrumental in conducting the first census in Russia in 1897. A member of fifty-three learned societies, Semyonov-Tyan-Shansky also headed the Russian Geographical Society from 1873 to his death in 1914, facilitating the exploration of inland Asia by Russian explorers.

By blood or marriage, Semyonov-Tyan-Shansky was related to the poet Vasily Zhukovsky, the philologist Yakov Grot, and the statesmen Yakov Rostovtsev, Nikolai and Dmitri Milyutin, Andrei Zablotsky-Desyatovsky , and Count Dmitri Tolstoy. Bunin completed the list.

2. Semyonov-Tyan-Shansky's grandmother was Maria Petrovna Bunina-Semyonova, who introduced her husband, Nikolai Petrovich Semyonov, a military officer, and his family into a far more educated and cultured milieu than they had known previously.

3. Bunin's claim is false. Semyonov-Tyan-Shansky's memoirs were published variously as *The Epoch of Emancipation in Russia, 1857–1867 in the Reminiscences of P. P. Semyonov-Tyan-Shansky*, in 1911; *Childhood and Youth*, in 1917; and the already noted *Traveling to Tyan-Shan in 1856–1857*, in 1948.

4. In truth, reforms in Russian orthography were put forth as early as 1904, with a formal commission advising changes in 1912. Tsarist ministers, however, so feared a backlash from the public that they failed to implement the recommendations.

On December 23, 1917, Lunacharsky decreed the removal of three letters from Russian writing, as well as that of the so-called hard sign that followed final consonants.

Unsurprisingly, many émigrés rejected the writing reforms of the Bosheviks, seeing them as a defamation of the prerevolutionary Russian they were determined to preserve. In 1951, Bunin refused to have his works published by Chekhov Publishers because the editors there insisted that they be printed in the new orthography.

5. Pyotr Semyonov-Tyan-Shansky first met Dostoevsky at military camp in early summer 1839.

6. The great reforms of Alexander II included the emancipation of the serfs in 1861, local self-government in towns and rural districts, and changes in the courts and the armed forces.

7. The Petrashevsky Circle was a group of progressive intellectuals who met in St. Petersburg during the 1840s to discuss Western philosophy and literature, as well as to oppose autocracy and serfdom.

8. The Kazan Cathedral in St. Petersburg was completed in 1811, its enormous scale and impressive stone colonnade modeled after the Basilica of St. Peter in Rome.

9. Fourierism, set forth by Charles Fourier, a utopian socialist, championed social communalism. Dostoevsky published *Poor Folk* in 1845 and *Netochka Nezvanova* in 1849.

10. Bunin has erred here. It was the circle of Sergei Durov, not Durasov.

11. The Main Engineering Academy was founded by Alexander I and, since 1823, was housed at the Mikhailovsky Castle in St. Petersburg.

12. The military camp that Dostoevsky and Pyotr Semyonov-Tyan-Shansky attended in June and July 1839 was located outside of St. Petersburg.

13. In these passages on Mikhail Petrashevsky and Dostoevsky, Bunin is quoting from Semenov-Tyan-Shansky's *Childhood and Youth*.

14. Anna Petrovna Bunina was the sister of Maria Bunina-Semyonova and thus Semyonov-Tyan-Shansky's great aunt.

15. See A. Chekhov, "Zamechatel'nye russkie zhenshchiny. Anna Petrovna Bunina," *Istoricheskii vestnik* 62, no. 10 (1865): 164–173.

16. The Russian Academy of Sciences was founded by Peter the Great in 1724 as part of his campaign to westernize Russia.

17. Anna Bunina was known as the Russian Sappho. Hence this couplet by the poet Konstantin Batyushkov:

> You are Sappho, and I am Phaon
> To this I will agree.
> But sad to say, you do not know
> The way to the sea.

See P. Semyonov-Tyan-Shansky, *Memuary P. P. Semenova-Tian-Shanskogo*, vol. 1, *Detstvo i iunost' (1827–1855 gg.)* (Petrograd, Tipografiia M. Statiuslevicha, 1917), 59.

18. In truth, Gavriil Derzhavin was ambivalent about Bunina, praising her work publicly but damning it privately. See W. Rosslyn, *Anna Bunina (1774–1829) and the Origins of Woman's Poetry in Russia* (Lewiston, NY: Edwin Mellen Press, 1997), 154.

Ivan Dmitriev, in a 1795 poem titled "On the Occasion of a Gift from an Unknown Woman," wrote about Bunina: "But who is she / Who with heart and hand / Honored an old and happy poet / She, the good genius of our land." See I. Dmitriev, *Polnoe sobranie stikhotvorenii* (Leningrad: Sovetskii pisatel', 1967), 433.

Ivan Krylov read in public Bunina's 1811 poem "The Fall of Phaethon." Also, Bunina is quoting from Nikolai Grech's 1821 work *An Attempt at a Short History of Russian Literature*.

Interestingly, Bunina objected to sentimentalist proscriptions of femininity as put forth by Nikolai Karamzin (and Jean-Jacques Rousseau). In her very first essay, titled "Love" and written in 1799, she objected to Karamzin's idea that man was virile and kind because he loved. Rather, she asserted just the opposite: it was precisely virility and kindness that enabled love. Bunin also asserted that a woman's love could not refashion an unworthy man.

19. Bunin's reference is to Alexander I. An edition of Bunina's works appeared in 1819. Also, Belinsky, in an 1843 review of Bunina's verse, cited her as adding to the "brilliant list of our old women writers." See V. Belinskii, *Polnoe sobranie sochinenii v trinadtsati tomakh* (Moscow: Akademiia nauk SSSR, 1955, 7:652–653.

20. Bunina's father was Pyotr Maximovich Bunin. Also, Ryazan is both a city and a province, roughly 120 miles from Moscow. Urusovo is located 80 miles southwest of Ryazan.

21. The individual in question is Ivan Petrovich Bunin.

22. The Russo-Swedish War between Catherine the Great and Gustav III took place between 1788 and 1790.

23. Bunina recalled: "My education was totally neglected. My uncle had an aversion for the French, for this was in the time of their massacres. . . . He was suspicious of all foreigners, and he refused to allow my aunt to keep a governess for me." See Rosslyn, *Anna Bunina*, 14.

24. Bunina's brother Vasily Petrovich Bunin, was a highly educated individual with an excellent knowledge of foreign languages, and also with a library, where she could read.

25. The *Moscow Journal* was a monthly literary periodical, published by Karamzin from 1791 to 1792.

26. Conversation of the Lovers of the Russian Word was a conservative and pre-Slavophile literary society, which began meeting in 1807 but moved to regular gatherings in 1811. In politics, the members of Conversation decried the liberalism of Alexander I. In literature, they championed folk and Old Church Slavonic words and expressions over French and European phrases and lexicons.

27. In opposition to the members of Conversation of the Lovers of the Russian Word, Karamzin, with his group Arzamas, sought to fashion the Russian literary language on the vocabulary and syntax of French, not Old Church Slavonic models. The fact, though, that the members of Conversation were more anti-French than anti-Karamzin allowed them to accept the writer as an honorary member of their group.

28. As Bunina herself wrote in a letter to her nephew Dmitri Bunin on December 4, 1827, she was beginning a new existence: "the miraculous childbirth of the transition of one kind of life to another." See A. Bunina. "Korrespondentsiia. Pis'mo Anny Petrovny Buninoi k Dmitriiu Maksimovichu Buninu," *Damskii zhurnal*, no. 1 (1931): 14.

29. Vasilievsky Island is located in the western part of St. Petersburg, boarded by the Bolshaya Neva and the Malaya Neva rivers in the south and northeast and by the Gulf of Finland in the west. Unsurprisingly, Bunina's first accommodations in the city were damp and cold, unpretentious and cheap.

30. *The Inexperienced Muse* appeared in 1809; it was the fourth book of poems to be published by a woman in Russia.

31. In truth, the four hundred rubles was an annual salary, thereby making Bunina the first professional woman writer in Russia.

32. Lipetsk is located approximately 230 miles southeast of Moscow.

33. Hugh Blair, a Scottish minister who is considered one of the greatest theorists of written discourse, published his *Sermons*, a guide to practical Christian morality, in five volumes from 1777 to 1801. Denisovka is about thirty miles north of Lipetsk.

12. Ertel

1. The cited edition of Ertel's works was published in Moscow in 1909. Mikhail Gershenzon published "The Worldview of A. I. Ertel" in M. Gershenzon, ed., *Pis'ma A. I. Ertelia* (Moscow: I. D. Sytin, 1909), iii–xxiv.

2. See L. Tolstoi, *Polnoe sobranie sochinenii v devianosta tomakh* (Moscow: Akademiia nauk, 1956), 37:243–244.

3. Smolensk is a city roughly 250 miles southwest of Moscow.

4. Koshchei the Immortal is a Slavic mythical figure in various tales. In Igor Stravinsky's 1910 ballet *The Firebird*, he is the villain and comes to an end when his soul, contained in an enormous egg, is destroyed by Prince Ivan.

The Travels of Pythagoras was written by Sylvain Maréchal in 1799, and Nikolai Kostomarov published *The Revolt of Stenka Razin* in 1858.

More accurately, *The Museum of Contemporary Foreign Literature* was published in St. Petersburg in 1847.

Finally, Pyotr Chaadaev, under the pseudonym Calderon de la Braca, published *Don Pedro Prokodurante, or The Punished Slacker* in 1794.

5. The *Kiev Paterikon* is a fourteenth-century anthology of stories, written about 1051 by the monks Simon and Polycarp at the Kiev-Pechersk Monastery, also known as the Monastery of the Caves, about the lives of the first inhabitants there. Preaching humility and meekness, the *Kiev Paterikon* also sheds light on the social and economic, religious, and cultural life of Kievan Rus.

The Monthly Readings, or *Menologian*, was the ambitious project of Saint Dmitri of Rostov, who, from 1684 to 1705, integrated all the lives of Russian saints into a single work. Stories in *The Monthly Readings* promoted Russian kenoticism: non-heroic suffering of the despised and humiliated Christ and his followers.

6. Usman is a city located some three hundred miles south of Moscow. Charles Darwin's *The Descent of Man and Selection in Relation to Sex* appeared in 1871. *Russian Word* was a monthly progressive scholarly and literary journal, published in St. Petersburg from 1859 to 1866.

7. Ertel married the highly educated Maria Fedotova in 1875, but the relationship did not last, Maria being more interested in reading and ideas than her husband. He arrived in St. Petersburg in 1879, courtesy of an invitation by Pavel Zasodimsky to manage a library he had opened recently there.

In St. Petersburg, Ertel established ties with revolutionary Populists, for which, in early 1884, he was arrested and imprisoned in the Peter-Paul Fortress for four months before he was exiled to Tver', where he lived under government surveillance until 1888.

The Peter-Paul Fortress was the original citadel for St. Petersburg. It was built from 1706 to 1740, initially to protect the area from attacks by the Swedish army and navy. From 1721 on, the fortress housed part of the city's garrison and, more notoriously, high-security political prisoners. Among its first inmates was Peter the Great's own rebellious son, Alexei. Other famous residents included Dostoevsky, Gorky, Trotsky, and Lenin's older brother, Alexander Ulyanov.

8. *Raznochintsy* were educated priests, merchants, peasants, minor officials, petty bourgeois, and impoverished noblemen who became reformers of various political colors and hues.

9. Bunin is referring to Kant's *The Critique of Practical Reason*, published in 1788.

10. Positivism is a philosophical system that rejects theism and metaphysics in claims that all rationally justifiable assertions can be verified scientifically, in logical or mathematical proofs.

11. Bunin is referring to the famine of 1891, which affected some thirty-six million people from the Urals to the Black Sea.

12. Nikolai Mikhailovsky was a Populist theoretician in Russia in the 1870s and 1880s. An extreme positivist, he, like Leo Tolstoy, accepted the Christian message only as nonresistance to evil.

13. Konstantin Pobedonostsev was the chief procurator of the Holy Synod and, as the official overseer of the Russian Orthodox Church, the éminence grise of imperial politics during the reign of Alexander III.

14. Ertel is referring to the Cossack Stenka Razin, who, in 1670–1671, led a major uprising against the nobility and the tsarist bureaucracy in southern Russia, and another Cossack, Yemelyan Pugachev, who, in 1773–1775, spearheaded a series of popular rebellions in Kazan and eastern Russia.

15. Ertel is referencing the *Thebaid*, a Latin epic written by Publius Papinius Statius in the late first century, and in which the author champions the Roman tyrant Domitian, as well as the cruelty and madness of his followers.

16. Bunin is paraphrasing the final line of Nekrasov's 1852 poem "On the Day of Gogol's Death."

17. Ertel is exaggerating grossly, revolutionaries perishing in Alexander II's reign being a few hundred at the most.

13. Voloshin

1. Bunin is referring, metaphorically, to *Landmarks,* also known as *Signposts,* a collection of essays published in Russia in 1909 in which leading intellectuals criticized their group for a host of ills: their failure of leadership in the 1905 revolution, their inability to respect the law and to develop a legal consciousness, their lack of respect for individual rights and personal freedoms, and, most seriously, their nihilistic utilitarianism, material progress, and national education only as means to ends.

2. Alexander Benois published this article in *Poslednie novosti* on August 28, 1932.

3. Bunin is citing, with some license, from Voloshin's 1901 poem "In the Carriage Car."

4. *Golden Fleece*, in print from 1906 to 1909, was a lavishly illustrated literary and artistic journal devoted to symbolism.

5. Voloshin was in Paris at various times between 1901 and 1916.

6. *Struggle* was a short-lived Bolshevik newspaper, published daily in Moscow, December 10–19, 1905.

7. Not quite. In his 1915 poem "On the Bombing of the Dardanelles," Bryusov wrote: "And on Hagia-Sophia in the full blue of seagulls / Justinian's cross will stand instead of the moon."

8. As noted in chapter 1, Voloshin wrote "Angel of Vengeance" in 1905.

9. With a flair for theater and masquerade, Yelena Glazer often dressed in boy's clothing, one individual taking her for her husband's son, not wife.

10. Voloshin arranged meetings in the Strasbourg Cathedral de Notre-Dame in August 1905.

11. Bunin is referring to M. Gofman, ed., *A Book about Russian Poets of the Last Decade*, published in 1907. Vagankovo cemetery is located roughly three miles north of the Kremlin. Zvenigorod is thirty miles west of Moscow. Koktebel is a popular resort town, located in southeastern Crimea, roughly 750 miles south/southwest of Moscow and 120 miles east of Sevastopol. Koktebel is also where Voloshin is buried. Finally, Voloshin was in Paris in 1901 and 1902.

12. The Bhagavad Gita is a major Sanskritt epic of ancient India. In it, a prince, facing battle, asks direct, uncompromising questions of his spiritual guide.

13. Having fallen under the influence of Rudolf Steiner in a visit to Dornach, Switzerland (the center of the anthroposophist movement), in summer 1914, Voloshin participated in the building of the First Goetheanum, a monumental, elaborate, double-domed wooden structure, which Steiner named after Goethe and which he designed and supervised in Dornach between 1913 and 1920. It was destroyed by fire on December 31, 1922.

14. More accurately, Voloshin was in Odessa from January 20 to May 10, 1919.

15. The Feodosian Literary-Artistic Circle, founded in fall 1919, was a group of well-known writers, actors, dancers, and musicians who sponsored lectures, readings, and concerts, as well as literary almanacs and other publications. Besides Voloshin, the other writers included Eduard Bagritsky, Ilya Ehrenburg, Osip Mandelshtam, and Tsvetaeva.

16. Most likely, Bunin has Mayakovsky in mind.

17. In Greek mythology, Priapus was a minor rustic god of fertility, often pictured with huge erections. Cachalot is another term for sperm whale.

18. For more on Bunin's stay in Odessa, see I. Bunin, *Cursed Days*, trans. T. Marullo (London: Phoenix Press, 2000).

19. Voloshin's image of Boris Savinkov as an elk appears in his 1915 poem "Ropshin," as part of a cycle of poems titled *Appearances* (not *Portraits*).

20. Voloshin translated many of Régnier's poems, believing that the writer embodied a "new realism" that synthesized symbolism, realism, and neoclassicism.

21. Anthroposophy, a system of belief put forth by Rudolph Steiner in 1912 to 1913, upheld knowledge via nonrational faculties. Anthroposophy accords a special place in Russia and its people: the alleged national sense of community, patience, and selflessness; the recourse to holistic thinking and rational mysticism; and the ability to accept higher truths will, circa the year 3500, in the sixth epoch of the "Spirit Self," give rise to a new civilization in the East to replace the rational and technological culture of the West.

It was the anthropolitical idea, though, that the life force of Russia was so anarchical and chaotic that, as a "female East," it needed to be impregnated by the "male West" to achieve viable consciousness and form, which, Steiner asserted, given the history of Russia and Europe, had every chance for success.

22. The meeting took place on April 11, 1919.

23. Voloshin entered the Masons in May 1905, but soon tired of the movement.

24. *Izvestia* was a daily broadsheet newspaper published from 1917 to 1991 in the former Soviet Union. The article appeared on April 25, 1919.

25. On January 13, 1913, an individual named Abram Balashov, an iconographer and Old Believer, slashed Repin's famous 1895 painting *Ivan the Terrible and His Son*.

Unsurprisingly, Repin charged that the futurists had bribed Balashov to destroy his work, in a first step toward a "general artistic pogrom."

Russian modernists came under siege. Editors of the newspaper *Russian Word* published testimonials from all over Russia, praising their country as the epitome of national artistic achievement. Professors exploited the controversy to lecture on patriotism and morally lax youth.

Voloshin fueled the fire in an essay titled "On the Significance of the Catastrophe that Befell Repin's Painting," in which he argued that Balashov had been motivated by the work itself, the culmination of two decades of shock and torment by viewers over the piece.

A month later, Voloshin, in a public lecture, added that praise for Repin's *Ivan* revealed what he considered to be a deplorable lack of taste in Russia and, more outrageously, that Balashov was a victim, not a violator of Repin's work.

Making matters worse was that Repin himself was in the audience, and he delivered a passionate but disjointed response to Voloshin's claim. (Balashov was placed in a mental hospital.)

26. Volshin left Odessa on May 10, 1919.

27. The individual in question is the poet Tatyana Tsemakh.

28. The Volunteers were an anti-Bolshevik army in southern Russia during the Russian Civil War.

29. Yevpatoria is seventy miles north of Sevastopol and roughly nine hundred miles southeast of Moscow. Kinburn Spit is roughly forty miles west of Odessa; Ochakov, five miles north of Kinburn Spit. Ak-Mechet is a district of Simferopol, approximately five hundred miles southwest of Odessa.

30. Feodosia is some 530 miles south of Odessa.

31. Voloshin's *Demons Deaf and Dumb* appeared in 1919 and contained the poem "Angel of Vengeance."

Centrag, or the Ukrainian Central Agency for the Dissemination of the Press and Literature, was founded by the Bosheviks in Kharkov in 1919. Osvag, or the Information Agency, was founded by Anton Denikin as the propaganda arm of the Volunteer Agency.

32. The individual in question is Leonid Grossman, who would later write extensively on drama, poetics, social thought, Western and Russian literature, and, most notably, the fiction of Dostoevsky.

33. *Southern Word* was a publication founded by members of the Volunteer Army in Odessa in 1919 and for which Bunin served as a coeditor for a short period of time. Voloshin wrote "Protopop Avvakum" in 1918, and "Saint Serafim" a year later.

34. Voloshin's *Masks* appeared in 1919.

35. The fifty-five-year-old Voloshin died on November 8, 1932.

36. Bunin is citing from Voloshin's 1921 poem "Slaughterhouse."

37. The work in question is Voloshin's 1920 poem "Northeast."

38. Bunin is citing Voloshin's 1921 poem "Readiness."

39. Salo is fatty cured pork popular in Russian and Eastern Europe.

14. The "Third Tolstoy"

1. Tolstoy wrote *Peter the First* from 1922 to 1941 (but did not complete it) and *Road to Calvary* between 1924 and 1941. He won the Stalin Prize for both works.

2. Tolstoy's *Prince Serebryanny* appeared in 1863.

3. Tolstoy returned to the Soviet Union on August 1, 1923.

4. Bunin is referring to Tolstoy's 1926 play *The Empress's Conspiracy*, about an attempt by Rasputin to carry out a palace revolution and to install Empress Alexandra as Russia's leader.

5. Alexei Tolstoy was a remote relative of Leo Tolstoy.

6. Bunin is quoting from a speech given by Molotov on November 29, 1936.

7. Alexei Bostrom was also a liberal, an atheist, and a bitter opponent of the gentry. Alexei Tolstoy was born in 1882.

8. As an officer in the cavalry, Nikolai Tolstoy overwhelmed even his fellow hussars with his excesses. Insanely jealous, he once shot his wife, Alexandra, but missed, eventually forcing the woman in 1882 and in the second month of a pregnancy with their fourth child—the future Alexei Tolstoy—to flee to Bostrom for protection.

Undeterred, Nikolai Tolstoy challenged Bostrom to a duel, but the latter refused. Later finding the couple on a train, Tolstoy shot Bostrom, wounding him. He was not charged with attempted murder, though, his action being seen by the court as unpremeditated. An ecclesiastical tribunal granted the couple a divorce, but on the condition that Alexandra never remarry. The woman, in order to keep the expected baby, also had to assert that the child was Bostrom's.

Ostracized by society and, for some years, also by her parents, Alexandra left with her lover for Nikolaevsky (now known as Pugachyov, some five hundred miles southeast of Moscow), where Bostrom maintained a small farm and held a modest post in local government. It was there that Alexei Tolstoy was born and officially registered as the son of Nikolai Tolstoy. Until the age of thirteen, though, the lad bore the name of Bostrom and believed the man to be his father.

9. Consider such works as Tolstoy's 1923 story "The Manuscript Hidden under the Bed" and his 1924 piece "The Adventures of Nevzorov, or Ibikus."

10. Between 1905 and 1906, Tolstoy wrote such "revolutionary" poems as "The Far-Off Ones," "The Dream," and "New Year." The book in question is Tolstoy's work *Lyrics*.

11. Tolstoy arrived in Berlin in late fall 1921. The *smenovekhovtsy* were Russian émigrés who came into being with the publication of the magazine *Change of Signposts* in 1921. They championed the October Revolution and the new Soviet state as logical and organic steps in the future and fate of Russia. They also exhorted exiles to return to the homeland, their claim being that the Bolshevik regime would give way to revived Russian nationalism.

12. See, for instance, Tolstoy's *Aelita* (1923), *The Gang of Five* (1925), *Engineer Garin's Death Ray* (1926), "The Unusual Adventures on a Volga Steamer" (1931), and *The Little Gold Key, or The Adventures of Buratino* (1931).

13. *New World* was and continues to be the most prestigious literary journal in Russia. It began to appear in Moscow in 1925 as an organ of the Union of Soviet Writers, publishing, for the next five years, the works of such writers as Babel, Mayakovsky, Gorky, Boris Pasternak, and Tolstoy.

14. *October* was founded in 1924 as an organ of the Union of Writers of the Soviet Union. It exists to this day.

15. See Iu. Zhukov, "Na Zapade posle voiny (Zapiski korrespondenta)," *Oktiabr'*, no. 10 (1947): 128.

16. Bunin is quoting from an untitled work that Blok wrote on September 8, 1914.

17. *Aurora Borealis* was a journal published in Moscow from 1908 to 1909.

18. Tolstoy published *Magpie Stories* in 1910.

19. In the first volume of *Road to Calvary*, Vadim Roshchi, one of the heroes of the work, is a bitter enemy of the Bolsheviks, but, by the last tome, he looks fondly on young Soviet workers and their belief in world revolution.

20. Tolstoy's *Bread*, published in 1938, focuses on the Russian Civil War, with flattering portraits of Stalin and damning ones of Trotsky. "Black Gold (Émigrés)" appeared in 1931.

21. Tolstoy never wrote such a work.

22. Bunin's first marriage to Anna Nikolaevna Tsakni in 1898 lasted eighteen months. Bunin's union with Vera Muromtseva, beginning in 1906, was legalized only in 1922. With Muromtseva, Bunin toured the Middle East in 1907, North Africa and Turkey in 1910, and Egypt, Lebanon, Ceylon, and Singapore in 1910 and 1911.

23. Sofya (Sonya) Dymshitz was from a wealthy Jewish family in St. Petersburg, but was disowned by her parents for eloping with Tolstoy in 1907. (At the time, Tolstoy had a wife and infant son. Dymshitz was also married but had stayed with her husband for only two weeks.)

The couple had a child in 1911, but the common-law marriage ended in 1914 when Tolstoy took up with the ballerina Margarita Kandaurova.

An artist in her own right, Dymshitz worked closely with Vladimir Tatlin and was among the first Russian modernists to embrace the revolution. Unlike so many artists of the time, she remained in the Soviet Union, enduring both the Great Terror and the Siege of Leningrad. (She was evacuated from the city in 1942.)

24. The reference here is to Gorky.

25. The Sukharev Tower, located roughly a mile north of Red Square, was built by Peter the Great from 1692 to 1701 to commemorate his triumph over his sister and rival, Sofya. The tower was named after L. P. Sukharev, whose regiment supported Peter in the struggle. It was destroyed by the Soviets in 1934.

26. "A Musical Snuffbox" was a literary café in Moscow 1918.

27. Blok wrote these excerpts in his diary on August 15, 1917.

28. On February 27, 1917, members of the Volynsky Regiment of the Petersburg Garrison, tired of suppressing and killing fellow citizens, rebelled against their officers and liberated rifles, supplies, and other materiel for insurrectionists. The Extraordinary Investigative Commission was established on March 17, 1917.

29. Beginning on May 8, 1917, Blok served as a verbatim reporter for the Extraordinary Commission, sometimes working up to ten hours a day, editing depositions, summarizing evidence, and keeping a notebook on interrogees, all of which were published in a 1921 work titled *The Last Days of Imperial Power*.

30. On November 28, 1917, Andrei Shingaryov and Fyodor Kokoshkin were arrested by the Bolsheviks and imprisoned in the Peter-Paul Fortress. After becoming seriously ill, they were taken to the Mariinsky Hospital on January 6, 1918, and, on the following night, murdered by Baltic sailors who had broken into the building.

31. Not quite. In the last two lines of "Intelligentsia and Revolution," Blok wrote: "The spirit is music. The devil sometimes ordered Socrates to listen to the spirit of music. With your entire body, heart, and consciousness, listen to the Revolution." Blok wrote "Intelligentsia and Revolution" on January 19, 1918. Also, Bunin's claim that Blok was Lunacharsky's personal secretary is false.

32. Bunin is referring to Blok's "Notes on 'The Twelve,'" written on April 1, 1920.

33. A *poema* is a long narrative poem.

34. Bunin has erred here. This event took place on May 27, 1917.

35. Simferopol is a city roughly five hundred miles southwest of Odessa. On November 14, 1918, the Bolsheviks captured the city and shot more than a thousand people, including hundreds of officers.

36. *Chastushki* are humorous, satirical, or ironic folk songs common in Russia and Ukraine.

37. Bunin is misquoting line 2575 of Goethe's *Faust*. The line reads: "Why talk this line to us? My head's near split in twos / It seems I head the chorus / Of a hundred thousand fools."

38. Bunin is quoting from Blok's poems "On the Field of Kulikovo" and "Russia," both of which were published in 1908.

39. Bunin is quoting from Blok's "Scythians."

40. Bunin is again quoting from Esenin's "Inoniia." As with Blok's "The Twelve," Bunin is citing "Scythians" with considerable departures from the original. Also, the Scythians were Iranian equestrian tribes who lived in large areas of the central European steppes from the seventh century BC to the fourth century AD.

41. Pushkin wrote "To the Slanderers of Russia" in 1831.

42. As a result of the German offensive into Russia, and after serious debate, Lenin persuaded his comrades in the Council of the People's Commissars to accept the harsh terms of the Brest-Litovsk treaty, which was signed on March 3, 1918, and ended the war between Germany and Soviet Russia.

Under the treaty, Russia lost control over most of the Baltic provinces, part of Belorussia, Ukraine, and the oil port of Batumi on the Turkish frontier. In economic terms, the treaty meant that Russia lost 26 percent of its population, 27 percent of its arable land and 32 percent of its yearly crops, 26 percent of its railways, 33 percent of its manufacturing facilities, 73 percent of its iron industries, and 75 percent of its coal fields. Further, the Russian army was to be demobilized completely, and the navy was disarmed and its warships detained in Russian ports.

43. The individual in question is Vladimir Friche, who later became a leading exponent of "sociological poetics" and "economic determinism" in literary studies.

44. Orsha is a small town directly south of Smolensk.

45. Bunin is wrong here. Natalya Krandievskaya was Tolstoy's third wife.

46. The Tolstoys left Odessa in April 1919 and arrived in Paris two months later.

47. In September 1919, Denikin's troops came within twenty miles of Moscow.

48. Stambul, also known as Tuzla, is the historical section of Constantinople, located in the southeastern part of the city.

49. Constantinople was occupied by British, French, and Italian forces from November 13, 1918, to September 23, 1920. In 1909, Bunin was elected an "Academician" by the Academy of Sciences in St. Petersburg, a designation that corresponded to the distinction of "Immortel" in France.

50. The Fields of the Dead was a necropolis, known for its vastness and beauty, with neighboring burial grounds for both Christians and Muslims.

51. Galata, known today as Karakoy, was a district in Constantinople. Sofia, the capital of Bulgaria, is located in the middle-western part of the country.

52. Denikin commanded Odessa from August 23, 1919, to February 8, 1920.

53. The Sea of Marmara connnects the Black and Aegean Seas, dividing the European and Asian parts of Turkey.

54. Having escaped during the Russian Civil War, Lvov made his way to Paris in late December 1918, where he engaged in anti-Bolshevik agitation, as well as assisted Russian émigrés in living in the West.

55. *Future Russia* appeared in two issues in 1920 and included Tolstoy among its editors.

56. Saint-Cloud and Sèvres are roughly seven miles west of Paris.

57. The novel in question is the first part of Tolstoy's *Road to Calvary*, titled *Sisters*, which appeared in the journal *Contemporary Notes* in 1920 and 1921.

58. *Old Times in Kashira* was a 1911 film. Kashira is located about eighty miles south of Moscow.

59. Prunier and Maison de la Poutine are legendary restaurants in Paris.

60. Bordeaux is in southwestern France, about 350 miles from Paris.

61. Freiburg is in extreme southwest Germany, about 500 miles from Berlin; Munich, in southeast Germany, is roughly 350 miles from the capital.

62. Münster is in east-central Germany, approximately three hundred miles from Berlin.

63. The Bolsheviks had forbidden the ringing of church bells since 1918.

64. Tsarskoe Selo (now Pushkin) is the site of the former Russian residence of the imperial family, about fifteen miles south of St. Petersburg.

65. Tolstoy recalled in a letter to Stalin: "In 1936, Bunin and I met by chance in a café. He was friendly and animated . . . still fresh and capable of work. His mood, though, was burdensome. . . . No one was reading him . . . he did not know whom to write for . . . [and] his books were being published in very small quantities. He said nothing about returning to the USSR, but he did not bear it any malice. Generally speaking, he has kept aloof from émigré life." See Iu. Krestinskii, "Pis'mo A. N. Tolstogo," in *Literaturnoe nasledstvo*, ed. V. Shcherbina et al., vol. 84, *Ivan Bunin* (Moscow: Nauka, 1973), bk. 2, 395.

Revealingly, an individual from the Office of Soviet Intelligence tells a different story. In a confidential report, written on July 24, 1937, he wrote: "Bunin's [1936] meeting with Tolstoy shows how weak his social spine is. . . . When Bunin saw Tolstoy, he threw himself on the writer's neck and smothered him with kisses—an act for which, to this day, Bunin's émigré friends have yet to forgive him." See M. Roshchin, *Ivan Bunin* (Moscow: Molodaia gvardiia, 2000), 304.

15. Mayakovsky

1. The thirty-six-year-old Mayakovsky committed suicide on April 14, 1930, allegedly after a dispute with his lover, the actress Veronika Polonskaya, who would not leave her husband for him.

2. Kaluga is both a city and an administrative center, located about one hundred miles southwest of Moscow. The Pamir Mountains are a range in Central Asia, known as the "rooftop of the world."

3. Bunin is quoting from Pasternak's 1930 poem "Death of a Poet."

4. Bunin is citing from Pasternak's 1922 poem "Poetry."

5. "A Cloud in Pants" was Mayakovsky's first important poem. It was recognized immediately by critics, most importantly by Gorky, as a new direction in Russian poetry.

6. At various times, Mayakovsky did portraits on scraps of paper, painted cubo-futurist works, and, during the First World War, drew cartoonlike pictures with anti-German and Turkish propaganda, to which he added his own verse. Mayakovsky also did large-scale, stenciled posters, informing barely literate viewers of the progress of the Red Army during the civil war, as well as of state-run campaigns and programs for public health and literacy.

7. Russia and Germany declared war on each other on August 1, 1914. The monument to the Russian general Mikhail Skobelev, raised in 1912, stood on Tverskaya Street, but was demolished in 1919 by a decree to demolish memorials to tsars and their servants. Actually, also, it was three days after war broke out between Russia and Austria-Hungary that Mayakovsky declaimed his poem "War Is Declared" at Skobelev's statue.

8. Bunin's allegation is true. Lenin suffered from rhotacism, the inability to pronounce *r* or the conversion of another consonant into *r*. Specifically, he could not roll or trill his *r*'s, often substituting vibrating *l*'s in their place. The citation is from Gorky's opening speech at the First All-Union Congress of Soviet Writers on August 17, 1934.

9. Bunin is paraphrasing Lenin's 1905 article "Party Organization and Party Literature."

10. Bunin is citing from Mayakovsky's 1918 poem "Left March" and the 1913 Futurist manifesto, "A Slap in the Face of Public Taste."

11. The *oprichniki* were a clandestine police group founded by Ivan the Terrible between 1565 and 1572.

12. Mayakovsky did so in his 1914 poem "Listen!"

13. The Terek is a major river in the northern Caucausus; the Aragvi, a river in eastern Georgia. Mayakovsky claimed to have spat in the Terek in his 1912 poem "Tamara and the Devil."

14. Bunin has the line wrong. In Mayakovsky's 1926 poem "To Sergei Esenin," the line is "Your name is sniveled into hankies."

15. Bunin is citing from Mayakovsky's 1925 poem "Broadway."

16. Bunin is quoting from Mayakovsky's 1924–1925 poem "Verlaine and Cézanne."

17. The citation is from Mayakovsky's 1925 poem "Summons."

18. The article in question is N. Atarov, "Dozornyi kommunizma," *Literaturnaia gazeta*, April 13, 1949, 3.

19. Bunin is citing two poems by Mayakovsky: the first stanza from his 1926 piece "A Letter from the Writer Vladimir Vladimirovich Mayakovsky to the Writer Alexei Maximovich Gorky" and the second, from his 1920 verse "Vladimir Ilyich." Also, the italicized line is from Bunin, not Mayakovsky.

20. An article in *Poslednie novosti*, dated July 18, 1922, reported: "P. P. Krylov, a former member of the first Duma, has fallen as a sacrifice to cannibalism. A doctor by profession, P. P. Krylov was summoned sometime in the evening to attend to a sick man. Horses were sent to get him. Not suspecting anything out of the ordinary, P. P. Krylov, faithful to the rules of his profession, set out for the sick man—and never re-

turned home. The next day members of a search party found that P. P. Krylov had been killed and eaten. A part of his body was found in a barrel."

21. The famine of 1921–1923, caused by a severe drought in southern Russia, resulted in over five million deaths in Russia, Ukraine, and Crimea, which Kalinin visited in 1922. "The percentage of mortality is rather high," Kalinin wrote callously in an article after a trip to Crimea. "In February 302,000 individuals were starving, of whom 14,413 died; in March 879,000, of whom 19,902 died; and in April 377,000, of whom 12,754 died." See M. Kalinin, "Po golodnomu Krymu," *Izvestia*, July 15, 1922, 2.

22. The reference is again to the poet Bednyi. Podmoskovye is a region around Moscow and is home to as many as 360 estates, including those of Pushkin, Chekhov, and Blok.

23. Bunin is quoting from Mayakovsky's 1927 poem "It Is Good."

24. Bunin is citing from a letter by Dzerzhinsky to his sister Aldona Dzierzynska-Bulhak, written on October 9, 1905.

25. The first two lines of the citation, Bunin is quoting from Mayakovsky's 1924 eulogy to Lenin, "Vladimir Ilyich Lenin"; the remaining lines, from his 1925 piece "Homeword!"

26. Bunin is citing from Mayakovsky's 1928 poem "A Letter to Tatyana Yakovleva."

27. There is no evidence for such an assertion, although Gorky recalls telling Bunin that he considered Mayakovsky "to be talented and greatly so at that." See N. Primochkina, *Gor'kii i pisateli russkogo zarubezh'ia* (Moscow: IMLI RAN, 2003), 58.

28. Gorky met Mayakovsky—alone at the Finnish resort at Mustomyaki, or "Black Hill" (now Gorkovskoe), some forty miles northwest of St. Petersburg in fall 1914. (Some accounts say that it was the first meeting between the two.)

Bunin is citing from Mayakovsky's autobiography: "I went to Mustomyaki. M. Gorky. I read fragments of 'Cloud.' Gorky, moved, wept all over my waistcoat. I moved him with my poem. This made me a little proud. It was the case, though, that Gorky weeps over a poetic waistcoat."

Others tells a different story of the encounter. Gorky's wife, Maria Andreeva, recalled that Mayakovsky was terrified at meeting the famous writer. "It was most interesting to see how nervous Mayakovsky became," she wrote. "His jaws were moving and he could not control them; his hands were in his pockets, out and in and out again."

Gorky himself claimed that it was Mayakovsky, not he, who shed tears at the event. "Mayakovsky read fragments of 'A Cloud in Pants' and 'The Backbone Flute,' along with other lyrical poems," he wrote to Ilya Gruzdyov in May 1930. "He read them splendidly, even cried like a woman, which frightened and agitated me considerably."

See V. Maiakovskii, "Ia sam," in *Polnoe sobranie sochinenii v trinadtsati tomakh* (Moscow: Khudozhestvennaia literatura, 1953), 1:3; Z. Papernyi, *V. Maiakovskii v vospominaniiakh sovremennikov* (Moscow: Khudozhestvennaia literatura, 1963), 117; and, V. Vialik, ed., *Perepiska A. M. Gor'kogo s I. A. Gruzdevym* (Moscow: Nauka, 1966), 227.

29. *Housewarming* was a monthly literary and artistic magazine published in New York from 1942 to 1950 and in Paris in 1950.

30. The article in question in "Neizvestnye stikhi Maiakovskogo," *Novosel'e*, no. 2 (1942): 57–62. *The Lay of the Host of Igor*, alternatively known as *The Tale of Igor's Campaign*, is an anonymous twelfth-century document of the failed attack against the Polovtsians in the region around the Don River.

Roman Jakobson joined the faculty of Harvard University as the Samuel Hazzard Cross Professor of Slavic Languages and Literatures and General Linguistics in 1949. Also, Bunin's claim that Jakobson and Mayakovsky were schoolmates is false.

16. Hegel, a Tailcoat, a Snowstorm

1. The Soviets had established power in Odessa on January 30, 1919, but German and Austrian troops occupied the city in March. The city fell to the Ukrainian nationalist Semyon Petlyura, who controlled the city December 11–18, 1918; to British and French troops, who held it until April 6, 1919; to Bolshevik forces, who occupied it for five months; and to General Denikin's White anti-revolutionary forces, who entered Odessa on August 24, 1919. The beleaguered city was ultimately retaken by the Soviets on February 9, 1920, three weeks after the Bunins left Russia.

2. Yelets is a city roughly 250 miles south of Moscow.

3. *Worker's Word* and its affiliate in Odessa were published by the Russian Social Democratic Party from 1902 to 1917 and reappeared as *Southern Worker* from 1917 to early 1920. Yushkevich is quoting from the section titled "Logic" in Hegel's 1871 *Encyclopedia of the Philosophical Sciences*. To his remarks, he added: "Then the Russian Revolution also makes sense!"

4. The publication in question is again *Southern Word*.

5. Bunin first visited Constantinople in 1901.

6. Following the signing of the armistice of Mudros on October 30, 1918, Allied forces occupied Constantinople from November 1, 1918, to September 23, 1923, with French troops overseeing the old city in the southwestern part of the old capital of the Ottoman Empire.

7. The Bunins left for Sofia around March 1, 1920.

8. In September 1918, French, British, Greek, and Serbian forces had invaded Bulgaria, forcing the country to sue for peace. In Sofia, the Bunins lived in the hotel Continental.

9. Besides money and his wife's diamonds, Bunin lost his academic gold medals. Stolen documents were returned to him by mail.

10. Bunin's Zouave could have been a member of the light infantry in the French army or one of the Turks who dressed like Zouaves in the Greco-Turkish war of 1919–1922.

11. Denikin's "bells" circulated on August 30, 1919, as the currency for the Russian White Volunteer Army, but soon depreciated into large-scale printings. (At one point, 150 "bells" equaled one French franc.)

12. Mikhail and Maria Tseitlin fled from Moscow first to Odessa in 1919 and then to Paris, where they became a center of Russian émigré life. Also, the Bunins arrived in Paris on March 28, 1920.

13. The nephew in question is Nikolai Pusheshnikov, a translator of Rudyard Kipling, John Galsworthy, and Jack London. Vasilievskoe is roughly sixty miles southwest of Moscow.

14. Sergei Malashkin was the son of poor peasants who took part in the Russian revolutions of 1905 and October 1917. Among the novels that brought him fame were *Two Wars and Two Worlds* and *The Notes of Ananiy Zhmutkin*, both of which were writ-

ten in 1927, and *The Composition of Evlampyi Zavalishin on the People's Commissar and Our Time*, appearing a year later. Several of Malashkin's works—for example, *The Sick Man* and *Moon from the Right Side, or An Unusual Love*, both penned in 1926—provoked controversy for depicting the ugly aspects of national life during the New Economic Policy.

15. Belevsky (also known as Belev) is roughly 75 miles southwest of Tula and 175 miles in the same direction from Moscow. The writer in question is the Soviet writer Panteleimon Romanov, best known for his 1931 work *Three Pairs of Silk Stockings*.

16. Romanov's *Rus* appeared in five volumes between 1925 and 1936.

17. Leonid Leonov visited Gorky in the second half of July 1927.

18. As noted in chapter 14, Bunin is quoting an excerpt from Blok's diary, written on August 15, 1917.

19. Bunin is citing from Blok's verse titled "Russian Raving," written in his diary sometime between February 1918 and April 1919.

20. Yuly Bunin died in Moscow in July 1921.

21. Rostov-on-Don is a city and administrative region roughly seven hundred miles south of Moscow.

22. Chekhov wrote this letter to Suvorin on March 31, 1892. Suvorin's article, "Anna Karenina," appeared in the newspaper *Novoe vremia* on May 13, 1877.

17. Nobel Days

1. Grasse, located roughly thirty miles from Nice in southeastern France, is known internationally as a leader of flavorings for food and of fragrances for perfume.

2. Belvedere was the name of the villa perched on a mountain slope about Grasse in southeastern France, where the exiled Bunin spent his summers, as well as the years of the Second World War. The Esterel Massif is a coastal mountain range in southeast France.

3. A reporter from the French communist newspaper, *l'Humanité*, noted succinctly: "The Nobel Prize in Literature had been awarded to Ivan Bunin, a White émigré. There is something comic in the fact that this award has been given to a relic of that old world that has been swept away by the proletarian revolution . . . and especially at a time when Russian literature in the USSR, having been sprinkled with the living water of revolution and of socialist construction, has attained a success that is well known to all." "La prix Nobel de littérture donné à un Russe blanc," *l'Humanité*, November 10, 1933, 3.

4. In 1901, Tolstoy was considered as the first recipient for the Nobel Prize (for literature), but Carl David af Wirsén, permanent secretary of the Swedish Academy, wrote to its members that although he admired the "immortal creations" of *War and Peace* and *Anna Karenina*, he could not condone Tolstoy's political and social ideas: his denial of self-defense to individuals and nations; his rewriting of the New Testament in a "half-mystical, half-rationalist spirit"; and his denunciation of "all forms of civilization . . . for some primitive form of life, disembodied from every precept of high culture."

As a result, the Nobel Prize was awarded to the French poet and essayist René Sully-Prudhomme, but not without protests from forty-two Swedish writers, artists, and scholars (including August Strindberg) that the award had not gone to Tolstoy.

In a letter to the group written on February 4, 1902, Tolstoy responded: "It [not winning the award] has saved me the painful necessity of dealing in some way with money . . . [something] that is regarded as very necessary and useful, but that I regard as the source of every evil."

Three years later, members of the Russian Academy of Sciences, believing that Tolstoy's work *The Great Sin*, published that year, enhanced greatly his standing as a writer, decided again to nominate him for the Nobel Prize. The nominating letter was approved by all of Russia's outstanding academic institutions and accompanied by a copy of *The Great Sin*.

Again, Tolstoy wanted nothing to do with the award. To Arvid Järnefelt, he wrote on September 26, 1906: "[If] it might happen that I will be judged to win the Nobel Prize, it would be very unpleasant to refuse. . . . Perhaps, you know some of the members [of the academy] and can write to the chair [of the group] asking . . . that they not give it to me."

Järnefelt sent a translation of the letter to the Nobel committee, and with Wirsén again determined to keep Tolstoy from winning the award, the Nobel Prize went to the Italian poet Giosuè Carducci, well known to only literary specialists.

It should be noted that Tolstoy was the only nominee for the Nobel Prize to have asked for the removal of his name from consideration and to have refused the $100,000 connected with the award. See N. Hedin, "Winning the Nobel Prize," *Atlantic Monthly* 186, no. 4 (October 1950): 75–76; and L. Tolstoi, *Polnoe sobranie sochinenii v devianosta tomakh* (Moscow: Akademiia nauk, 1954), 70:147–153; also vol. 73 (1954), 273–274; vol. 76 (1956), 201–202.

5. At the time of the award, Bunin added: "But I think that the Swedish Academy chose me because of *The Life of Arseniev*." Bez podpisi, "Inostrannaia pechat' ob I. A. Bunine," *Poslednie novosti*, November 12, 1933, 4.

6. As noted in chapter 4, Bunin was in England in 1925 as a guest of the PEN Club.

7. Alfred Nobel died on December 10, 1896. Emanuel Nobel died on May 31, 1932. Interestingly, it was Emanuel who, over the objections of several members of the Nobel family, ensured that his deceased uncle's wishes regarding both the Nobel Foundation and the Nobel Prize would be fulfilled.

8. Compare the shirt stud that kills the hero in "The Gentleman from San Francisco."

9. More accurately, Bunin is referring to the Stockholm Concert Hall, completed in 1926.

10. The individual is Gustaf V, an ardent foe of communism.

11. As Galina Kuznetsova, wrote in her diary on December 10, 1933: "When Ivan Alexeevich climbed up onto the stage, he was terribly pale. He had such a solemn and tragic look, as if he were going to take Communion or die on the scaffold. His pallid, ashen face . . . attracted a great deal of attention. . . . When he reached the pulpit, he bowed with an exaggerated sense of his worth." See G. Kuznetsova, *Grasskii dnevnik* (Washington, DC: Victor Kamkin, 1967), 308.

12. There were other complications. As Sedykh recalled in his memoirs: "The journalists [in Sweden] . . . wanted to know who would present Bunin to the king. According to tradition, this was to be done by the ambassador of the laureate's home

country. But the ambassador was the Soviet [Alexandra Kollontai]. . . . I said that such a thing was not proper . . . and caused a sensation. . . . Kollontai announced that she would not be attending the ceremonies, [an act] that only increased Swedish sympathy for Bunin." See A. Sedykh, "I. A. Bunin," in *Dalekie, blizkie* (New York: Novoe Russkoe Slovo, 1962), 195–196.

Index

Printed in the USA
CPSIA information can be obtained
at www.ICGtesting.com
CBHW031346260624
10697CB00002B/65